Construction Drawings and Details for Interiors:
Basic Skills

Construction Drawings
and Details for Interiors:
Basic Skills

SECOND EDITION

W. Otie Kilmer, AIA   ■   Rosemary Kilmer, ASID, IDCE LEED® AP

WILEY

JOHN WILEY & SONS, INC.

LIBRARY OF CONGRESS CATALOGING-IN-PUBLICATION DATA:

Kilmer, Rosemary.
  Construction drawings and details for interiors : basic skills / Rosemary Kilmer, W. Otie Kilmer. — 2nd ed.
    p. cm.
  Rev. ed. of: Construction drawings and details for interiors : basic skills / W. Otie Kilmer, Rosemary Kilmer. c2003.
  Includes index.
  ISBN 978-0-470-19041-8 (pbk.)
  1. Building—Details—Drawings. 2. Interior architecture. 3. Structural drawing. I. Kilmer, W. Otie. Construction drawings and details for interiors. II. Title.
  TH2031.K54 2009
  729.022—dc22
                              2008016846

Book design by Richard Oriolo

CONTENTS

Writing a second edition of a book is much like writing the original one, however, the process is a little easier since we've been through it once. In an effort to keep up with the rapidly advancing technology in the interior design and architectural professions, it has taken the knowledge and skills of several people to bring this second edition to fruition. The authors wish to express their sincere thanks to the following people, who helped in the development of new material, revision of existing information, and preparation of this second edition.

First, we would like to thank our current and former students, who continue to show their enthusiasm to learn more and more each year, which challenges us to keep abreast of the issues and best practice standards facing the interior design profession. This edition includes work by the following talented and hardworking students: Lisa Tillman, Lamis Behbehani, and Lisa Vanzee.

Special appreciation is expressed to the professionals and organizations that provided us with illustrations and permissions to use their materials to make this edition a truly visual experience. We are especially thankful to KJG Architecture, Inc., Gettys Chicago, Maregatti Interiors, Studio 3 Design, Bob Hosanna, Courtney Johnston, AutoDesk, The Construction Specifications Institute, KraftMaid Cabinetry, and Hewlett-Packard Company.

Every effort has been made to correctly supply the proper credit information.

We are grateful to a number of interior design educators throughout the country for their helpful suggestions as to what needed to be revised or included in this edition to truly be helpful to the students and instructors in interior design.

We are deeply grateful to the dedicated staff at John Wiley & Sons for their guidance, assistance, and dedication to this edition. We are particularly indebted to Paul Drougas for his support, understanding, and perseverance to complete this project. Thank you, Paul, for believing in us.

A special thanks to Lisa Vanzee, our daughter, whose expertise and skills in computer graphic technology enriched this edition immensely. We would also like to thank Jeff and Courtney Johnston, our daughter and son-in-law, for their professional experience, as to contemporary standards and practices.

Most of all, we would like to acknowledge each other (Otie and Rosemary), as we have been constant companions and colleagues for many years. Without the love, support, and motivation that we share with each other we would not be able to continue to explore new horizons.

ACKNOWLEDGMENTS

The second edition of this book builds upon the foundations of the first edition and expands on current practices and information not included in that edition. The authors wish to thank the many students, teachers, and professionals who used the first edition and gave us valuable input as to what needed to be expanded, revised, or added.

The design process for architectural interiors involves a series of phases, each of which may call for drawings. At the outset, these may include programming, schematics, preliminary, and design development drawings. Such presentation drawings are created to convey elements, spatial relationships, materials, color schemes, furniture, furnishings, and equipment, as necessary to set the design concept for an interior. Construction drawings are produced that follow the design intent developed through these earlier drawings. Construction drawings, also known as working drawings, are graphic representations that communicate how to construct, remodel, or install a project. These drawings also include related information, such as room designations; door, window, and fixture locations; dimensions; materials; and other details.

Construction drawings involve considerable time and attention to detail. In many professional design firms, over 50 percent of a project fee (payment from the client to the designer) might be allocated to preparing construction drawings and the related specifications. This attests to the importance of construction drawings in the overall process of designing and construction environments.

Interior designers are playing a larger role in coordinating interior projects and producing construction drawings. Interior design and construction requires some unique types of drawings not commonly found in textbooks or curricula. It is to speak to this need that this book was created—as a handbook to preparing construction drawings solely for the field of interior design.

This book has been designed for two groups of users: students in interior design schools and interns in the offices that design interiors; and professional interior designers and architects who need a basic, yet comprehensive set of standards and techniques. For students or interns, these pages are best used with an instructor or mentor who can present the published materials, but augment them with supplemental information and other exercises.

Computer-aided drawing (CAD) programs are tools that have become integral to interior design. This book thus provides a general introduction to using the computer. It briefly discusses electronically storing and retrieving the documents for current and future projects. Many elements of a current project can be copied and easily modified for future application in other projects. In this manner, designers can build a design database. Today, images, drawings, and other information are sent electronically to clients, consultants, suppliers, builders, and other professionals. This is a leap ahead of such past methods as copying and mailing or sending telephonic facsimile. Working electronically has changed many of the ways designers communicate their work, and is continually evolving.

However, this is not a textbook on how to draft with the computer, or on the use of specific drafting software. Computer hardware and software are constantly being upgraded and improved. For this reason, this book focuses on how to incorporate a generic CAD approach to the drawing process. Examples are presented throughout the book of both electronic and hand-drawn creations. Although many designers use CAD heavily in their work, a significant number do not fully use it for all aspects of the drawing process. Well-executed hand drawings can still be effective design exploration and communication tools, and sometimes they are even works of art.

This book is organized in two parts. Part 1 (Chapters 1 through 4) first discusses graphic language as a communication tool in design and architecture. Chapter 1 (Drawing as Communication) has been expanded to include information on universal design, sustainable design, Leadership in Energy and Environmental Design (LEED), and Building Information Modeling (BIM).

Chapters 2 and 3 present basic drafting and equipment needs for the beginning student. Chapter 4 presents the drawing classification systems and how they are used for idea generation and communication.

Part 2 (Chapters 5 through 17) detail the construction document process. Overall concepts and organization are discussed, as are specific examples. A new Chapter 6 has been added to include field measuring existing buildings and interiors, as-built drawings, and preparing demolition plans.

Chapter 7 has been expanded to include modular information, wall and partition types, and construction.

A new Chapter 8 has been added to include fire and life-safety plans. This chapter also discusses preparing drawings for specific building code compliance and review by the various authorities who have jurisdiction over new buildings and remodeling of existing ones.

Chapter 10 of the first edition has been made into a new chapter specifically on doors and windows. Door types, frames, and hardware have been expanded upon in this edition.

Room finish schedules and more detailed finish plans have been incorporated into a new Chapter 13.

Chapter 16 has been expanded to include ceiling systems, sustainability, LEED, daylighting, and energy conservation.

Most checklists at the end of each chapter have been expanded in scope and referenced to building code and ADA requirements. Many new illustrations have been added and older drawings have been replaced with new ones to more clearly show the specifics discussed in the writings.

Chapter 18 discusses the use of computers and the various systems for reproducing construction drawings.

Examples used in the book include both residential and commercial interiors. However, more emphasis is placed on commercial projects, as these installations usually require more in-depth detailing, coordination, and often multiple drawings/sheets due to the larger spaces and number of building trades required. The illustrations represent high standards and can serve as guides for design: line work, lettering, notation, and dimensioning that students can aspire to in their own work. In addition to the authors' drawings, examples are included from practicing professionals.

Drawings and details of interiors are included from a variety of geographical areas—as design ideas, material, environmental factors, and accepted standards vary throughout the world. Projects are also shown in relation to their compliances with the Americans with Disabilities Act (ADA) and other code requirements. Dimensions shown are often indicated in feet and inches, with metric equivalents for Canadian and international applications.

Appendices and a glossary are included listing commonly used terms, graphic standards, and other information related to the preparation of construction drawings for interiors.

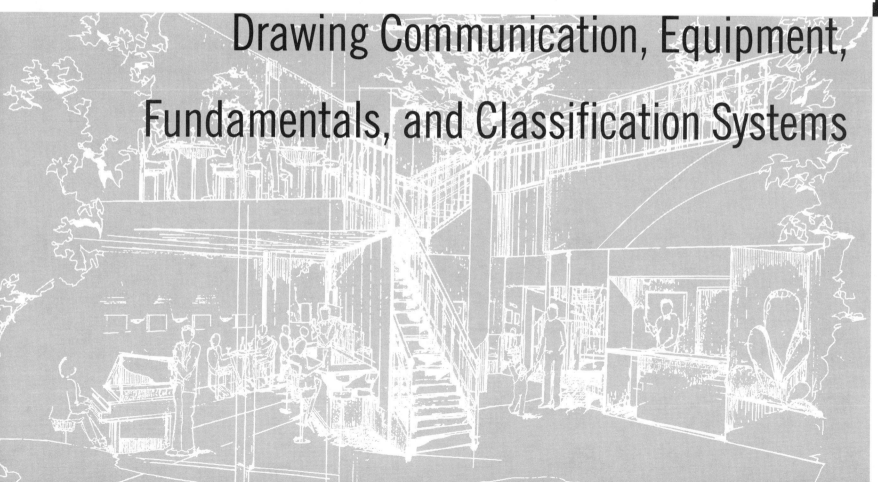

PART ONE

Drawing Communication, Equipment, Fundamentals, and Classification Systems

Drawing as Communication

Ideas and plans are formed in the interior designer's mind, but to be transformed into reality, they have to be communicated to others. Although a designer may have a great idea, it must be effectively communicated or it will remain just an idea and never move beyond conception. Interior designers and other professionals in the building industry use drawings as the primary means of developing and sharing their ideas. Interior designers and architects do a lot of sketching and drawing. They develop their skills in freehand drawing by sketching existing objects and spaces in the environment (Figure 1-1).

These same skills of observation and sketching are then used in visualizing designs for new spaces and objects (Figure 1-2).

This process of brain, eye, and hand coordination is an intrinsic part of design. Architectural drawings can be grouped into three basic types: drawing as idea generation, drawing as a design and presentation medium, and drawing as a guide for the construction process. There are distinct differences between each of these types, yet they all contain some common drawing tools, techniques, standards, and graphic language.

Design communication is also influenced by issues that regulate the building industry, such as building codes that protect the health, safety, and welfare of the public. Currently, other issues,

FIGURE 1-1 **Sketching existing objects and spaces help designers develop their freehand drawing skills.**

such as universal design, sustainability, and LEED (Leadership in Energy and Environmental Design), and Building Information Modeling (BIM) affect the way designers communicate their ideas.

FIGURE 1-2 Designers can use their freehand drawing skills to visualize and sketch new spaces and objects.

Drawing for Idea Generation

Idea generation assists the designer in working through and visualizing the solution to a problem. Designers use many different types of drawings to generate and bring to reality their creative ideas. These drawings can be in the form of quick freehand sketches illustrating different kinds of views (Figure 1-3).

Many times these types of drawings are not shown to clients but are used solely to help designers shape their ideas into a visual form. The drawings are not intended to be the final solution to an idea, but rather to allow the designer to explore alternatives or refine an idea. They also help to record designers' two- and three-dimensional thinking. These concept sketches and drawings are part of a sequence of design steps referred to as the design process (Figure 1-4).

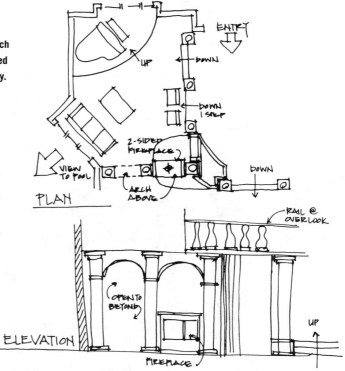

FIGURE 1-3 Quick freehand sketches such as this floor plan and elevation can be used to bring designers' creative ideas to reality.

PLAN

ELEVATION

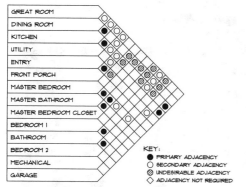

ADJACENCY MATRIX

| | GREAT ROOM | DINING ROOM | KITCHEN | UTILITY | ENTRY | FRONT PORCH | MASTER BEDROOM | MASTER BATHROOM | MASTER BEDROOM CLOSET | BEDROOM 1 | BATHROOM | BEDROOM 2 | MECHANICAL | GARAGE |

KEY:
● PRIMARY ADJACENCY
○ SECONDARY ADJACENCY
◐ UNDESIRABLE ADJACENCY
◇ ADJACENCY NOT REQUIRED

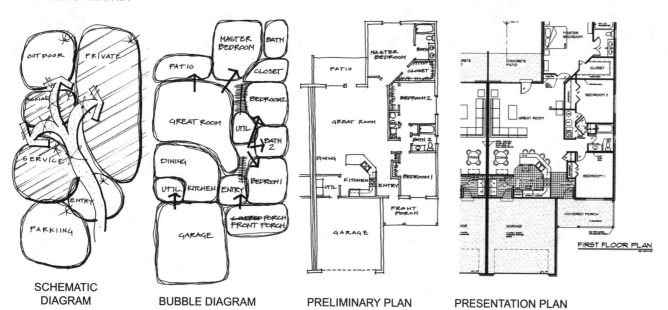

SCHEMATIC DIAGRAM

BUBBLE DIAGRAM

PRELIMINARY PLAN

PRESENTATION PLAN

FIGURE 1-4 Analysis charts, concept sketches, and drawings are part of a sequence of design steps known as the design process.

FIGURE 1-5 **Design drawings such as this pictorial rendering show ideas in more detail.**

Drawing as Design and Presentation Media

Once a designer has developed an idea to a point that visual communication is needed to show it to the client or others, new drawings must be created for use as presentation media. These drawings depict the parameters of an idea in more detail, yet are not totally worked out to a point that they serve as an accurate construction guide. Design drawings can range from pictorial renderings of an idea (Figure 1-5) to rendered plan views of a building's interiors (Figure 1-6). In the first example, a rendering is often done as a perspective view (Chapter 4), which resembles a photograph. The receding lines of an object are purposely drawn to a distant vanishing point—similar to the effect of railroad tracks that appear to touch at the horizon. Design drawings are also done using techniques other than perspectives, such as the isometric shown in Figure 1-7. Different types of drawings are discussed further in Chapter 4.

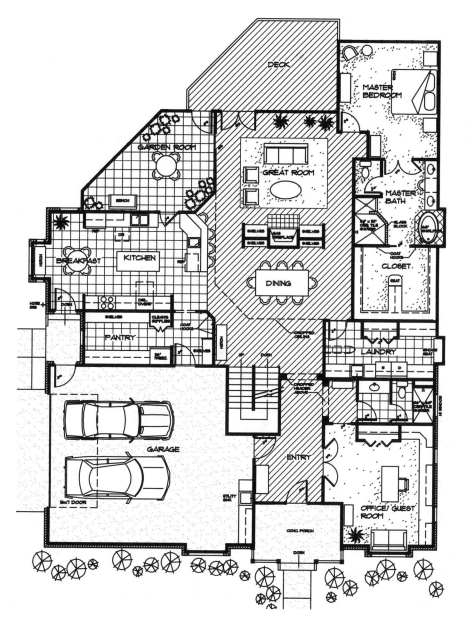

FIGURE 1-6 **Design drawings can also show more detail in the form of rendered plan views of a building.**

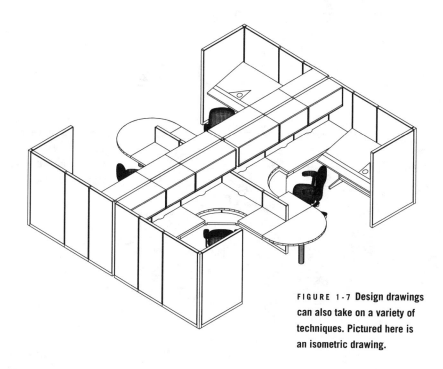

FIGURE 1-7 **Design drawings can also take on a variety of techniques. Pictured here is an isometric drawing.**

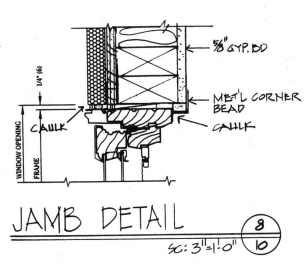

JAMB DETAIL

5/8" GYP. BD

MET'L CORNER BEAD

CAULK

1/4" (6)

WINDOW OPENING

FRAME

CAULK

SC: 3"=1'-0"   8 / 10

FIGURE 1-9 Designers use graphic conventions to indicate sizes, material, and related information needed to turn ideas for objects or spaces into reality.

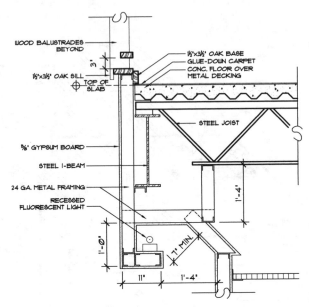

WOOD BALUSTRADES BEYOND

1½"x3½" OAK SILL

TOP OF SLAB

3"

1½"x3½" OAK BASE
GLUE-DOWN CARPET
CONC. FLOOR OVER METAL DECKING

STEEL JOIST

5/8" GYPSUM BOARD

STEEL I-BEAM

24 GA. METAL FRAMING

RECESSED FLUORESCENT LIGHT

1'-4"

7" MIN.

1'-0"

11"   1'-4"

SECTION @ BALCONY

SCALE: 1"=1'-0"   12 / 14

FIGURE 1-8 Drawings used to communicate how something should be constructed are scaled, detailed, and more accurate; they also show materials to be used.

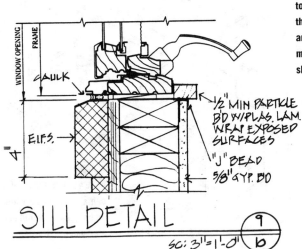

SILL DETAIL

WINDOW OPENING

FRAME

CAULK

E.I.F.S.

4"

1/2" MIN. PARTICLE BD W/PLAS. LAM. WRAP EXPOSED SURFACES

"J" BEAD

5/8" GYP. BD

SC: 3"=1'-0"   9 / 6

FIGURE 1-10 Clear, concise drawings of an object, such as this section, help a builder to construct the object as the designer envisioned.

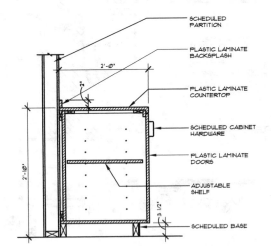

SCHEDULED PARTITION

PLASTIC LAMINATE BACKSPLASH

2'-0"

2"

PLASTIC LAMINATE COUNTERTOP

SCHEDULED CABINET HARDWARE

PLASTIC LAMINATE DOORS

ADJUSTABLE SHELF

2'-10"

3 1/2"

SCHEDULED BASE

SECTION OF BASE CABINET

SCALE: 1" = 1'-0"

Drawing as a Guide for Construction

Drawings serve as the prime means of communication for constructing buildings, interior spaces, cabinets, furniture, and other objects. Construction drawings are scaled, detailed, and accurate representations of how an object looks and how it is constructed, as well as the materials used (Figure 1-8). The drawings follow established architectural graphic conventions to indicate sizes, material, and related information that is needed to bring the objects or spaces into reality (Figure 1-9). The builder needs clear, concise drawings that are directly related to the different views of an object, such as plans, elevations, sections (Figure 1-10), and other drawing types that are discussed in later chapters.

Issues Affecting How Interior Designers Communicate

Interior design is a constantly changing discipline that is affected by societal, environmental, and technological changes. Issues affecting how interior designers communicate today are influenced by universal design concepts, sustainability, and digital technology as they apply to design practice within the building industry.

Universal Design

Universal design is a worldwide belief that encompasses the design of environments, objects, and communication with the intent of serving the widest range of users. Universal design should not be used interchangeably with accessible design, which specifically focuses on people with disabilities and their right of access to entities. Universal design is more than providing minimal compliance with set accessibility guidelines and requirements. Universal design integrates accessible features into the design of the building,

interiors, and objects. It attempts to address usability issues of spaces and equipment versus setting standards and minimum requirements. Figure 1-11 illustrates an example of the international symbol for accessibility regardless of the user's abilities.

The Center for Universal Design at North Carolina State University, in collaboration with a consortium of universal design researchers and practitioners, developed seven principles of universal design that were copyrighted in 1997. Funding for the project was provided by the U.S. Department of Education's National Institute on Disability and Rehabilitation Research. These principles are useful in guiding designers in the creation of environments that are accessible to all people, whether they have a disability or not. Good examples of universal design are almost invisible as they are so well blended into the design that they seem commonplace.

FIGURE 1-11 **This is the internationally recognized symbol for compliance for wheel chair access.**

Sustainability and LEED

The built environment has a profound impact on our natural environment, economy, health, and productivity. Based on this impact, the design, creation, and maintenance of the built environment presents both challenges and opportunities for design professionals. Sustainable design and green design have become common terminology in the design field and involve using methods and products that cause the lowest possible impact upon the ability of the natural environment to maintain its natural balance. Interior designers must practice in an environmentally responsible manner, and must advance their knowledge and application of sustainable design in order to advance sustainable practice. One way this can be accomplished is through an understanding of LEED (Leadership in Energy and Environmental Design) and the Green Building Rating System™, which was developed by the U.S. Green Building Council (Figure 1-12). This system encourages and accel-

1: Principle One: Equitable Use

The design is useful and marketable to people with diverse abilities

GUIDELINES

- Provide the same means of use for all users: identical whenever possible; equivalent when not.
- Avoid segregating or stigmatizing any users.
- Provisions for privacy, security, and safety should be equally available to all users.
- Make the design appealing to all users.

2: Principle Two: Flexibility in Use

The design accommodates a wide range of individual preferences and abilities.

GUIDELINES

- Provide choice in methods of use.
- Accommodate right- or left-handed access and use.
- Facilitate the user's accuracy and precision.
- Provide adaptability to the user's pace.

3: Principle Three: simple and intuitive

Use of the design is easy to understand, regardless of the user's experience, knowledge, language skills, or current concentration level.

GUIDELINES

- Eliminate unnecessary complexity.
- Be consistent with user expectations and intuition.
- Accommodate a wide range of literacy and language skills.
- Arrange information consistent with its importance.
- Provide effective prompting and feedback during and after task completion.

4: Principle Four: Perceptible Information

The design communicates necessary information effectively to the user, regardless of ambient conditions or the user's sensory abilities.

GUIDELINES

- Use different modes (pictorial, verbal, tactile) for redundant presentation of essential information.
- Provide adequate contrast between essential information and its surroundings.
- Maximize "legibility" of essential information.
- Differentiate elements in ways that can be described (i.e., make it easy to give instructions or directions).
- Provide compatibility with a variety of techniques or devices used by people with sensory limitations.

5: Principle Five: Tolerance for Error

The design minimizes hazards and the adverse consequences of accidental or unintended actions.

GUIDELINES

- Arrange elements to minimize hazards and errors: most used elements, most accessible; hazardous elements eliminated, isolated, or shielded.
- Provide warnings of hazards and errors.
- Provide fail safe features.
- Discourage unconscious action in tasks that require vigilance.

6: Principle Six: Low Physical Effort

The design can be used efficiently and comfortably and with a minimum of fatigue.

GUIDELINES

- Allow user to maintain a neutral body position.
- Use reasonable operating forces.
- Minimize repetitive actions.
- Minimize sustained physical effort.

7: Principle Seven: Size and Space for Approach and Use

Appropriate size and space is provided for approach, reach, manipulation, and use regardless of user's body size, posture, or mobility.

GUIDELINES

- Provide a clear line of sight to important elements for any seated or standing user.
- Make reach to all components comfortable for any seated or standing user.
- Accommodate variations in hand and grip size.
- Provide adequate space for the use of assistive devices or personal assistance.

FIGURE 1-12 **This is the logo for the United States Green Building Council, who developed the LEED rating systems.**

erates global adoption of sustainable green building and development practices through the creation and implementation of universally understood and accepted tools and performance criteria. LEED promotes a whole-building approach to sustainability by recognizing performance in five key areas of human and environmental health: sustainable site development, water savings, energy efficiency, materials selection, and indoor environmental quality.

Additionally, LEED has six different rating systems based on the nature of the project. These are LEED-EB (Existing Building), LEED-NC (New Construction), LEED-CI (Commercial Interiors), LEED-CS (Core and Shell), LEED-H (Homes), and LEED-ND (Neighborhood Development). At the time of this writing, rating systems for Schools, Retail, and Healthcare are being developed.

Interior designers, along with architects, real estate professionals, facility managers, engineers, landscape architects, construction managers, lenders, and government officials are encouraged to use LEED to help transform the built environment to sustainability. Federal agencies, as well as state and local governments across the country are adopting LEED for public-owned and public-funded buildings. Sustainable considerations within the built environment begin at the design phase of a project and are carried through in the specifications and construction drawings. It is therefore important that students in interior design learn how to design and apply LEED standards in an environmentally responsible manner. Sustainable issues and LEED standards are incorporated into relevant chapters where appropriate.

Digital Technology and Building Information Modeling

Digital technology continues to evolve at a rapid pace in the production of new software for two- and three-dimensional modeling programs for use by interior designers and others involved in the building industry. While this book is not about any specific software, there must be some discussions of the most widely used programs and their specific details as the majority of designers are using computers in the production of design and construction drawings.

Autodesk's AutoCAD® has been the most widely used CAD program in interior design and architectural firms in the United States for the production of construction drawings. Other popular programs used by the building and design industry include Archi-CAD® (by Graphisoft) and MicroStation (by Bentley). At this point in time, it appears these software programs will not be discarded anytime soon; however, it appears that the architecture and design industry is headed toward a new technology known as Building Information Modeling, or BIM.

Autodesk Revit® Building, a BIM technology, is leading a new CAD industry standard for interior design and architectural practice. BIM is not a specific program, but an integrated approach to design and construction drawings. It is an approach that produces database-driven, 3-D parametric models of proposed projects that address geometry, spatial relationships, sectional perspectives, unit-cost impacts, and detailed documentation with unprecedented speed. Once mastered, the technology facilitates the entire multidisciplinary interactions of a project team. An advantage of BIM is that revisions made in one view or drawings are automatically integrated into related drawings and/or schedules, as illus-

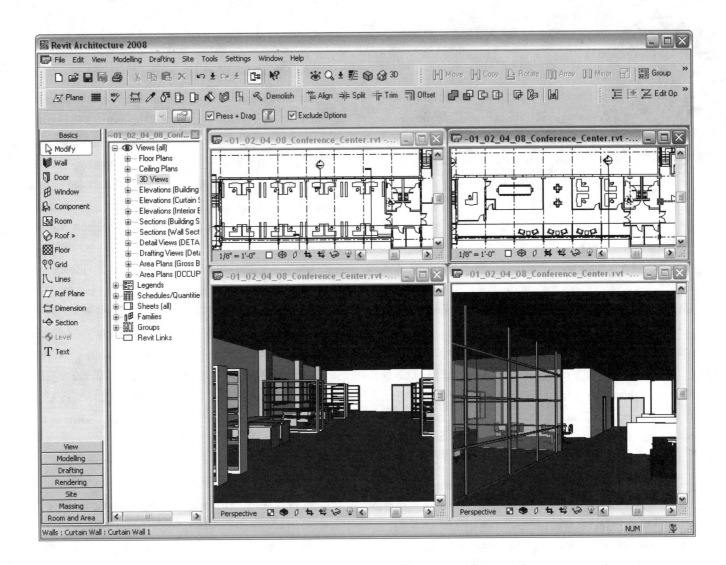

FIGURE 1-13 Autodesk's Revit software program presents CAD as a building information modeling (BIM) system.

trated in Figure 1-13. In the AutoCAD platform this would require the changes made to one drawing be "X-referenced" to the other base drawing.

As many large design firms across the country begin to imple-ment BIM technology into their practice, it will be essential to edu-cate design students in this technology.

Drafting Equipment and Their Care

To do any job accurately and expediently, a designer must have the proper tools. Tools are important in any work—whether it be surgery or carpentry, designing or drafting. Quality tools and equipment will also make drawing and drafting more enjoyable. Investing in good equipment for designing and drafting can benefit both students and professionals.

The advent of computer-aided design and drafting, or commonly referred to as CAD, has reduced the need for much of the basic equipment described in the following pages. However, many students and professionals still prefer to draw manually in some situations, such as sketching initial design concepts or construction details. To this end, basic manual equipment and techniques are described in the next few chapters.

A designer or draftsperson need not buy every piece of new equipment or software available. However, one should buy a new product if it will improve one's work, both in quality and efficiency. Manufacturers often produce a range of models of varying quality. One can decide which model will produce the best effects in relation to the purchase price—sometimes not the top-of-the-line model. One should purchase tools and equipment of good quality, as they are an investment that will pay off throughout one's career.

Drawing Tables and Surfaces

To produce quality drawings for interior design projects, it is necessary to establish a dedicated workplace. Designs can be drawn manually on a drawing board set on a tabletop surface, on a hand-made drafting table, or on a ready-made drafting table. Or they can be drawn using computer drafting hardware and software that augments a drawing board or replaces it totally. In this chapter, commonly used manual drafting tables, equipment, and tools are discussed.

For interior designers, a fairly large layout and drawing surface is needed most of the time. It is vital to have a drawing surface that will hold large presentation boards and standard sheets up to 24 x 36 inches (731 mm x 914 mm). Even larger sheets may be necessary for perspective drawings and full-size furniture drawings. A drawing board or table approximately 30 x 50 inches (762 mm x 1.27 m) should be obtained if possible. This would allow adequate space around the actual drawing sheet to place and maneuver the drawing tools and materials.

Ready-made drafting tables are manufactured in a wide variety of shapes, sizes, materials, and prices (Figure 2-1). Some styles have an adjustable top and rest on four legs. Other models have a single or double pedestal base with a top that can be raised or low-

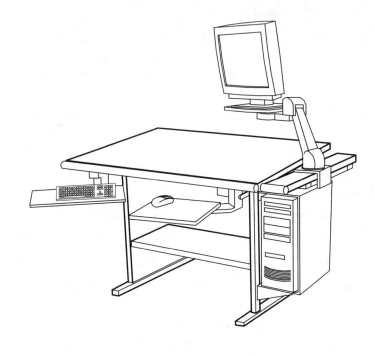

ered according to the chair or stool height. This enables drafters to sit in a chair with a comfortable back and thus to work with less fatigue. The newer models also allow the top to tilt at various angles for comfort. This allows the drafter to work whether sitting or standing. Space-saving folding tables are also produced, although they are not generally as sturdy as the fixed models.

Manufactured tables have drawing surfaces that range in size from 30 x 48 inches (762 mm x 1.21 m) to 30 x 60 inches (762 mm x 1.52 m) and are usually made of wood or hardboard over a cellular core. However, a wood drawing surface can become scored and grooved over time, which affects the drawing quality of the surface. It is best to cover the bare wood top with a protective finish such as plastic melamine or a vinyl drawing-board cover that gives a bit of resiliency and is easy to keep clean. The latter cover-

ing is often produced with an off-white and colored side. Which side to leave face up, is left to the individual.

Drawing-board and table surfaces do not have to be manufactured, as a self-made surface can also be satisfactory and less expensive. For example, a hollow-core, flush door can be supported on blocks or handmade legs made of 2 x 4 lumber with metal brackets. However, the height and angle that suits individual work habits must first be determined, as this type of drawing area will be fixed and not adjustable.

Drawing Papers and Plastic Film

Interior design drawings can be produced on paper or plastic films. The quality paper or film will help determine the quality of line work. A variety of papers and plastic films are manufactured today in many standard sheet sizes and rolls. The choice of which to use is dependent upon the designer's overall intent, office standards, and the intended method selected to making a copy from the original.

Papers

Drafting papers are made in a large variety of types, based on stability, translucency, permanence, strength, and cost. There are two basic categories: opaque and translucent. Opaque papers are thicker than translucent ones and cannot be reproduced through methods such as the diazo printing process, which is being phased out. Therefore, they are not suitable for construction drawings that are to be copied in this manner. They are more suitable for plotting directly from a computer (in single sheets or rolls) and for concept and presentation drawings, as they are available in a variety of colors. Some opaque papers are made smooth on one side and rough on the other. The smooth side is more appropriate for inking and the rough side for pencil drawings. Most papers will accept ink or pencil. However, the quality of their application and possible bleed-through varies according to the composition of the paper and its thickness.

Translucent papers, such as tracing paper and vellum, are used for drawings that are to be reproduced through the diazo process. However, they can also be reproduced photostatically. Tracing paper is generally a natural, untreated translucent paper. It is used primarily for exploratory ideas and sketches. It is commonly sold in inexpensive rolls (in white or yellow shades) and is called "trace," "trash," "flimsy," or "bum wad." It is fairly strong and durable, but not as transparent as vellums and will not produce line work as crisp and clear as vellums.

Table 2-1: Standard Paper Sizes

TYPE	ARCHITECTURAL DRAWING SIZES (IN.)	TYPE	METRIC SIZES (MM)
A	8 ½ x 11	A4	21- x 297
B	11 x 17	A3	297 x 420
C	17 x 22	A2	420 x 594
D	24 x 36	A1	594 x 841
E	36 x 48	A0	841 x 1189

Vellum is a translucent tracing paper that is treated to improve strength, surface texture, and transparency. Vellums have a high rag content that gives them strength so they can withstand erasing. Vellum is sold in rolls or standard sheet sizes and can be used for hand or computer drafting. Standard sheet sizes for architectural drawings are shown in Table 2-1.

Plastic Films

Plastic drafting films are tough, translucent, polyester sheets. Their common thickness ranges from 0.002, 0.003, 0.004, 0.005, and 0.0075 inch to 0.05, 0.08, 0.10, 0.14, and 0.19 mm. The sheets may be frosted on one side and smooth on the other or frosted on both sides. Drawing is done on the frosted side, which accepts pencil or pen more readily than the smooth side.

Special plasticized lead pencils were at one time commonly used with plastic films, but they are not as prevalent as they once were. These are discussed in the paragraph under leads in the next section. Special ink is also available for drawing on plastic film. Both pencil and ink lines are very clear and crisp on plastic films and produce very clear, clean prints. Plastic films are sold in rolls and standard sheet sizes. The films are generally more expensive

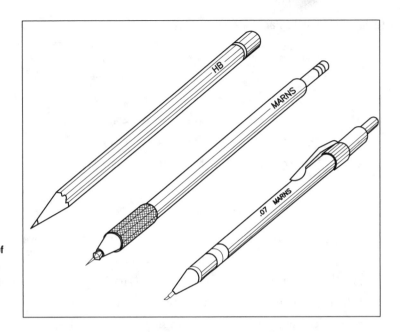

FIGURE 2-2 The three types of pencils available for designers are the wood-cased pencil, the traditional leadholder, and the fine-line mechanical pencil.

Table 2-2: Pencil-lead Weights*

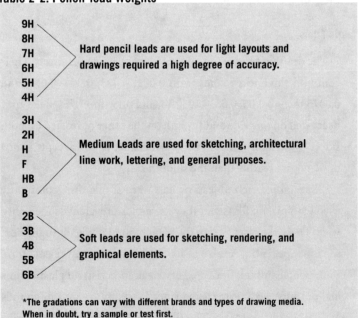

9H 8H 7H 6H 5H 4H	Hard pencil leads are used for light layouts and drawings required a high degree of accuracy.
3H 2H H F HB B	Medium Leads are used for sketching, architectural line work, lettering, and general purposes.
2B 3B 4B 5B 6B	Soft leads are used for sketching, rendering, and graphical elements.

*The gradations can vary with different brands and types of drawing media. When in doubt, try a sample or test first.

than tracing paper or vellum and are used primarily for permanent records or tough originals for multiple reproductions.

Pencils, Leads, and Pens

Pencils are one of the most basic and primary drawing tools of the professional designer. There are three basic types of pencils available to a designer for producing quality drawings (Figure 2-2). The selection is a matter of preference and the particular level of performance needed by the user.

Wood-cased pencil. The oldest manufactured pencil is of wood with a lead encased inside. It is seldom used for repetitive work in today's offices, yet is still a reliable tool for occasional use for convenience and when pencil line control is needed. To expose the lead, the wood shell is cut away by a draftsman's pencil sharpener. However, the sharpener only cuts the wood and does not touch the lead. To "point" the lead, the designer can use a lead pointer, which forms the lead into a conical point. If a wedge point is desired, rubbing the lead on sandpaper can form it. Wood-cased pencils come in a variety of different lead weights, ranging from 9H (extremely hard) to 6B (extremely soft). These leads are explained later in this chapter.

Traditional leadholder. This type of mechanical pencil is made of metal or plastic, with special individual leads inserted in a permanent holder. Different lead weights may be inserted to produce a variety of sharp line weights. Pencil leads are graded from 9H (hard) to F (firm) to 6B (soft). Beginners should sharpen the point frequently for a clear, sharp line until they develop the ability to rotate the pencil while drawing to wear the point more evenly. The lead is sharpened by rubbing and rotating on sandpaper, on regular paper, or in a special mechanical lead pointer. When using sandpaper to sharpen the lead, it should be slanted at a low angle to achieve a good taper and point.

Fine-line mechanical pencil. This type of mechanical pencil does not require sharpening and is loaded with multiple leads of the same diameter and hardness. The pencil generally is made to hold 0.3-, 0.5-, 0.7-, or 0.9-mm diameter lead. The size of the lead determines the line width. This type of pencil is also generally rotated while drawing, and capable of producing consistently sharp, clean lines. Like the traditional leadholder, the mechanical pencil offers the convenience of a steady supply of lead, as the leads are inserted in the bottom of the holder and pushed out the tip by pressing a button on the end of the pencil. It is the most widely used pencil in today's schools and offices for sketching, note-taking, and even drafting.

Leads. A variety of leads are available for both wood and mechanical pencils. Leads used on tracing paper and drafting paper are composed of graphite. Leads range in grades from 9H (extremely hard) to 6B (extremely soft), see Table 2-2.

The softer the lead, the darker the image or line it will produce. For most drafting work, where clean, crisp lines are necessary, H and 2H leads are used. For sketching, softer leads are better, such as F and HB. Very soft leads, such as the B grades, are best for pencil renderings and shadowing work. For light, preliminary layout work, 3H and 4H leads are best.

Generally, the more "tooth" or roughness a paper has, the harder the lead should be. Also, the harder the drawing surface, the softer the lead feels. If you are in high humidity conditions, the apparent hardness of the lead tends to increase.

As noted before, there are special plastic-leaded pencils avail-able for drawing on plastic drafting film. These plastic leads are available in five grades of hardness, ranging from E1 (soft) to E5 (super hard). They are water-resistant and bond well to the plastic film. A vinyl eraser is also available for use with these special leads.

Pens. Some designers prefer ink and use a technical fountain pen (Figure 2-3), as it is capable of precise line width. It can be used for both freehand and drafted ink drawings. As with the drafting pencils, pens are available in a variety of forms and price ranges. However, most technical drawing pens consist of a tubular point, which has an ink-flow-regulating wire inside it. The size of the tubular point is what determines the finished width. Standard widths of ink lines are measured according to a line-width code, such as .30/00, which means the line width is .30 mm or the American standard size of 00. Metric widths range from .13 to 2.0 mm, while the American Standard widths range from 000000 to 6. These sizes

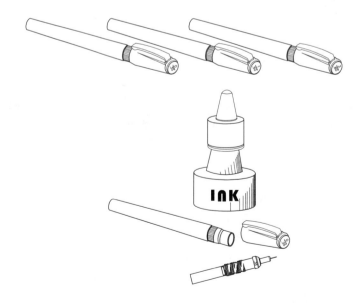

FIGURE 2-3 Technical fountain pens and ink refill.

correspond to line-width designations developed by the American National Standards Institute (ANSI) and are coordinated with metric sizes. For a good starter pen set, a good range of point sizes would be 3 x 0 (.25 mm), 2 x 0 (.3 mm), 1 (.45 mm), and 3 (.80 mm). Technical pens that produce the same line widths are also produced with felt tips. These are less costly, however their felt tips tend to wear out faster than the metal tips.

An advantage to using ink, especially on plastic drafting film, is that it will last for several years longer than pencil, will not smudge, and will produce excellent reproductions. When using technical pens, remember to keep points screwed in securely to prevent the ink from clogging. Always replace the cap firmly after each use to keep the ink from drying, and store the pens with their points up when not in use.

Use a good waterproof, black drawing ink. Good nonclogging ink that is specially made for use in fountain pens and technical pens is the best choice.

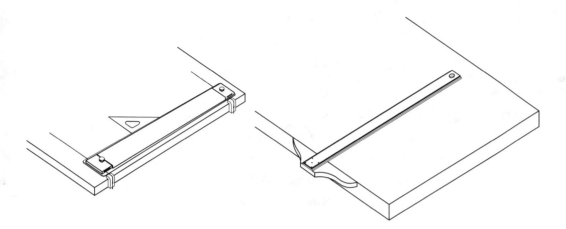

FIGURE 2-4 **The T-square and the parallel bar are used to create straight lines, whether they are horizontal or vertical.**

Parallel Bar, T-square, and Drafting Machines

It is extremely important to make sure lines on design drawings and construction drawings are exactly straight and, when required, parallel. To make sure lines are straight in a horizontal, vertical, and angular direction, there are several tools available. The most common of these instruments are the T-square and parallel bar (Figure 2-4).

Another device, called a drafting machine (Figure 2-5) is also sometimes used.

T-square. A T-square consists of a straightedge with a head set at right angles that can be set flush against the edge of a drawing

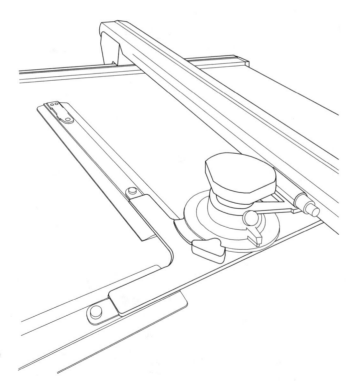

FIGURE 2-5 **An arm-track drafting machine can produce horizontal, vertical, and angular lines.**

board or table. The head is generally very sturdy and immovable. T-squares come in different lengths to coordinate with various drawing board sizes. The most common sizes are 36 and 42 inches (.91 m x 1.06 m). They are available with opaque or transparent edges, the latter making it easier to see through to existing lines when spacing them by eye. To use a T-square, one holds it with one hand (usually the left) at the head so it can be moved into position and held in place while a line is drawn along the straightedge with the other hand. The T-square is inexpensive and portable, which makes it convenient for students. However, in modern practice the T-square has been replaced by the parallel bar and the drafting machine, as they do not require a constant hand to steady the head.

Parallel bar. A parallel bar is attached by cleats and pulleys to a particular drawing surface. The bar moves up and down on thin wire that runs over pulleys inside the bar. When properly installed, the bar can be moved up and down the drawing board and always be parallel with the top of it. Parallel bars are available in a variety of lengths to fit different drawing board sizes. The parallel bar is easy to use. It permits the drafter to draw long horizontal lines and serve as a base for the placement of triangles and other instruments for precision drawing.

Drafting machine. A drafting machine is a combination of several conventional drafting tools. It is fixed to the drawing board and consists of vertical and horizontal blades that serve as scales for linear measurement, eliminating the need for a triangle and T-square for drawing vertical and horizontal lines. There is also a scale in angular degrees on the head that replaces the protractor.

There are two basic types of drafting machines—the arm type and the track type. The arm type has two arms that pivot in the center with a head at the end of the lower arm which is clamped to the top edge of the drafting table. The drafter moves the head up and down and right and left. The head and the scales on it remain parallel to their original setting. The track type has a horizontal track mounted to the top edge of the drafting table with a vertical track attached to it that slides left and right. The head with the scales on it is fastened to the vertical track and slides up and down.

Drafting machines are available for right- or left-handed people. Right-handed people hold the head in place with the left hand. Left-handed people hold the head in their right hand with the scales facing the opposite direction.

The scales on drafting machines can be set at angles by releasing a lock, pressing a release button, and turning the head. Frequently used angles, such as 30, 45, and 60 degrees have positive set points. Scales are available in several lengths, in either architectural or metric measurements. They are also available in either plastic or aluminum finishes.

Triangles, Templates, and Compasses

A variety of other drawing tools are available for constructing vertical or inclined lines as well as circles, curvilinear shapes not based on fixed-radius circular forms, and other special shapes, such as representations of furniture, plumbing fixtures, and other interior equipment and furnishings.

Triangles. A triangle is a three-sided instrument used with the T-square or parallel straightedge for drawing vertical and angular lines (Figure 2-6). The most common are 45-degree and 30/60-degree triangles, each named for the angles they form. A range of sizes is available, with a size of 8 or 10 inches (203 mm x 254 mm)

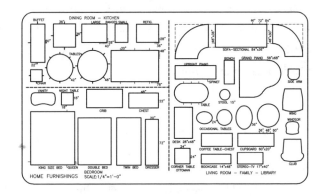

FIGURE 2-6 Triangles are also used to create straight lines when drawing. When used with a parallel bar or T-square, angular and vertical lines can drawn. Shown on the left is a fixed 30-60 triangle; on the right is an adjustable triangle.

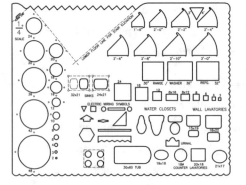

FIGURE 2-7 Templates are used to speed up the drafting process by tracing the punched shapes directly onto a drawing. Templates come in a variety of patterns and scales.

being in the middle of the range. Their size is based on the length of the longest side of the right angle. It is best to begin with these; then larger and smaller sizes can be added as needed. For example, small triangles, such as 4 inches (101 mm), are useful for hand lettering and crosshatching small areas.

Adjustable triangles can be set for any angle from 0 to 45 degrees. The adjustable triangle is convenient for situations requiring a variety of sloping lines, such as for stairs or slanted ceilings.

Some triangles are available with recessed edges for use when inking. This keeps the edge up off the paper so the ink doesn't run under the triangle and become smeared. Triangles are available in a clear (nonyellowing) or colored plastic. They are scratch-resistant and generally have good edge retention. They should not be used as a cutting edge as they are easy to nick, and they must be used and stored carefully.

Templates. Templates are in prepunched patterns representing various shapes commonly used in interior design and architectural plans (Figure 2-7). Templates help to speed up the drafting process and aid in the production of accurate drawings. There are a variety of templates available, some of which are used regularly, while others are needed for special purposes only. There are templates that are used to draw circles, squares, windows, doors, electrical symbols, plumbing fixtures, furnishings, and hundreds of other features.

The circle template is a very basic and highly useful timesaving device for drawing accurate circles or various sizes as well as curves that are parts of circles. Circles range in size from $\frac{1}{16}$ inch (1.58 mm) up to 2 inches (50.8 mm) in diameter. Ellipse templates come in similar sizes, but since ellipses vary from near flat to near circular, a series of templates may be needed for each size. How-

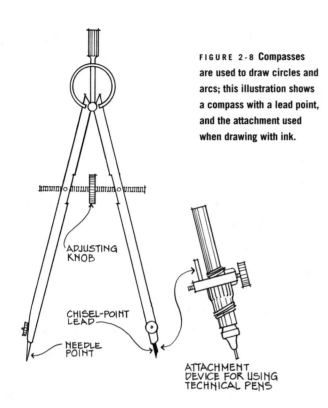

FIGURE 2-8 **Compasses are used to draw circles and arcs; this illustration shows a compass with a lead point, and the attachment used when drawing with ink.**

ADJUSTING KNOB

CHISEL-POINT LEAD

NEEDLE POINT

ATTACHMENT DEVICE FOR USING TECHNICAL PENS

available, but even though they may be convenient they often appear stiff and are not frequently used in design offices. Lettering templates are best used for very large letters and numbers that may be difficult to form freehand.

Compass. A compass is an inverted V-shaped instrument used for drawing circles and arcs (Figure 2-8). It has a pin at the end of one leg and a leadholder at the end of the other. A special device will allow technical pen points to be used with the compass. The best way to use a compass is to mark a center point and the radius desired on a piece of paper and adjust the compass to that measurement by setting the pin on the center point and setting the pencil or pen point on the radius mark. Hold the compass firmly at the top, leaning it a little in the direction the circle will be drawn, then rotate it. Generally, rotating it in a clockwise direction is easier. Press hard enough to get the desired line weight. Be careful to match line weights of circles or arcs to the rest of the drawing.

Scales

ever, a single guide with the most commonly used proportions is available.

French curved templates are excellent tools for drawing irregular curved lines that are not part of a circle or ellipse. These guides consist of at least a dozen traditional forms that can help a designer draw almost any flowing curve needed. There are also flexible drawing curves available that can be bent as needed to fit an irregular curved line. They can hold the shape as the line is drawn, then straightened out after use.

Other useful templates include forms for both residential and commercial furniture, as well as plumbing fixtures, retail fixtures, and lighting and electrical symbols. Lettering templates are also

Measuring tools are extremely important to the interior designer, because a designer's plans, elevations, sections, and details must always be drawn with all their dimensions at the same fractional part of their real (full-size) dimensions. Architectural and interior design line work generally represents objects that are much larger than the drawing paper; therefore, a proportional measuring system must be used. This *scale* of the drawing is always stated on the drawing. When a drawing is drawn *to scale*, this means that all dimensions on the drawing are related to the real object, or space, by an appropriate selected scale ratio. For example, when drawing at a scale of $\frac{1}{8}$" = 1'-0", each $\frac{1}{8}$-inch increment in the drawing represents a foot in the full-size object.

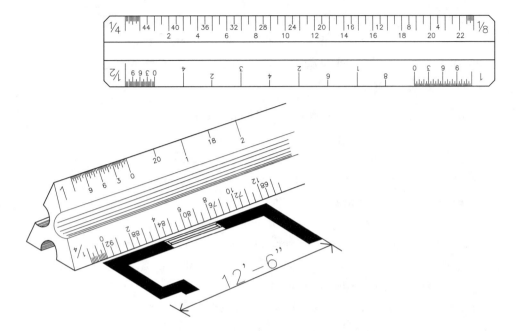

FIGURE 2-9 Scales are special rulers designed to measure in a variety of units, enabling objects to be drawn at various sizes. Scales are available in English and metric units, and in various shapes and sizes. Scales should never be used as a straightedge.

The term "scale" also refers to the physical measuring device used by designers to accurately reduce linear distances to their correct scaled lengths. Scales are special rulers that can be used for measuring in a variety of units and that enable the designer to draw an object larger than, smaller than, or the same size as the real (full-size) object. Scales are calibrated in inches or millimeters much like a regular ruler. They are available in either a flat or triangular shape (Figure 2-9). Triangular scales are very popular because as many as four scales can be printed on each face. Generally, a triangular scale has as many as 11 different scales on it. The shape also makes them convenient to pick up and use. Flat scales generally have either a two-bevel or four-bevel edge, depending on the number of scales they carry. Good-quality scales must have sharply defined graduations that are close to the edge for accurate measurements. Scales are not meant to be a straight

edge, and should never be used as a pencil or inking guide when drawing a straight line.

There are several different types of scales, but the interior designer will mainly use the architect's scale, engineer's scale, and metric scale.

The architect's scale is the one most frequently used by an interior designer. It is used for laying out accurate design and construction drawings in feet and inches. Architectural scales generally contain 11 different divisions where each major division represents 1 foot. The major divisions are indicated as $3/32$, $1/16$, $1/8$, $3/16$, $1/4$, $3/8$, $1/2$, $3/4$, 1, 1-$1/2$, and 3. Each one of these divisions represents 1 foot on the scale. For example, the $1/4$ scale means $1/4$ of an inch on the scale represents 1 foot.

When using the architect's scale, begin at the 0 point, then count off the number of feet, using the major subdivisions that are marked along the length of the scale. The scaled inches are located on the other side of the 0 point.

The engineer's scale is a full divided scale, as it has the inches marked along its edge, which are then divided into decimal parts of an inch. The engineer's scale generally contains six different divisions/scales. These divisions are indicated as 10, 20, 30, 40, 50, and 60. These divisions mean "parts to an inch." For example, the 40 scale means 1 inch = 40 feet. As there are 40 subdivisions within an inch, each mark represents 1 foot. This scale can also be used to represent larger units such as 400 or 4000 feet per inch. Engineer's scales are generally used for drawing large-scale site plans and maps.

Metric scales are used when drawing architectural and interior plans in metric units. The millimeter is the basic unit of the metric scale. Metric scales are based on ratios, such as 1:50, which means 1 mm on the scale represents 50 mm. Typical ratios are 1:10,

1:25, 1:50, 1:100, 1:200, and 1:500. To enlarge a drawing, scales are available in 2:1 and 5:1 ratios. Since metric scales are based on the metric system, using the base 10, it is possible to use single-ratio scales for other ratios. For example, a 1:1 scale with 1-mm markings could also be used to represent 1 mm, 10 mm, 100 mm, or 1000 mm. A 1:2 metric scale could be used for 1 mm to represent 20 mm, 200 mm, and so forth.

Erasers, Erasing Shields, and Brushes

To be able to erase errors and correct drawings is very important to the interior designer. Erasability is one of the key advantages of using a pencil or pen for drawings. Erasers, erasing shields, and brushes are convenient tools of almost equal importance.

Erasers. A wide variety of both rubber and synthetic erasers is available. A good eraser must be capable of completely removing pencil or ink lines without leaving smudge marks or roughing the surface of the paper. For vellum drafting paper, soft rubber erasers should generally be used. There are also special erasers designed to

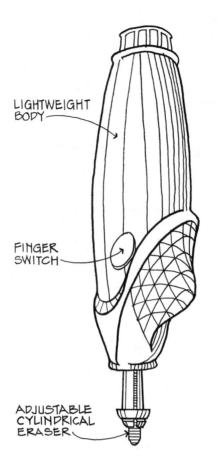

LIGHTWEIGHT BODY

FINGER SWITCH

ADJUSTABLE CYLINDRICAL ERASER

FIGURE 2-11 An electric eraser can be very handy when erasing large areas of a drawing and is especially convenient when cordless.

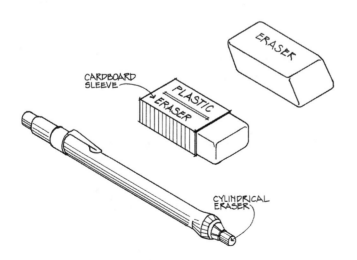

ERASER

CARDBOARD SLEEVE

PLASTIC ERASER

CYLINDRICAL ERASER

remove ink. However, be careful, as these erasers are too abrasive for some drawing surfaces. Some ink erasers claim to have a solvent incorporated into them for better erasing of ink. Erasers are available in either block form or stick form inserted into a holder much like a leadholder (Figure 2-10). Vinyl and other plastic erasers are designed for use on plastic drafting film.

Electric erasers are extremely useful when a great amount of erasing is necessary. Electric erasers are small handheld tools that hold long round lengths of eraser that are rotated when turned on. The cordless variety is the most convenient (Figure 2-11).

FIGURE 2-10 Erasers come in various shapes and sizes, and different kinds can erase pencil or ink. Shown are a mechanical eraser-holder, a plastic block eraser in a sleeve, and a basic block eraser.

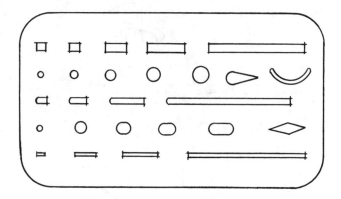

FIGURE 2-12 An eraser shield allows for precise erasing, as it shields the parts of the drawing that is to remain. The prepunched holes allow the designer to erase only those lines needing to be erased.

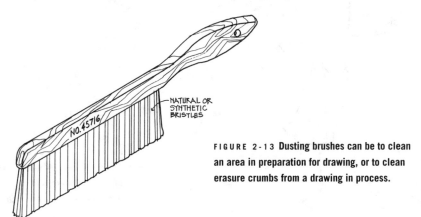

NATURAL OR SYNTHETIC BRISTLES

NO. 45716

FIGURE 2-13 Dusting brushes can be to clean an area in preparation for drawing, or to clean erasure crumbs from a drawing in process.

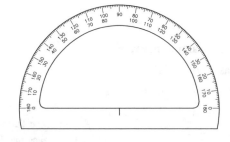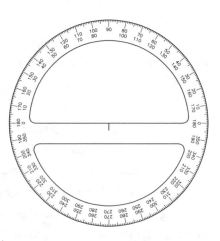

FIGURE 2-14 Protractors aid designers in laying out and measuring angles. They come in a variety of sizes and materials.

Erasing shields. A small metal or plastic card with prepunched holes and slots is used to erase precise areas of a drawing, as shown in Figure 2-12. The prepunched holes come in a variety of sizes and shapes, allowing the designer to erase small details and control the erasure up to a particular point. It is also helpful in protecting the drawing surface while using an electric eraser. Although the transparency of a plastic shield can be convenient, a metal shield generally lasts longer.

Brushes. A dusting brush is useful for keeping drafting surfaces clean and free of debris (Figure 2-13). Erasure crumbs are sometimes left on a drawing surface to help prevent smudges, but if they become too abundant they can cause lines to skip, so it is helpful to brush the drawing surface often.

Additional Equipment

A number of additional tools may assist the designer. For example, full-circular (360 degrees) and half circular (180 degrees) protractors aid in the layout and measuring of angles on a drawing. They are manufactured in a variety of sizes in both metal and plastic (Figure 2-14).

Other equipment includes flexible drawing curves that are made as a vinyl-covered length of extrusion with a lead center. They can be bent to the required radii or curve to serve as a guide for drawing smooth curved lines with a pencil or pen. The curve holds its position until it is reshaped into another curve.

Drawing and Drafting Fundamentals 3

Drawing and drafting are forms of visual language that use lines, pictorial images, and symbols to convey specific meanings. Like spoken language, written language, and body language, this visual language has its own unique applications. In the design field, drawing, also called sketching or idea generation, is used as a technique for developing and communicating ideas. Preliminary sketches are used to initiate and explore basic concepts, as illustrated in Figure 3-1. These can be presented to others as is, or refined into presentation drawings that are developed to scale and rendered in more detail. Drawing is thus a means of communication used by designers to effectively convey ideas and converse with one another about how to turn them into reality.

Drafting is a particular type of drawing that conveys specific information about something's size, composition, assembly, and other exacting characteristics. Drafting is usually a means to an end; that is, it serves as a guide on how to make something. For these reasons, drafting is founded on a number of basic premises and rules. A draftsperson's specialized drawings, generally referred to as working drawings or construction drawings, help the designer to develop ideas and communicate to the builder the exact parameters of their design concepts—assisting in the construction of a physical interior environment or building (Figure 3-2).

Construction drawings require a great deal of effort to draw,

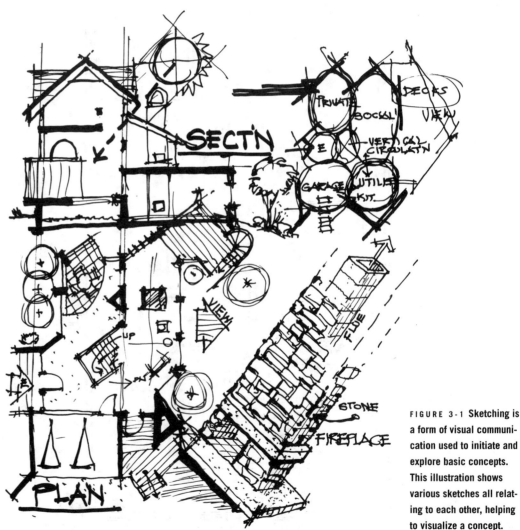

FIGURE 3-1 **Sketching is a form of visual communication used to initiate and explore basic concepts. This illustration shows various sketches all relating to each other, helping to visualize a concept.**

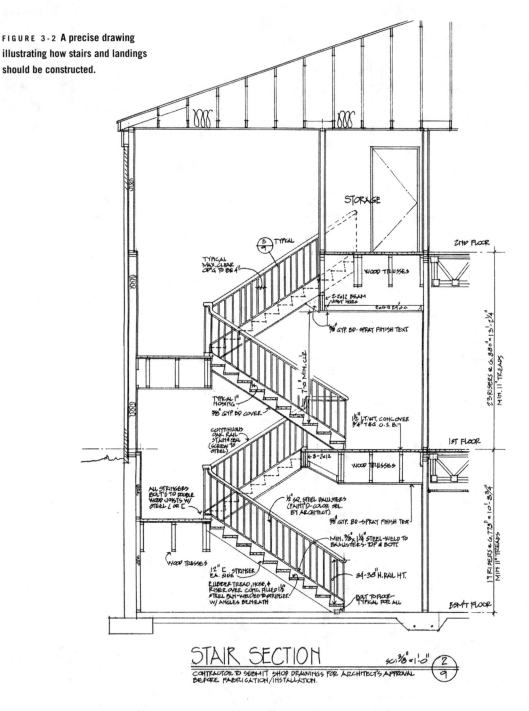

STAIR SECTION

CONTRACTOR TO SUBMIT SHOP DRAWINGS FOR ARCHITECT'S APPROVAL BEFORE FABRICATION/INSTALLATION.

as they must be clear, concise, and accurate, with high-quality lines and legible dimensions and notes.

To draw and draft at a professional level, one must learn some basic skills and techniques. This chapter will introduce the basics needed to produce quality and easily readable drawings to effectively communicate with others.

Starting the Drawing

Drawings are executed on a paper or plastic sheet that is placed on the drawing board or surface. It is usually held in place on the drawing surface with drafting tape placed at the four corners, as illustrated in Figure 3-3. The opposite corners are pulled and taped alternately to stretch and flatten the sheet. When one is finished with the drawing or needs to remove it for a short period of time, the tape is carefully removed and discarded. The sheet can then be stored flat or rolled for convenience. There is a tendency for beginners to roll original drawings and prints with the original line work or printed side on the inside, probably in an effort to protect the line work. However, the preferred way to roll a drawing is to do it with the printed information on the outside. In this way, as the drawing is unrolled, it will tend to curl away from the viewer and toward the surface it is placed on (Figure 3-4). This keeps the drawing from constantly curling up toward the viewer. This technique is also effective for multiple copies stapled together in sets.

Drawings are produced on a variety of surfaces with varying types of media, as discussed in Chapter 2. One of the first steps in composing a properly scaled drawing is to select the best size and format for the surface. To do this effectively, a number of variables must be taken into account. These include the complexity and

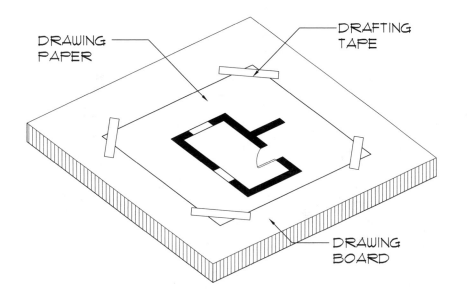

DRAWING PAPER

DRAFTING TAPE

DRAWING BOARD

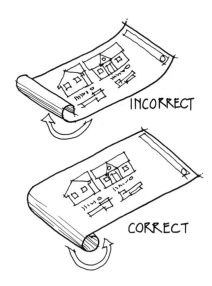

INCORRECT

CORRECT

FIGURE 3-3 (left) The drawing paper is held in place on the drawing surface with small pieces of drafting tape.

FIGURE 3-4 (right) Rolling drawings with the printed information on the outside causes them curl and hide the drawing from the viewer when unrolled and laid flat. Rolling them with the information on the outside allows the viewer to look at the drawings without having the paper curl up and hide the drawing.

scale of the drawing, the reproduction technique selected, and the viewing conditions the reader will be under.

Drawing Page Layout

Original drawings, particularly those done in pencil, need to be kept clean to provide for the clearest reproduction. Smudged drawings will often produce smudged prints that are difficult and time consuming to read. Graphite from pencils is the greatest threat to drawing cleanliness. Sliding hands, elbows, and equipment over pencil lines will blur them and produce an undesirable patina over the entire drawing surface. The same is true with ink drawings, whether they are done by hand or computer. Time must be allowed for the ink to dry. Equipment should be lifted and placed over drawings, not slid from one area to another. Regular washing of hands and equipment will also help prevent smudging of line work.

In manual drawing, one should start with very light lines and darken those as needed for the final drawing (Figure 3-5). On the computer, "pen" settings determine the value or thickness of a line (Figure 3-6). There is no preliminary stage of drawing with light lines. In manual drawings, it is good practice to start drawing at the upper portion of the sheet and progress toward the bottom of the paper. In this way, most drawings will not be disturbed as you move the equipment and hands down the sheet. Of course, computer drawing allows one to begin almost anywhere on the sheet, compose the drawings, and print out the results in one clean plot. The machine doesn't worry about top to bottom or left to right—it follows the composition set by the designer.

Line Types

Lines are drawn to describe objects, hidden conditions, and important relationships between components and space. A line drawn on a surface has both direction and weight. The weight of a line

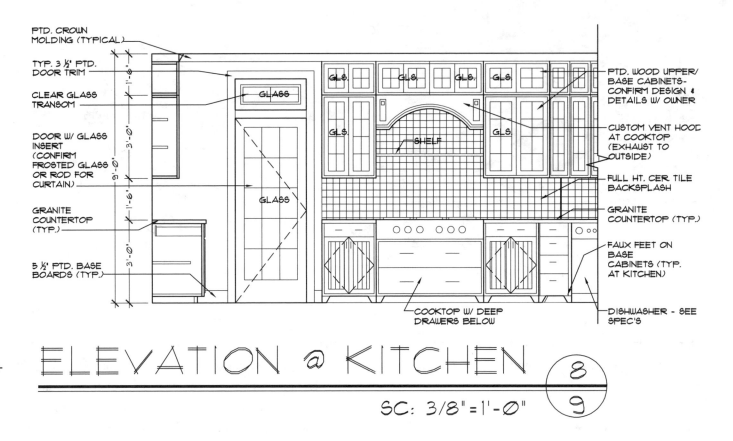

PTD. CROWN
MOLDING (TYPICAL)

TYP. 3½' PTD.
DOOR TRIM

CLEAR GLASS
TRANSOM

DOOR W/ GLASS
INSERT
(CONFIRM
FROSTED GLASS
OR ROD FOR
CURTAIN)

GRANITE
COUNTERTOP
(TYP.)

5½' PTD. BASE
BOARDS (TYP.)

GLASS

GLASS

GLS.   GLS.   GLS.   GLS.

GLS.   SHELF   GLS.

PTD. WOOD UPPER/
BASE CABINETS-
CONFIRM DESIGN &
DETAILS W/ OWNER

CUSTOM VENT HOOD
AT COOKTOP
(EXHAUST TO
OUTSIDE)

FULL HT. CER TILE
BACKSPLASH

GRANITE
COUNTERTOP (TYP.)

FAUX FEET ON
BASE
CABINETS (TYP.
AT KITCHEN)

COOKTOP W/ DEEP
DRAWERS BELOW

DISHWASHER - SEE
SPEC'S

ELEVATION @ KITCHEN

8/9

SC: 3/8" = 1'-0"

FIGURE 3-6 When using the computer to create a drawing, various "pen" weights/widths can be assigned to lines for the desired line hierarchy.

refers to its thickness and intensity; a line can also be continuous or dashed. The direction can be straight, curved, diagonal, or a combination of these. In drafting, continuous lines of various weights are used to represent objects and major elements such as structural walls or columns. Dashed lines are usually used to denote objects hidden from view. However, they can also be used to denote other things, such as a wheelchair turning radius or ceiling height changes on a floor plan. The following are the most commonly used line types. Examples are shown in Figure 3-7.

- **Cutting lines: show major slices in a building or object.**

- **Object lines: show major outlines of building elements or objects.**

- **Hidden lines: indicate areas or objects not visible on the surface, or objects hidden behind others. They are also used to show objects above the cutting plane of a floor plan, such as wall cabinets, beams, arches, etc.**

- **Centerlines: locate the symmetrical center of objects such as windows, doors, beams, and walls.**

- **Dimension lines and extension lines: indicate the physical distances of objects. Dimensions are placed directly above the dimension line or inserted within it.**

- **Leaders: extend from text and end with an arrow, pointing to an object**

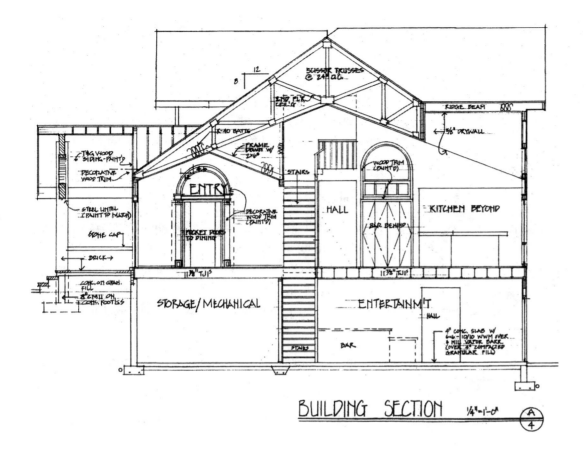

BUILDING SECTION ¼"=1'-0" A/4

(labels on drawing): 12, 8, SCISSOR TRUSSES @ 24" O.C., 2ND FLR. CEIL'G, RIDGE BEAM, ⅝" DRYWALL, R-40 BATTS, FRAME DOWN W/ 2x6", T&G WOOD SIDING-PAINT'D, DECORATIVE WOOD TRIM, STEEL LINTEL (PAINT TO MATCH), STONE CAP, BRICK, CONC. ON GRAN. FILL, 8" CMU ON CONT. FOOTING, ENTRY, STAIRS, HALL, WOOD TRIM (PAINT'D), DECORATIVE WOOD TRIM (PAINT'D), KITCHEN BEYOND, BAR BEHIND, POCKET DOORS TO DINING, 11⅞" TJI, 11⅞" TJI, STORAGE/MECHANICAL, ENTERTAINM'T, HALL, STAIRS, BAR, 4" CONC. SLAB W/ 6x6-10/10 WWM OVER 6 MIL VAPOR BARR. OVER 3" COMPACTED GRANULAR FILL

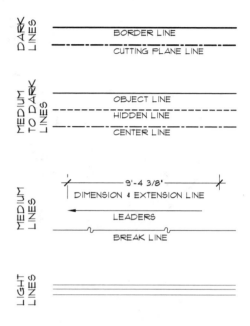

(line type chart labels): DARK LINES — BORDER LINE, CUTTING PLANE LINE; MEDIUM TO DARK LINES — OBJECT LINE, HIDDEN LINE, CENTER LINE; MEDIUM LINES — 9'-4 3/8" DIMENSION & EXTENSION LINE, LEADERS, BREAK LINE; LIGHT LINES

FIGURE 3-7 These are common line types used in drawings to describe objects, hidden conditions, and the importance of relationships between components and space.

or place.

- **Break lines:** indicate where an object or area is not drawn in its entirety.
- **Layout lines:** are used in the preliminary blocking out of components and for lettering guidelines.

Line Weights and Uses

Line weight refers to the blackness (intensity) and width of a line on the drawing surface. In general, heavy (dark) lines are used to represent cutting planes and contours (or outer boundaries) of an object. In a floor plan view, it is often the walls that are drawn with the darkest lines in order to define the spaces (Figure 3-8). These lines appear to be the closest to the viewer and are perceived as major elements. Medium and lighter lines appear to be farther away from the viewer and are used for secondary emphasis.

Drawings for interior design projects generally use three line widths, thick (dark), medium, and thin (light). Thick lines are generally twice as wide as thin lines, usually ¹⁄₃₂ inch or about 0.8 mm wide. Thin lines are approximately ¹⁄₆₄ inch or 0.4 mm wide. Medium lines fall between these two extremes. In pencil drawings,

1ST FLOOR PLAN

SC: 1/4"=1'-0"

FIGURE 3-8 In a floor plan, the walls are often drawn the darkest to define the spaces. The viewer tends to see these lines first, and thus they are perceived as major elements.

are also used to emphasize an object or element.

Medium Lines

Medium-weight lines are used for hidden objects and are usually drawn dashed or dotted. They are also used for outlining the planes of objects and for centerlines, as well as for furniture and equipment.

Thin, Light Lines

Thin, light lines are generally used as guidelines, drawn to help line up certain details or to help with lettering height. These lines should be barely visible and should disappear when a print or copy is made. Light lines, that are a little darker, are used for dimension and extension lines, leaders, door swings, and break lines.

Drafting Standards, Abbreviations, and Symbols

A designer's drawings are used to communicate specific information to many other individuals, such as owners, architects, engineers, and builders. To do this effectively, a number of drafting standards, abbreviations, and symbols have been developed over time that have become uniformly acceptable in the building industry. Although an office may use variations of the standard conventions presented here, most follow some version of these conventions. Many construction terms are abbreviated to save drawing space and eliminate the need for detailed drawings or notes. For example, a W8 x 31 is a standard steel beam whose exact physical and structural properties are detailed out in industrywide steel manuals. Another example is the commonly used term "above finished floor," which is abbreviated as A.F.F. and used in floor plans and electrical plans. The most commonly used abbre-

each type can be further broken down, depending on the variety of lead and level of pressure. With the variety of mechanical pencils on the market today, it is easy to control line widths. As discussed in Chapter 2, fine-line mechanical pencils are available in a 0.3, 0.5, 0.7, or 0.9 mm lead. By switching to different pencils, the drafter can vary line weight easily.

Thick, Dark Lines

Thick, dark lines are used for major sections (Figure 3-9), details, borderlines, and cutting plane lines. A thick, intense line can represent the walls on a floor plan or structural members, such as fireplaces or stairways, the outline of a ceiling on a reflected ceiling plan or the outline of a building on a site plan. Thick, intense lines

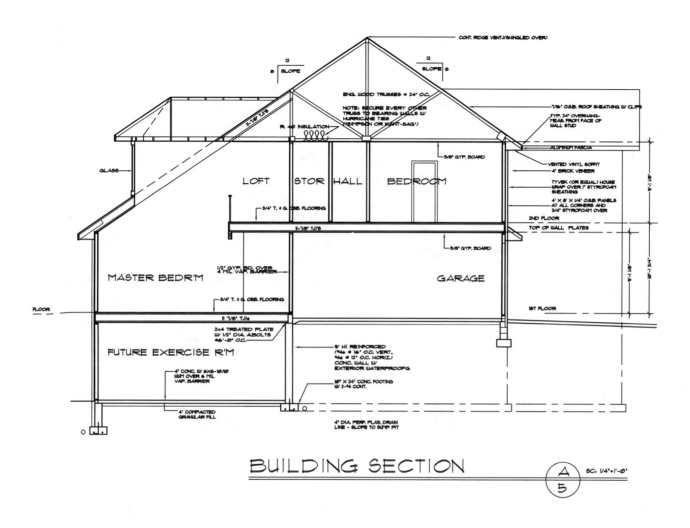

CONT. RIDGE VENT.(SHINGLED OVER)

12
8 SLOPE

12
SLOPE 8

ENG. WOOD TRUSSES @ 24" O.C.
NOTE: SECURE EVERY OTHER
TRUSS TO BEARING WALLS W/
HURRICANE TIES
(SIMPSON OR KANT-SAG')

7/16" O.S.B. ROOF SHEATHING W/ CLIPS
TYP. 24" OVERHANG-
MEAS. FROM FACE OF
WALL STUD

R-40 INSULATION

ALUMINUM FASCIA
VENTED VINYL SOFFIT
4' BRICK VENEER

3/8" GYP. BOARD

GLASS

LOFT   STOR HALL   BEDROOM

TYVEK (OR EQUAL) HOUSE
WRAP OVER 1" STYROFOAM
SHEATHING
4' X 8' X 1/4" O.S.B. PANELS
AT ALL CORNERS AND
3/4" STYROFOAM OVER

3/4" T. & G. O.S.B. FLOORING

2ND FLOOR
TOP OF WALL PLATES

11-7/8" TJI'S

3/8" GYP. BOARD

MASTER BEDR'M

1/2" GYP. BD. OVER
4 MIL VAP. BARRIER

GARAGE

3/4" T. & G. O.S.B. FLOORING

FLOOR

1ST FLOOR

11 7/8" TJI's

2x4 TREATED PLATE
W/ 1/2" DIA. ABOLTS
@6'-0" O.C.

9' HI REINFORCED
(#4's @ 16" O.C. VERT.
#4's @ 12" O.C. HORIZ.)
CONC. WALL W/
EXTERIOR WATERPROOF'G

FUTURE EXERCISE R'M

4" CONC. W/ 6X6-10/10
W.M OVER 6 MIL
VAP. BARRIER

18" X 24" CONC. FOOTING
W/ 2-#4 CONT.

4" COMPACTED
GRANULAR FILL

4" DIA. PERF. PLAS. DRAIN
LINE - SLOPE TO SUMP PIT

BUILDING SECTION

A
5
SC: 1/4"=1'-0"

FIGURE 3-9 Dark, thick lines are commonly used in building sections to denote where a plane is cut.

viations are discussed in Chapter 5 and are shown in Appendix D.

Symbols are used to represent objects that cannot be depicted accurately or would take too much time to draw. For example, the details of a window in plan or a wall electrical outlet are impractical to draw with clarity at such a small scale. These are represented in the plan by an acceptable symbol that is cross-referenced to a legend or note to more clearly define the object (Figure 3-10). Various components such as sinks, doors, windows, and electrical devices are drawn as symbols. These will be discussed in more depth in later chapters.

Sections cut through the building and materials are depicted using common symbols to represent their elements rather than drawing them as they might appear. For example, a section through a piece of plywood is shown schematically instead of drawn realistically to show the intricate layers of cross-grained wood veneers and glue. Symbols for materials are often drawn differently in a plan view and section view. In most cases, an attempt is made to portray as closely as possible what the actual cross-section would look like (Figure 3-11). Again, typical symbols for architectural materials are discussed more in Chapter 5.

Lettering

Lettering is used to communicate ideas and to describe elements that cannot be effectively explained with just drawings. In some cases, words are actually a clearer and more economical way to communicate. To ensure written words are quickly understood, a universal lettering style is commonly employed by designers and architects (Figure 3-12). This style, based on the Roman alphabet, generally consists of all capital letters for ease of reading. Although

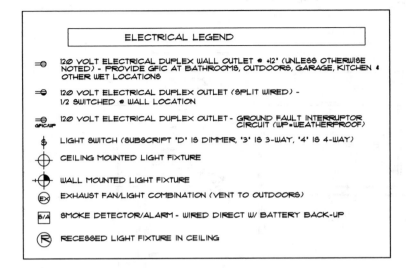

ELECTRICAL LEGEND

⊸ 120 VOLT ELECTRICAL DUPLEX WALL OUTLET @ +12' (UNLESS OTHERWISE NOTED) - PROVIDE GFIC AT BATHROOMS, OUTDOORS, GARAGE, KITCHEN & OTHER WET LOCATIONS

⊸ 120 VOLT ELECTRICAL DUPLEX OUTLET (SPLIT WIRED) - 1/2 SWITCHED @ WALL LOCATION

⊸GFIC/WP 120 VOLT ELECTRICAL DUPLEX OUTLET - GROUND FAULT INTERRUPTOR CIRCUIT (WP=WEATHERPROOF)

$ LIGHT SWITCH (SUBSCRIPT 'D' IS DIMMER, '3' IS 3-WAY, '4' IS 4-WAY)

⊕ CEILING MOUNTED LIGHT FIXTURE

⊢⊕ WALL MOUNTED LIGHT FIXTURE

(EX) EXHAUST FAN/LIGHT COMBINATION (VENT TO OUTDOORS)

(S/A) SMOKE DETECTOR/ALARM - WIRED DIRECT W/ BATTERY BACK-UP

(R) RECESSED LIGHT FIXTURE IN CEILING

PARTIAL ELECTRICAL PLAN

FIGURE 3-10 In this illustration, an electrical plan is shown with various symbols, and the legend above describes what each symbol represents.

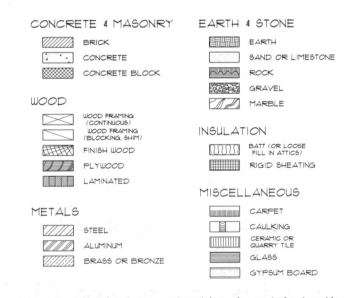

CONCRETE & MASONRY
- BRICK
- CONCRETE
- CONCRETE BLOCK

WOOD
- WOOD FRAMING (CONTINUOUS)
- WOOD FRAMING (BLOCKING, SHIM)
- FINISH WOOD
- PLYWOOD
- LAMINATED

METALS
- STEEL
- ALUMINUM
- BRASS OR BRONZE

EARTH & STONE
- EARTH
- SAND OR LIMESTONE
- ROCK
- GRAVEL
- MARBLE

INSULATION
- BATT (OR LOOSE FILL IN ATTICS)
- RIGID SHEATING

MISCELLANEOUS
- CARPET
- CAULKING
- CERAMIC OR QUARRY TILE
- GLASS
- GYPSUM BOARD

FIGURE 3-11 Materials that are cut through in section are depicted graphically. An attempt is made to represent the material, but in general it is simplistically, since drawing all the intricate details would be too time-consuming.

TOO WIDE TOONARROW TOOCLOSE TOOLOOSE
ABCDEFGHIJKLMNOPQRSTUVWXYZ 1234567890
ABCDEFGHIJKLMNOPQRSTUVWXYZ

STYLE	SAMPLE
ARCHSTYL.SHX	A B C D E F G H I J K L M N O P Q R S T U V W X Y Z 1 2 3 4 5 6 7 8 9 0
ARIAL	ABCDEFGHIJKLMNOPQRSTUVWXYZ 1234567890
BELL MT	ABCDEFGHIJKLMNOPQRSTUVWXYZ 1234567890
BERLIN SANS FB	ABCDEFGHIJKLMNOPQRSTUVWXYZ 1234567890
BOOK ANTIQUA	ABCDEFGHIJKLMNOPQRSTUVWXYZ 1234567890
CENTURY	ABCDEFGHIJKLMNOPQRSTUVWXYZ 1234567890
CITY BLUEPRINT	ABCDEFGHIJKLMNOPQRSTUVWXYZ 1234567890
COPPERPLATE GOTHIC	ABCDEFGHIJKLMNOPQRSTUVWXYZ 1234567890
COUNTRY BLUEPRINT	ABCDEFGHIJKLMNOPQRSTUVWXYZ 1234567890
ERAS MEDIUM ITC	ABCDEFGHIJKLMNOPQRSTUVWXYZ 1234567890
GILL SANS MT	ABCDEFGHIJKLMNOPQRSTUVWXYZ 1234567890
LUCIDA CONSOLE	A B C D E F G H I J K L M N O P Q R S T U V W X Y Z 1 2 3 4 5 6 7 8 9 0
ROMANS	A B C D E F G H I J K L M N O P Q R S T U V W X Y Z 1 2 3 4 5 6 7 8 9 0
STYLUS BT	ABCDEFGHIJKLMNOPQRSTUVWXYZ 1234567890
TAHOMA	ABCDEFGHIJKLMNOPQRSTUVWXYZ 1234567890
TIMES NEW ROMAN	ABCDEFGHIJKLMNOPQRSTUVWXYZ 1234567890
VERDANA	ABCDEFGHIJKLMNOPQRSTUVWXYZ 1234567890

most designers employ a universal-looking style, individual styles do develop and are often recognized and associated with the person who uses them. However, stylistic differences must not be so extreme that letters and words become difficult or time-consuming to read. The intent of architectural lettering is to communicate quickly and clearly. Many firms attempt to unify lettering among their personnel by adopting an office standard.

Today, computer software quickly produces lettering in many styles that appear to be hand-lettered or typed (Figure 3-13). Some of these are so realistic it is difficult to tell whether they really are done by hand or by computer. However, this does not mean that there is not a need for a student or designer to learn and produce

good hand-lettering. The ability to hand-letter is still much alive and needed. We still need to have effective handwriting when communicating with clients, builders, and many others in the field. A designer's lettering style can also be a kind of professional trademark that distinguishes him or her as a creative individual.

Basic Guidelines for Lettering

Good lettering is made by consistency. This includes height of letters, style, and spacing between letters. To maintain consistency in height, hand-lettering is always done using two or more horizontal guidelines. To maintain consistency between lines of lettering, the distance between these lines should be measured with a scale

FIGURE 3-14 (left) Horizontal guidelines can be used for height consistency when lettering. Two or three guidelines can be used, and these lines can remain on the drawing if produced lightly.

FIGURE 3-15 (right) Lettering should be consistent throughout a drawing; the shapes and proportions should be similar.

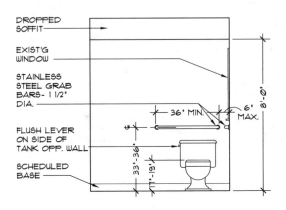

or other device. Then, when the draftsperson gains more proficiency, this distance can be fairly accurately "eyeballed" in. The two lines serve as the upper and lower limits of the letters. A third line can serve as a consistent guide for parts of letters or even lowercase letters (Figure 3-14). The draftsperson must endeavor to keep the letters within the top and bottom lines and not let parts of the letters extend beyond these. In most cases, the guidelines are produced with such a light line that they are left in and not erased. In pen-and-ink drawings, these lines might be laid out in nonreproducible blue pencil lines.

Most designers prefer vertical strokes in lettering, although slanted characters are often faster to produce. Letters should be produced with bold strokes, not drawn with a series of sketched and ragged lines. There should be a distinctive start and stop to each line stroke within a letter. Shapes and proportions of lettering should be consistent throughout a drawing (Figure 3-15). Close attention should be given to the width of a letter, as well as the proportional spaces between letters. This spacing is very important, as it gives words good visual formation and clarifies their relationship to other words. In general, spacing between letters in a word should be made approximately equal in the beginning of the designer's career. However, this rule can be modified as the designer gains confidence, as proportional spacing can vary a bit,

depending on the shapes of the letters.

One shortcut used for lettering by some designers is the aid of a small triangle carried along the parallel bar (or other horizontal device) and quickly brought into play for vertical strokes within a letter. This technique produces a very consistent vertical style, but some designers see it as a crutch. If this technique is used, it should be discontinued once the draftsperson gains the ability and confidence to produce accurate vertical lines.

To effectively learn proper lettering, one should produce words and numbers, not just individual letters. Practice by copying phrases from articles and books, or writing a story. This will give you better skills in forming properly proportioned letters and spaces between them.

Design drawings enable the professional designer to visualize and communicate the features of a three-dimensional object or interior space. Then, detailed construction drawings are made to accurately describe what materials are to be used and how the object or space is to be constructed. The design drawing can be a three-dimensional pictorial sketch that shows what the object looks like in reality (Figure 4-1), or a series of related yet different views of the object, such as a plan or top view and an elevation, as illustrated in Figure 4-2. The first approach, the single view, attempts to portray the object as the eye would see it. The second approach, the multiview, relies on the eye to view a series of images and the mind to then put these views together into a whole. For example, a floor plan shows width and length of objects within a space. An elevation view is then drawn to illustrate height, but no third dimension or true depth is visually indicated. Figure 4-3 classifies the various drawing systems according to these two broad categories. Many computer software programs now can produce some very convincing single-view drawings from multiviews, which allow designers to quickly flip back and forth between these two types of drawings.

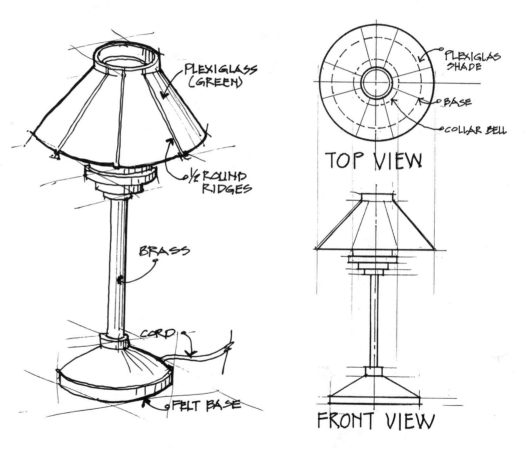

FIGURE 4-1 (left) Design drawings may consist of pictorial sketches that show an object as the eye might see it.
FIGURE 4-2 (right) Different views of an object help the eye to understand the object as a whole.

CLASSIFICATION OF DRAWING SYSTEMS

	TYPE	APPLICATION – OBJECT	APPLICATION – INTERIORS	RELATIONSHIP OF OBJECTS TO PICTURE PLANE
MULTIVIEW	ORTHOGRAPHIC	PLAN/ELEVATION	PLAN / ELEVAT'N SECT'N	AN OBJECT'S RECTANGULAR FACES ARE PARALLEL TO THE PICTURE PLANE.
SINGLE VIEW — PARALINE — AXONOMETRIC	ISOMETRIC			THE THREE PRINCIPAL AXES MAKE EQUAL ANGLES (30°) WITH THE PICTURE PLANE. ALL LENGTHS ARE EQUAL.
	DIMETRIC			THE TWO PRINCIPAL AXES MAKE EQUAL ANGLES WITH THE PICTURE PLANE, AND TWO LENGTHS ARE EQUAL. OBJECTS CAN BE ROTATED AT VARIOUS ANGLES.
	TRIMETRIC			EACH OF THE TWO PRINCIPAL AXES MAKES A DIFFERENT ANGLE WITH THE PICTURE PLANE. HEIGHT IS REDUCED, SIMILAR TO A DIAMETRIC.
SINGLE VIEW — PARALINE — OBLIQUE	ELEVATION			THE FACE (ELEVATION) OF THE OBJECT IS PARALLEL TO THE PICTURE PLANE. DEPTHS ARE USUALLY REDUCED IN RATIO.
	PLAN			THE TOP VIEW (OR PLAN) OF THE OBJECT IS PARALLEL TO THE PICTURE PLANE. HEIGHTS ARE USUALLY REDUCED.
SINGLE VIEW — PERSPECTIVE	ONE-POINT			ONE FACE IS PARALLEL TO THE PICTURE PLANE. PROJECTOR LINES CONVERGE TO ONE POINT.
	TWO-POINT			VERTICAL FACES ARE AT AN ANGLE TO THE PICTURE PLANE. PROJECTOR LINES CONVERGE TO TWO POINTS.
	THREE-POINT			VERTICAL FACES ARE AT AN ANGLE TO THE PICTURE PLANE. PROJECTOR LINES CONVERGE TO THREE POINTS.

(MULTIVIEW: Parallel lines remain parallel to each other. PARALINE: Parallel lines remain parallel to each other. PERSPECTIVE: Parallel lines appear to converge to vanishing points.)

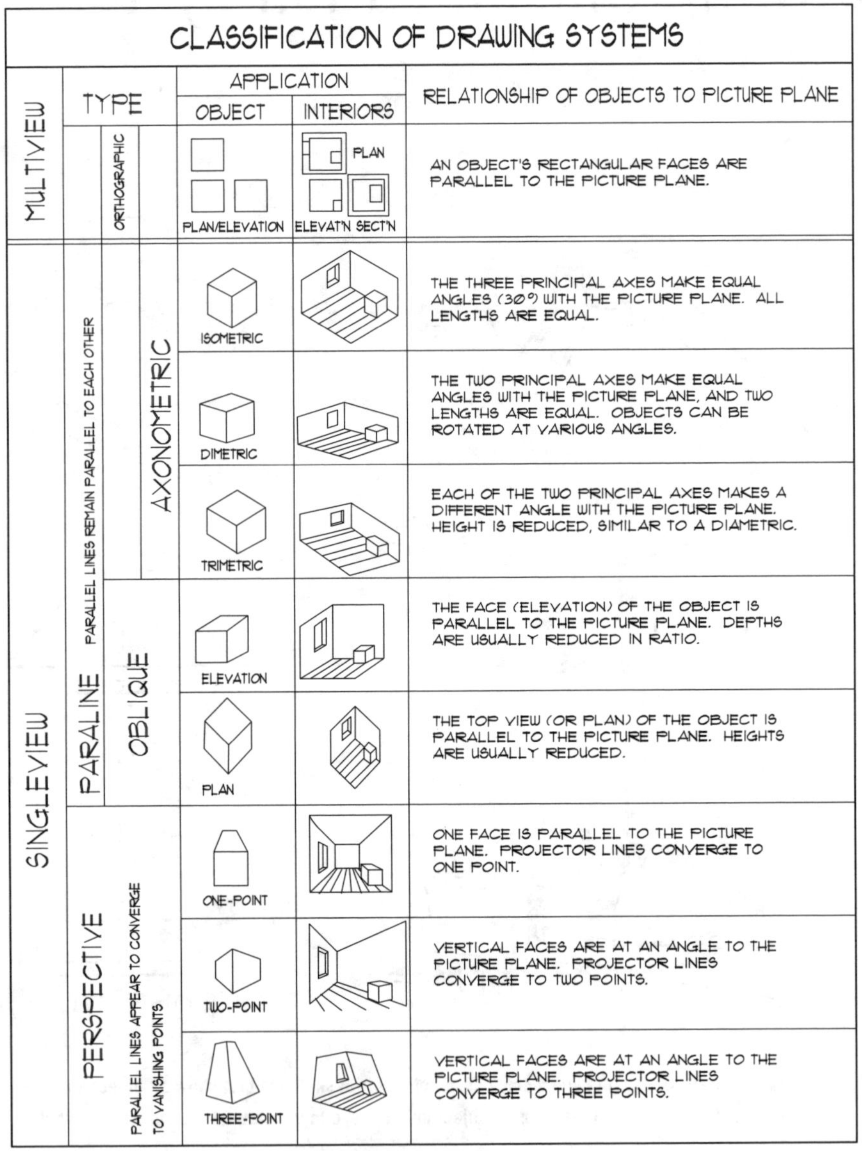

FIGURE 4-3 This chart classifies various drawing systems into two broad categories: single view and multiview.

Multiview Drawings

Multiview drawings can be visualized by what is commonly called the glass box theory. In this process, a three-dimensional object is imagined to be surrounded by a clear glass box (Figure 4-4). If the viewer looks along the perpendicular through any plane on the glass box, the object can be imagined to be a flat, two-dimensional image on that particular glass pane. The object can be viewed from above (called a plan view) or the side (called an elevation view). In turn, if these images are drawn separately, the viewer reverses the process and projects (by imagining) these various multiviews onto a whole three-dimensional object.

Orthographic Projections

The word *orthographic* refers to the projection system that is used to derive multiview drawings based on the glass box model. Drawings that appear on a surface are the view a person sees on the transparent viewing plane that is positioned perpendicular to the viewer's line of sight and the object. In the orthographic system, the object is placed in a series of positions (plan or elevation) relative to the viewing plane.

The most common types of orthographic drawings are the plan, elevation, and section (Figure 4-5). However, no single one of these drawings can communicate the actual configuration of a three-dimensional object or space. They must be used together to accurately depict spatial and solid elements. In fact, more complex objects and spaces will require several more of each of these drawings. Multiview drawings lack the pictorial effect of perspectives (which are a type of single-view drawings), yet are more accurate for conveying correctly scaled objects, interiors, and buildings.

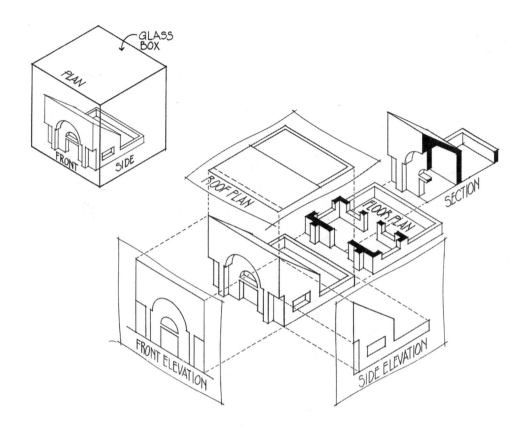

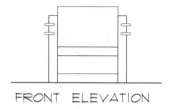

FRONT ELEVATION

SIDE ELEVATION

PLAN

FIGURE 4-4 (left) The glass box theory portrays a three-dimensional object as though surrounded by a clear glass box, with the corresponding view projected to the glass plane.

FIGURE 4-5 (right) The plan, elevation, and section are the most common multiview drawings.

Single-view Drawings

Single-view drawings attempt to picture an object or space as we normally see it in reality with all three dimensions appearing simultaneously. They present relationships of objects, space, and materials in a realistic or photographic-looking manner. Single-view drawings can be either paraline or perspective views. In paraline drawings, lines are drawn parallel to one another, and object features retain this relationship as they appear to recede in the distance (Figure 4-6). This parallel phenomenon is what gives this drawing system the name *paraline*.

The perspective view produces a more realistic picture as it attempts to duplicate the way our eyes actually see objects and space. In perspective drawing, parallel lines in space or on an object appear to converge to a common distant vanishing point, as illustrated in Figure 4-7. Perspective drawings resemble a photograph and are the most convincing of the drawing systems. They generally take more time to produce by hand, but computer generation has made the process less time-consuming.

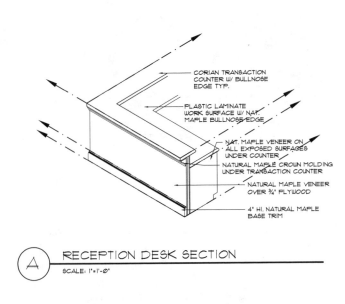

RECEPTION DESK SECTION

Ⓐ SCALE: 1"=1'-0"

CORIAN TRANSACTION
COUNTER W/ BULLNOSE
EDGE TYP.

PLASTIC LAMINATE
WORK SURFACE W/ NAT.
MAPLE BULLNOSE EDGE

NAT. MAPLE VENEER ON
ALL EXPOSED SURFACES
UNDER COUNTER

NATURAL MAPLE CROWN MOLDING
UNDER TRANSACTION COUNTER

NATURAL MAPLE VENEER
OVER ¾" PLYWOOD

4" HI. NATURAL MAPLE
BASE TRIM

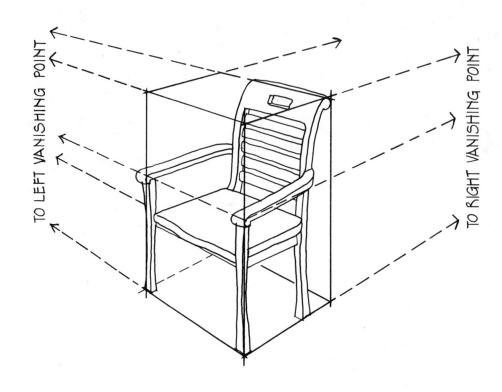

TO LEFT VANISHING POINT

TO RIGHT VANISHING POINT

FIGURE 4-6 (left) Lines are drawn parallel to one another in paraline drawings, a form of single view drawings.

FIGURE 4-7 (right) In a perspective, horizontal lines appear to visually recede to a point in the distance.

Paraline Drawings

Paraline dawings are usually faster and easier to develop than perspectives, as receding horizontal lines can be drawn with instruments, without calculating depths or drawing lines to a common vanishing point as is necessary in perspective drawings. However, when using computer-aided design (CAD), the speed of the rendering programs will govern which of these is produced the quickest. Paraline drawings are categorized according to the projection method used to develop them, and can be subdivided into two distinct types, axonometric and oblique (Figure 4-8).

Axonometric Projections

Some interior designers refer to all paralines as axonometrics; however, axonometric drawings are technically just one form of paraline drawing. *Axonometric* means "measurable along the axes." Axonometric drawings include three axes that relate to width, depth, and height. Each line drawn parallel to these axes is drawn at an exact scale with the true length of the object depicted. The axonometric projection system consists of three primary views: isometric, dimetric, and trimetric. These views are distinguished by the degree of variation visible of the principal faces of the object. In the isometric view, all faces represent true scales. The latter two systems show one or more faces in a reduced scale.

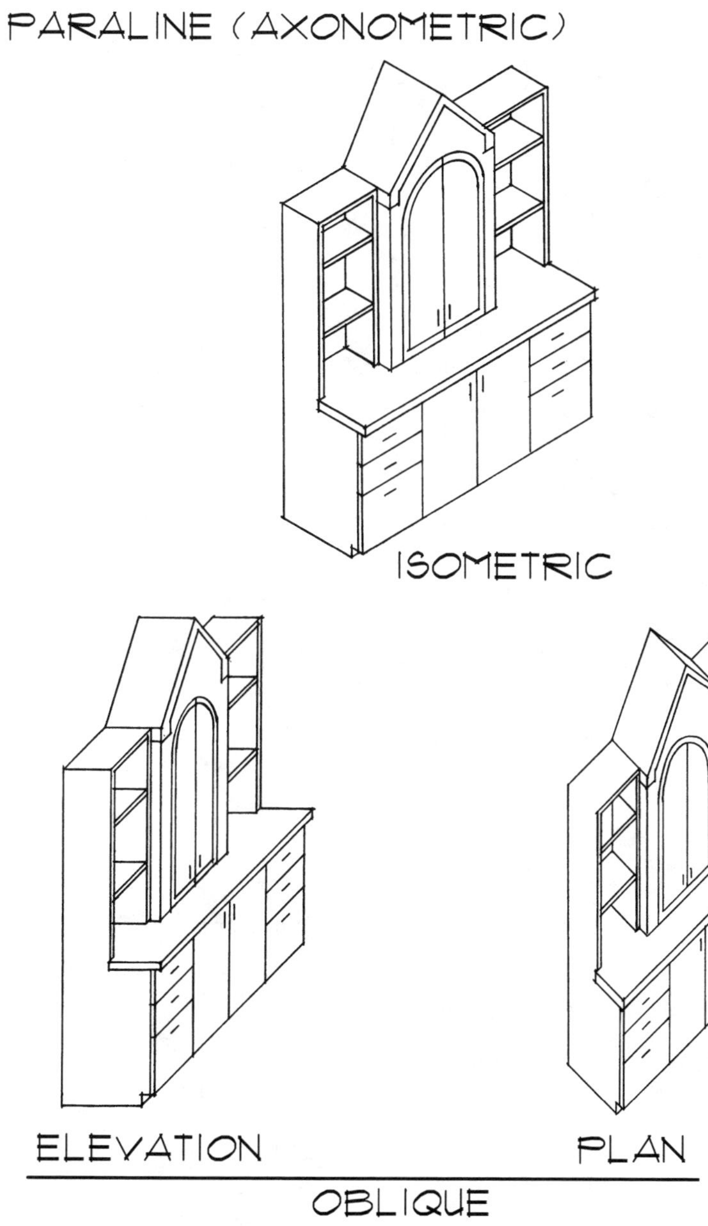

PARALINE (AXONOMETRIC)
ISOMETRIC
ELEVATION
PLAN
OBLIQUE

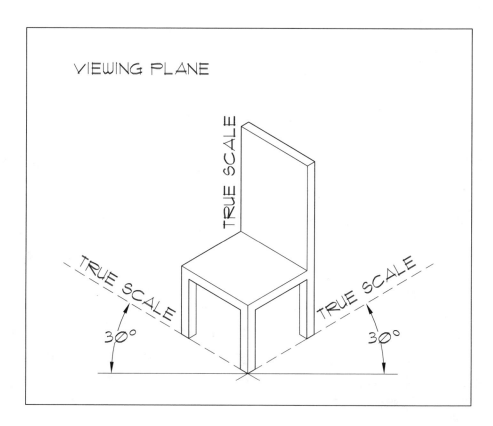

VIEWING PLANE
TRUE SCALE
TRUE SCALE
TRUE SCALE
30°
30°

FIGURE 4-9 **Isometric drawings present the three primary faces of an object equally and at the same angle with the viewing plane.**

FIGURE 4-8 **There are two types of paraline drawings: isometric and oblique.**

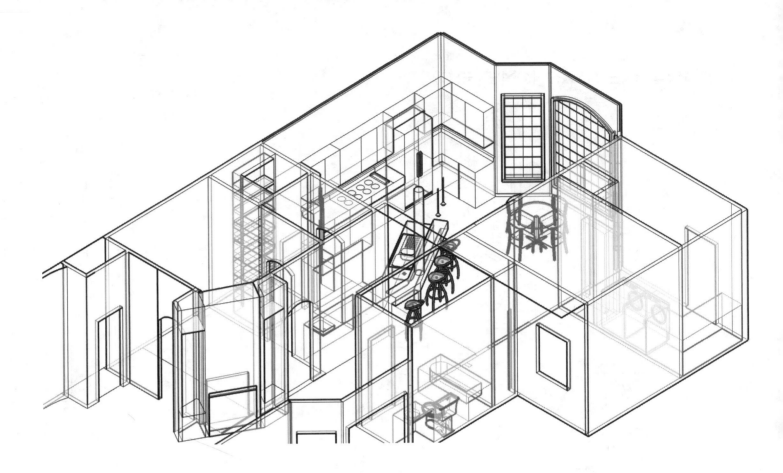

FIGURE 4-10 Isometric drawings are generally constructed as "wire frames" showing the construction lines.

Isometric (derived from the Greek words meaning "equal measure") drawings present the three primary faces of an object equally and at the same angle with the viewing plane. The planes of width and depth are drawn at 30 degrees and the height is held vertical (Figure 4-9). Dimensions are scaled equally along all three axes.

Isometric drawings are the easiest of the axonometric systems to construct, but the visual distortion caused by parallel lines not appearing to converge to a distant vanishing point gives them a distinct pictorial effect. Computer software now allows the designer to program in true scale for width, height, and depth. Then, isometric "wire frames" that show the construction lines can be quickly generated on the screen, as illustrated in Figure 4-10. Hidden or unwanted lines can also be easily turned off or removed from the image.

In the dimetric and trimetric drawings, all principal faces are not held at equal angles to the picture plane (Figure 4-11). The dimetric drawing makes two faces equally visible and shortens the third face. The trimetric rotates an object so that all three faces are at different angles to the picture plane.

In both the dimetric and trimetric drawings, the scale along one or more of the principal faces is reduced proportionately to emphasize or deemphasize a feature of the object. Both dimetric and trimetric drawings are more time-consuming to construct than the isometric drawings, but have the advantage of presenting an object's best features and more closely resemble the perspective-type drawings.

Oblique Projections

Oblique projections are popular among interior designers. Although there are several types of oblique drawings, the plan oblique and elevation oblique are the most commonly used. In these drawings, the floor plan or elevation serves as the true face on the picture plane, and parallel lines are projected vertically or horizontally at an angle other than 90 degrees from this face. The viewer's lines of sight are parallel, but are not at right angles with the viewing plane (Figure 4-12). Oblique drawings also have the feature that one face of an object is always parallel to the viewing plane and represented in true proportion, such as an elevation or plan view. These parallel lines are sometimes reduced in scale (shortened) from true size to reduce the visual distortion. With the use of specialized computer software, these views can be generated or extruded from a plan or elevation view with the click of a mouse.

To produce a plan oblique, the true shaped plan can be rotated at any angle, although the 30/60 degree and 45/45 degree are the most popular. The advantage of the plan oblique is that the building's floor plan can be used directly to generate this kind of drawing. By contrast, isometrics are more time-consuming because of the extra projections and dimensioning required. A floor plan or elevation cannot be used directly to produce an isometric drawing.

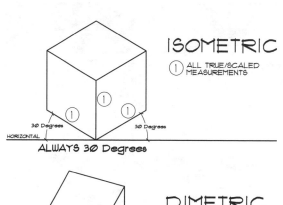

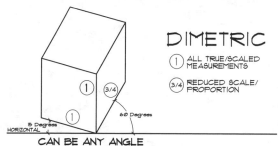

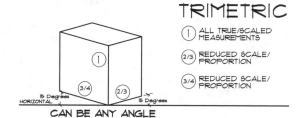

FIGURE 4-11 In diametric and trimetric drawings, all principal faces of an object are not held at equal angles to the picture plane.

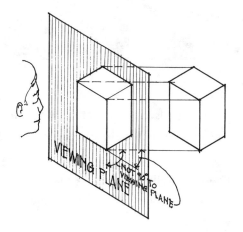

FIGURE 4-12 In a plan oblique drawing, the true plan can be rotated at any angle, although the 30-60 degree and 45-45 degree are most popular.

Perspective Drawings

FIGURE 4-13 Perspective drawings are the most realistic looking and are often used as presentation drawings.

A perspective drawing is a type of single-view drawing that is more realistic looking than an oblique or axonometric drawing. In a perspective drawing, objects appear to diminish in size as they recede into the distance, and lines that are parallel in the actual object appear to converge at some distant point on the horizon (termed the *vanishing point*). Perspectives are used primarily as presentation drawings to portray a finished object, building, or interior space (Figure 4-13). Perspectives most closely duplicate what our eye or a camera sees.

Perspectives have characteristics that distinguish them from paraline and orthographic drawings. These characteristics are:

1. **Convergence of parallel lines**
2. **Diminution of size**
3. **Foreshortening**
4. **Overlapping of forms**

These properties, as illustrated in Figure 4-14 help make perspectives very realistic compared to the other types of drawings. Perspective drawings are broken into three basic categories according to the number of vanishing points used to construct them (Figure 4-15). To construct perspectives, an imaginary picture plane is placed between the observer and the object (or interior) to be drawn. If this plane can be placed parallel to one plane of an object, parallel lines will appear to converge to only one point, producing the one-point perspective, as shown in Figure 4-16. If the picture plane is placed parallel to only one set of lines (the vertical lines, for example), the results are termed a *two-point perspective* (Figure 4-17). The parallel lines then appear to converge to two vanishing points. A three-point perspective is produced when all the lines or faces of an object are oblique (not parallel) to the picture plane. This method is not often used for interior spaces, but rather for tall buildings. Each of these perspective types can be hand-drawn in a number of different ways. A projection system can be used to produce an individualistic drawing for a specific object or space (Figure 4-18). Or a preconstructed perspective grid can be made and overlay sheets placed over it to draw a perspective. One method for constructing a grid is shown in Figure 4-19. Perspective grids can be drawn for each project, or preprinted grids can be made with the lines already

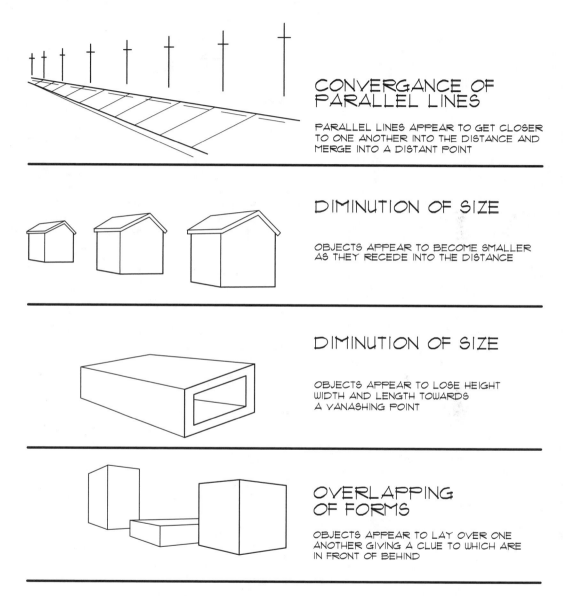

CONVERGANCE OF PARALLEL LINES

PARALLEL LINES APPEAR TO GET CLOSER TO ONE ANOTHER INTO THE DISTANCE AND MERGE INTO A DISTANT POINT

DIMINUTION OF SIZE

OBJECTS APPEAR TO BECOME SMALLER AS THEY RECEDE INTO THE DISTANCE

DIMINUTION OF SIZE

OBJECTS APPEAR TO LOSE HEIGHT WIDTH AND LENGTH TOWARDS A VANASHING POINT

OVERLAPPING OF FORMS

OBJECTS APPEAR TO LAY OVER ONE ANOTHER GIVING A CLUE TO WHICH ARE IN FRONT OF BEHIND

FIGURE 4-14 Perspective drawings use four properties that make them more realistic than paraline and orthographic drawings.

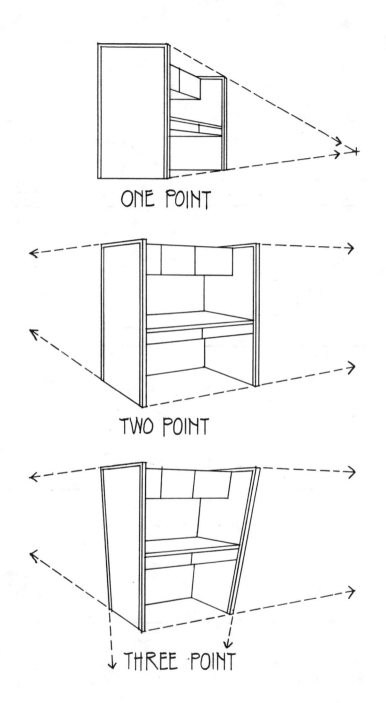

ONE POINT

TWO POINT

THREE POINT

FIGURE 4-15 There are three basic categories of perspective drawings, depending on the number of vanishing points.

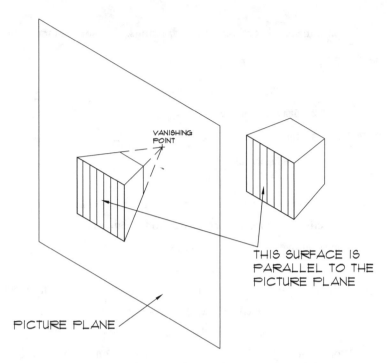

VANISHING POINT

THIS SURFACE IS PARALLEL TO THE PICTURE PLANE

PICTURE PLANE

FIGURE 4-16 In a one-point perspective, the picture plane is parallel to an object, and the parallel lines will appear to converge to only one point.

drawn in true perspective. These grids can be generated by hand or computer, or one can purchase preprinted grids.

One-point Perspective

Of the three types of perspective, the one-point is perhaps the easiest to understand and construct. In one-point perspectives, receding lines or sides of an object appear to vanish to a single point on the horizon. These types of perspectives are often used to produce room interiors, either from an elevation (front view) or plan (top view), depending on where the observer is standing (called the *station point*), as illustrated in Figure 4-20. The set-up for both of these is exactly the same, the difference being whether the observer

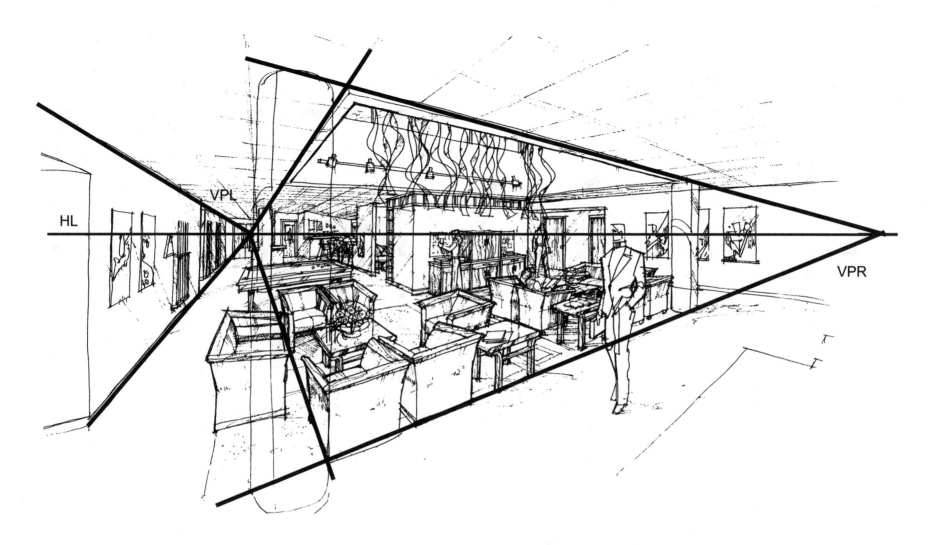

HL

VPL

VPR

is positioned above or at the horizon. The station point can also be moved to the left or right to emphasize the particulars of the space.

Two-point Perspective

The two-point perspective is one of the most widely used of the three types, as it portrays the most realistic view for the observer (Figure 4-21). By placing the object at unequal angles from the right and left vanishing points (which corresponds to the viewer's position in the space), dynamic views can be produced. However, if the viewer's position is moved too far over to one side or the other, distortions can occur in the final drawing. In most interior views, the eye-level perspective is the preferred choice. Two-point perspectives are more difficult to hand-draw than one-point perspectives, as planes must be projected to two vanishing points, as illustrated in Figure 4-22.

FIGURE 4-17 In a two-point perspective, the picture plane is placed parallel to only one set of lines (the vertical lines in this example) and the parallel lines appear to converge to two vanishing points.

PLAN PROJECTION METHOD

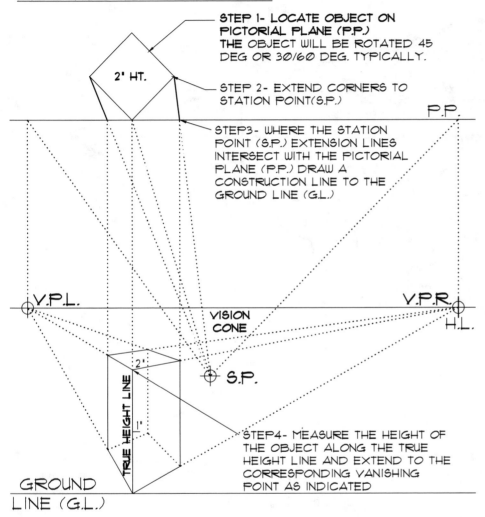

STEP 1- LOCATE OBJECT ON PICTORIAL PLANE (P.P.) THE OBJECT WILL BE ROTATED 45 DEG OR 30/60 DEG. TYPICALLY.

2' HT.

STEP 2- EXTEND CORNERS TO STATION POINT(S.P.)

P.P.

STEP3- WHERE THE STATION POINT (S.P.) EXTENSION LINES INTERSECT WITH THE PICTORIAL PLANE (P.P.) DRAW A CONSTRUCTION LINE TO THE GROUND LINE (G.L.)

V.P.L.

V.P.R.

VISION CONE

H.L.

S.P.

2'

TRUE HEIGHT LINE

1"

STEP4- MEASURE THE HEIGHT OF THE OBJECT ALONG THE TRUE HEIGHT LINE AND EXTEND TO THE CORRESPONDING VANISHING POINT AS INDICATED

GROUND LINE (G.L.)

FIGURE 4-18 In the hand-drawn method of three-point perspectives, a projection system is used to produce an individualistic drawing for a specific object or space.

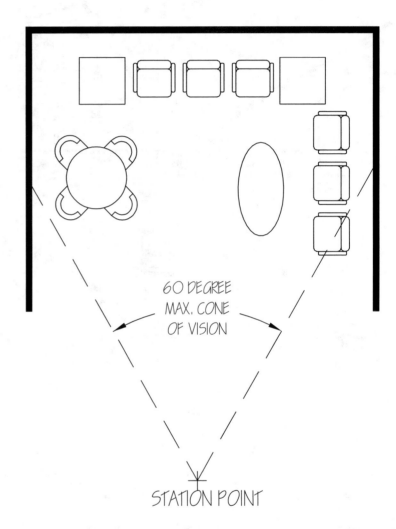

60 DEGREE MAX. CONE OF VISION

STATION POINT

FIGURE 4-20 The station point, shown in this plan view, represents the point from which the interior of the room will be seen in perspective.

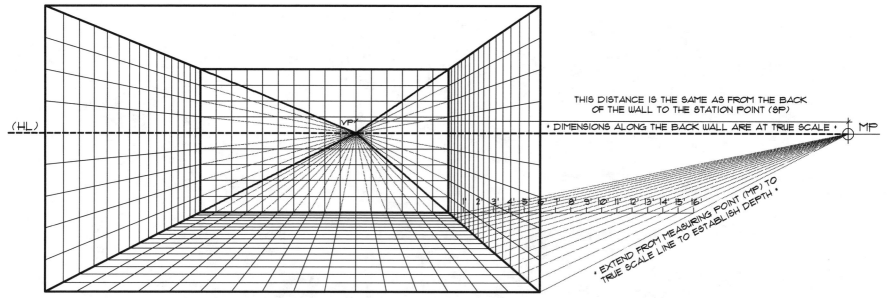

THIS DISTANCE IS THE SAME AS FROM THE BACK
OF THE WALL TO THE STATION POINT (SP)

• DIMENSIONS ALONG THE BACK WALL ARE AT TRUE SCALE •   MP

• EXTEND FROM MEASURING POINT (MP) TO
TRUE SCALE LINE TO ESTABLISH DEPTH •

(HL)   VP

STEP 1- DRAW A FLOOR PLAN TO ANY SCALE AND SELECT WALL THAT IS TO BE TRUE SCALE OR
BACK PARALLEL WALL IN THE PERSPECTIVE. PICK STATION POINT SP OF OBSERVER IN
PLAN, NOTING THIS POINT SHOULD BE APPROXIMATELY A 30-60 DEG. CONE OF VISION
TO INCORPORATE SOME OF THE SIDE WALLS. MEASURE & RECORD THIS DISTANCE (IN
SCALED FEET) FROM SP TO WALL B, WHEN CONSTRUCTING A PERSPECTIVE GRID WITHOUT
PLAN MEASUREMENT, THIS DISTANCE CAN OFTEN BE ASSUMED TO BE 1 TO 1 1/2 TIMES THE
WIDTH OF WALL B.

STEP 2- MAKING THE GRID: TO WHATEVER SCALE DESIRED (OFTEN 1/2' = 1'-0') DRAW WALL B IN
TRUE VERTICAL PROJECTION AND MARK OFF IN ONE FOOT INCREMENTS. DRAW A
HORIZON LINE FIVE FEET ABOVE THE FLOOR OR BASELINE. PLACE A DOT ON HORIZON
LINE CORRESPONDING TO YOUR POSITION FROM SIDEWALLS ON FLOOR PLAN (SAME
DISTANCE FROM WALLS B & C), AND CALL THIS THE VANISHING POINT VP. DRAW LINES
FROM ROOM CORNERS (WALL B) THROUGH VP.

STEP 3- EXTEND BASELINE AT WALL B AND MARK IN ONE FOOT INCREMENTS (SAME SCALE AS
WALL B). MEASURE DISTANCE FROM VP TO MEASURING POINT MP EQUAL TO DISTANCE
FROM SP TO WALL B (STEP 1).

STEP 4- DRAW LINES FROM MP THROUGH THE ONE FOOT INCREMENTS ALONG BASELINE AND
EXTEND TO FLOOR AND WALL C JUNCTION. FROM THESE MARKS, DRAW HORIZONTAL
LINES ALONG THE FLOOR, WHICH MARK OFF ONE FOOT INCREMENTS RECEDING TOWARD
WALL B. DRAW VERTICAL LINES ON WALLS A & C FROM ENDS OF EACH OF THESE FLOOR
LINES. EXTEND THESE LINES HORIZONTALLY TO GRID OFF THE CEILING.

STEP 5- EXTEND LINES FROM THE VP THROUGH THE FOOT INCREMENTS ON THE PERIMETER OF
WALL B, FINISHING THE GRID PERSPECTIVE TO BE ONE FOOT SQUARES AS THEY LOOK IN
PERSPECTIVE.

STEP 6- IF YOU DREW THE GRID NICE AND NEAT, TRACE IT IN INK AND KEEP IT FOR FUTURE
USAGE WITH OVERLAY PAPER. MAKE A SERIES OF GRIDS WITH VARYING STATION
POINTS, DIMENSIONS, ETC. FOR VARIETY. NOTE THAT YOU CAN TURN THE GRID ON END,
UPSIDE DOWN, OR REVERSE TO PRODUCE DIFFERENT ROOM AND VANISHING POINT
CONFIGURATIONS.

FIGURE 4-19 An example of how to
draw a one-point perspective grid.

FIGURE 4-21 The two-point perspective is used more often than the one-point and three-point perspectives, because it portrays a more realistic view of an object or space.

Three-point Perspective

Three-point perspectives are generally drawn with the viewer at a distance above the horizon (bird's-eye view) or below the horizon (worm's-eye view). The three-point perspective is used mostly for very tall buildings and is rarely used in interior spaces, unless they are multi-storied. Three-point perspectives are more complicated than the former two types, as a third vanishing point is introduced, which prevents any lines from becoming parallel.

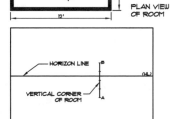

MEASURE THE DIMENSIONS OF THE ROOM AND ASSUME YOUR DIRECTION OF VIEW (AND YOUR GENERAL LOCATION IN THE ROOM.)

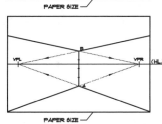

USE A LARGE SHEET OF PAPER FOR YOUR DRAWING AND SCALE THE PERSPECTIVE TO THE PAPER. SCALE THE HEIGHT OF THE FAR CORNER OF THE ROOM (LINE AB) ON THE PAPER AT A CONVENIENT SCALE, SAY ½"=1'-Ø". DRAW THE HORIZON LINE (HL) AT APPROXIMATE EYE LEVEL (5'-Ø') AND EXTEND ACROSS THE PAPER.

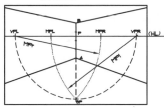

SKETCH IN THE APPROXIMATE CORNER VIEW YOU WOULD SEE IN THE ROOM BY EXTENDING THE LINES TO THE HL TO GAIN YOUR LEFT AND RIGHT VANISHING POINTS (VPL & VPR)

A GOOD RULE OF THUMB ON PLACING THE VANISHING POINTS IS TO PLACE THE CLOSEST VP APPROXIMATELY 1½ TIMES THE WIDTH OF THE BACK WALL OF THE ROOM (NOT THE WALL ADJACENT TO YOU) FROM THE VERTICAL LINE AB ON THE HL. PLACE THE OTHER VP AT A FATHER DISTANCE THAN THIS. THIS WILL ASSURE THAT THE ENTIRE BACK WALL WILL BE IN THE PICTURE.

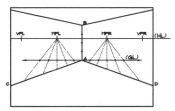

MEASURE A POINT (P) MIDWAY BETWEEN VPL & VPR ON THE HORIZON LINE. CONSTRUCT AN ARC CONNECTING VPL & VPR USING POINT P AS THE CENTER OF THE ARC. LOCATE YOUR STATION POINT (SP) ON THAT ARC, DIRECTLY VERTICAL FROM THE FAR CORNER OF THE ROOM. SWING AN ARC FROM THIS STATION POINT (SP) TO THE HORIZON LINE USING EACH VANISHING POINT (VP) AS THE CENTER TO LOCATE THE MEASURING POINT LEFT (MPL) AND THE MEASURING POINT RIGHT (MPR).

ALONG THE GROUND LINE (GL), SCALE THE WIDTH AND DEPTH OF THE ROOM FROM POINT A USING THE SAME SCALE AS LINE AB. DRAW LINES FROM THE MPL & MPR THROUGH THE INCREMENTS ALONG THE GL UNTIL THEY TOUCH THE LINES AC & AD (JUNCTION OF EACH WALL WITH THE FLOOR)

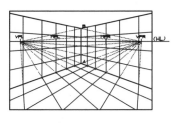

FROM THESE POINTS ALONG AC & AD EXTEND LINES ON THE FLOOR TOWARD YOU FROM THE RESPECTIVE VANISHING POINTS, CREATING A PERSPECTIVE OF SQUARE GRIDS ON THE FLOOR. EXTEND VERTICAL LINES FROM THE POINTS ALONG AC & AD TO PRODUCE LINES RECEDING IN PERSPECTIVE ALONG THE WALL. DRAW LINES FROM THE SCALED POINTS ALONG LINE AB THAT EXTEND TO THE PROPER VANISHING POINTS, PRODUCING PERSPECTIVE GRIDS ON THE WALLS

FIGURE 4-22 **How to draw a two-point perspective grid.**

PART TWO

Contract Documents

Construction Drawings, Specifications, and Contracts 5

Specifications, contracts, and construction drawings are an integral part of what is referred to as the contract documents. These documents form a guide for the various workers and suppliers to follow in constructing the project. The construction drawings show the location, size, and particulars of a structure to be built. The specifications set the standards of the workmanship and materials in writing. The drawings and specifications complement one another and are used together. For example, the drawings show the color and location of paint to be applied to a wall surface, but do not tell how it is to be applied (sprayed, rolled, or brushed) and the resulting quality of workmanship required. In this case, the subsurface must first be prepared to receive the paint, adjacent areas need to be protected from the painting, the minimum skills of the painter must be specified, and the cleanup needed must be called out. These particulars are all detailed in written specifications for the painting, and similar instructions are prepared for all the other work to be carried out on the project.

Specifications

Specifications are written documents that clearly describe the required materials, requirements for the execution of the work, and workmanship expected. Generally, for small, simple projects the written specifications may be placed directly in the drawings, either typed on transparent adhesive film or in text form in CAD on a separate drawing sheet. However, for most projects, the specifications are included in a "job book" or "project manual" and issued with the contract agreements and construction drawings as the complete set of contract documents.

The job book can be a bound or loose-leaf manual and contains the technical specifications. A project manual may include the specifications as well as other documentation for the total project, such as the contract(s), bidding requirements (if needed), and general and supplementary conditions of the contract.

Specification Types

Specifications should complement the construction drawings, not duplicate them. Their main purpose is to describe the type and quality of materials and finishes; quality and method of construction and installation; acceptable testing methods; alternate provisions; and warranties and their requirements. Specifications are referred to as "closed" or "open" for bidding purposes. "Closed" means no product can be used on the project other than what is specified. Open specifications allow for the substitution of products specified, or for the contractor to suggest a number of products for the item that is specified or being bid on. There are four

Table 5-1: Sample Proprietary Specifications

LOUNGE AREA		
ITEM	QUANTITY	DESCRIPTION
1	3	Manufacturer #10-123, Black Leather Lounge Chair
2	4	Manufacturer # 9-321, Dark Oak, Side Table

main types of specifications: proprietary, descriptive, reference, and performance.

Proprietary

Proprietary specifications, which are closed, call out a specific manufacturer's products by name, model or part number, and color or finish, if applicable. Proprietary specifications are the most restrictive, as they give the interior designer complete control over what is to be installed in a project. Sometimes the specifications include an "or equal" clause (sometimes referred to as a base-bid specification), which means the substitution of other products will be allowed if the contractor thinks they are equal to the one specified. Proprietary specifications tend to be easier to write as the designer needs to provide only the basic descriptive information, such as the manufacturer, product number, and finish/fabrics, as shown in Table 5-1.

If more detail is needed, the manufacturer will supply the information to the designer so that it can be incorporated into the specifications.

Descriptive

Descriptive specifications are open, and do not specify a manufacturer or trade name for the materials and/or finishes required for a project. Descriptive specifications call out in detail the mate-rials, finishes, fabrication methods, acceptable workmanship, and installation methods. Descriptive specifications may be more difficult to write, because all the pertinent information and requirements for the construction and installation of a product must be specified. However, when a tremendous number of similar products are on the market, descriptive specifications allow the designer to prescribe the exact standards he or she wants for a project without selecting a particular manufacturer.

Reference

Reference specifications are similar to the descriptive ones, insofar as they describe a material, finish, or other product based on the designer's requirements rather than a trade name. However, reference specifications are generally based on standards that are set by an established authority or testing facility, such as the American Society for Testing and Materials (ASTM) or the American National Standards Institute (ANSI).

These authorities provide minimum performance criteria for various materials and products. Reference specifications are generally short, because only the standard must be stated, and they are fairly easy to write. Chances for error are minimal, as industry standards and generally recognized methods of building are being used. However, the designer must be completely familiar with and updated on the standard and how to write the appropriate specification. Sometimes the standard includes more provisions than are needed for a particular project.

Performance

Performance specifications describe the expected performance of the item(s) being specified. This type of specification is also considered open, as no trade names are included. Any item that meets the performance criteria can be used in the project. The means by which the required results are met is not specified, but left up to the contractor, subcontractor, or vendor. Performance specifications are often used for custom components when the designer wants to achieve a particular result that is not already manufactured. This type of specification can be more difficult to write, because the designer must know all the criteria expected as well as methods for testing (if required). Also, there is a risk that the designer could lose his or her original design concept along with control over the products used if it is not carefully written.

Organization of Specifications

The organization of written specifications has been standardized in accordance with the building trades. Many architects and interior designers use the specification system developed by the Contract Specifications Institute (CSI) and Construction Specifications Canada (CSC), known as the MasterFormat™ system. This system was revised in the fall of 2004 and standardizes the format and numbering of project information used in specifications and cost estimating, and organizes the job book or project manual. The MasterFormat™ 2004 system establishes a way of organizing the parts of project manuals that contain any combination of procurement requirements, contracting requirements, or construction specifications. The MasterFormat™ structure is divided into two groups and five subgroups. The first group, "Procurement and Contracting Requirements" (Division 00) contains introductory information and procurement requirements and contracting requirements. The second group is the "Specification Group" and contains the following subgroups:

General Requirements Subgroup: Division 01

Facility Construction Subgroup: Divisions 02-19

Facility Services Subgroup: Divisions 20-29

Site and Infrastructure Subgroup: Divisions 30-39

Process Equipment Subgroup: Divisions 40-49

Groups are not numbered, but are divided into Subgroups. Subgroups are not numbered, but are divided into numbered Divisions. Divisions are the top Level (Level 1) in the hierarchy of the classification system, as shown in Table 5-2.

The subgroups contain 50 divisions that are based on major categories. Each of these major divisions is coded with a six-digit number, such as 09 30 00 for Tiling. Each division, known as the Division or Level 1, is then subdivided into Level 2 and Level 3 categories. The first two digits (09) represent the Division or Level 1, the next pair of numbers, in this case "30", represent Level 2, and the third pair, "00" represents Level 3. For example, under Painting and Coating, 09 90 00 is a Level 1 category that includes several different types of painting and coating finishes. Specifications, within a job book or project manual could also incorporate Level 2 and Level 3 categories, such as 09 94 13 Textured Finishing. The level of information the designer uses depends on the complexity of the job and specifications.

The designer or specifier (if they are different) can select the areas of the MasterFormat™ that are appropriate for the materials, finishes and other products to be specified for their project and utilize this information to complete a job book or project manual where the information can be easily and reliably found. See Appendix A for Example Numbering for a Simple Interior Project Table of Contents. Appendix B shows the complete listing of Level 1 and Level 2 numbers and titles.

Table 5-2: Master format by Contract Specifications Institute

General Divisions

PROCUREMENT AND CONTRACTING REQUIREMENTS GROUP

Division 00 - Procurement and Contracting Requirements

Specifications Group

GENERAL REQUIREMENTS SUB-GROUP

Division 01 - General Requirements

FACILITY CONSTRUCTION SUB-GROUP

Division 02 - Existing Conditions

Division 03 - Concrete

Division 04 - Masonry

Division 05 - Metals

Division 06 - Wood, Plastic, Composites

Division 07 - Thermal & Moisture Protections

Division 08 - Openings

Division 09 - Finishes

Division 10 - Specialties

Division 11 - Equipment

Division 12 - Furnishings

Division 13 - Special Construction

Division 14 - Conveying Equipment

Division 15 - RESERVED

Division 16 - RESERVED

Division 17 - RESERVED

Division 18 - RESERVED

Division 19 - RESERVED

FACILITY SERVICES SUB-GROUP

Division 20 - RESERVED

Division 21 - Fire Suppression

Division 22 - Plumbing

Division 23 - Heating, Ventilating & Air-Conditioning

Division 24 - RESERVED

Division 25 - Integrated Automation

Division 26 - Electrical

Division 27 - Communications

Division 28 - Electronic Safety & Security

Division 29 - RESERVED

SITE AND INFRASTRUCTURE SUB-GROUP

Division 30 - RESERVED

Division 31 - Earthwork

Division 32 - Exterior Improvements

Division 33 - Utilities

Division 34 - Transportation

Division 35 - Waterway and Marine Construction

Division 36 - RESERVED

Division 37 - RESERVED

Division 38 - RESERVED

Division 39 - RESERVED

PROCESS EQUIPMENT SUB-GROUP

Division 40 - Process Integration

Division 41 - Material Processing and Handling Equipment

Division 42 - Process Heating, Cooling and Drying Equipment

Division 43 - Process Gas and Liquid Handling, Purification and Storage Equipment

Division 44 - Pollution Control Equipment

Division 45 - Industry Specific Manufacturing Equipment

Division 46 - RESERVED

Division 47 - RESERVED

Division 48 - Electrical Power Generation

Division 49 - RESERVED

For a complete listing of all sub-divisions visit
http://www.csinet.org/s_csi/docs/9400/9361.pdf

Contracts

Various contractual agreements are needed between the parties involved in a building project. These agreements detail each party's responsibilities and can be in oral or written form. However, it is preferable to put down in writing the responsibilities of each party and what is expected. This can prevent future disagreements and serves as a legal contract binding the various parties. Contracts can be simple written agreements, or preprinted documents, such as those provided by the A.I.A. (American Institute of Architects), A.S.I.D. (American Society of Interior Designers), and I.I.D.A.

(International Interior Design Association). Figure 5-1 shows an example of what A.S.I.D.'s Agreement Between Designer and Client For Design Services contains in its Table of Contents. One important contract is that between the owner and contractor to do the work based on the drawings and specifications. There may also exist a whole series of other contracts between the contractor and subcontractor, or contractor and material supplier.

Construction Drawings

Construction drawings (often called working drawings) visually communicate the design and the information required to bring a building or space into reality to everyone who is involved in the building process. These drawings generally follow a set of architectural drawing conventions that are widely accepted in the industry. However, there is not just one right way to do construction drawings. The office staff and project size, office standards, and the detail needed for custom fabrications can require construction drawings that vary from the conventions.

Organization of Construction Drawings

A variety of types of drawings are needed to accurately describe a project to the various tradespeople who will do the work. The main types are what are generally called architectural and engineering drawings. For example, a concrete wall may be described as to its size and finish on the architectural drawings, but an engineering drawing is also needed to spell out the exact structural components, such as size and spacing of steel reinforcing in the wall. In addition to these two categories of drawings, there might be other specialty drawings that do not fit neatly within either one. For example, an

AMERICAN SOCIETY OF
INTERIOR DESIGNERS, INC.

ASID DOCUMENT 301 · 2008

AGREEMENT BETWEEN DESIGNER AND CLIENT FOR DESIGN SERVICES
Small/Medium Commercial Contract 2008

TABLE OF CONTENTS

2

FIGURE 5-1 A preprinted ASID contract document.

FURNITURE SCHEDULE

MRK	ITEM	QTY.	MANUF.	DESCRIP.	FABRIC/ FINISH	REMARKS
T₃	TABLE	15	JOHNSON	2'x2' RECT. PLAM. TOP #474-J95 30"H	BASE: CHROME PED. W/ DISK BASE I 1/4" VINYL BULL EDGE TOP: NEVAMAR PLAM. W-8-352V REGENCY MAHOGANY	
T₄	TABLE	41	JOHNSON	4'x4' SQ. PLAM. TOP #608-J95 30"H	BASE: CHROME PED. W/ DISK BASE I 1/4" VINYL BULL EDGE TOP: NEVAMAR PLAM. W-8-352V REGENCY MAHOGANY	
T₅	TABLE	9	JOHNSON	36" DIA. PLAM. TOP #533-J95 30"H	BASE: CHROME PED. W/ DISK BASE I 1/4" VINYL BULL EDGE TOP: NEVAMAR PLAM. W-8-352V REGENCY MAHOGANY	
T₆	TABLE	8	JOHNSON	48" DIA. PLAM. TOP #533-J95 30"H	BASE: CHROME PED. W/ DISK BASE I 1/4" VINYL BULL EDGE TOP: NEVAMAR PLAM. W-8-352V REGENCY MAHOGANY	
C₂	CHAIR	206	LOWENSTEIN	PROFILI SIDE CHAIR W-18.5" D-21" H-35" SEAT H-18"	PAUL BRAYTON DESIGNS C8-26 CHECKMATE W-54" REPEAT-1-3/4" HOR, 2' VERT.	FINISH-MAHOG.
G₁	GLASS WALLS	33	GOLDRAY	CUSTOM CURVED GLS. WALL (ETCHED) SIZE PER PLANS	BOILER PLATE ETCHING, FROSTED	SUBMIT SHOP DRAW'G

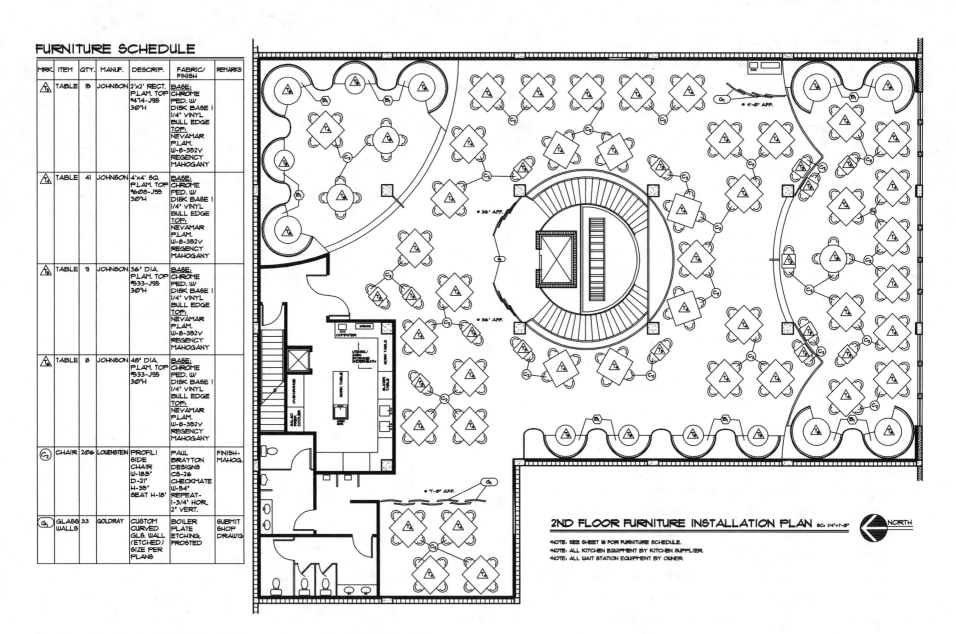

2ND FLOOR FURNITURE INSTALLATION PLAN SC: 1/4"=1'-0'

•NOTE: SEE SHEET 18 FOR FURNITURE SCHEDULE.
•NOTE: ALL KITCHEN EQUIPMENT BY KITCHEN SUPPLIER
•NOTE: ALL WAIT STATION EQUIPMENT BY OWNER.

NORTH

FIGURE 5-2 A furniture installation plan included in a set of construction drawings for a restaurant.

Table 5-3: Sequence of Construction Drawings

Note: depending on project type, some of the below sheets might not be included

SHEET NO.	DESCRIPTION OF SHEET (S)
1.	**TITLE/COVER SHEET**
	Client, project, designer information
	Index of sheets, professional stamps
	Architectural symbols & abbreviations
	Perspective or other visuals
	Design factors and applicable codes
2.	**LOCATION OR SITE PLAN** (Civil engineer's drawings might include these)
	This information might be on cover sheet
3.	**FIRE AND LIFE SAFETY PLAN** (might be included on another sheet)
	Exits, firewalls, square footages, and other code compliances
4.	**FOOTING AND FOUNDATION PLAN** (If required)
	Might be part of the structural engineer's drawings
5.	**DEMOLITION PLANS** (If required)
6.	**FLOOR PLAN (S)**
	Begin with lowest floor first
7.	**BUILDING SECTIONS**
	Key to floor plans
8.	**EXTERIOR ELEVATIONS** (If required)

SHEET NO.	DESCRIPTION OF SHEET (S)
9.	**WALL SECTIONS, STAIR SECTIONS**
	Drawn at large scale
10.	**INTERIOR ELEVATIONS**
	Show most prominent elevations
11.	**DETAILS**
	Drawn at large scale
12.	**FINISH PLAN (S) or FINISH SCHEDULE**
	Include legend and specific finishes
13.	**FURNITURE INSTALLATION PLAN (S)**
	Include legend and furniture placement
14.	**FURNISHINGS AND EQUIPMENT PLAN (S)** (If required)
15.	**REFLECTED CEILING PLAN (S)**
	Include legend and coordinate with Electrical & Mechanical
16.	**ELECTRICAL PLAN (S) AND/OR POWER/COMMUNICATION PLAN (S)**
	Include legend and reference to reflected ceiling plan
17.	**MECHANICAL PLAN (S)** including plumbing
18.	**SPECIFICATIONS** (If required or put in separate booklet)

architectural floor plan might show exact information about rooms, doors, windows, and other particulars, but items such as the exact placement of office desks and files would be found on a separate furniture installation plan, as seen in Figure 5-2.

In interior projects, the interior partition plans, details, and furniture drawings could be included with the architectural set, or they could be a completely separate set of drawings. Another type of specialized drawing might be a drapery installation plan for detailing specific window coverings.

Construction drawings are sequentially arranged by major components, as illustrated in Table 5-3. This sequence generally follows how the building is constructed, from the ground to the

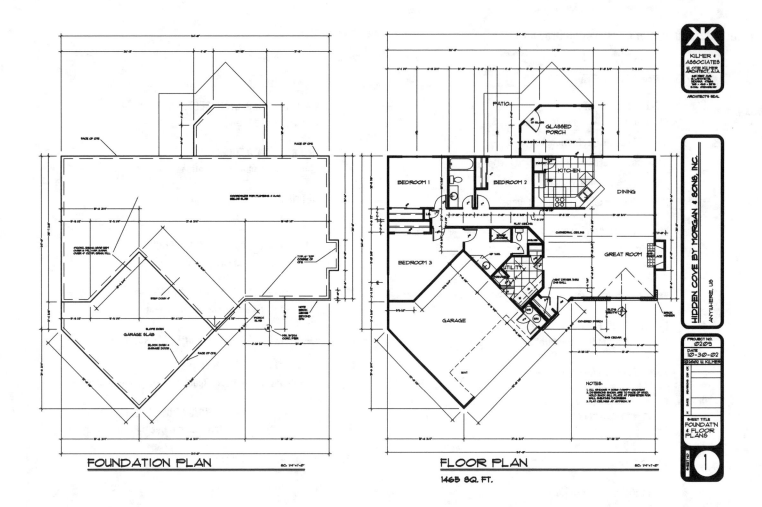

FOUNDATION PLAN

FLOOR PLAN

1465 SQ. FT.

FIGURE 5-3 This small set of construction drawings consists of only 3 sheets. Sheet 1 of 3 includes the foundation plan, floor plan, and a footing detail.

shell of the building to the interiors. However, the exact sequence of drawings and their content will vary from project to project and office to office. For example, the number of sheets of construction drawings for a small residence may be smaller than for a commercial project. Figures 5-3, 5-4, and 5-5 show the example of a small model home where only three sheets comprise the whole set of construction drawings. A more complex commercial project

might include as many as 21 sheets of drawings, as illustrated in Figure 5-6, which shows the cover sheet for a restaurant project with a table of contents listing the 21 sheets. In both cases, however, the sheet order remains. The sheets are numbered and bound sequentially as a set, for clarity and ease of use by contractors, subcontractors, and others involved in the project.

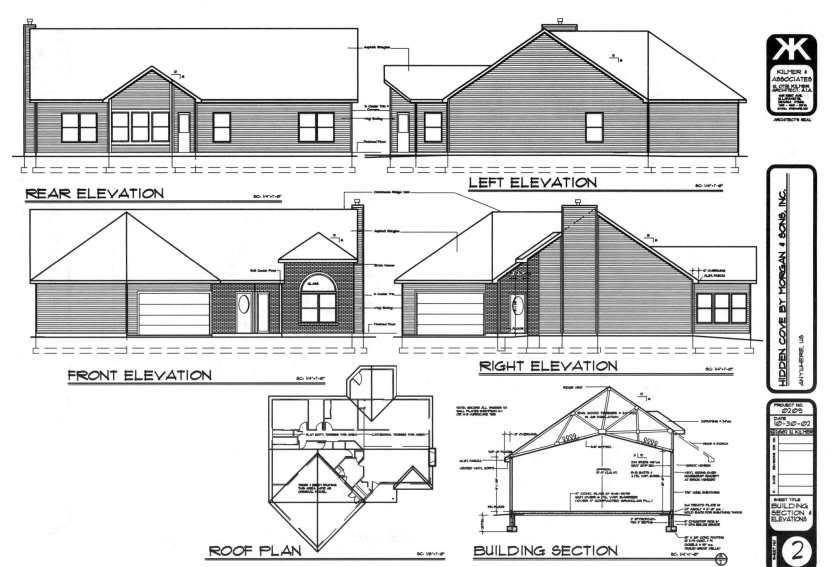

REAR ELEVATION   SC: 1/4"=1'-0"

LEFT ELEVATION   SC: 1/4"=1'-0"

FRONT ELEVATION   SC: 1/4"=1'-0"

RIGHT ELEVATION   SC: 1/4"=1'-0"

ROOF PLAN   SC: 1/8"=1'-0"

BUILDING SECTION   SC: 1/4"=1'-0"

KILMER &
ASSOCIATES
W. OTIS KILMER
ARCHITECT, A.I.A.

ARCHITECT'S SEAL

HIDDEN COVE BY MORGAN & SONS, INC.
ANYWHERE, US

PROJECT NO.
0209
DATE
10-30-02
©2002 W. KILMER

SHEET TITLE
BUILDING
SECTION &
ELEVATIONS

SHEET NO
2

FIGURE 5-4 Sheet 2 of 3 for this small house includes four exterior elevations, a roof plan, and a building plan.

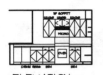

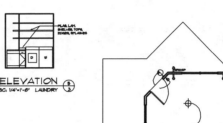

ELEVATION ①/3
SC: 1/4"=1'-0" KITCHEN

ELEVATION ②/3
SC: 1/4"=1'-0" KITCHEN

ELEVATION ③/3
SC: 1/4"=1'-0" BATHROOM

ELEVATION ④/3
SC: 1/4"=1'-0" M. BATH

ELEVATION ⑤/3
SC: 1/4"=1'-0" LAUNDRY

FIGURE 5-5 Sheet 3 of 3 includes the electrical plan, electrical legend, and several interior elevations.

FIGURE 5-6 (facing page) This cover sheet for a set of construction drawings for a commercial restaurant and lounge indicates the set consists of 21 sheets. The table of contents lists what can be found on each sheet.

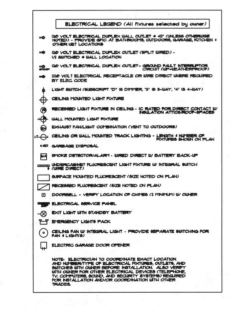

ELECTRICAL LEGEND (All fixtures selected by owner)

→ 120 VOLT ELECTRICAL DUPLEX WALL OUTLET @ 42" (UNLESS OTHERWISE NOTED) - PROVIDE GFIC AT BATHROOMS, OUTDOORS, GARAGE, KITCHEN & OTHER WET LOCATIONS

→ 120 VOLT ELECTRICAL DUPLEX OUTLET (SPLIT WIRED) - 1/2 SWITCHED @ WALL LOCATION

→ 120 VOLT ELECTRICAL DUPLEX OUTLET - GROUND FAULT INTERRUPTOR CIRCUIT (WP=WEATHERPROOF)

→ 220 VOLT ELECTRICAL RECEPTACLE OR WIRE DIRECT WHERE REQUIRED BY ELEC. CODE

$ LIGHT SWITCH (SUBSCRIPT "D" IS DIMMER, "3" IS 3-WAY, "4" IS 4-WAY)

⊕ CEILING MOUNTED LIGHT FIXTURE

⊕ RECESSED LIGHT FIXTURE IN CEILING - IC RATED FOR DIRECT CONTACT W/ INSULATION ATTIC/ROOF-SPACES

⊢⊕ WALL MOUNTED LIGHT FIXTURE

⊕ EXHAUST FAN/LIGHT COMBINATION (VENT TO OUTDOORS)

⊢⊙⊙ CEILING OR WALL MOUNTED TRACK LIGHTING - LENGTH & NUMBER OF FIXTURES SHOWN ON PLAN

GD GARBAGE DISPOSAL

SD SMOKE DETECTOR/ALARM - WIRED DIRECT W/ BATTERY BACK-UP

▭ UNDERCABINET FLUORESCENT LIGHT FIXTURE W/ INTEGRAL SWITCH (WIRE DIRECT)

▭ SURFACE MOUNTED FLUORESCENT (SIZE NOTED ON PLAN)

▱ RECESSED FLUORESCENT (SIZE NOTED ON PLAN)

▣ DOORBELL - VERIFY LOCATION OF CHIMES (2 MINIMUM) W/ OWNER

▪ ELECTRICAL SERVICE PANEL

⊗ EXIT LIGHT WITH STANDBY BATTERY

⊢ EMERGENCY LIGHTS PACK

⊙ CEILING FAN W/ INTEGRAL LIGHT - PROVIDE SEPARATE SWITCHING FOR FAN & LIGHT(S)

▢ ELECTRIC GARAGE DOOR OPENER

NOTE: ELECTRICIAN TO COORDINATE EXACT LOCATION AND NUMBER/TYPE OF ELECTRICAL FIXTURES, OUTLETS, AND SWITCHES WITH OWNER BEFORE INSTALLATION. ALSO VERIFY WITH OWNER FOR OTHER ELECTRICAL DEVICES (TELEPHONE, TV, COMPUTERS, SOUND, AND SECURITY SYSTEMS) REQUIRED FOR INSTALLATION AND/OR COORDINATION WITH OTHER TRADES.

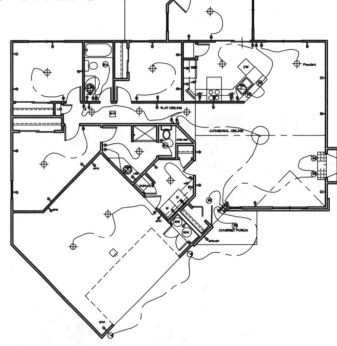

ELECTRICAL PLAN   SC: 1/4"=1'-0"

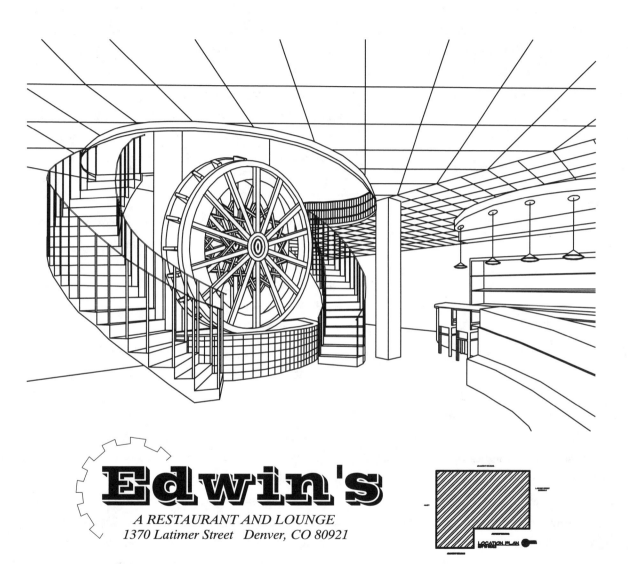

DESIGN FACTORS

OCCUPANCY CLASSIFICATIONS: A-3
CONSTRUCTION TYPE: II
ZONING: CB
SOIL BEARING CAPACITY = 2000 PSF
ROOF LOAD = 30 PSF
FLOOR LOAD = 100 PSF
WIND LOAD = 25 PSF
FLOOR AREA: FIRST FLOOR = 6711 SQUARE FEET
             SECOND FLOOR = 6606 SQUARE FEET
             TOTAL = 13317 SQUARE FEET

TABLE OF CONTENTS

ABBREVIATIONS

A.F.F.	ABOVE FINISHED FLOOR
CONC.	CONCRETE
C.M.U.	CONCRETE MASONRY UNIT
DIA.	DIAMETER
EXT'G	EXISTING
FIN.	FINISHED
FLR.	FLOOR
GLS.	GLASS
G.F.I.C.	GROUND FAULT INTERUPT CIRCUIT
GYP. BD.	GYPSUM BOARD
O.C.	ON CENTER
PLAS. LAM.	PLASTIC LAMINATE
R.	RISER
RAD.	RADIUS
T	TREAD
TYP.	TYPICAL

SYMBOLS

SECTION NUMBER — SECTION SYMBOL — SHEET DRAWN ON
ELEVATION NUMBER — ELEVATION SYMBOL — SHEET DRAWN ON
DETAIL NUMBER — DETAIL SYMBOL — SHEET DRAWN ON

INDICATES A LEVEL — FINISH FLOOR LEVEL / CEILING HEIGHT
DOOR NUMBER OR TYPE
COLUMN REFERENCE — NUMBERS IN ONE DIRECTION / LETTER IN THE OTHER
WINDOW NUMBER OR TYPE

Edwin's

A RESTAURANT AND LOUNGE
1370 Latimer Street   Denver, CO 80921

LOCATION PLAN

DESIGN GROUP

SHELLY BARHYDT
COURTNEY KILMER
THERESA LABUS

Edwin's

A RESTAURANT AND LOUNGE
1370 Latimer Street, Denver, CO 80921

SKL Enterprises, Inc.: Mr. David Lord, President
2650 Collin Plaza Suite 34, Houston, TX

DATE:
29 APRIL 1999

PROJ. #
999101

REVISIONS

TITLE:
TITLE PAGE

SHEET
1
OF 21

The sheet numbering system can vary according to the complexity of the project and office preference. For small projects, a simple numeric system can be used. Most offices prefer to use a system that identifies each area of specialty by a prefix, such as "A" for the architecture or "S" for structural. A list of the most common prefixes follows; however, other prefixes may be added as needed.

A – Architecture

S – Structural

M – Mechanical

E – Electrical

P – Plumbing

I – Interiors

F – Finishes or Furniture

Q – Equipment

Guidelines for Preparing Construction Drawings

Before construction drawings are executed, a considerable amount of work must precede their preparation, such as programming, preparing schematic drawings, and developing the design. The overall design of the project, general materials, finishes, and other particulars must already be established. Preliminary information from other consultants, such as electrical and acoustical engineers, must be collected and available for input into the drawings. A building-code analysis must be done to confirm the project meets requirements for the protection of the public's health, safety, and welfare.

Before the construction drawings are drafted up, a mock-up set is first created to give an overview of the sequence of sheets and their individual contents, as shown in Figure 5-7. This process helps to organize the drawings and reduces the risk of overlooking important information and relationships between drawings. These mock-up drawings are generally drawn at small scale, such as half-size, quarter-size, or even smaller. Each drawing to be placed on a separate sheet is blocked out as a rectangle at the properly scaled size with its title, reference number, and the scale it is to be drawn to. This mock-up set of drawings serves as a guide for the individual or team when preparing the construction drawing set. On a small project, a small number of mock-up drawings may be required, whereas larger projects demand a carefully planned mock-up set, which usually requires a greater number of drawings and more details.

Sheet Size

The size of sheets that drawings are done on can vary among professional firms, depending upon the office standards, the type of project, and the form of reproduction selected for the drawings. Generally, sheets are composed in a horizontal format, and multiple sheets (which comprise a set) are bound on the left side, as for a book. In this case, the left border of the sheet becomes the binding side, and drawings are placed no closer than 1 to 1-½ inches (25 – 38 mm) from this edge. Drawings, lettering, and dimensions are composed so they can be read from the bottom of the sheet when viewed in the horizontal position, as illustrated in Figure 5-8. It occasionally becomes necessary to arrange for dimensions and some notes to be read from the right side of the sheet, but never from the top or left-sided orientation.

The most common sheet sizes used by offices are 18 x 24 inches (457 x 609 mm), 24 x 36 inches (609 x 914 mm), and 36 x 48 inches (914 x 1218 mm). Small drawings, such as revisions or additions to a large drawing, are typically drawn on 8-½ x 11 inches (213 x 275 mm), 8-½ x 14 inches (213 x 350 mm), or 11 x 17 inches (275 x 425 mm). These smaller sizes are based on standard photocopier, inkjet, and laser printer machines.

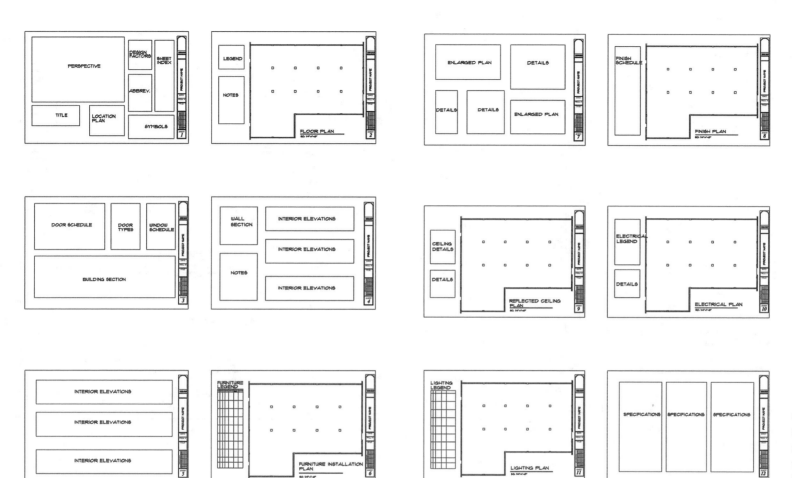

FIGURE 5-7 A small mock-up set of construction drawings is very helpful for indicating what will be drawn on each sheet and its sequence in the set.

Standard paper sizes include A, B, C, D, and E in inches in architectural sizes. Metric sizes are measured in millimeters and include A4, A3, A2, A1, and A0. (See Table 2-1, page 15.).

Sheet Composition

When sheets are bound into a set and a person leafs through the sheets, the information on the right-hand side of the sheet is gen-

erally seen first. For this reason, title blocks and important information are often placed to the right side of the sheet, as seen in Figure 5-9. This is particularly important if the sheet is not completely filled with drawings, schedules, etc. The blank, unused areas should appear to the left. As mentioned, the left-handed side has the largest margin, while the other sheet margins should be held to a minimum of ½ inch (12 mm). Some firms prefer to draw

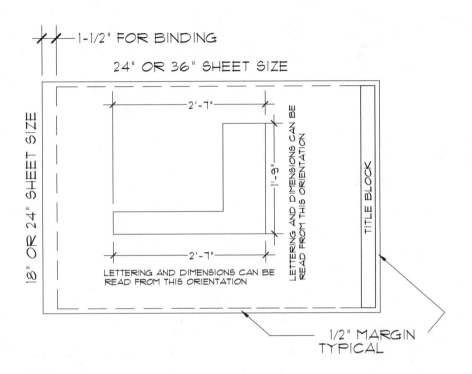

1-1/2" FOR BINDING

24" OR 36" SHEET SIZE

18" OR 24" SHEET SIZE

2'-7"

1'-9"

2'-7"

LETTERING AND DIMENSIONS CAN BE
READ FROM THIS ORIENTATION

LETTERING AND DIMENSIONS CAN BE
READ FROM THIS ORIENTATION

TITLE BLOCK

1/2" MARGIN
TYPICAL

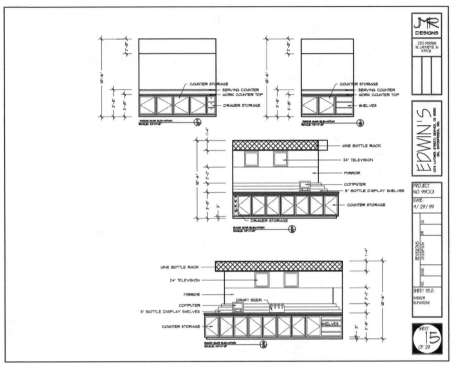

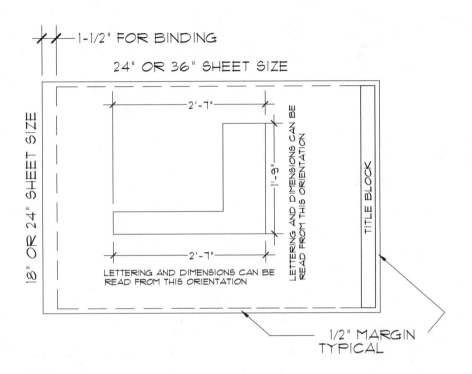

FIGURE 5-8 (left) Most information on the sheets is preferably read from the bottom, similar to a bound book. However, some information can also be read from the right side of the sheet.

FIGURE 5-9 (right) Important information is placed on the lower right of the sheet for ease of finding. Sets of drawings can then be "thumbed" through as in pages in a book.

a borderline around the entire sheet, which graphically "surrounds" or encompasses all the drawings. In that case, the borderline is held to the same margins as discussed above.

Title Blocks

Title blocks on a construction-drawing sheet serve a number of key functions. These blocks are standardized for each office and are generally placed along the right side of the sheet, running the full height of that edge, minus the ½ inch (12 mm) top and bottom borders or margins. Title blocks can also be placed along the bottom of the sheet, or in the case of engineering drawings might be simply a block in the lower right-hand corner. Figure 5-10 illustrates the most common placement of title blocks.

These title blocks are drawn in a variety of ways. Many firms have them preprinted on the sheets, or programmed into the computer to print out when the drawings are produced. Other methods include making reproducible title blocks with photocopiers on transparent sticky-back sheets and individually adding them to the drawing sheets. In these latter cases, additional information can be filled in with pencil, pen, or other transfer mediums.

Title blocks typically contain information that identifies the project, its location, the name of the client, the designer's (or firm's) name and address, names or initials of the drafters and checkers, revision blocks, and space for professional seals. It might also include information on others involved in the project, such as consulting engineers. The title block tells contractors, suppliers, and other interested parties the location of the project and who to contact for specific information. Title blocks, as shown in Figure 5-11 generally include:

- **Design firm's name/logo, address, telephone/fax number, and e-mail address (if applicable)**
- **Date, professional seals, sheet title, sheet number**
- **Job number and how many sheets comprise a set**

Title blocks might also include an area for initials of the person who drew the sheet, and the person who checked it. The block generally includes a "revisions" section (Figure 5-12) to indicate changes made to the original drawing after the initial date it was issued to the various parties. When several revisions are made to a sheet, they are listed as Revision A, B, etc., to indicate which changes are most recent.

Lettering on Drawings

The most important aspect of lettering in construction drawings is its readability. It should be consistent in style and easy to follow. Most offices use uppercase lettering for quick readability, but a clear lowercase alphabet can also be employed. When several drafters are working on a set of drawings, it is important that all the lettering from the design firm appear in the same style. In both manual and computer-aided lettering, a consistent style or font should be selected and used by all participants.

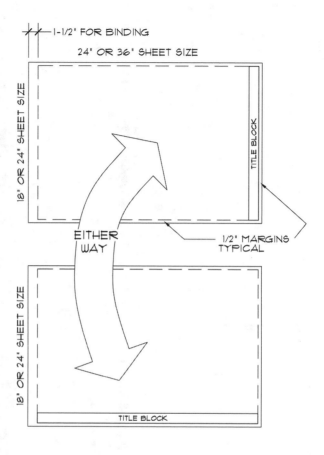

FIGURE 5-10 Title blocks are generally placed on the lower edge of the sheet, and in most cases to the right side.

The height of lettering on construction drawings varies according to the hierarchy of the information being presented and the type of reproduction being used. If the drawings are to be reproduced at the same size, the following standards are generally used:

1.	Sheet numbers in the title block	½ in. (12 mm)
2.	Main titles under individual drawings	3/16 – ¼ in. (5 – 6 mm)
3.	Subtitles, such as room names	3/16 in. (5 mm)
4.	Majority of lettering, such as notes and dimensions	3/32 – ⅛ in. (2.4 – 3 mm)

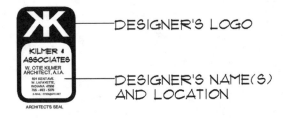

DESIGNER'S LOGO

DESIGNER'S NAME(S) AND LOCATION

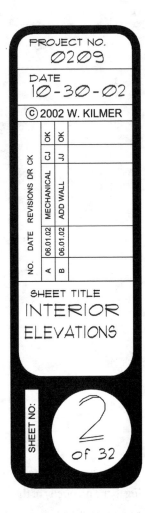

OWNER AND PROJECT INFORMATION

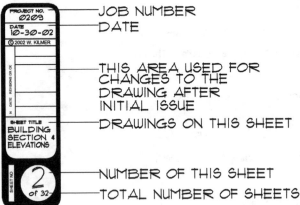

JOB NUMBER

DATE

THIS AREA USED FOR CHANGES TO THE DRAWING AFTER INITIAL ISSUE

DRAWINGS ON THIS SHEET

NUMBER OF THIS SHEET

TOTAL NUMBER OF SHEETS

FIGURE 5-11 (left) Professionals design their own unique title blocks, but most include common information, as shown in this example.

FIGURE 5-12 (above) A revision block clearly indicates the date and type of changes made to the drawings after the initial issuance date of the sheet.

If the drawings are to be reduced by photocopying, plotting, or other means, the lettering sizes should be increased, depending upon the reduction ratio, in order for the final notes, dimensions, etc., to be clear and readable.

Notes

Notes are used on construction drawings for the identification of features or information that cannot be conveyed by drawings or by a symbol. Notes should be concise, easy to read, and clear in their meaning. Notes should be grouped and aligned vertically to the right or left side, as illustrated in Figure 5-13. They should also be placed close to the elements described in order to keep leaders as short and direct as possible. Leaders are drawn away from the beginning or end of the note and generally end in an arrow pointing to the object the note refers to. Leaders can be either straight or curved lines, depending upon the office standards. If curved lines are used, they should be gradual sweeping curves, and not crooked or wavy. Leaders should never cross one another, as this can create visual confusion. Notes that pertain to several items, such as the height of electrical outlets, can be pulled out separately and organized below the drawing. If there is more than one note, they should be numbered and organized chronologically on the drawing sheet, as shown in Figure 5-14.

Notes should be placed in open areas of the drawings so line work, textures, and dimensions will not be drawn over them (Figure 5-15).

Drawing Conventions and Representations

Construction drawings communicate how something is built by showing specific assemblies and employing architectural drawing conventions. These conventions are fairly standard throughout the industry and are used to reduce the drawing time and space needed to convey information. For example, in Figure 5-16, a graphic symbol with an arrow drawn on a cabinetry section denotes the exact place the section was cut and the direction of the view taken in the resulting section drawing.

Abbreviations, graphic symbols, keys, and legends are used as shorthand to reduce drawing time while conveying important information. Another convention governs how dimensions are recorded in a drawing. Dimensioning standards ensure that the exact sizes and placement of assemblies are communicated by using a system that is recognized by both the designer and the builder.

Abbreviations

Abbreviations for words and short phrases are often used in construction drawings. Commonly used abbreviations can be found in Appendix D, but it should be noted they are not universal. Abbreviations can vary among the different trades, as, for example, QT can mean "quarry tile" or "quart." The architect, engineer, interior designer, drafter, and contractor must all be able to recognize what each abbreviation stands for. The drafter should include a legend of abbreviations (often shown on the title sheet of a set of drawings) to insure their meaning is understood. See Figure 5-17 for an example of abbreviated terms used in a set of construction drawings. See Appendix D for an expanded list.

Graphic Symbols

Graphic symbols are used in construction drawings as a pictorial shorthand language to reduce drawing time and coordinate separate drawings. For example, symbols can be used on a floor-plan drawing to indicate placement and type of specific equip-

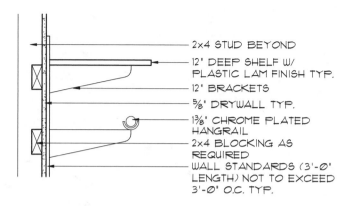

- 2x4 STUD BEYOND
- 12" DEEP SHELF W/ PLASTIC LAM FINISH TYP.
- 12" BRACKETS
- ⅝" DRYWALL TYP.
- 1⅜" CHROME PLATED HANGRAIL
- 2x4 BLOCKING AS REQUIRED
- WALL STANDARDS (3'-∅" LENGTH) NOT TO EXCEED 3'-∅" O.C. TYP.

SHELF & GARMENT ROD DETAIL
SCALE: ⅜" = 1'-∅"

ment such as electrical outlets and wall light switches (Figure 5-18). Although symbols may vary from office to office, there are generally accepted types used by all architectural and interior design firms. Each symbol must communicate clearly specific directives to be followed. Symbols are divided into several types: material symbols, line symbols, graphic symbols, and component symbols.

Material symbols are used in drawings to represent the type of construction materials used in a component. Designers should use the symbols most widely accepted in the industry, such as those shown in Figure 5-19, indicating materials cut in section. Symbols are also used to indicate materials in elevation drawings, as illustrated in Figure 5-20. .

Line symbols use the graphic look, line weight, and thickness of elements represented in the drawings to communicate information to the viewer. For example, a dashed line can indicate a

FIGURE 5-13 It is good drafting practice to align lettering where possible (preferably to the left), and minimize the length of leaders.

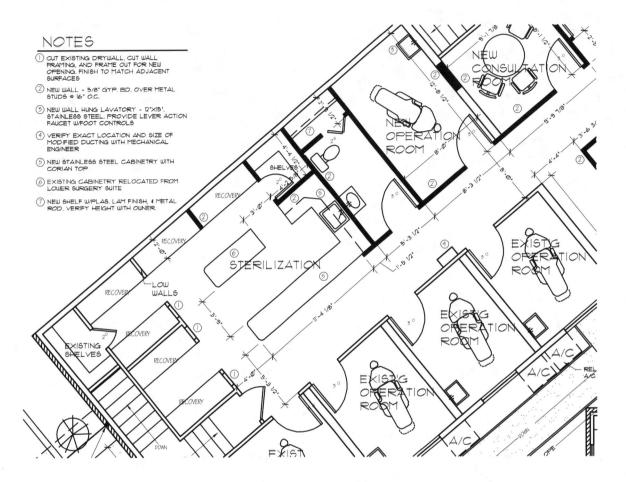

NOTES

1. CUT EXISTING DRYWALL, CUT WALL FRAMING, AND FRAME OUT FOR NEW OPENING. FINISH TO MATCH ADJACENT SURFACES
2. NEW WALL - 5/8" GYP. BD. OVER METAL STUDS @ 16" O.C.
3. NEW WALL HUNG LAVATORY - 12"X15", STAINLESS STEEL. PROVIDE LEVER ACTION FAUCET W/FOOT CONTROLS
4. VERIFY EXACT LOCATION AND SIZE OF MODIFIED DUCTING WITH MECHANICAL ENGINEER
5. NEW STAINLESS STEEL CABINETRY WITH CORIAN TOP
6. EXISTING CABINETRY RELOCATED FROM LOWER SURGERY SUITE
7. NEW SHELF W/PLAS. LAM FINISH, & METAL ROD. VERIFY HEIGHT WITH OWNER.

FIGURE 5-14 Notes can be numbered, organized into a block, and cross-referenced to the plan.

hidden feature or object. See Figure 5-21 for typical line symbols and their meanings.

Graphic symbols can be used to index related parts of drawings, either on the same sheet or multiple sheets. Letters, numbers, and notes can be placed within the symbol to organize it with other symbols and refer to other sheet numbers. Symbols can also be used to denote a specific height of a floor elevation or structural column designation. These basic symbols are shown in Figure 5-22.

Legends

Construction drawing legends combine graphic symbols with notes. They are used on a variety of drawings, such as floor plans, furniture plans, electrical plans, and lighting plans. For example, a wall legend (Figure 5-23) can be used on a floor plan to designate a specific wall construction assembly. An electrical legend is used in conjunction with an electrical plan to denote specific equipment. Figure 5-24 illustrates an electrical

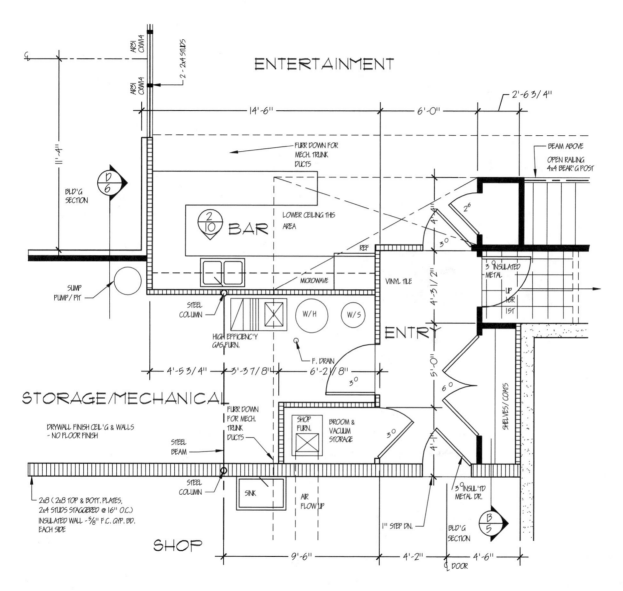

ENTERTAINMENT

AR51 COM4

2 - 2x4 STUDS

14'-6"

6'-0"

2'-6 3/4"

FURR DOWN FOR
MECH. TRUNK
DUCTS

BEAM ABOVE

OPEN RAILING
4x4 BEAR'G POST

11'-4"

BLD'G
SECTION

D 6

2 10 BAR

LOWER CEILING THIS
AREA

2⁸

4'-1"

3⁰

REF

SUMP
PUMP / PIT

STEEL
COLUMN

MICROWAVE

VINYL TILE

3 9 INSULATED
METAL

4'-5 1/2"

UP
FOR
1ST

W/H

W/5

HIGH EFFICIENC'Y
GAS FURN.

F. DRAIN

ENTRY

5'-0"

6⁰

SHELVES/ COATS

3 9 INSUL'TD
METAL DR.

4'-5 3/4"

3'-3 7/8"

6'-2 1/8"

3⁰

STORAGE/MECHANICAL

DRYWALL FINISH CEIL'G & WALLS
- NO FLOOR FINISH

STEEL
BEAM

FURR DOWN
FOR MECH.
TRUNK
DUCTS

SHOP
FURN.

BROOM &
VACUUM
STORAGE

3⁰

4'-1"

2x8 (2x8 TOP & BOTT. PLATES,
2x4 STUDS STAGGERED @ 16" O.C.)
INSULATED WALL - 5/8" F.C. GYP. BD.
EACH SIDE

STEEL
COLUMN

SINK

AIR
FLOW UP

SHOP

1" STEP DN.

BLD'G
SECTION

B 5

9'-6"

4'-2"

4'-6"

G DOOR

PARTIAL PLAN OF LOWER FL'R

SCALE: 1/ 4"=1'-0"

FIGURE 5-15 Notes should be
placed in positions that do not
block dimensions or other arts
of the drawings.

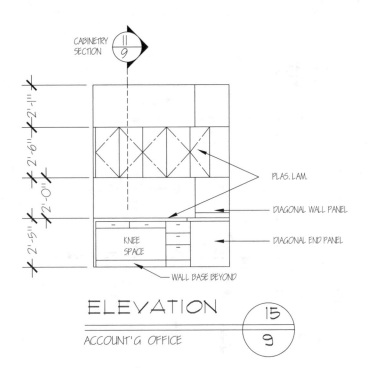

CABINETRY SECTION 11/9

PLAS. LAM.

DIAGONAL WALL PANEL

DIAGONAL END PANEL

KNEE SPACE

WALL BASE BEYOND

ELEVATION

ACCOUNT'G OFFICE

15/9

ABBREVIATIONS

A.F.F.	ABOVE FINISHED FLOOR
CONC.	CONCRETE
C.M.U.	CONCRETE MASONRY UNIT
DIA.	DIAMETER
EXT'G	EXISTING
FIN.	FINISHED
FL'R	FLOOR
GLS.	GLASS
G.F.I.C.	GROUND FAULT INTERRUPT CIRCUIT
GYP. BD.	GYPSUM BOARD
O.C.	ON CENTER
PLAS. LAM.	PLASTIC LAMINATE
R.	RISER
RAD.	RADIUS
T	TREAD
TYP.	TYPICAL

FIGURE 5-16 (left) Example of a graphic symbol showing where a cabinet is cut through for a section drawing.

FIGURE 5-17 (right) To reduce the amount of space needed for notes, abbreviations are commonly accepted in the design fields.

legend in conjunction with additional electrical notes.

Although there are many commonly recognized legends and graphic symbols, the drafter should always include the specifics of what is being shown. Legends should be concise and graphically presented: as small as possible on the sheet, yet easily readable in the field by the builder.

Dimensioning

Dimensioning involves incorporating numerical values in a drawing to accurately locate and size various objects and assemblies in buildings and interiors. Dimension lines and arrows (or tick marks) are used to identify exactly where the dimension begins

and ends, as shown in Figure 5-25. Dimensions are grouped, where possible, and ordered in a hierarchical manner. First the overall, or outside, dimension of a space or object is indicated, then the dimension of smaller details within the space are noted, as illustrated in Figure 5-26.

Dimensions are required on all construction drawings and must be accurate, complete, and readable. At the present time, most construction drawings are dimensioned in the English or metric systems, using feet and inches, or meters.

When feet and inches (English system) are used for dimensioning, the symbol (') is used for feet and (") for inches. Dimensions less than 12" are specified in inches with no zero before them.

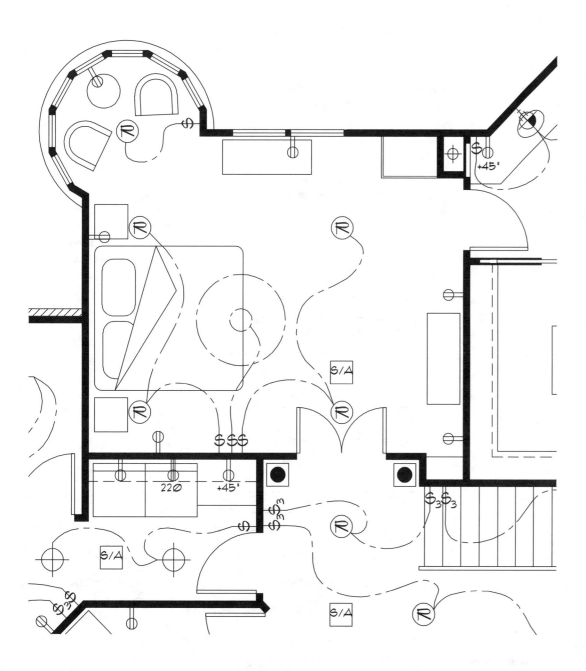

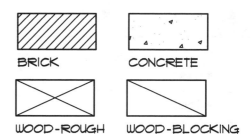

BRICK   CONCRETE

WOOD-ROUGH   WOOD-BLOCKING

FIGURE 5-19 Materials shown in section view are rendered with commonly recognized marks, as seen in this partial example.

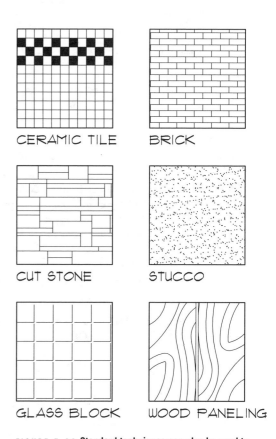

CERAMIC TILE   BRICK

CUT STONE   STUCCO

GLASS BLOCK   WOOD PANELING

FIGURE 5-20 Standard techniques can also be used to represent material seen in elevation views.

LINE USE	LINE SYMBOL	LINE WIDTH
CENTERLINE	————————	THIN
OBJECT LINE	————————	MEDIUM
HIDDEN FEATURE	— — — — — —	MEDIUM
BREAK LINE	———∿————	THIN
DIMENSION LINE	←———————→	THIN
LEADER LINE	————————→	THIN
SECTION OR CUT LINE	— — — — —	THICK
LAYOUT & GUIDELINES	————————	VERY THIN, LIGHT
LETTERING	A B C D E F	THICK
BORDER LINES	————————	THICK
WALLS IN PLAN VIEW	══════ POUCHED ══	THICK OR POUCHED
TEXTURES IN PLAN & ELEVATION VIEW	▦ ～ ▤	THIN

FIGURE 5-21 Line widths and types are used as graphic symbols with specific meanings.

WALL LEGEND

██████████ 2x4 WALLS W/ ½" GYP. BD. EACH SIDE

▥▥▥▥▥▥ 2x4 OR 2x6 INSULATED WALLS W/ FULL BATTS & ½" GYP. BD.
EXISTING WALL TO REMAIN

▭▭▭▭ 1-HR FIRE RATED WALL-W/⅝" GYP. BD. EACH SIDE
EXISTING WALL TO BE REMOVED

= = = = = = =

FIGURE 5-23 A wall legend is helpful for designating specific wall types in a floor plan drawing.

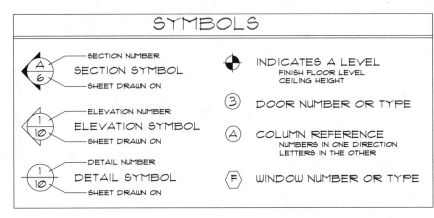

SYMBOLS

SECTION NUMBER
SECTION SYMBOL
SHEET DRAWN ON

ELEVATION NUMBER
ELEVATION SYMBOL
SHEET DRAWN ON

DETAIL NUMBER
DETAIL SYMBOL
SHEET DRAWN ON

INDICATES A LEVEL
FINISH FLOOR LEVEL
CEILING HEIGHT

DOOR NUMBER OR TYPE

COLUMN REFERENCE
NUMBERS IN ONE DIRECTION
LETTERS IN THE OTHER

WINDOW NUMBER OR TYPE

FIGURE 5-22 This example shows a few of the most commonly recognized architectural symbols.

ELECTRICAL NOTES

1. ALL ELECTRICAL OUTLETS TO BE GROUNDED

2. G.C. TO PROVIDE 3/4" PLYWOOD PANEL FOR TELEPHONE EQUIP. WHERE INDICATED

3. WR DESIGNS AND THEIR ARCHITECT ARE NOT RESPONSIBLE FOR ANY ELECTRICAL ENGINEERING. POWER AND COMMUNICATIONS LAYOUT IS TO SHOW OUTLET AND SWITCH LOCATIONS ONLY

ELECTRICAL LEGEND

⊖ 110 VOLT DUPLEX WALL RECEPTACLE

⊖D.C. 110 VOLT DUPLEX RECEPT. ON DEDICATED CIRCUIT

⊖GFI DUPLEX RECEPT. W/ GROUND FAULT INTERRUPTER

◀ TELEPHONE WALL RECEPTACLE

◉ TELE/COMMUNICATION OUTLET

A.F.F. ABOVE FINISH FLOOR

FIGURE 5-24 The electrical legend details out the information represented by symbols on the electrical plan.

Dimensions 12" or above are specified in feet and inches, with a dash placed between the feet and inches, such as 2'-6". If a dimension is an even number of feet, the inches are generally shown as a zero, such as 5'-0". However, some firms prefer to leave the inches off when they are zero, such as 5'. If a distance is a fraction of an inch without a whole number before it, some prefer to put a zero before it for clarity, such as 0'-⅜". In drawings using the metric system, all dimensions are in millimeters, such as 5 mm.

Dimensioning should remain consistent with respect to how materials and assemblies are measured, whether to subsurface or finish surfaces. For example, if a wall is dimensioned to the finished face, subsequent walls should also be dimensioned to their finished faces. A note should be placed on the drawing to denote how items are to be measured. If there are any exceptions to this overall rule, these should be called out on the sheet.

The most common method of dimensioning is the framing technique. The advantage of this system is that it most closely follows the construction sequence in the field and informs the particular trades of dimensions most important to their area of construction. The framing technique is to the face of a stud, concrete, or masonry wall, as illustrated in Figure 5-27. With this technique, the builder first locates the framing or foundation wall, to which other assemblies or finish materials are applied at a later date. The dimension can be placed to either the face of the subwall (depending on the location and how easy it is for the builder to make a mark), or to each side, with an indication of the total subwall thickness.

For example, a wood stud partition wall on a plan with a layer of ½ inch (12 mm) gypsum board on each side is dimensioned as 3-½ inches (88 mm). This is the actual stud width, and not the total wall thickness, which would be 4-½ inches (100 mm). This way,

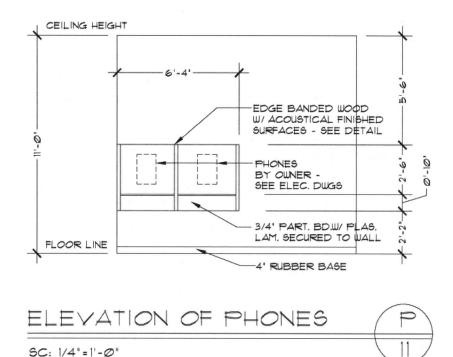

ELEVATION OF PHONES

SC: 1/4" = 1'-0"

P
11

the builder who is erecting the wall does not have to be concerned with the finish materials at this time and can mentally subtract these thicknesses to arrive at the exact location for the wall stud. However, if there indeed is a critical dimension that needs to be maintained relative to the finish material, typically for fit with another object (such as a wall or cabinet to be installed later), a note can be added to the dimension stating it is a "clear" or "face of finish" dimension, as shown in Figure 5-28.

The other method of dimensioning involves locating the centerline of a wall. In this case the builder must subtract from the centerline to find where to run the face of the wall studs, or make a center mark on the stud. This takes extra time and introduces

FIGURE 5-25 The 45-degree slash marks in this example show where a dimension begins and ends.

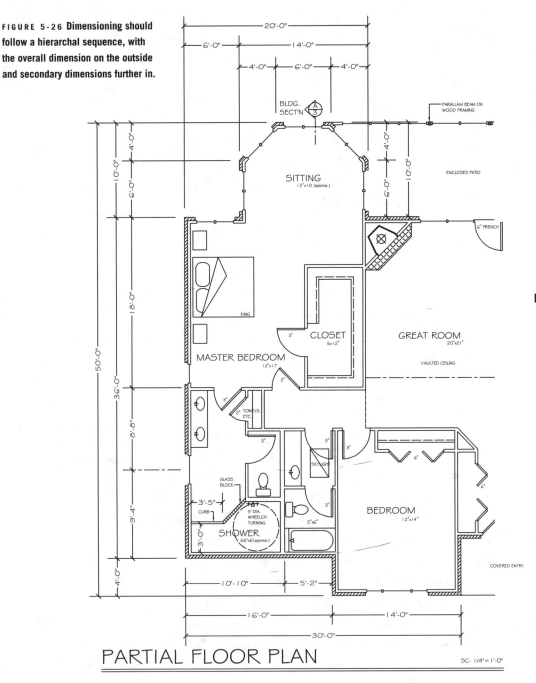

FIGURE 5-26 Dimensioning should follow a hierarchal sequence, with the overall dimension on the outside and secondary dimensions further in.

PARTIAL FLOOR PLAN

SC: 1/4"= 1'-0"

the possibly of errors. However, this method is appropriate where one wants to locate a wall in the exact center of a space, or in the center of a structural frame gridwork.

Dimension standards discussed here primarily apply to the floor plan. Different drawings, such as elevations, ceiling plans, details, etc., have their own unique dimension standards, but are similar to the floor-plan font size, style, and units. These other drawing types might be dimensioned to the frame member or the finished face of a material. In the field of kitchen design, specialized cabinetry is almost exclusively dimensioned in only inches (or millimeters) instead of feet and inches, to the finish faces (Figure 5-29).

English and Metric Dimensioning Systems

Although many plans are dimensioned using the English system (feet and inches), the metric system is slowly replacing it as the preferred method. In the metric system, units are based on the standard meter, which is then subdivided by tenths to arrive at decimeters, centimeters, and millimeters. This system is easy to use, as the decimal can simply be moved to the right or left to change from one unit to the other. There are no fractions to memorize or convert when adding. In architectural drawings, the meter or millimeter is used more than the decimeter or centimeter.

Converting from the English to metric system can be done in several ways. The choice will depend upon whether one is dealing with elements still manufactured under the English system and on what accuracy is required in the final assembly, which will be a judgment call on the designer or builder.

In the first and most accurate method, if a piece of metal is made at ½ inch thickness (as the manufacturer has not converted to the metric system), the ½ inch must be converted to metric

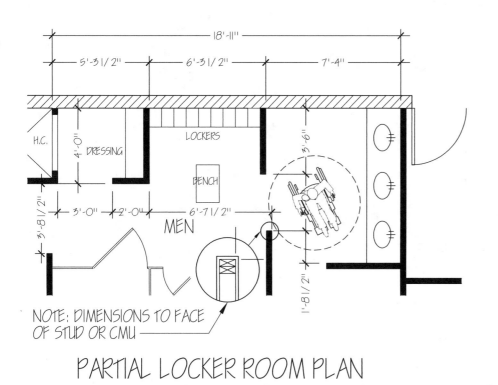

NOTE: DIMENSIONS TO FACE OF STUD OR CMU

PARTIAL LOCKER ROOM PLAN

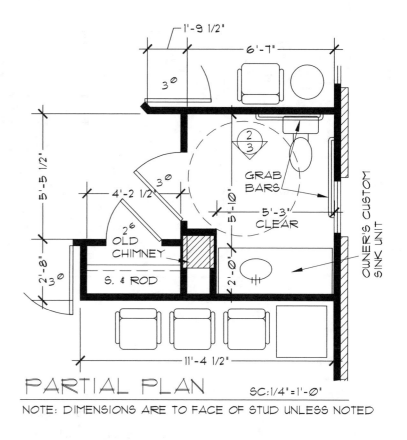

PARTIAL PLAN   SC:1/4"=1'-0"

NOTE: DIMENSIONS ARE TO FACE OF STUD UNLESS NOTED

by multiplying ½ x 2.54, which would equal 1.27 cm or 0.0127 meters.

Another method of converting is to estimate the number in the metric system according to a scale one is familiar with. Note that 1 inch equals 2.54 centimeters, and that ½ inch is a bit more than 1 centimeter. Also, ¼ inch is more than half a centimeter, and ⅟₁₆ inch is more than 1 millimeter. Using these rough guides, the final number in metrics can be estimated to a tolerance that is acceptable in the field during construction.

Another factor to consider when converting is whether the item or detail dimension can be rounded up or down to arrive at the metric number. For example, if the current spacing of some fastening anchors is 6'-0" on center, one cannot round up in metrics, because then one will exceed the specified spacing. In this case, the dimension would have to be rounded down. Typically, when conversions are needed, one should round off fractions to the nearest 5 millimeters, inches to the nearest 25 millimeters, and feet to the nearest meter.

FIGURE 5-28 (right) This example shows how dimensions are applied to the face of the finish where the "clear" opening is critical.

FIGURE 5-27 (left) This example shows how dimensions are applied to the face of a stud, concrete or masonry wall.

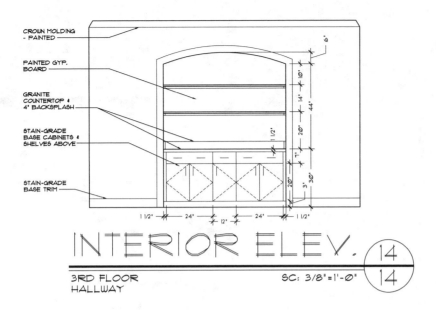

Labels in figure:
CROWN MOLDING - PAINTED

PAINTED GYP. BOARD

GRANITE COUNTERTOP & 4" BACKSPLASH

STAIN-GRADE BASE CABINETS & SHELVES ABOVE

STAIN-GRADE BASE TRIM

INTERIOR ELEV. (14/14)

3RD FLOOR HALLWAY

SC: 3/8"=1'-0"

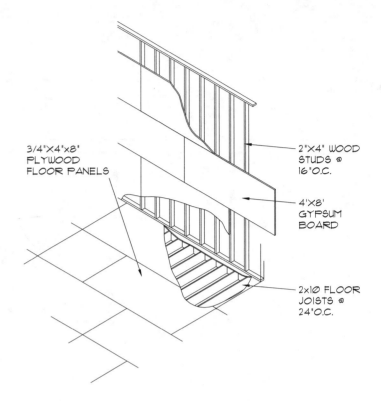

3/4"X4"X8' PLYWOOD FLOOR PANELS

2"X4" WOOD STUDS @ 16"O.C.

4'X8' GYPSUM BOARD

2x10 FLOOR JOISTS @ 24"O.C.

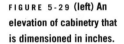

FIGURE 5-29 (left) An elevation of cabinetry that is dimensioned in inches.

FIGURE 5-30 (right) Building materials are manufactured and installed based on modular units.

Modular Units

Buildings can be constructed using modular components that are manufactured in common standard sizes. This process eliminates considerable waste of materials, labor, and time. Modules manufactured in the English system of dimensioning come in 16-, 24-, and 48-inch (40.6-, 60.9-, and 121.9-cm) sizes, as shown in Figure 5-30.

Even brick and concrete block are installed on approximately 4-inch (101.1-cm) and 8-inch (20.32-cm) modular coursing.

A modular grid (based on common building material sizes) can be used in the design process to conform to the floor plan (or section when working vertically) to a standard module. For example, if a small building is placed on a modular dimension of 28 feet (8.53 m) by 40 feet (12.19 m), its dimensions correspond to the 2-foot (.6-m) module. However, if the building is 27 feet (8.22 m) by 39 feet (11.88 m), it falls short of the module. In this situation,

approximately 1 foot (.3 m) must be cut off the modular material, resulting in wasted material and increased labor costs for cutting.

During the construction drawing process, the modular should also be followed where possible. When dimensioning new spaces, walls, and other elements, it is preferable to set the dimensions on the module, to avoid creating more work for the carpenter and wasting material. For example, if a wall is to be located in a new space, it should be placed at 12 feet (3.65 m) from an existing wall rather than 11 feet, 10-⅛ inches (3.6 m).

It is good design practice to try to always design with a modular unit in mind. In the design of corporate spaces, the spacing of the windows generally sets the modular unit, which is generally a 5'-0" (1.52 m) or 6'-0" (1.83 m) module.

As-Built Drawings and Demolition Plans 6

It can be difficult to ascertain what effect an existing structure and building elements might have on decisions made later in the design process and in the preparation of the construction drawings. However, each building, its interiors, and the components often have unique and distinct entities that can be utilized in future remodeling plans. First, it is necessary to document the layout and general character of the building, its spaces, and unique features in order to analyze the existing elements. These might be something like large-scale, classically styled columns in the interior that serve as a major design element representing strength and an iconic design style. In these cases, these assemblies might indeed need to be carefully measured and cataloged, in order to be preserved and referenced in the design of the new space.

Important aspects in the preparation of construction drawings for remodeling or additions to existing structures are the areas of creating "as-built" drawings and demolition plans. As-built drawings are also called measured or recorded drawings. Through careful measuring and other documentation such as notes, sketches, and photographs, the as-built drawings accurately portray an existing building and its interior spaces. Sometimes an owner of a building may have existing drawings that were used for the original construction, or updated existing drawings that record the changes during former construction. However, if no former

drawings exist, new drawings must be made on the existing structure and spaces, done through a process commonly called "field measuring." The as-built drawings are generally composed first, and any demolition that may need to be completed prior to new construction is then outlined as a demolition plan. Demolition plans precede the construction drawings detailing the particulars of new or remodeled construction.

As-Built Drawings

If a structure or tenant space is going to be remodeled or have a new addition, the original construction drawings, prepared by a design firm or qualified designer, are the guiding documents from which the structure and its interiors are built. During construction, these drawings might be updated as conditions, assemblies, or materials change during the construction phase. Many times, the former contract documents may require the various contractors to mark up (often in color) features in the project that were revised during subsequent construction. In many large projects, particularly those involved with federal or state governing agencies, these marked up drawings are incorporated into a revised set of construction documents, showing all of the additions and corrections. These are usually filed with the owners or their desig-

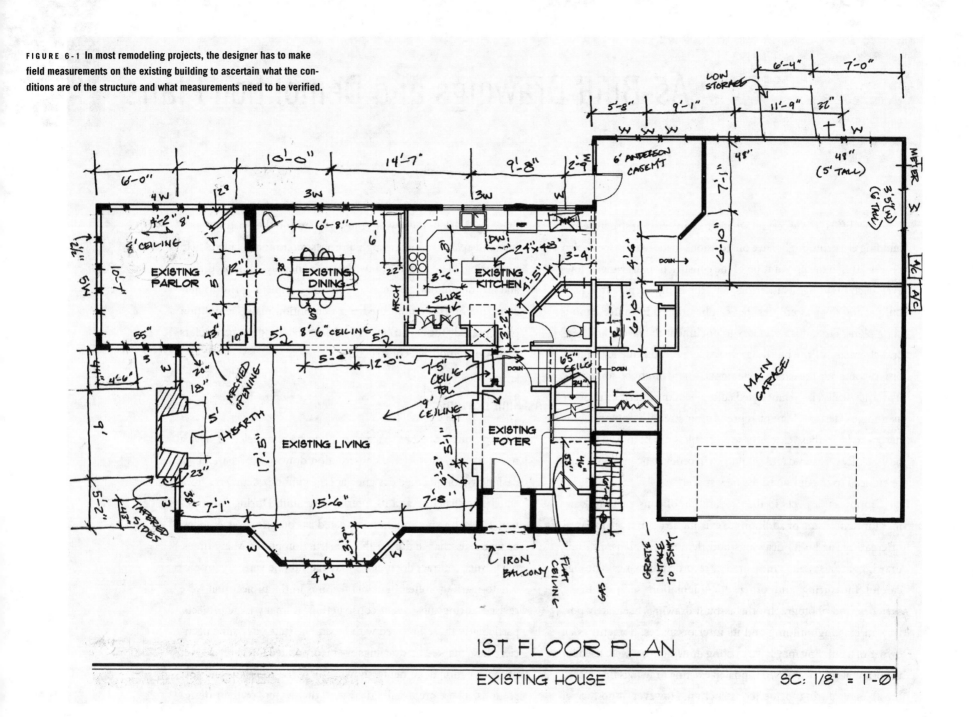

1ST FLOOR PLAN

EXISTING HOUSE

SC: 1/8" = 1'-0"

nated agents as "AS-BUILT" documents and given a new date. These revised drawings might eventually include all of the changes during construction and serve as excellent guides for future remodeling or additions. However, these construction drawings must be carefully compared to existing building conditions if they are to be used for new spaces or remodeling. In these cases, many changes may have been made over time that are not reflected in the construction drawings and must be updated. The interior designer is generally responsible for checking the as-built drawings that might be provided by others.

Field Measurements

In a number of cases, there may be no existing or as-built drawings available, as they were never made in entirety or in great detail, such as in many older structures. In other cases, drawings may have been lost or are no longer accessible—for a number of reasons. In these cases, new drawings must be made from accurate "field measurement," notes, and photographs to serve as the as-built drawings (Figure 6-1).

To make clear and usable as-built drawings, there are no shortcuts to doing this process. It can be a slow, tedious process as almost every existing condition in a building must be verified, inspected, and carefully measured. Even so, some responsibility must be assigned to the contractors to double-check the as-built drawings with the actual conditions on the job site. For this reason, the dimensions placed on any as-built drawings are noted as field measurements and often require the contractor to verify these dimensions before or during the remodel/construction process. This verification process will reduce the chances of discrepancies in the drawings and actual conditions on the job site. For example, the designer might measure some variation in wall heights, assum-

ing the ceiling or roof structure is not exactly level. However, during the construction process, the contractor might use a laser-measuring device and find that the ceiling is indeed level, but the floor is not. This could have a direct influence on either re-leveling the floor or the ceiling—whichever is the preferred choice.

Field measurements might be a series of new small individual drawings and photographs that are combined for the basis of the new design. Or, the measurements, notes, and photos might be incorporated into the original existing construction documents such as computer generated files that are available that can be modified directly. The new drawings and documentations can then serve as the base drawings from which demolition and new construction can be completed.

Measuring in the field should be done by a competent design professional who knows what major and minor information is needed. If other individuals are needed in the measuring and recording process, the experienced design professional must head the team. This will reduce the amount of time that might be needed to go back and re-measure missing information. It can also insure that the measuring process is not overdone with a lot of un-needed details. When field measuring existing spaces, a systematic plan of attack should be made in distinct phases. In large projects, an overall plan or reference plan should be done of the total space or building first, then a measurement taken of the outer or perimeter walls of the space(s) (Figure 6- 2). In interior rooms, the "exterior" walls are assumed to be the major limits of the space. Any central corridor or major walls and/or columns are measured next and referenced to the exterior dimensions. Once the reference plan is in place, each room or space is measured from established door or window openings, and cross-referenced to the reference plan (Figure 6-3). This insures that any error in a room

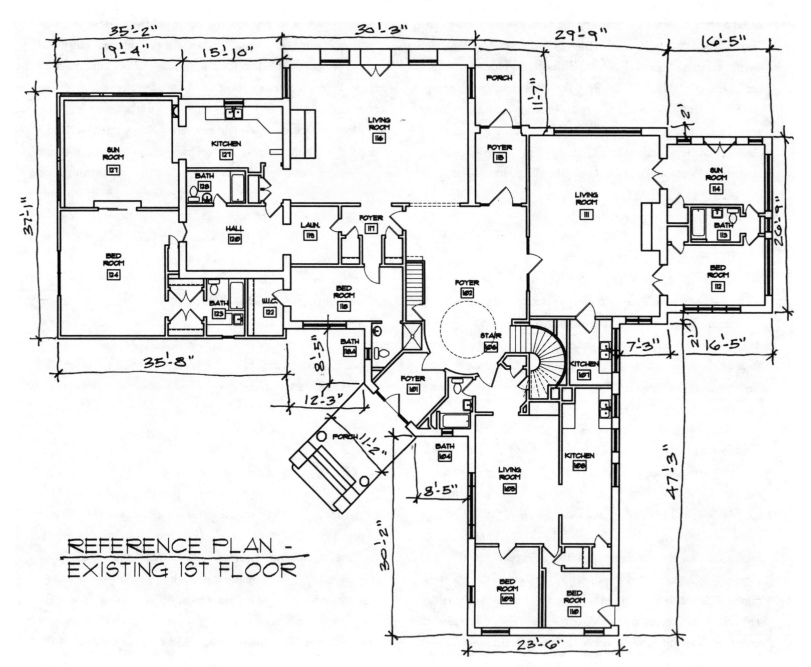

REFERENCE PLAN -
EXISTING 1ST FLOOR

FIGURE 6-2 The designer
creates a scaled reference
plan that keys rooms to
other large scale measured
drawings of each area.

measurement is isolated from the overall plan, which could build up inaccuracies if the entire building is measured from one space to the next.

This phasing method also allows more than one or two persons to do the measuring and recording, as spaces within the reference plan can be assigned to different individuals, thus speeding up the process, yet preventing miscommunication and errors. Field measurements are often done in pencil, as any errors or modifications can be done immediately to the drawing. However, in small or simple room configurations, many designers just use their handy felt-tip pen, as it makes clear and legible line work and lettering. They can be clearly photocopied or electronically scanned for sharing with individuals involved in the project. The preferred paper is a tablet with gridded paper, generally in ¼ inch (6.35 mm) squares, which helps the designer quickly use the squares to draw straight lines and use multiple squares to get the space in scale and proportion on the paper (Figure 6-4). A small reference plan can be made on a master sheet and keyed to other sheets that contain individual room measurements. Care should be made to record every major feature that might have an impact on new or remodeled construction. These would include items such as window dimensions, including the height of the sill and head. Ceiling heights, dropped soffits, protruding pilasters, baseboard heights, and openings in walls should be accurately measured and referenced to a floor, ceiling, or wall plane/corner. Care should be made to reduce inaccuracies such as the rounding off of too many measurements as that can compound errors. Also, a long wall with many doors, windows, or offsets should be measured to distinct reference points versus maintaining a continuous string of measurements from one element to the other, as any small error will be carried along in the string of measurements. At least one full-

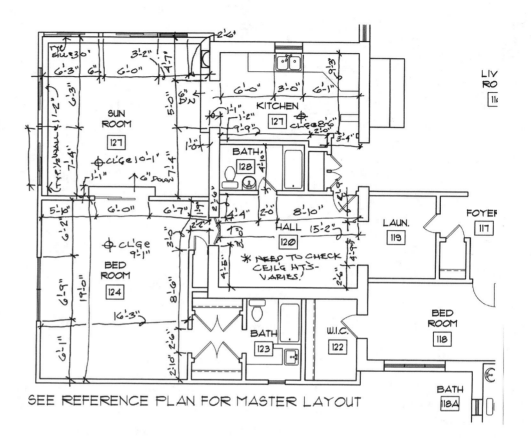

SEE REFERENCE PLAN FOR MASTER LAYOUT

length measurement should be made of the overall wall or space dimension, as it can serve as a check against smaller incremental measurements (Figure 6-5).

Notes made on the field drawings and photography serve as excellent documentation to help the designer or draftsperson remember existing elements and conditions of a space (Figure 6-6). These might be simple notes recording the condition of a door or the location of a hanging light directly over the nosing of a stairway. Digital photography can further document existing conditions by doing numerous shots and recording the room or

FIGURE 6-3 Each room of the existing building is carefully measured to wall and window openings. Other minor measurements can then be referenced to these control points.

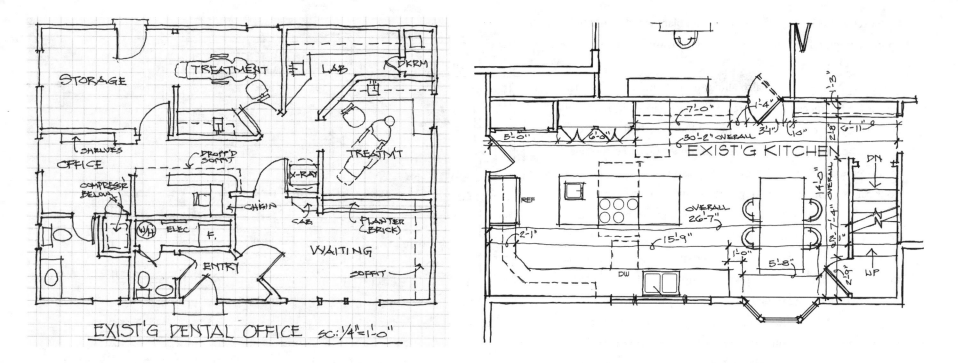

EXIST'G DENTAL OFFICE sc:¼"=1'-0"

EXIST'G KITCHEN

FIGURE 6-4 (left) Preprinted paper is a helpful guide to making a scaled existing floor plan. The paper helps the designer estimate distances based on the grid spacing.

FIGURE 6-5 (right) The designer should always measure the overall dimensions of a room to ensure the smaller increment measurements do not introduce accumulative errors.

reference plan roughly where the picture was made. Digital cameras also give the people in the field the opportunity to make sure the photo came out clear and indeed capture enough of the space or objects to insure accurate representation later in the design and construction drawing process. Digital images can be transferred to a job file for the draftsperson to quickly review on the computer monitor when drawing up the as-built drawings from the field measurements.

Although it is preferred for the person making the measurements in the field to also draft up the drawings, it is not always possible due to time or budget constraints. In these instances, it is imperative that the field measurements, notes, and photos be made systematically with a clear understanding when viewed by others. No doubt there are always small errors in field measurements, as

sometimes when drawing up the final plans, something just doesn't quite align or fit according to the measurements. In the actual spaces, rooms may not be perfectly square or a measurement is off more than an inch. This is where doing many measurements and tying them to established reference points such as columns and major walls will ensure accurate drawings.

Scale of As-Built Drawings

Most often, the initial field measurement drawings and notes are made at a scale that is appropriate to fit on the designer's drawing tablet. They might be proportional to the preprinted squares on the sheet, but not necessarily drawn at a true scale. The reference plan might be done as a small sketch and the other rooms or spaces are keyed to this unscaled plan (Figure 6-7). Rooms or spaces can

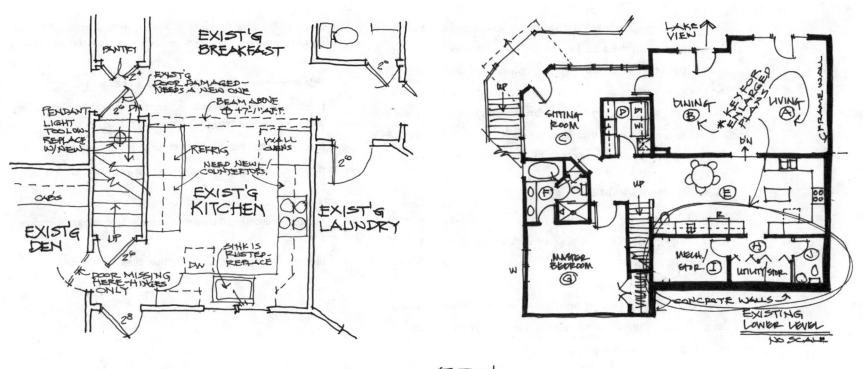

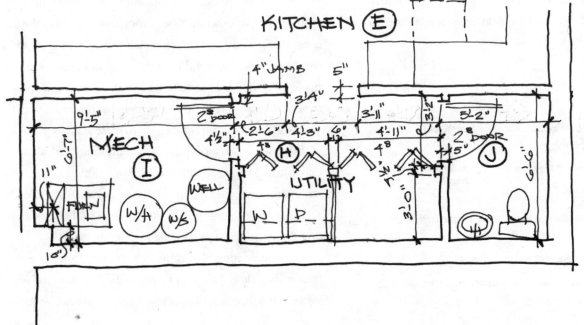

FIGURE 6-6 (top left) Notes can be added directly to the field sketch to denote conditions of materials and other concerns to be aware of for the new remodel.

FIGURE 6-7 (top right) This small plan sketch is keyed with room names and numbers to reference to other enlarged drawings (as seen in Figure 6-6).

FIGURE 6-8 (left) This large scale drawing permits more information to be added to the spaces that were keyed in Figure 6-7.

be drawn on separate sheets, trying to maintain some form of scale and proportion to the actual space and elements. Some of these spaces could take several sheets to encompass all the features of the spaces as particular elements may be needed to be drawn at a much larger scale than the small plan drawings. In these cases, match lines, reference points, or notes can be made to accurately move from one sketch to the other, as illustrated in Figure 6-8.

Dimensioning As-Built Drawings

As-built drawings made from field measurements and placed into CAD drawings do not need a lot of dimensioning—other than major areas and features such as column spacing, or overall wall locations. This is due to the fact that the field measurements were made primarily with a tape measure or an electronic measuring device that does not ascertain if walls were exactly straight and at right or other assumed angles. Most as-built drawings will contain one or more notes that call for a field verification of the dimensions and conditions at the actual site before construction begins.

Checklist for As-Built Drawings

General

- Title the drawings, note their scale, and identify north (or reference direction).
- Cross-reference the drawings to other drawings or details as needed.

Notations

- Draw in and note walls, columns, doors, windows, openings, stairs, and cabinetry.
- Note room names, floor changes, and materials.
- Note finished ceiling heights and other assemblies above finished floor (A.F.F.).

- Locate ceiling grids, light fixtures, smoke detectors, soffits, HVAC ceiling units, speakers, sprinkler heads, ceiling access doors, and drapery pockets.
- Note door sizes, window widths, heights to head and sill.
- Locate electrical wall receptacles, switches, telephone/data ports, and other wall-mounted items.
- Note floor drains, plumbing fixtures, water heaters, and other devices.
- Note furniture, and other items that are not apparent in the drawings.

Dimensions

- Dimension controlling factors such as walls, columns, and doors/windows.
- Dimension room widths, stairs, and floor changes.

Demolition Plans

Many new interiors are constructed in spaces of existing buildings or the existing interior environment is remodeled for updating, spatial needs, or other factors. In most cases, some of the existing construction and elements will remain, others taken out, and some will be reworked. Careful consideration and evaluation must be made as to what is to remain, what is to be removed, and what is in need of modification for new work to be compatible with the old or existing conditions (Figure 6-9). In these situations, some or all of the existing interiors and other features must be clearly identified that are in need of being removed or modified before new construction, assemblies, components, or materials are added. This may require one or more separate drawings in the set of construction drawings and are called the demolition plan(s).

The demolition plan is the primary instrument for the contractors to follow. This plan serves as the base drawing (or drawings if more than one floor is involved), for other drawings,

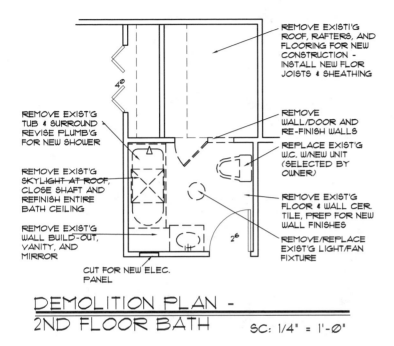

REMOVE EXISTI'G ROOF, RAFTERS, AND FLOORING FOR NEW CONSTRUCTION - INSTALL NEW FLOR JOISTS & SHEATHING

REMOVE EXIST'G TUB & SURROUND REVISE PLUMB'G FOR NEW SHOWER

REMOVE WALL/DOOR AND RE-FINISH WALLS

REPLACE EXIST'G W.C. W/NEW UNIT (SELECTED BY OWNER)

REMOVE EXIST'G SKYLIGHT AT ROOF, CLOSE SHAFT AND REFINISH ENTIRE BATH CEILING

REMOVE EXIST'G FLOOR & WALL CER. TILE, PREP FOR NEW WALL FINISHES

REMOVE EXIST'G WALL BUILD-OUT, VANITY, AND MIRROR

REMOVE/REPLACE EXIST'G LIGHT/FAN FIXTURE

CUT FOR NEW ELEC. PANEL

DEMOLITION PLAN - 2ND FLOOR BATH   SC: 1/4" = 1'-0"

FIGURE 6-9 Notes and dashed lines on the demolition plan indicate what items are to be removed or prepared for new construction.

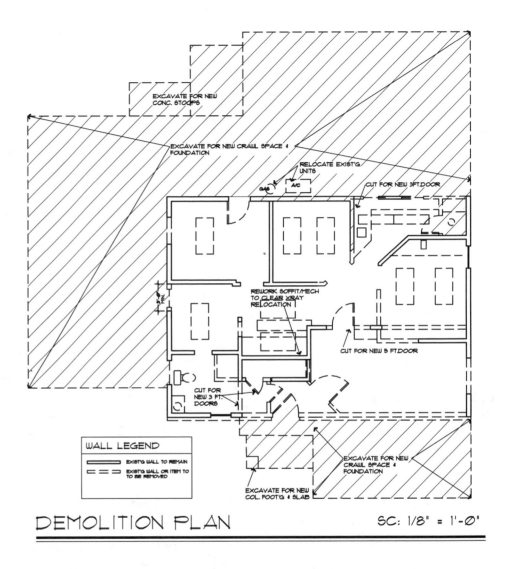

EXCAVATE FOR NEW CONC. STOOPS

EXCAVATE FOR NEW CRAWL SPACE & FOUNDATION

RELOCATE EXIST'G. UNITS

CUT FOR NEW 3FT.DOOR

REWORK SOFFIT/MECH TO CLEAR X-RAY RELOCATION

CUT FOR NEW 3 FT.DOOR

CUT FOR NEW 3 FT. DOORS

EXCAVATE FOR NEW CRAWL SPACE & FOUNDATION

EXCAVATE FOR NEW COL. FOOT'G & SLAB

WALL LEGEND

EXIST'G WALL TO REMAIN

EXIST'G WALL OR ITEM TO TO BE REMOVED

DEMOLITION PLAN   SC: 1/8" = 1'-0"

FIGURE 6-10 Cross hatch patterns are used on the demolition plan to show the extent of areas to be demolished or excavated for new construction.

such as elevations and enlarged details, to be referenced to. In addition to the architectural and interior elements to be removed or modified, there must also be other information sufficient to identify the location and extent of all plumbing/mechanical/electrical equipment and fixture demolition.

There are several ways to note what items are to be removed and the extent of the operation. The most common is a plan view with the removed items being graphically highlighted in some fashion such as cross-hatching the specifics to be taken out with an accompanying note (Figure 6-10). In most cases of large-scale drawings and simple demolition, this is the easiest way. In some cases where there are a lot of particulars that need to be noted in

the demolition, or the plan is drawn at a small scale (and the notes will not fit on the drawing), symbols or letters are assigned on the plan and accompanied by a legend (Figure 6-11). Or, the small drawing can be referenced to one or more larger-scale drawings that can more clearly show the work to be done.

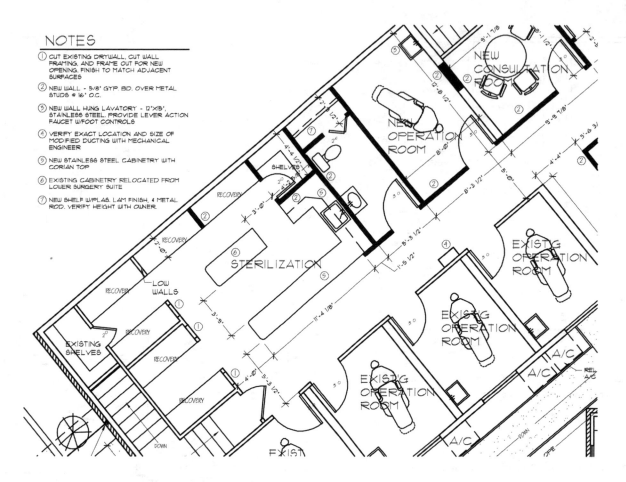

NOTES

1. CUT EXISTING DRYWALL, CUT WALL FRAMING, AND FRAME OUT FOR NEW OPENING. FINISH TO MATCH ADJACENT SURFACES

2. NEW WALL - 5/8" GYP. BD. OVER METAL STUDS @ 16" O.C.

3. NEW WALL HUNG LAVATORY - 12"X15", STAINLESS STEEL. PROVIDE LEVER ACTION FAUCET W/FOOT CONTROLS

4. VERIFY EXACT LOCATION AND SIZE OF MODIFIED DUCTING WITH MECHANICAL ENGINEER

5. NEW STAINLESS STEEL CABINETRY WITH CORIAN TOP

6. EXISTING CABINETRY RELOCATED FROM LOWER SURGERY SUITE

7. NEW SHELF W/PLAS. LAM FINISH, & METAL ROD. VERIFY HEIGHT WITH OWNER

FIGURE 6-11 In small scale plans, demolition notes are keyed to the plan versus trying to write within each space.

Scale of Demolition Plans

Generally, the demolition plan(s) is drawn at the same scale as the floor plans, allowing the viewer to ascertain the scale of objects and features. The most common scale for drawing small commercial projects is ¼" = 1'-0" (1:50 metric) and ⅛" = 1'-0" (1:100 metric) for larger commercial spaces. However, in very large spaces, such as a tenant development plan, the entire plan might be shown and keyed as to where to find enlarged drawings of specific areas or items. In some instances, a "match line" is placed on the partial drawing, and their continuation is found on another sheet(s).

The scale of the drawing is placed directly beneath the title of the drawing, or in the sheet title block—if the office sets a standard for this. When enlarged details are developed to show a feature, a key with a symbol or note is placed on the demolition plan and cross-referenced to a separate enlarged drawing. Additional

clearly what demolition work and other details need to be done.

Dimensioning Demolition Plans

There may not be a lot of dimensioning required on the demolition plan, as most items to be removed can readily be identified in the plan view and with adjoining notes. Items such as walls are generally removed to specific points, such as the abutment with an adjacent wall. However, in some cases such as floor material, dimensions may be needed if the removal occurs in a large open area that has no apparent reference location and is in need of dimensioning from a recognizable base point. In these situations, demolition plans need to be carefully dimensioned to indicate the extent of assemblies and items to be removed, as well as those to remain, as illustrated in Figure 6-12.

Dimensions should be established from objects that are easily obtainable on the construction site, such as wall or column locations. Demolition plans are dimensioned primarily to the finish dimensions versus the underlying framing members, as these are most apparent. However, if the frame dimensions are the controlling factors, a note is added to the drawings to clarify this, and demolition may require removal of surface coverings to the underlying assembly.

Drafting Standards for Demolition Plans

The demolition plan shows the limits of removal for features such as the floors, walls, ceilings, and objects that penetrate or touch it. Assemblies such as soffits, walls, and partitions that are to remain or be removed should be shown as well as the changes in materials and ceiling heights. Draw in lights, HVAC equipment, etc., that must be taken into consideration for removal or remodeling. Note that a line weight hierarchy is established for existing items to

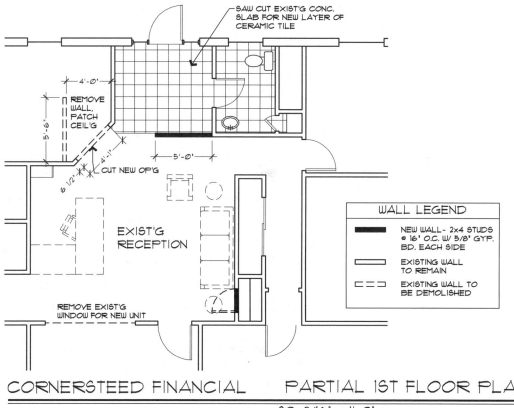

remain versus items to be removed—with the latter often shown with lighter and dotted line weights.

Designation of Materials

The designer is challenged with noting all of the specific materials that are to remain, be re-worked, or removed in the project. This is achieved by placing notes on the demolition plan to indicate materials, symbols inserted into the plan and keyed to an accompanying legend, or a combination of these. CAD programs now offer the designer many options to designate materials on the

FIGURE 6-12 Notes and dimensions show the exact location and limits of items to be removed. In small projects, the demolition plan might also show some walls to be added, if one drawing will cover both removal and new construction.

demolition plan by defining specific "hatching" patterns as related to a material.

Checklist for Demolition Plans

General

■ Check plans for **LEED** certification credits, if applicable.

■ Title the drawings, note their scale, and identify north (or reference direction).

■ Cross-reference the drawings to other drawings or details as needed.

■ Establish a line-weight hierarchy and wall key of walls and other items to be removed versus items to remain.

■ Show doors and windows that remain versus those to be removed.

■ Show the extent of any stairs and ramps to be removed or to remain.

■ Show ceilings, light fixtures, and **HVAC** ceiling registers to be kept or removed (or refer to a separate ceiling demolition plan).

■ Show sections of floors and framing to be removed (after first consulting with the architect or engineer).

■ Show electrical devices (wall switches and outlets) to be removed or to remain.

■ Show plumbing fixtures, floor drains, and other related items to be removed or to remain.

■ Show any built-in cabinetry and equipment that is to remain or be removed.

Notations

■ Note room names, existing floor changes, and materials.

■ Note any new structural components (beams, columns, joists) to be added before demolition (refer to engineer's drawings).

■ Note any existing areas or items that need to be protected during demolition, or must remain in use by the owner(s).

■ Add notes for contractor to field-verify existing conditions and dimensions. Notify the designer of any discrepancies in the field conditions and the drawings—before demolition occurs.

Dimensions

■ Dimension extents of demolition to controlling factors such as walls, columns, and doors/windows.

■ Dimension cuts (widths and lengths) into existing floors, walls, and ceilings.

The floor plan is perhaps the most significant architectural drawing, as it contains a tremendous amount of information about the design and construction of a building or space (see Figure 7-1). It also serves as the primary drawing to which many of the other specialty drawings can be keyed.

A floor plan is an orthographic view of a total building or an area within a building, seen as if a horizontal cutting plane were passed through it at a height of approximately 4 feet (1219 mm) above the floor line (Figure 7-2). In some cases, it may be necessary to assume a higher cutting plane to show an item such as a high window or the space above a tall cabinet. The viewer is looking straight down into the building, as illustrated in Figure 7-3. In multiple-level buildings, a separate floor plan is drawn for each level. In turn, each level is aligned with the one above for bearing walls, stairways, ductwork, and other vertical elements related to both floors. Stairways are labeled "up" on one level and "down" on the level above. When viewing a floor plan of a building that includes a mezzanine or loft, the upper level is shown in plan, with the lower level also shown or simply labeled "open" (Figure 7-4).

In construction drawings, floor plans are drawn to scale and detailed to show walls, doors, windows, plumbing fixtures, appliances, stairs, cabinetry, and any other built-in or free-standing interior features. Most of these items are drawn, as viewed from

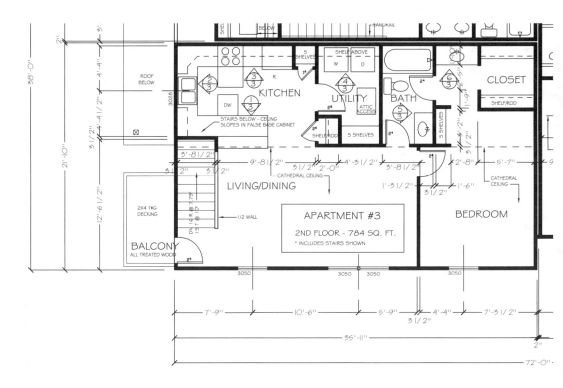

2ND FLOOR PLAN

SC: 1/4"= 1'-0"

1. ALL WALLS TO BE 2X4 STUDS @ 16" O.C. GYP. BOARD - UNLESS NOTED OTHERWISE
2. FIELD VERIFY ALL CABINETRY BEFORE ORDERING/INSTALLING

FIGURE 7-1 A construction drawing of a floor plan conveys a significant amount of information to the builder, such as dimensions, door/window locations, cabinetry, and symbols that correspond to interior elevations.

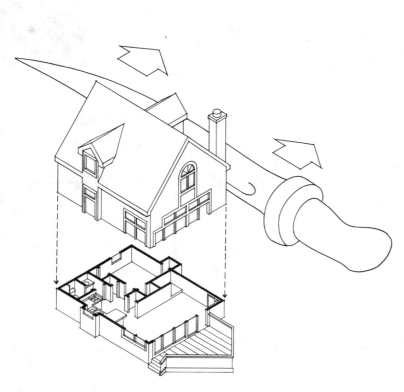

FIGURE 7-2 A floor plan drawing is visualized as if an imaginary knife sliced approximately 4 feet (1219 mm) above the floor.

FIGURE 7-3 This is the construction drawing of the floor plan produced by the imaginary knife cut in Figure 7-2.

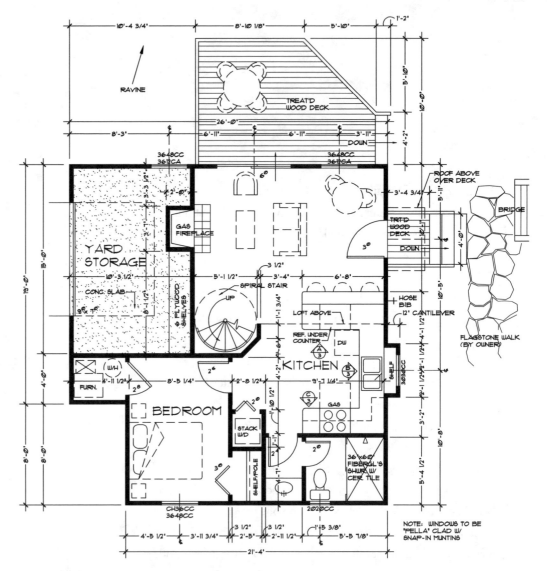

FIRST FLOOR PLAN
514 SQ. FT.

SC: 1/4"=1'-0"

NORTH

above. Figure 7-5 illustrates how a lavatory, appliances, and plumbing fixtures are drawn in several rooms. Doors are drawn in the plan view in an open position showing the direction of their operation. Their size might be called out simplistically in plan, such as 3°, denoting the door is 3 feet (91.4 cm) wide, as shown in Figure 7-6. More detailed information regarding doors are shown in a door schedule (see Chapter 12) and keyed on the plan. Windows and their operation are difficult to describe in just a floor-plan view. They are drawn simplistically in plan and referenced with specific symbols that relate to the type of their action and listed in a window schedule (see Chapter 12 for examples of window schedules).

In addition to symbols, line weights and different types of lines can be used to relay information with the floor-plan drawing. For example, broken lines can denote items such as upper cabinets and high windows that are above the cutting plane, as shown in Figure 7-7. Also, a different pattern can be used on the floor plan to denote a change in the floor treatment, such as the grid pattern in the kitchen and utility room in Figure 7-7. Much of the other information given on a floor plan is more general, with the items spelled out in more detail in other drawings or specifications. For example, a water heater or handrail is designated as such on the plan, and their detailed specifications are found elsewhere in the construction drawings or written specifications.

Floor Plans in Modular Units

It is good design practice to try to always design with a modular unit in mind, as most buildings are constructed using predetermined modular grids and components as manufactured in common standard sizes. The designer tries to create spaces and objects

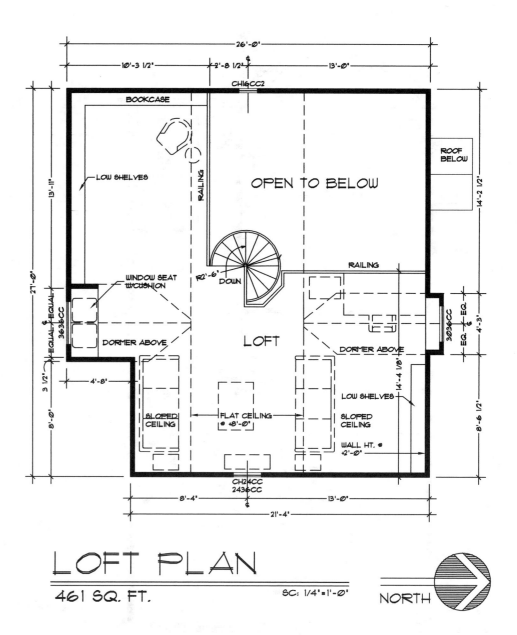

FIGURE 7-4 **A second-level floor plan can also show part of the space below. This helps to visualize what one can see when looking from this upper floor to the lower one.**

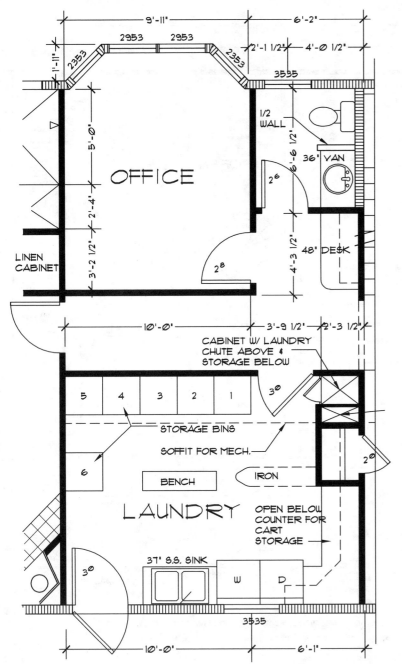

FIGURE 7-5 Built-in features such as sinks, cabinetry, and water closets are drawn as viewed from above.

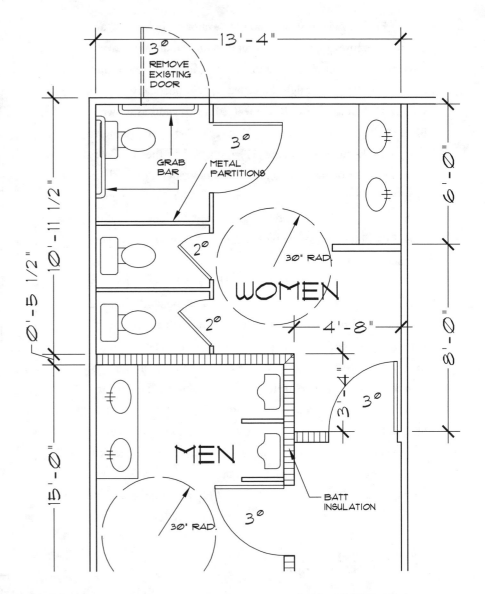

FIGURE 7-6 In this partial floor plan, doors are drawn simply, just showing their size and direction of swing. For example, 3 means a door that is 3 feet in width.

with standard materials, to eliminate considerable waste of materials, labor, and time.

Typically, a modular grid is used over the floor plan to insure a standard module. The current module in the English system of dimensioning and manufacturing is the 16, 24, and 48-inch size and spacing of materials (40.6, 60.9, and 121.9 cm). Even brick and concrete block are installed on approximately 4-inch (10.1-cm) and 8-inch (20.32-cm) modular coursing.

A modular grid spacing (based on common building material sizes) is used in the design process to conform the floor plan to a standard module. For example, if an interior space is 20 feet (6.1 m) by 30 feet (9.14 m), its dimensions correspond to the 2-foot (.6-m) module. However, if the building is 19 feet (5.79 m) by 29 feet (8.84 m), it falls short of the module. In this situation, approximately 1 foot (.3 m) must be cut off the modular material, resulting in increased labor costs for cutting and discarded materials.

In turn, the modular layout should also be followed in the construction drawing phase wherever possible. When dimensioning new spaces and walls, it is preferable to set the dimensions on the module to avoid creating more work for the builder and resulting in wasted material. For example, if a wall is to be located in a new space, it should be ideally placed at 10 feet (3.05 m) from an existing wall rather than 9 feet-10-1/8 inches (3.04 m). In the design of commercial spaces where corporate environments may be included, the spacing of the exterior windows and columns generally set the modular unit, which is usually 5 feet-0 inches (1.52 m) or 6 feet-0 inches (91.83 m) as illustrated in Figure 7-8.

In commercial interior spaces, there are also structural columns within the interior that are generally placed in a modular pattern. These are located by using a system of column refer-

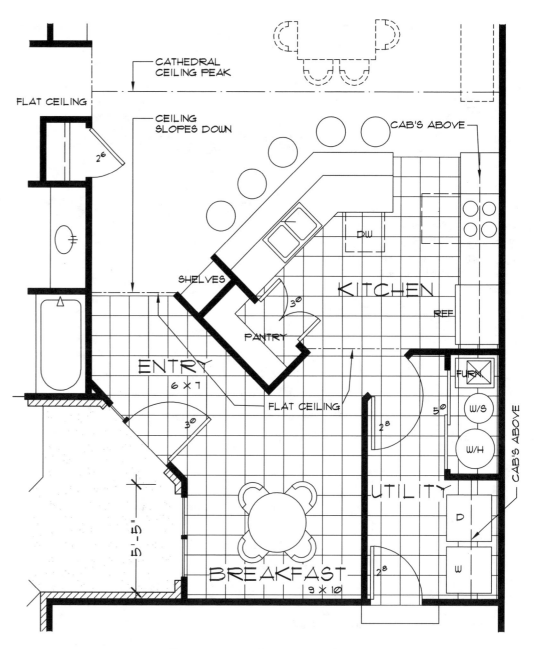

FIGURE 7-7 Dashed and dotted lines are used in this floor plan to indicate upper cabinets in the kitchen and utility areas, as well as ceiling changes.

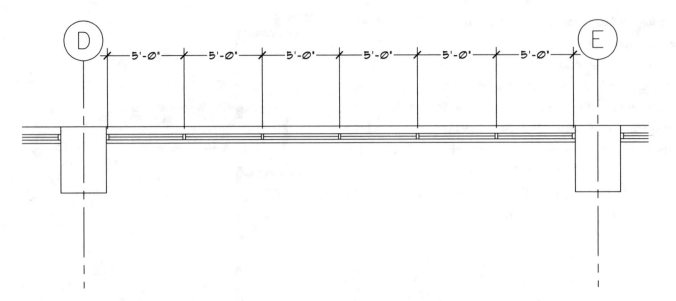

FIGURE 7-8 In this commercial building the windows are set in a 5'-0" module which would influence the placement of the interior wall partitions.

ence grids. The grid runs both in a horizontal and vertical direction. The horizontal grid identifies each row of columns by numbers or letters from left to right. Then, the opposite symbols are used to identify the location of each column in the vertical direction, beginning from the top. This system facilitates locating each column on the grid by a reference such as column B3, as illustrated in Figure 7-9.

Wall and Partition Types and Construction

There are three commonly used interior partition types in building design. These are wood frame, steel frame, and masonry partitions; or a combination of these (Figure 7-10).

Wood Frame Partitions

Wood construction for interior partitions generally consists of 2′4 wood studs [actual size is 1-½" x 3-½" (38.1 mm x 88.9 mm)]

spaced 16 inches (406 mm) or 24 inches (610 mm) on center; the 16-inch spacing being more common. Gypsum wall board of various thicknesses is nailed or screwed directly to the wood studs on one or both sides of the partition depending on the design intent, use of space, fire and sound rating.

Steel (Metal) Frame Partition

Steel construction with metal studs is more common for large commercial buildings and consists of galvanized steel. Metal studs are available in several thicknesses, referred to as gages. The most common thickness used for studs and other metal framing is 25-gage (0.0175" or 0.455 mm). Heavier gages are used for load-bearing partitions, framing door openings, or very tall partitions. Metal studs are manufactured in a "U" shape with small flanges and have precut openings for the passage of electrical conduit and other cables. They are attached to a top and bottom metal channel or "runner."

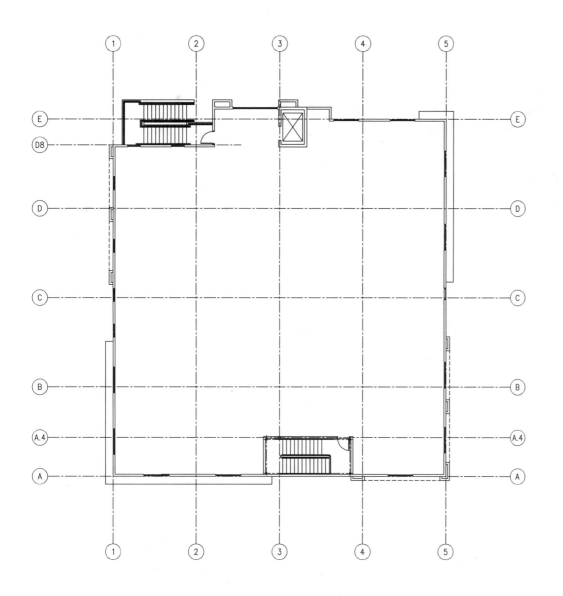

FIGURE 7-9 Structural columns within a commercial interior space are placed in a modular pattern and are identified by a system of column reference grids, such as C2.

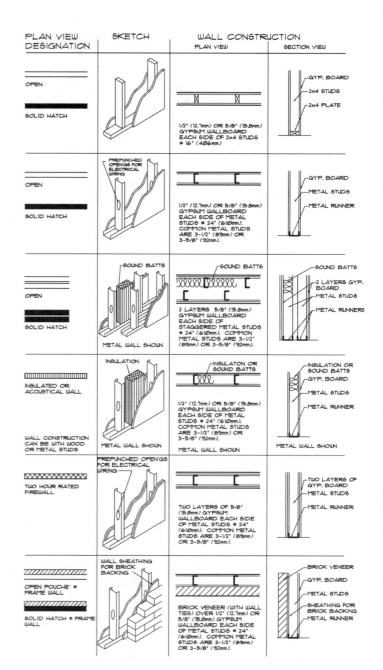

FIGURE 7-10 Typical interior wall construction types seen in different views.

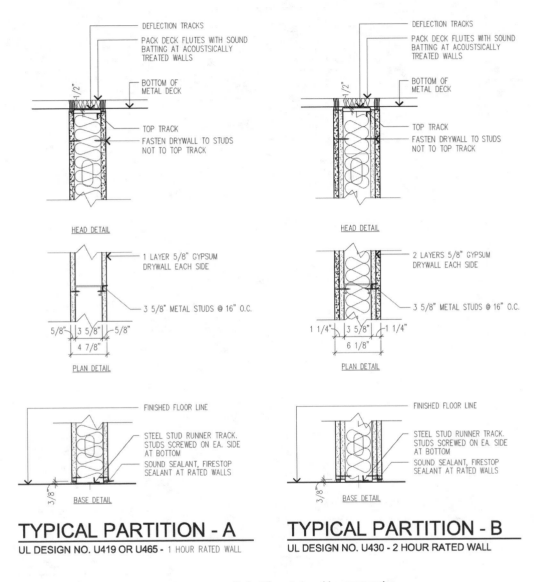

DEFLECTION TRACKS

PACK DECK FLUTES WITH SOUND BATTING AT ACOUSTSICALLY TREATED WALLS

BOTTOM OF METAL DECK

1/2"

TOP TRACK

FASTEN DRYWALL TO STUDS NOT TO TOP TRACK

HEAD DETAIL

1 LAYER 5/8" GYPSUM DRYWALL EACH SIDE

3 5/8" METAL STUDS @ 16" O.C.

5/8" | 3 5/8" | 5/8"

4 7/8"

PLAN DETAIL

FINISHED FLOOR LINE

STEEL STUD RUNNER TRACK. STUDS SCREWED ON EA. SIDE AT BOTTOM

SOUND SEALANT, FIRESTOP SEALANT AT RATED WALLS

3/8"

BASE DETAIL

TYPICAL PARTITION - A
UL DESIGN NO. U419 OR U465 - 1 HOUR RATED WALL

DEFLECTION TRACKS

PACK DECK FLUTES WITH SOUND BATTING AT ACOUSTSICALLY TREATED WALLS

BOTTOM OF METAL DECK

1/2"

TOP TRACK

FASTEN DRYWALL TO STUDS NOT TO TOP TRACK

HEAD DETAIL

2 LAYERS 5/8" GYPSUM DRYWALL EACH SIDE

3 5/8" METAL STUDS @ 16" O.C.

1 1/4" | 3 5/8" | 1 1/4"

6 1/8"

PLAN DETAIL

FINISHED FLOOR LINE

STEEL STUD RUNNER TRACK. STUDS SCREWED ON EA. SIDE AT BOTTOM

SOUND SEALANT, FIRESTOP SEALANT AT RATED WALLS

3/8"

BASE DETAIL

TYPICAL PARTITION - B
UL DESIGN NO. U430 - 2 HOUR RATED WALL

FIGURE 7-11 Typical fire-rated partition construction.

Metal studs are similar in size to wood studs and are available in widths of 1-⅝, 2-½, 3-⅝, 4, and 6 inches (41.3, 63.5, 92.1, 101.6, and 152.4 mm). Like wood studs, they are spaced 16 inches or 24 inches (406 mm or 610 mm) on center. For most commercial interior partition construction 24-inch spacing is used.

Masonry Partition

Masonry partitions refer to walls constructed of concrete block, glass block, brick structural clay tile, terra cotta, and gypsum block. Generally, masonry partitions form the exterior walls that are what the building is constructed of. However, depending on the design intent, there may be interior masonry partitions required for special purposes such as a bearing wall, fire resistive construction, or acoustical barrier.

Fire-rated Partitions

A fire resistive partition is one of the most important types of construction assemblies the interior designer will detail in building design. A fire partition is defined as a wall assembly of materials designed to restrict the spread of fire. Exterior walls and interior partition fire ratings are specified in hour(s) of resistance, such as 1-hour, 2-hour, 3-hour, and 4-hour. This means that for a 2-hour rated partition, it will prevent fire and smoke from passing through the partition for a period of at least two hours. Fire ratings are established by an independent testing laboratory and then these ratings are adopted by the building code. Various partitions are constructed and subjected to a standard test fire, and the results are measured in order to establish a rating. The International Building Code specifies the exact requirements for the various types of fire-rated walls and partitions. See Figure 7-11 for some typical fire-rated partition construction.

For interior construction generally 1-hour rated partitions, and occasionally 2-hour rated partitions, will be required for separating corridors from lease space, and separating one type of occupancy from another. Interior partitions that are used to enclose vertical circulation, such as stairwells and elevators are generally required to be 2-hour rated, according to the International Building Code. Some occupancy separations require 3-hour or 4-hour protection.

Acoustical Partitions

The acoustical quality of an interior space can affect how it is used and how successful it is as much as its colors, finishes, furniture, and shape. Spaces can be distracting if they are too noisy or inaudible sounds or speech can't be heard clearly. Interior partition construction design decisions can affect the resulting acoustical quality of a space. In order to control unwanted noise (sound), the designer must prevent or minimize the transmission of sound from one space to another by selecting construction elements and detailing partition assemblies. Interior partitions can be designed and constructed in a variety of ways to modify their acoustical or sound transmission quality. Transmission of sound through interior partitions is primarily accomplished by the mass of the partitions.

Generally, the sound rating of an interior partition is a number that represents the sound transmission class (STC) as established by laboratory testing. The sound transmission class is an average rating of the resistance to transmission over a wide range of frequencies. The higher the STC rating, the better the partition is at minimizing or stopping sound. See Figure 7-12 for some common STC ratings and their control of various sounds.

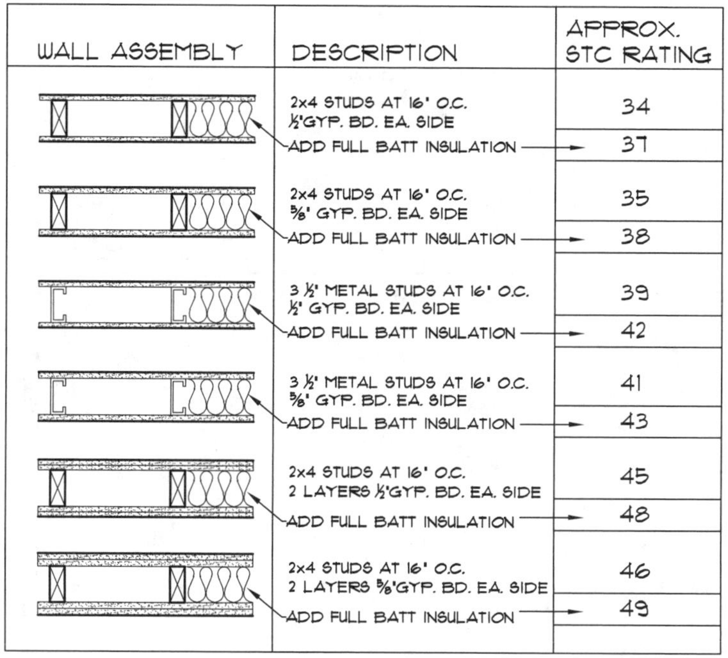

WALL ASSEMBLY	DESCRIPTION	APPROX. STC RATING
	2x4 STUDS AT 16' O.C. ½'GYP. BD. EA. SIDE	34
	ADD FULL BATT INSULATION	37
	2x4 STUDS AT 16' O.C. ⅝' GYP. BD. EA. SIDE	35
	ADD FULL BATT INSULATION	38
	3 ½' METAL STUDS AT 16' O.C. ½' GYP. BD. EA. SIDE	39
	ADD FULL BATT INSULATION	42
	3 ½' METAL STUDS AT 16' O.C. ⅝' GYP. BD. EA. SIDE	41
	ADD FULL BATT INSULATION	43
	2x4 STUDS AT 16' O.C. 2 LAYERS ½'GYP. BD. EA. SIDE	45
	ADD FULL BATT INSULATION	48
	2x4 STUDS AT 16' O.C. 2 LAYERS ⅝'GYP. BD. EA. SIDE	46
	ADD FULL BATT INSULATION	49

FIGURE 7-12 **Common acoustical wall partitions and their STC ratings.**

Scale of Floor Plans

The floor plan tends to be one of the largest single drawings in a construction set and often is placed on a sheet by itself. However, if space permits, other minor elements might be drawn around it to fill up the sheet. The sheet size a floor plan is drawn on is often the governing factor of the scale of that drawing. Floor plans are drawn at a scale that best presents the information to be conveyed without being too small to read. Residential floor plans are relatively small in overall square footage and are generally drawn at a scale of ¼" = 1'-0" (1:50 in metric scale). As commercial spaces can be quite large, a scale of ⅛" = 1'-0" (1:100 metric) or even 1/16" = 1'-0" (1:200 metric) might be more appropriate. In these latter examples, auxiliary enlarged plans can be drawn and keyed to the base

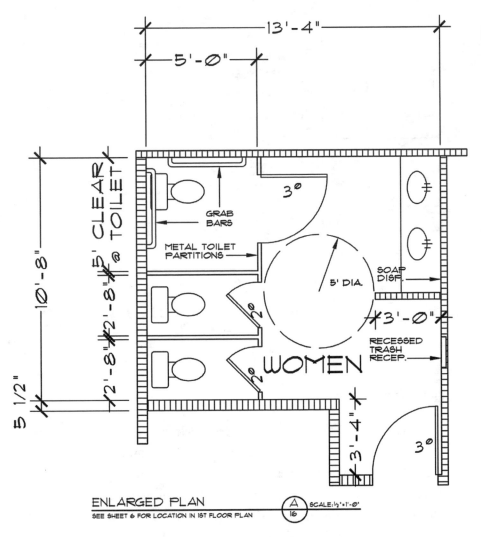

ENLARGED PLAN
SEE SHEET 6 FOR LOCATION IN 1ST FLOOR PLAN
$\frac{A}{16}$ SCALE: ½"=1'-0"

Drafting Standards

Many decisions must be made before a floor plan is complete and the designer will probably spend more time drafting the floor plan than any other drawing in the construction drawing set. Drafting floor plans is more efficient if a logical sequence is followed, such as layout of walls, openings, door swings, fixtures, cabinets, dimensions, symbols, and any necessary notes.

Generally in drawing floor plans for commercial interior spaces, the shell of the buildings will have already been designed by an architect and the exterior walls and columns have been determined. The interior designer then begins with a "base building" drawing that consists of the exterior walls and core of the building that includes public restrooms and vertical egress systems, such as stairwells and elevators, as seen in Figure 7-14.

The primary purpose of the floor plan is to locate interior partitions, doors, windows, stairs, and any other major built-in components. The amount of information shown in a floor plan construction drawing depends on the size and complexity of the proposed project. In commercial design, the construction drawings are supplemented by a set of written specifications that describe in detail the scope of the work, materials to be used, method of installation, and quality of workmanship required. The specifications are coordinated with the set of construction drawings that make up part of the total construction documents. As the specifications are more detailed as to any particular item, there is no need to include detailed information on the floor plan that would be included in the specifications. Therefore, generic terms are used on the floor plan drawing to describe an item, such as a water closet, utility sink, or other equipment.

FIGURE 7-13 Some spaces can be drawn at a large scale, such as ½" = 1'0" (1:20 metric), to convey detailed information. These are then cross-referenced to a smaller-scale floor plan.

floor plan, as shown in Figure 7-13. If a building is too large to draw the entire floor plan on one sheet, it can be broken into two or more parts using match lines and drawn on several sheets. One should always indicate the scale of the floor plan on the sheet, generally placed under the title.

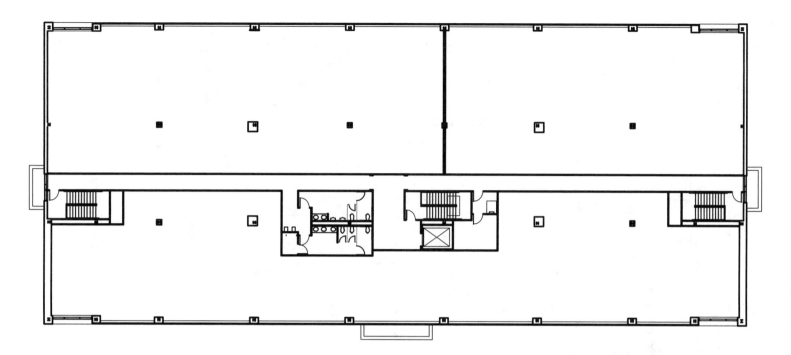

Walls in Plan View

Floor plans should be drawn with a hierarchy of line weights for easy reading and for graphic excitement. Generally, a minimum of three line weights should be used, as illustrated in Figure 7-15. Walls should be drawn with the darkest and thickest lines

These lines can be doubled or filled in to indicate the thickness of the wall. The actual wall thickness will vary with the type of construction, but there are some typical widths. Most walls in residential and small commercial construction are built with 2 x 4 wood studs which are actually 3-½ inches (8.89 cm) in width. When ½-inch gypsum board is added on each face, the wall thickness becomes 4-½ inches (11.43 cm) finished. The same wall thick-

LIGHT LINE WEIGHT _____

MEDIUM LINE WEIGHT _____

HEAVY LINE WEIGHT _____

FIGURE 7-15 A minimum of three distinct line weights should be used in floor-plan drawings.

ness is also often used in large commercial interiors where the studs are made of steel, although steel stud widths are produced in many different sizes, as well. For both residential and commercial projects, interior 2 x 4 walls are generally drafted at approximately 5 inches (127 mm) thick in plan view. Exterior walls are

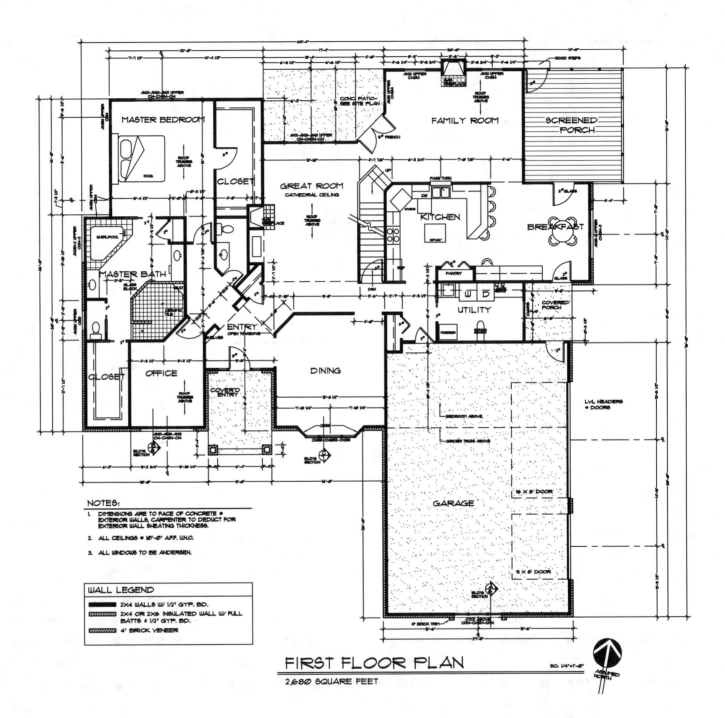

FIGURE 7-16 In this drawing,
walls are drawn with heavy lines.
Built-in furniture, cabinetry, and
other objects are drawn with
medium lines. Textures are represented with light lines.

FIRST FLOOR PLAN

2,680 SQUARE FEET

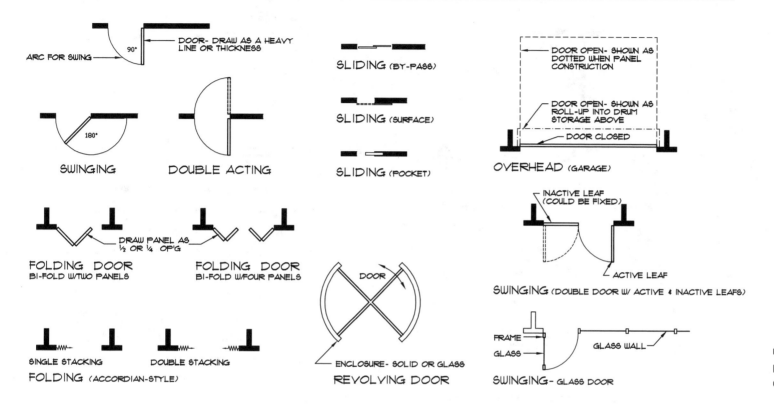

FIGURE 7-17 **Doors drawn in plan view show their method of operation.**

drawn at about 6 to 8 inches (152 to 203 mm) thick, depending upon what materials they are constructed of.

Built-in and free-standing objects such as countertops, plumbing fixtures, stairs, furniture, and other items that have contours should be drawn with slightly lighter line weights than the walls. Finally, textures, door swings, and dimension lines are the thinnest and lightest lines, as shown in Figure 7-16.

Doors and Windows in Plan View

Doors and windows are drawn in the floor plan using various symbols and images, and are further dimensioned and referenced to schedules in the construction drawings. The symbols used will depend upon the operating action of the door or window, the specifics needed to describe it, and the scale of the floor-plan drawing. In hand-drafting, these symbols are generated for each new

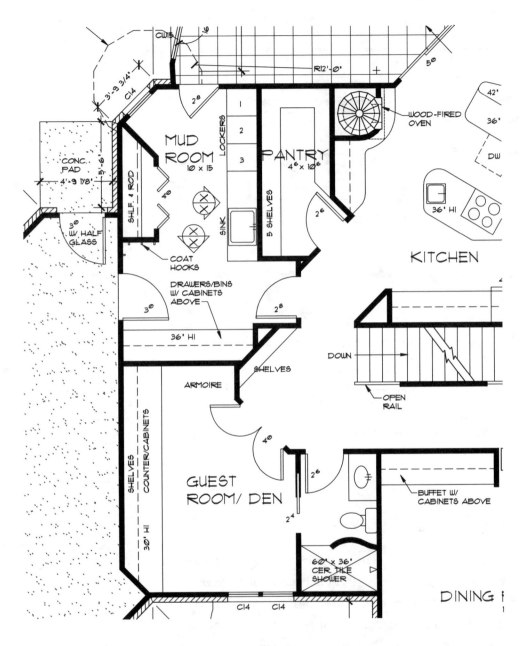

FIGURE 7-18 The doors in this floor plan are generically called out according to their widths, such as 3°. They all are of the same materials, style, and other matching features.

project. However, when using a computer, door and window symbols can be stored in a symbol library and merely called up and inserted in the proper location. Many door and window manufacturers have their full library of products on the Internet and the designer can download a specific product and insert it directly into his or her drawing.

Doors

Doors are generally classified by their action, as illustrated in Figure 7-17, and whether they are interior or exterior units. Although a wide variety of styles exists within these general classifications, it is difficult to denote the specific style in a plan view. Refer to Chapter 12 for the most common door types, their operation, styles, hardware, and other features. Generally doors are drawn in the plan view in an open position showing the direction of their operation (such as a swinging door). Doors are drawn in plan view as a heavy line in small-scale drawings or as a double line, to indicate their thickness, in larger-scaled plans. A swing door has a thinner curved line drawn to denote the direction of its swing. In small projects (particularly residential work) the door size is noted on the plan, such as 3°, denoting the door is 3 feet wide (0.11 m), as shown in Figure 7-18.

In larger and commercial projects, openings that are to receive doors can be addressed in basically two methods. The first and simplest is to treat openings generically. Doors might be labeled "A," for example, and all be of the same type, finish, frame, and hardware. "B" doors would represent another group. The other method is to address each opening as a unique design feature and assign each door with its own independent number, as shown in Figure 7-19. A circle is drawn within the door swing and the door number is placed within it. In turn, this number is referenced to a

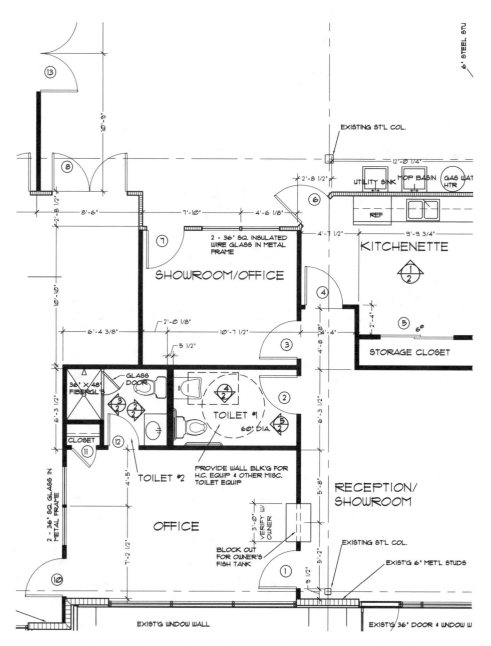

FIGURE 7-19 Each door in this partial plan is assigned an individual number that can be found on an accompanying door schedule indicating all the details of each door.

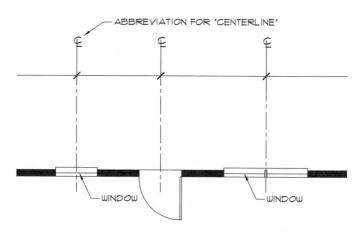

FIGURE 7-20 In frame walls, doors and windows are dimensioned to their centerlines, noted as a C/L. From these, the builder estimates the "rough" opening.

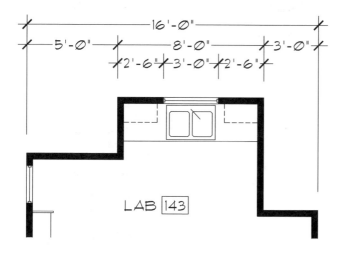

FIGURE 7-21 In masonry walls, door and window openings are dimensioned to the edges rather than the centerline. The door or window unit is centered in the space.

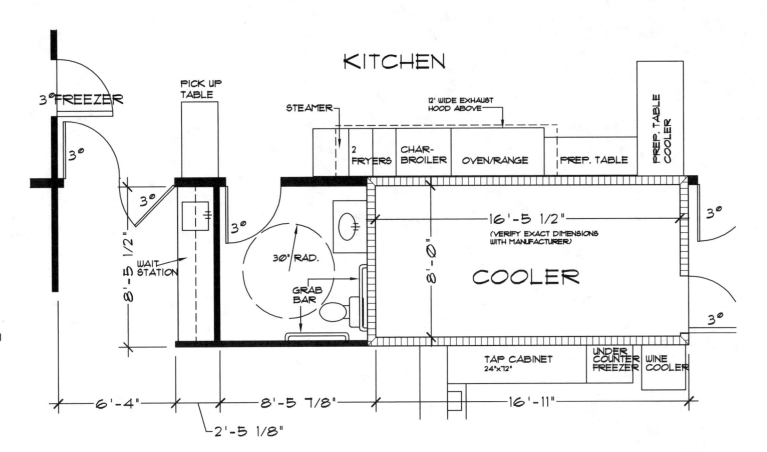

KITCHEN

3° FREEZER

PICK UP TABLE

STEAMER

12' WIDE EXHAUST HOOD ABOVE

PREP. TABLE COOLER

3°

3°

3°

WAIT STATION

8'-5 1/2"

30" RAD.

GRAB BAR

2 FRYERS

CHAR-BROILER

OVEN/RANGE

PREP. TABLE

16'-5 1/2"

(VERIFY EXACT DIMENSIONS WITH MANUFACTURER)

8'-0"

COOLER

3°

3°

TAP CABINET 24"x72"

UNDER COUNTER FREEZER

WINE COOLER

6'-4"

8'-5 7/8"

16'-11"

2'-5 1/8"

FIGURE 7-22 When a door is adjacent to a wall, as in this partial restaurant plan, it is often not necessary to dimension the door location. The builder knows the door is to be located tight to the adjacent wall and will provide the proper details and clearances.

door schedule that provides the details for that distinct door. This information is then cross-referenced to a door schedule as explained in Chapter 12.

Doors and windows in plan view are generally dimensioned to the centerline of the door or window and frame unit as shown in Figure 7-20. This method allows the designer to locate the door fairly accurately, leaving the actual rough opening, trim, and other clearance details to the builder. In masonry, the door or window assembly (which has an exact unit size) is listed. The builder provides (in both cases) a slightly larger size, to set and shim the unit

to fit the opening. The rough opening size is listed on the plan or in the schedule and abbreviated "R.O." This R.O. includes the door, frame, and proper clearances to install the unit within the frame wall, as illustrated in Figure 7-21.

In many cases where a door hinge is close to an adjacent wall, it is not necessary to dimension the center of the door (or frame). The builder knows the door is to be located tight to the wall and will allow the proper exact clearances for operation and trim work, as shown in Figure 7-22.

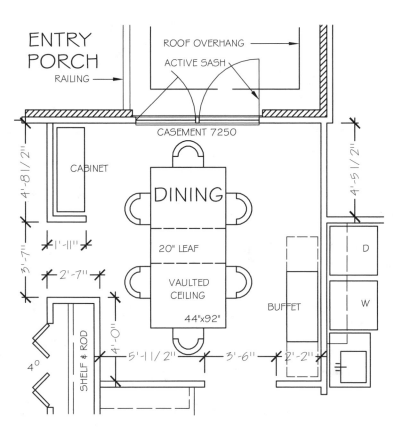

FIGURE 7-23 **The windows in the dining room of this partial plan are drawn in some detail, as the scale of the drawing is fairly large.**

Windows

Windows are drawn in floor plans in a variety of ways according to the scale of the plan and office standards. Generally, if the scale is large enough, windows are drawn in based on their style and type of operation. A double casement window is shown in Figure 7-23. See Figure 7-24 for a complete list of the different styles of windows and how they would be drawn in plan view. If the scale of the drawing is small, such as ⅛" = 1'0 (1:100 metric) or 1/16" = 1'-

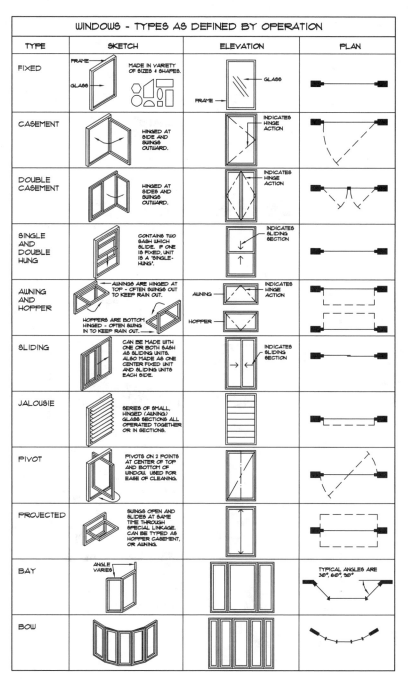

FIGURE 7-24 **Different types of windows defined by their operation are illustrated in plan view and elevation.**

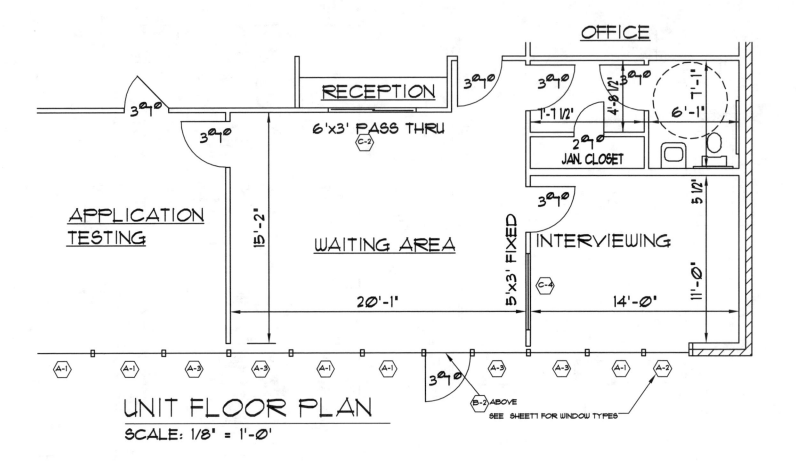

OFFICE

RECEPTION

6'x3' PASS THRU
C-2

APPLICATION TESTING

WAITING AREA

INTERVIEWING

JAN. CLOSET

5'x3' FIXED
C-4

15'-2'

20'-1'

14'-0'

11'-0'

5 1/2'

1'-1 1/2'

4'-8 1/2'

6'-1'

7'-1'

A-1   A-1   A-3   A-3   A-1   A-1   A-3   A-3   A-1   A-2

B-2 ABOVE
SEE SHEET1 FOR WINDOW TYPES

UNIT FLOOR PLAN
SCALE: 1/8' = 1'-0'

FIGURE 7-25 In commercial plans, such as this tenant space drawn at ⅛" scale, windows are shown as a single line. A symbol is added that is referenced to a detailed window schedule.

0" (1:200 metric) on large commercial projects, then a simple single line should be used with a symbol referring to the window schedule for more detailed information (Figure 7-25).

Graphic and Text Notation on Floor Plans

As a floor plan is the central, or core, drawing of any set of construction documents, it must be cross-referenced to other drawings and background materials. Graphic symbols and text notation are incorporated into the floor plan to make it as clear as possible.

Room Names and Notes

There are a number of items in a floor plan drawing that cannot be portrayed graphically and need to be noted. These will vary according to the scale of the floor plan, its complexity, and whether it is a design or construction drawing (Figure 7-26).

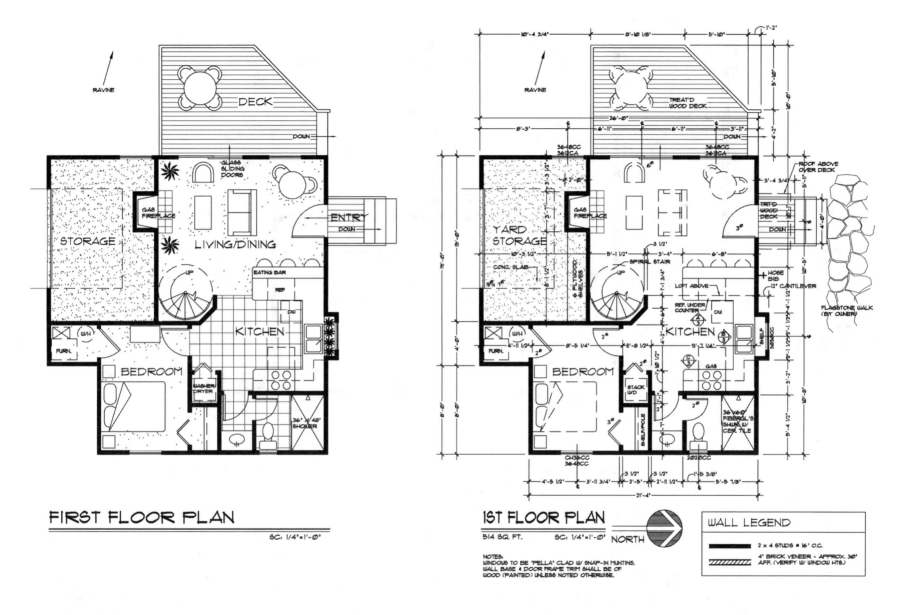

FIRST FLOOR PLAN

SC: 1/4"=1'-0"

PRESENTATION DRAWING

1ST FLOOR PLAN

514 SQ. FT.   SC: 1/4"=1'-0"   NORTH

NOTES:
WINDOWS TO BE "PELLA" CLAD W/ SNAP-IN MUNTINS.
WALL BASE & DOOR FRAME TRIM SHALL BE OF
WOOD (PAINTED) UNLESS NOTED OTHERWISE.

WALL LEGEND

▬▬▬ 2 x 4 STUDS @ 16" O.C.

▨▨▨ 4" BRICK VENEER - APPROX. 30"
A.F.F. (VERIFY W/ WINDOW HTS.)

CONSTRUCTION DRAWING

FIGURE 7-26 A presentation drawing, as shown on the left, shows spaces, furniture, and other items, including some textures. A construction drawing indicates the exact dimensions and other particulars in more detail.

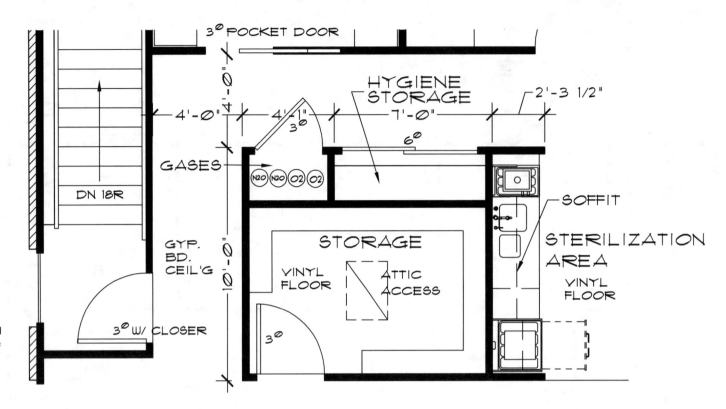

3⁰ POCKET DOOR

HYGIENE STORAGE

7'-0"

2'-3 1/2"

4'-0"

4'-1"

3⁰

GASES

6⁰

N2O N2O O2 O2

DN 18R

SOFFIT

STERILIZATION AREA

GYP. BD. CEIL'G

STORAGE

VINYL FLOOR

VINYL FLOOR

ATTIC ACCESS

3⁰ W/ CLOSER

3⁰

FIGURE 7-27 **The small gas and hygiene storage rooms in this partial floor plan are labeled just outside of the space as the lettering is too large to fit within it.**

Room use is generally spelled out in both design and construction drawings. In small projects, only the room name is listed, whereas in large commercial spaces, a number might be assigned (or both a name and number). If the room is too small to write in the name or number on the floor plan, it is written just outside the space with a leader pointing to the room, as seen in Figure 7-27. Approximate room size is sometimes indicated beneath the room name; however, this is done mostly in presentation drawings, as the dimension is generally not accurate enough for a construction drawing. In a construction drawing, other dimensions noted on the plan will govern the size of the rooms, as it controls the exact

placement of the studs. The finishes placed over the studs reduce the dimensions of the room by the material thickness. Some materials such as ceramic tile have an uneven base, which varies the room dimensions slightly.

Various notes are also added to the floor plan to convey specific information to the client or builder. These items might include handrails on stairs, soffits above, floor-level changes, and so forth, as shown in Figure 7-28. However, these notes are kept to a minimum in order not to clutter the drawing and are lettered at a smaller height than the room names. Figure 7-29 shows an example of how notes might be added to floor plan drawings.

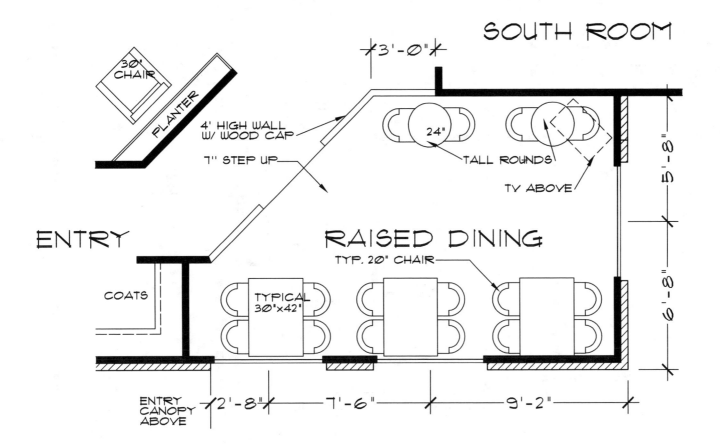

SOUTH ROOM

30" CHAIR

PLANTER

4' HIGH WALL W/ WOOD CAP

7" STEP UP

3'-0"

24"

TALL ROUNDS

TV ABOVE

5'-8"

ENTRY

RAISED DINING

TYP. 20" CHAIR

COATS

TYPICAL 30"x42"

6'-8"

ENTRY CANOPY ABOVE

2'-8"   7'-6"   9'-2"

9'-0"

FIGURE 7-28 In addition to room names, this plan has notes added at a small scale to call out various items in the space.

Architectural Symbols

A number of specialized symbols are used on the floor plan. For example, columns are usually assigned a grid number and referenced to the column centerline for dimensioning purposes (Figure 7-30). The grid consists of numbers along one axis and letters of the alphabet along the other, so that one can easily pinpoint a specific column, such as D-2 or C-4. A centerline is drafted as a series of single dashes and long lines passing through the column. A column designation bubble (sized for the appropriate lettering within

it) is placed at the end of this line. In some cases, such as at an end column, the reference line might be to the face of a column, instead of the center. In this case, a notation is added to point out this exception, as shown in Figure 7-31.

Wall and building section cuts are shown on the floor plan with a symbol that indicates the approximate location of the cut and the direction of view, as illustrated in Figure 7-32. A circle is generally used that is divided in two sections. The top portion a

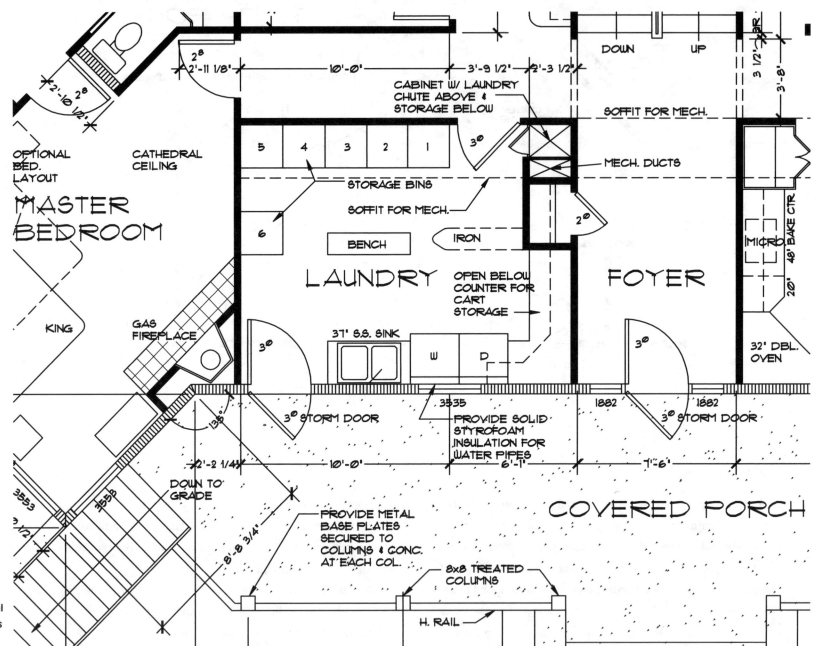

OPTIONAL BED. LAYOUT

CATHEDRAL CEILING

MASTER BEDROOM

KING

GAS FIREPLACE

2'-11 1/8'

2'-10 1/2'

2^8

2^8

10'-0'

3'-9 1/2'

2'-3 1/2'

3 1/2'

3'-8'

DOWN   UP

CABINET W/ LAUNDRY CHUTE ABOVE & STORAGE BELOW

SOFFIT FOR MECH.

3^0

5   4   3   2   1

6

STORAGE BINS

SOFFIT FOR MECH.

BENCH

IRON

MECH. DUCTS

2^0

MICRO

48' BAKE CTR

20'

LAUNDRY

FOYER

OPEN BELOW COUNTER FOR CART STORAGE

3^0

3^0

37' S.S. SINK

W   D

32' DBL. OVEN

135'

3^0 STORM DOOR

3535

1882

1882

3^0 STORM DOOR

PROVIDE SOLID STYROFOAM INSULATION FOR WATER PIPES

2'-2 1/4'

10'-0'

6'-1'

7'-6'

3553

355B

3 1/2'

DOWN TO GRADE

8'-8 3/4'

PROVIDE METAL BASE PLATES SECURED TO COLUMNS & CONC. AT EACH COL.

COVERED PORCH

8x8 TREATED COLUMNS

H. RAIL

FIGURE 7-29 Several notes are added to this partial floor plan for clarity.

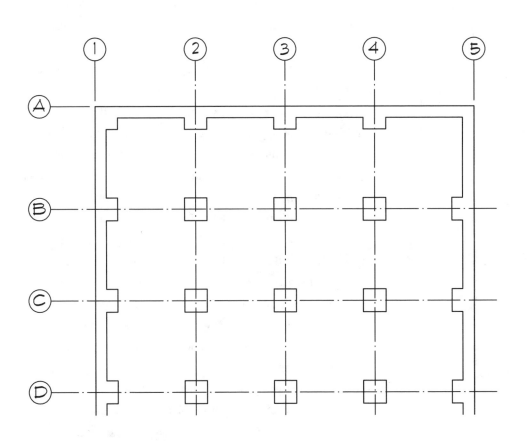

FIGURE 7-30 Columns can be identified in a floor plan by assigning numbers and letters to a grid locating their centerlines or faces.

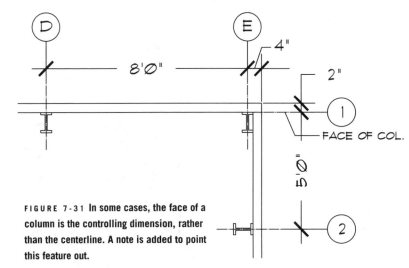

FIGURE 7-31 In some cases, the face of a column is the controlling dimension, rather than the centerline. A note is added to point this feature out.

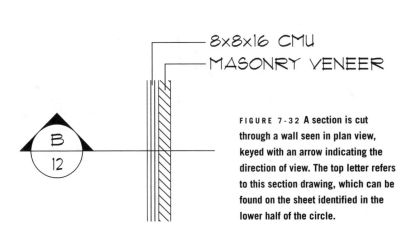

8x8x16 CMU
MASONRY VENEER

FIGURE 7-32 A section is cut through a wall seen in plan view, keyed with an arrow indicating the direction of view. The top letter refers to this section drawing, which can be found on the sheet identified in the lower half of the circle.

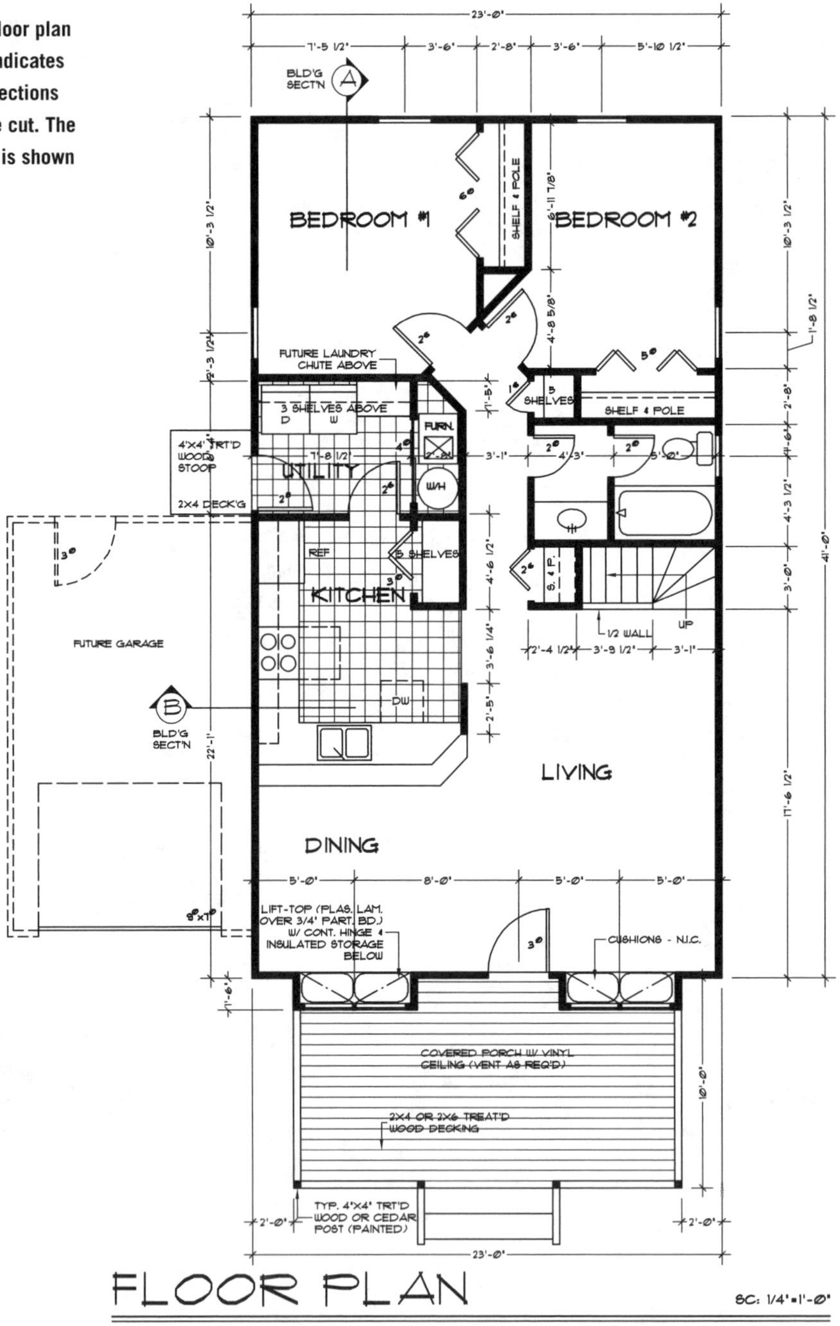

FIGURE 7-33 **The floor plan of this small house indicates where two building sections (labeled A and B) are cut. The direction of the view is shown by the arrow.**

FLOOR PLAN

SC: 1/4" = 1'-0"

letter, such as A, B, and C, generally indicates how many sections are cut. (Numbers can also be used.) The bottom section of the circle contains a number that refers to the sheet number this section is drawn on. In small projects where there are a limited number of sheets, bottom numbers are not used. The circle is just big enough to contain the letter and number. If more than one building section cut is needed, the symbols are drawn at a similar size to adhere to a uniform standard. Figure 7-33 shows how building section cuts are indicated on floor plans.

Interior and exterior elevations are noted on the floor plan in much the same way as building section cuts (Figure 7-34). Once again, a circle containing numbers is used, with an arrow indicating the direction of view. Some designers prefer to make a distinct visual difference between sections and elevations to help the viewer easily distinguish them. In Figure 7-35, for example, the arrow is blackened in on sections and not elevations. Another way to denote the difference is to use an arrow on the section cut and eliminate the arrow "tails" on an elevation mark.

Sometimes, the scale of the floor plan is too small to place all the required detail or notes within a small space such as toilet rooms and stairs. In such situations, an enlarged plan is drawn elsewhere of these spaces and cross-referenced on the plan. The area to be enlarged can simply have a note within (or adjacent) that says "see sheet *x* for enlarged plan." In most cases, however, a heavy broken line is placed around the area to be enlarged, as illustrated in Figure 7-36. A circle and number(s) are assigned to it, similar to the section or elevation symbol. This enlarged plan can appear on the floor-plan sheet or another sheet. This same method can also be used to show detail on other features, such as a column or another specialized assembly.

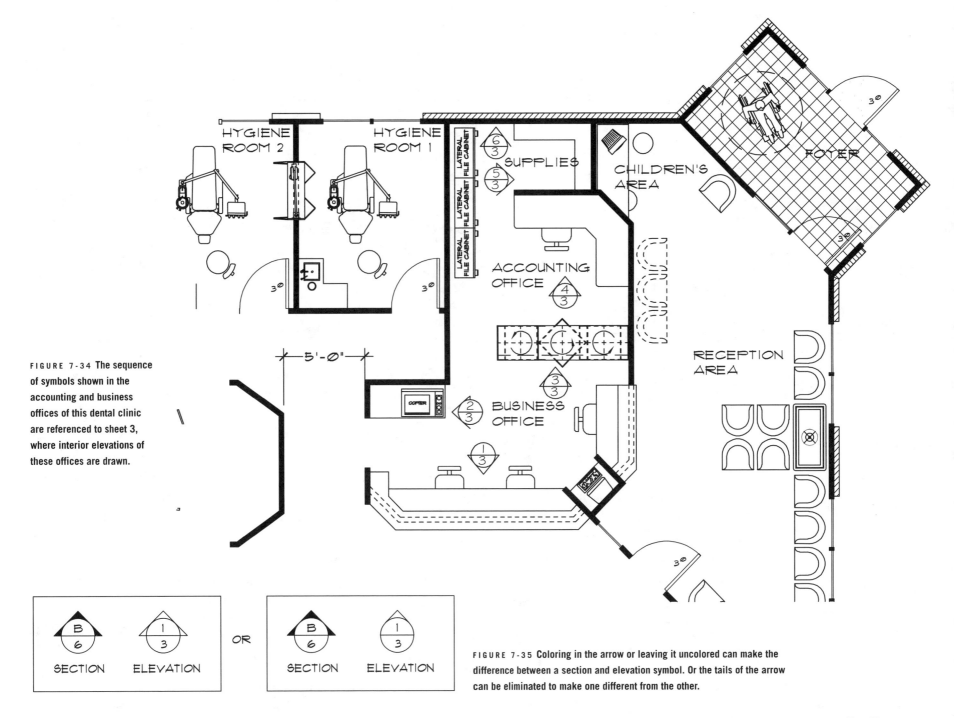

HYGIENE ROOM 2

HYGIENE ROOM 1

LATERAL FILE CABINET
LATERAL FILE CABINET
LATERAL FILE CABINET

SUPPLIES

CHILDREN'S AREA

FOYER

3⁰

3⁰

3⁰

ACCOUNTING OFFICE

RECEPTION AREA

5'-0"

COPIER

BUSINESS OFFICE

3⁰

3⁰

FIGURE 7-34 The sequence of symbols shown in the accounting and business offices of this dental clinic are referenced to sheet 3, where interior elevations of these offices are drawn.

SECTION   ELEVATION   OR   SECTION   ELEVATION

FIGURE 7-35 Coloring in the arrow or leaving it uncolored can make the difference between a section and elevation symbol. Or the tails of the arrow can be eliminated to make one different from the other.

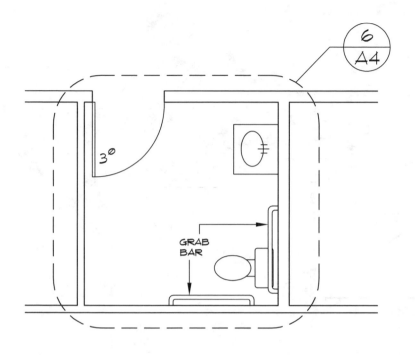

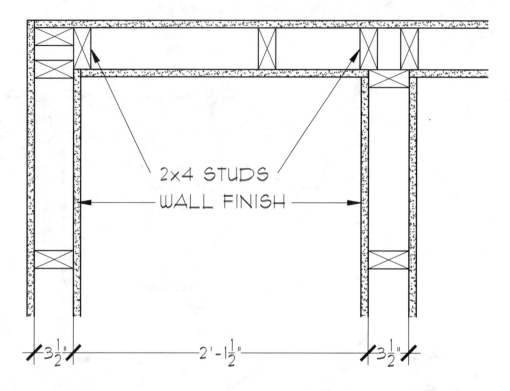

FIGURE 7-36 (left) A portion of a floor plan can be keyed with a symbol to a larger, more detailed plan that is drawn elsewhere. For example, this part of the plan is referenced as area 6 and enlarged on sheet A4.

FIGURE 7-37 (right) Dimensions on a floor plan generally locate the framework of the building, such as the face of these 2x4 studs.

Dimensioning Floor Plans

A floor plan is carefully dimensioned to ensure items such as walls, columns, doors, windows, openings, stairs, and other particulars are correctly located for construction. Sometimes after a plan is drawn accurately to a scale, its reproduction causes a slight enlargement or reduction of the drawing. In such cases, the floor plan is slightly out of true scale, but this is acceptable because the written dimensions are the controlling factors. In fact, most designers add a note on the drawing that says, "Do not scale drawing, follow written dimensions."

Generally, elements such as walls are dimensioned to the frame (Figure 7-37), as the builder first erects this and then adds the finishes to it. This dimensioning technique gives the exact location of the studs, columns, and beams and is generally placed to one side of the face of these. In some cases, however, the centerline of the wall might be located and dimensioned, as illustrated in Figure 7-38.

As noted in Chapter 5, dimensioning is done in a hierarchical manner. Buildings, structural framework, rooms, and fixtures are dimensioned in decreasing size order. The actual number of dimensions on a plan is dependent upon how much latitude the designer affords the contractor. A very detailed and dimensioned plan gives the builder little room for deviation from the original design. However, if only a few key dimensions are shown, the

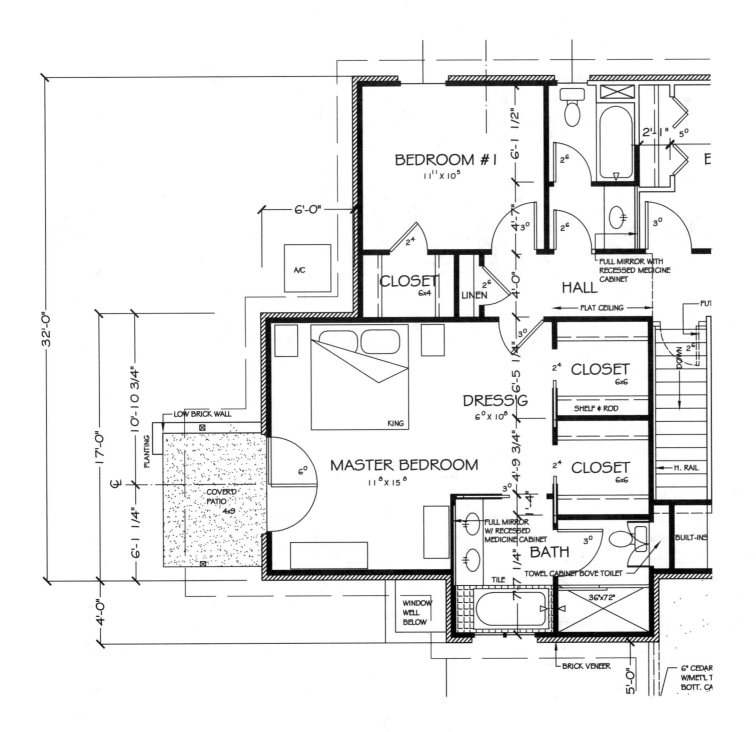

BEDROOM #1
11¹¹ x 10⁵

6'-0"

A/C

6'-1 1/2"

2⁶

2'-1" 5⁰

E

4'-7"

3⁰

2⁶

CLOSET
6x4

LINEN

2⁶

2⁴

4'-0"

HALL

FULL MIRROR WITH
RECESSED MEDICINE
CABINET

FLAT CEILING

FU

3⁰

DOWN

2⁶

CLOSET
6x6

2⁴

DRESS'G
6⁰ x 10⁸

SHELF & ROD

32'-0"

10'-10 3/4"

17'-0"

6'-1 1/4"

4'-0"

LOW BRICK WALL

PLANTING

6⁰

6'-5 1/4"

4'-9 3/4"

CLOSET
6x6

2⁴

H. RAIL

KING

MASTER BEDROOM
11⁸ x 15⁸

COVER'D
PATIO
4x9

3⁰

1'-4"

FULL MIRROR
W/ RECESSED
MEDICINE CABINET

3⁰

BUILT-INS

7'-1 1/4"

1/4"

BATH

TOWEL CABINET 'BOVE TOILET

TILE

WINDOW
WELL
BELOW

36"x72"

BRICK VENEER

5'-0"

6" CEDAR
W/MET'L T
BOTT. CA

FIGURE 7-38 All dimensions in this floor plan are to the face of a stud, except for the wall between the closets. It is dimensioned to the centerline of the wall. The centerline technique can also be used to locate exterior windows and doors, as seen in this example.

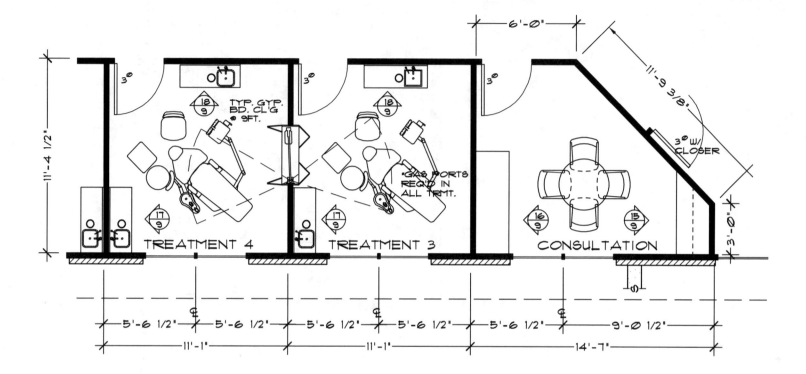

builder is trusted to determine exact locations of interior components. A good guideline for dimensioning falls somewhere between these two approaches. An over-dimensioned plan allows the builder little freedom to make field adjustments or substitute cost-saving techniques. However, too few dimensions can produce a lot of guesswork and increase the chances for error in the field and coordination between subcontractors.

Dimensioning Techniques

Dimensions are placed on the floor plan as shown in Figure 7-39. Note that the dimension lines are drafted lighter than wall lines and are generally done as a continuous group or string of numbers along a line. The extension line begins slightly away from the object (a minimum of $\frac{1}{16}$" or 1.58 mm) never touching it. It extends about $\frac{1}{8}$ inch (3.17 mm) beyond the dimension line. Arrows, dots, or 45-degree tick marks (most common) are used at the extension line and dimension line junction (Figure 7-40). The arrows, dots, or tick marks are drawn with a thicker and/or darker line to make them stand out graphically. The 45-degree tick marks are drawn in a consistent direction, generally sloping left to right. However, some draftspersons slope the tick marks for vertically read dimensions from left to right and horizontally read dimensions from right to left. When using the computer, any of these three graphic symbols (arrows, dots, or ticks) can be called up and consistently inserted for all dimensions.

Dimensioning on a floor plan usually requires two or three

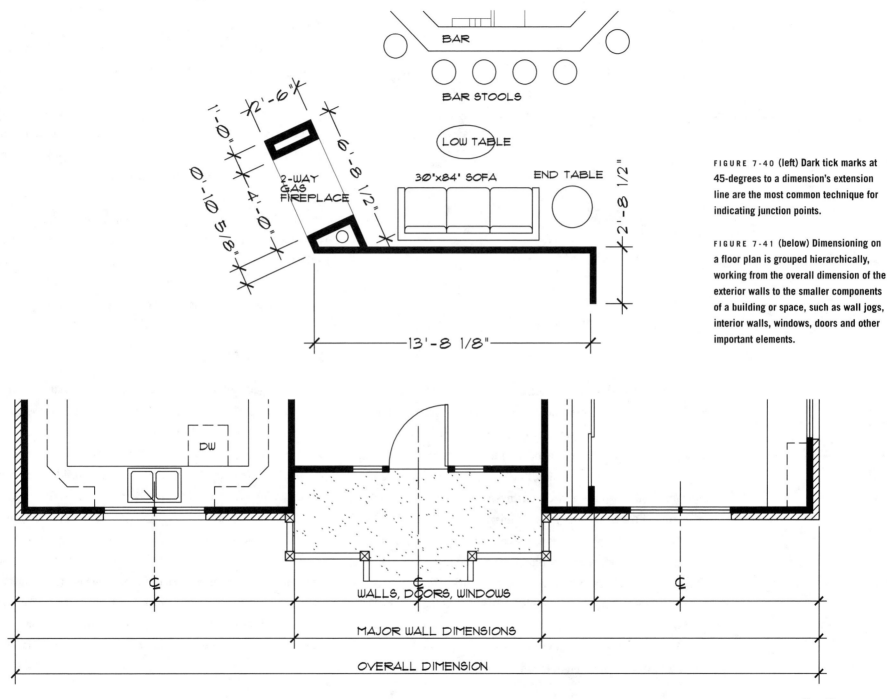

BAR

BAR STOOLS

LOW TABLE

2-WAY
GAS
FIREPLACE

30"x84" SOFA

END TABLE

2'-6"

1'-0"

0'-10 5/8"

6'-8 1/2"

4'-0"

2'-8 1/2"

13'-8 1/8"

FIGURE 7-40 (left) Dark tick marks at 45-degrees to a dimension's extension line are the most common technique for indicating junction points.

FIGURE 7-41 (below) Dimensioning on a floor plan is grouped hierarchically, working from the overall dimension of the exterior walls to the smaller components of a building or space, such as wall jogs, interior walls, windows, doors and other important elements.

DW

WALLS, DOORS, WINDOWS

MAJOR WALL DIMENSIONS

OVERALL DIMENSION

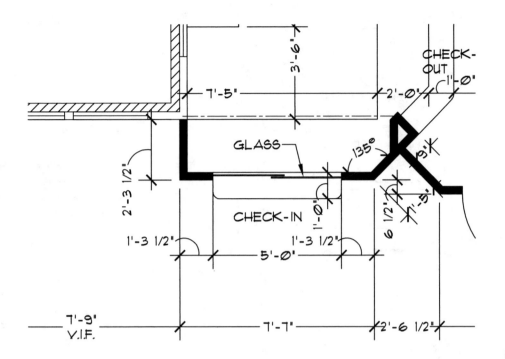

The numbers do not rest on the dimension line, as they might blend in with the line and become unreadable. In computerized drafting, the machine is often programmed to automatically place the numbers centered in the broken dimension line, rather than above it. Dimensions are oriented to read from the base or right side of a drawing. When an area is too small for the dimension to go in the usual place, the numbers are placed outside (or sometimes below) the extension line and a leader is used to point to the dimensioned area (see Figure 7-42).

The preferred area for dimensioning all items on a floor plan is outside the walls where possible, as it tends to keep the interior of the floor plan uncluttered. However, it is difficult to accurately dimension most projects without having some dimension lines within the floor plan. This is especially true of interior projects.

Designation of Materials

Floor plans generally are not used to designate specific materials, as finishes might be too small to show in plan and their selections might be changed later. The amount of material information provided on a floor plan depends on the size and complexity of the proposed construction. The plans for a small residential project may contain more detailed information, such as the finished floor materials, because the design may be simpler and very few materials used, as illustrated in Figure 7-43.

The few materials that might be designated on the floor plan are the walls, which can be pouched to indicate wood or other wall material designations such as block, brick, or concrete. Floor and wall finish materials are better indicated on the finish plans. See Chapter 13 for further explanation on drafting finish plans.

continuous dimension lines to locate exterior walls, wall jogs, interior walls, windows, doors, and other elements, as shown in Figure 7-41. Exterior walls of a building are dimensioned outside the floor plan. The outermost dimension line is the overall building dimension. The next dimension line, moving toward the plan, indicates wall locations and centerlines to doors and windows (depending on the wall type). Other miscellaneous details in the plan (such as minor offsets, jogs, or cabinetry and fixtures) are located on a third dimension line. This hierarchy of line work allows the carpenters and other trades to quickly locate major framing elements and minor details by referring to the appropriate dimension line.

Numerals are placed above and centered on the dimension line, being drafted at a height of ⅛ to ³⁄₁₆ inch (3.17 to 4.76 mm).

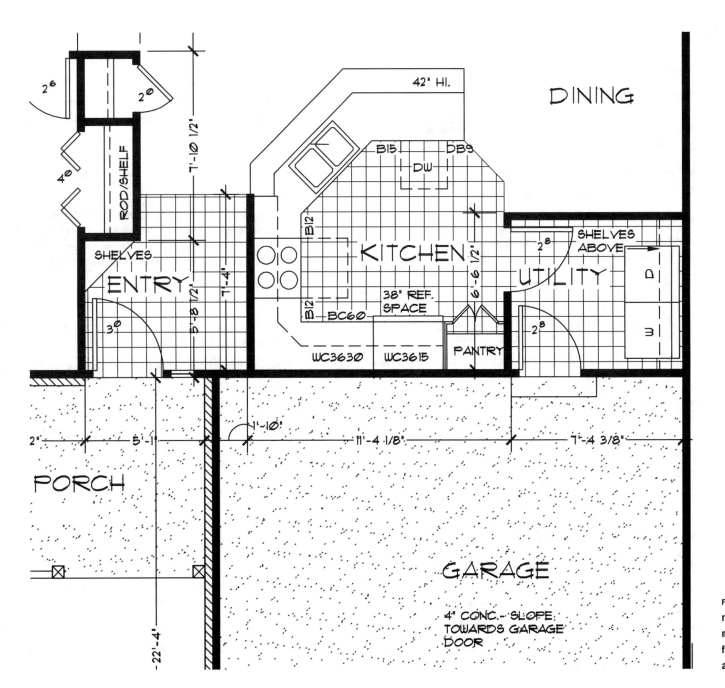

DINING

42" HI.

B15   DB9

DW

ROD/SHELF

2⁶

2⁰

4⁰

SHELVES

ENTRY

3⁰

B12

KITCHEN

38" REF.
SPACE

B12   BC60

WC3630   WC3615

PANTRY

2⁸

SHELVES
ABOVE

UTILITY

D

W

2⁸

7'-10 1/2'

7'-4'

5'-8 1/2'

6'-6 1/2'

PORCH

2"   5'-1"   1'-10'   11'-4 1/8'   7'-4 3/8'

22'-4'

GARAGE

4" CONC.- SLOPE
TOWARDS GARAGE
DOOR

FIGURE 7-43 **Floor plans in small
residential projects often depict
material finishes, such as this tiled
floor in the entry, kitchen, breakfast
area, and utility room.**

Checklist for Floor Plans

General

- Title the drawing, note its scale, and indicate north (or reference) direction.

- Draw with a minimum of three line weights indicating space, objects, and textures (or other elements).

- Draw all doors and direction of operation (swings, folding, etc.).

- Draw all windows to scale and show mullions.

- Number and symbol code all doors and windows.

- Check door swings and window operations for possible conflicts with other elements and views.

- Number or name all rooms/spaces.

- Show stairways and include an arrow to indicate up or down from that floor level. Call out the number of risers and treads and cross-reference if a detailed drawing is made of the stairs elsewhere.

- Draw dashed lines for major soffits or openings above and call them out in a note, including attic and other access panels.

- Draw dashed lines for wheelchair access circles to show compliance with ADA standards (where applicable).

- Draw handrails, guardrails, and half-height walls, and call out with a note, where necessary.

- "Balloon" or note areas of the floor plan that need to be enlarged for more detail and key them with a symbol to indicate where those drawings can be found.

- Pouche walls and reference to a wall type legend.

- Draw in fixed cabinets, shelves, plumbing fixtures, and other built-in items.

- Check plan for code compliance and ADA requirements and clearances.

- Check plan for LEED certification credits, if applicable.

- Are the drawings clear and readable when reproduced or printed? If not, correct as necessary.

Notations

- Note any floor level changes, slopes, and ramps.

- Call out floor drains where applicable.

- Cross-reference the floor plan with section and elevation symbols for information about the building structure, walls, ceilings, floors, and built-in items such as cabinetry.

- Label major components such as fireplaces, bookcases, built-in furniture, refrigerators, dishwashers, compactors, furnaces, and water heaters.

- Call out miscellaneous items such as medicine cabinets, drinking fountains, and other built-in items. Include here or reference to another drawing information and locations of towel dispensers, soap dispensers, waste containers, electric hand dryers, mirrors, and towel bars.

- Label shelves and rod(s) in closets.

- Note ceiling heights here (small projects) or on the Reflected Ceiling Plan (larger projects).

- Note/draw items if supplied by owner or contractor, or "Not in Contract" (NIC).

Dimensions

- Dimension all wall locations, and place a general note indicating whether the dimensions are to face of a wall, centerline, or other surface (such as face of a stud, concrete, etc.).

- Dimension walls and other items to structural components such as columns or existing walls.

- Give the angle in degrees of walls that are not placed 90 degrees to one another and supply exact reference points where these walls start and end.

- Give radius or diameter of all circular elements such as curved walls, openings, curved handrails, etc.

- Dimension all horizontal openings, partitions, and general cabinetry.

- Locate all stairs and dimension properly. See Chapter 11 for stair details and dimension standards.

Fire and life safety codes and regulations are set to establish the minimum requirements that will provide a reasonable degree of safety from fire and other hazards encountered in buildings. When plans are prepared for new or remodeled buildings (or sometimes the interior only), they are submitted to various plan review authorities to insure the proposed work is in compliance with national, state, and city fire and life safety codes. These divisions look over the drawings submitted by the designer to insure the project will meet the minimum requirements that can provide a reasonable degree of safety from a fire or other life safety concerns encountered in the building. The designer prepares a building code compliance plan, which also can be combined with a fire and life safety plan (for commercial projects) to demonstrate the project meets the required building and fire codes. The plans are then reviewed by the governing building inspector and coordinated with a fire prevention bureau, such as the local fire marshal. Once the review is completed, the plans are released for construction.

Although some designers might call the review process a design constraint, the purpose of these codes and drawings are to insure the health, safety, and welfare of not only the users, but others such as the visitors, clients, and public who use the building and its interiors. In this view, meeting the codes is not a hindrance to the designer, but a concern for designing for people and its implications.

Building Code Compliance Analysis

A building code compliance analysis is developed by the designer or architect to illustrate how the building and its parts meet the various ordinances. In some cases, this is shown in written summation of code compliance in narrative form (Figure 8-1).

Or, the information can also be shown in a graphical manner and combined with the fire and life safety plan drawing (Figure 8-2). The process involves the designer, architect, or engineer preparing a document that can be clearly understood by the individuals who perform the code review for the various cities and states that must first review the project and then issue the proper permit for construction.

Code compliance, fire and life safety plans should show:

- **OCCUPANCY CLASSIFICATION: New and remodeled buildings are classified according to the description that best describes the use of the building, such as residence, assembly, business, hospital, or school. Each of these occupancy groups is directly related to potential fire hazards and other concerns for protection and egress. The greater the number of people in a building, the greater concern for safety and pro-**

BUILDING CODE ANALYSIS

TENANT SQUARE FOOTAGE = 3,718
CONSTRUCTION TYPE II-B
OCCUPANCY B
APPLICABLE BUILDING CODE:
  2003 INDIANA BUILDLING CODE (2000 INTERNAT'L BUILD'G CODE, 3RD ED.
  2003 INDIANA FIRE CODE (200 INTERNAT'L FIRE CODE, 4TH PRINT'G
  1997 INDIANA ELECTRIC CODE (1996 NAT'L ELECTRIC CODE)
  2003 INDIANA MECHANICAL CODE (2000 INTERNAT'L MECH. CODE)
  1999 INDIANA PLUMBING CODE (1997 UNIFORM PLUMBING CODE)

SHEET INDEX

1 - FLOOR PLAN, DOOR SCHEDULE
2 - BLD'G SECTION & ELEV'S
3 - ELECTRICAL & LIGHTING PLANS
4 - PLUMBING PLANS

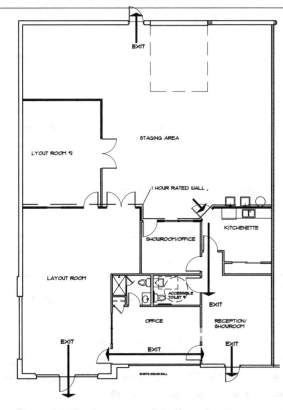

LIFE SAFETY PLAN

SCALE: 3/32" = 1'-0"

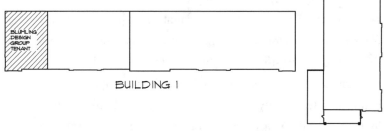

BUILDING 1

LOCATION PLAN

SCALE: 1/64" = 1'-0"

WALL LEGEND

▬▬▬▬	3.5" MET'S STUDS @ 16" O.C. W/ $\frac{5}{8}$" GYP. BD. EA. SIDE
▥▥▥▥	1 HR. RATED WALL (SLAB TO ROOF) ASSEMBLY - 3.5" OR 6" MET'L STUDS @ 16" O.C. W/ $\frac{5}{8}$" F.C. GYP. BD. EA. SIDE
▨▨▨▨	2 HOUR RATED TENANT WALL - 6" MET'L STUDS @ 16" O.C. W/2 LAYERS $\frac{5}{8}$" GYP. BD. EA. SIDE & SOUND BATTS
▦▦▦▦	EXISIT'G EXTERIOR CMU WALL

FIGURE 8-2 The building code analysis can also be combined with the life safety plan to show compliance with both requirements.

tection. The building codes assign a number to occupancy classification, which is compared to the square footage of that usage. This produces an occupancy load that determines the maximum number of people permitted for that specific group. In some instances, a building might incorporate more than one occupancy group or use. In these cases, the plans must show the protection and egress particular to the specific group.

- **BUILDING LOCATION ON PROPERTY:** The distances of property lines, building structures, and separation distances relate to the spread of fire from one building to another and the fire resistive requirements of the building and its components.

- **FLOOR AREA AND HEIGHT:** Buildings are limited in maximum floor areas and height according to the fire zone they are in, occupancy use, number of stories, and type of construction. These areas can often be increased by segmented "fire-resistive barriers" or sprinkler systems in the building.

- **BUILDING TYPE AND CONSTRUCTION:** Buildings are classified by type of construction, which refers to the materials, how they are assembled, and their known fire-resistive qualities. These types range from the non-fire-resistive wood construction often used in residences to the highly fire-resistive concrete and steel structures. The supplemental coverings used in the interiors of a building are also taken into consideration as possible fire and smoke hazards, particularly where there are high concentrations of people (such as a movie theater lobby).

- **OCCUPANCY AND FIRE-RESISTIVE SEPARATIONS (IF ANY):** A building, its interiors, and components are required by most building codes to resist the effects of a fire for a specific minimum amount of time, protecting the safety of occupants as they find their way to the exits. These fire-resistive assemblies are commonly referred to as firewalls, and fire-resistive floor/ceiling assemblies. A building housing more than one occupancy or desiring to increase areas and heights above those determined by the codes must show how additional fire barriers will allow such variances to the codes, and still protect the occupants.

- **EGRESS:** Exiting from a building in an emergency is determined by a variable number of relationships, such as the fire resistance and occupancy load of a building. Codes are also set for minimum numbers, widths, and door swing. Most codes in commercial buildings now specify at least two separate exits per floor (depending on the occupant load) in the case of an emergency. Residential buildings have fewer

BUILDING CODE ANALYSIS

TENANT SQUARE FOOTAGE = 6,251 (INSIDE BUILDING)
CONSTRUCTION TYPE II-B
OCCUPANCY A-2
OCCUPANT LOAD DETERMINATION
    KITCHEN   1,986 SQ. FT. / 200 = 9.9 OR 10
    DINING AREA   2,927 SQ. FT. / 15 = 195 OCCUPANT LOAD
    TOTAL A-2 OCCUPANCY = 4,913 SQ. FT. (LESS THAN 5,000 REQUIRING SPRINKLERS)
    TOILETS & BANQUET AREA   1,338 SQ. FT.
      (SEPARATED FROM DINING W/ 1-HOUR RATED WALLS)
    INDOOR AREAS DO NOT EXIT THRU COVERED OUTDOOR AREA
      (THEREFORE, NOT ADDED TO INDOOR OCCUANT LOAD)

SQUARE FOOTAGE TOTALS

KITCHEN	1,986 SQ. FT.
TOILETS	336 SQ. FT.
BANQUET	1,002 SQ. FT.
DINING/BAR	2,927 SQ. FT.
COVERED OUTDOOR DINING	817 SQ. FT.
TOTAL RESTAURANT	6,977 SQ. FT.
UNCOVERED OUTDOOR DINING	1,135 SQ. FT.

APPLICABLE BUILDING CODE:
    2003 INDIANA BUILDING CODE (2000 INTERNAT'L BUILD'G CODE, 3RD ED.
    2003 INDIANA FIRE CODE (200 INTERNAT'L FIRE CODE, 4TH PRINT'G)
    1997 INDIANA ELECTRIC CODE (1996 NAT'L ELECTRIC CODE)
    2003 INDIANA MECHANICAL CODE (2000 INTERNAT'L MECH. CODE)
    1999 INDIANA PLUMBING CODE (1997 UNIFORM PLUMBING CODE)

specific exit requirements, but do set minimum standards for location, size, and sill heights for escape windows in sleeping areas.

- **EMERGENCY SIGNAGE:** In addition to clearly marked and illuminated "exit signs," most commercial buildings also must have an evacuation or egress plan posted in visible site for the occupants to refer to in an emergency. A good example of this is the "route of escape" posted on the interior side of hotel and motel rooms.

- **FIRE DETECTION AND ALARM SYSTEMS:** Residential buildings have fewer safeguards for fire detection and alarms than commercial ones do. However, most codes now require smoke detectors and alarms inside and just outside of a sleeping room. In large commercial build-

FIGURE 8-1 A building code analysis shows the project compliance with the various ordinances.

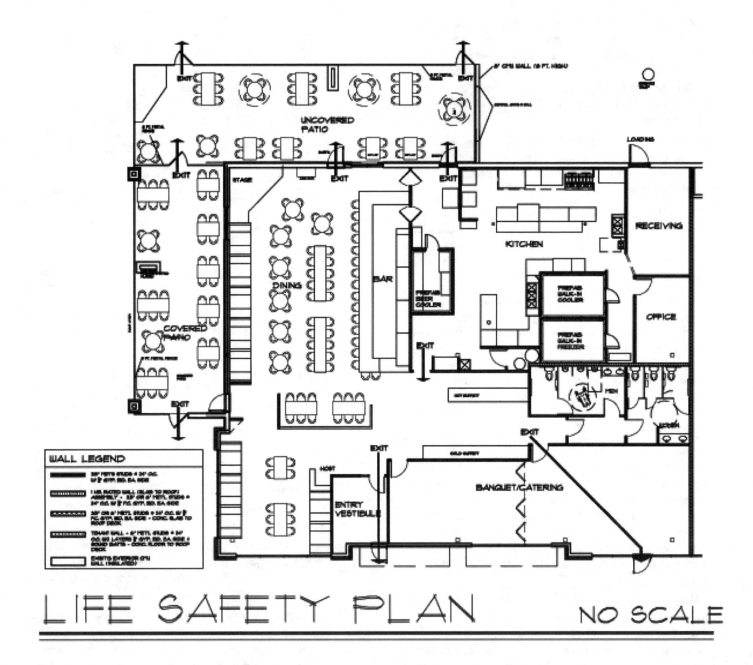

LIFE SAFETY PLAN   NO SCALE

FIGURE 8-3 The fire and life safety plan shows the exit routes out of the building and identifies the fire ratings of the walls.

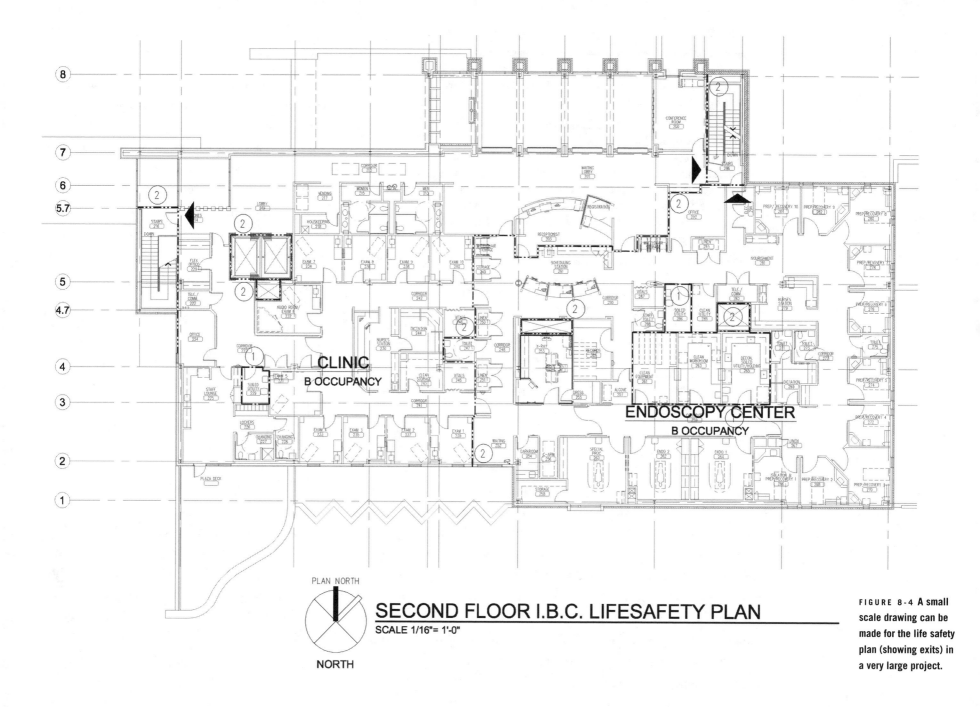

PLAN NORTH

NORTH

SECOND FLOOR I.B.C. LIFESAFETY PLAN
SCALE 1/16"= 1'-0"

CLINIC
B OCCUPANCY

ENDOSCOPY CENTER
B OCCUPANCY

FIGURE 8-4 A small
scale drawing can be
made for the life safety
plan (showing exits) in
a very large project.

ings, including high-rises, there are a series of systems to give the occupants early warning of the possibility of a fire hazard. These include audible and visual alarms, as well as some that immediately send a signal to the local fire department.

- **FIRE SUPPRESSION:** To suppress a possible outbreak of fire, most buildings use some form of a sprinkler system, often tied to the alarm system. In these systems a sprinkler head detects a heat temperature related to a fire outbreak, causing that sprinkler to spray water on the fire source. In turn, if the fire spreads, other sprinkler head fuses activate those heads to release water spray directed at the fire to contain its spread. Other fluids and gases can be substituted for water if large amounts of water could cause major damage.

- **BARRIER-FREE ACCESS:** Building code compliance and fire and life safety must also include provisions for freedom of access and egress for all individuals. This precedence was set with the passing of the Americans with Disabilities Act (1990) and has now become a standard in all building codes and creates these barrier-free environments, whether it be a new or remodeled building. Barrier-free access is specified from the order of the route an individual takes upon arriving at a site, entering a building, and moving through the designated accessible route and features. See Appendix C for more detailed information and graphic guides.

Fire and Life Safety Plans

A Fire and Life Safety Plan is prepared to clearly show graphically or by legend the rating and location of building elements, and the egress exits (Figure 8-3). Within the Fire Plan, compliance is shown that includes the interior building systems such as fire barriers, fire detection, and fire suppression. A Fire and Life Safety Plan should identify all exits, primary and secondary evacuation routes, and accessible routes, areas of refuge, fire alarm boxes, fire extinguishers, fire hose stations, and fire enunciator panels. An area of refuge is a designated area that provides safety from fire and smoke for people awaiting help or rescue.

Scale of Fire and Life Safety Plans

The scale of the Fire and Life Safety Plan is dependent on the size of the project, extent of fire code separations and protection, and required means of egress.

As there is often not a lot of detailed information that needs to be drawn in the plan view, a scale of ¹⁄₁₆" = 1'-0" (1:200) can be sometimes used (Figure 8-4), although a scale of ⅛"=1'-0" (1:100 metric) is the most preferred. If more detail is needed to clarify exact fire, life safety, and egress issues, a scale of ¼"=1'-0" (1:50 metric), or larger can be used.

Dimensioning Fire and Life Safety Plans

A lot of dimensions are not needed on the Fire and Life Safety Plans, as they are meant to graphically show compliance with the various codes. Most of the dimensioning will be shown on the floor plan drawings of the project. However, situations such as dead end corridors (usually a maximum of 25 feet (7.62 m), maximum distances to exits, wheelchair turning circles and clearances, and exit corridor widths should be dimensioned in the plan.

Drafting and Designation of Assemblies for Fire and Life Safety Plans

A lot of the miscellaneous information required for construction (shown on the floor plans) can be turned off or "ghosted" with a lighter layer in CAD. This enables the code compliance information to be graphically shown and noted in darker line weights, which makes the code compliance more readable. Wall designations can be coded with different line types and weights to indicate fire walls and assemblies.

Checklist for Code Compliance and Fire and Life Safety Plans

General

- Title the drawing and note the scale it is drawn at, either below the title or in the sheet title block.

- Cross-reference drawing (with correct symbols) to floor plans and/or other drawings as needed to assist the reviewer in locating exact details of a particular assembly that must be checked for code compliance.

- Graphically show locations and fire ratings of any required fire walls or other barriers.

- Graphically show the fire ratings of any other rated wall assemblies such as horizontal exits, corridors, exit enclosures, and exit shafts (elevators).

- Graphically show the exit sign locations or means of egress and illuminated egress path. Note minimum light levels and source of backup power supply for these exit lights.

- Check plan for code compliance and ADA requirements and clearances.

- Check plan for LEED certification credits, if applicable.

- Are the drawings clear and readable when reproduced or printed? If not, correct as necessary.

Notations

- Prepare a code summary that shows: occupancy classification, floor area(s), occupant load factor, occupant load, building type and construction, occupancy and fire-resistive separations (if required), fire-detection systems/alarms, and fire-suppression systems (if required).

- Clearly label each area or room, such as office, corridor, storage, etc.

- Note locations of doors required to have panic hardware.

- Spell out the plumbing fixture requirements for restrooms as based on the occupant loads and use of the building.

Dimensions

- Dimension any areas such as dead end corridor lengths, to show compliance with the codes.

- Dimension or note the maximum travel distance for exiting (if required).

- If dimensioning is required to detail items such as stair widths, handrail locations and widths, ramp widths and slopes, this can often be done on the floor plans. The code compliance reviewer can then look for these particulars on other sheets in the drawing set.

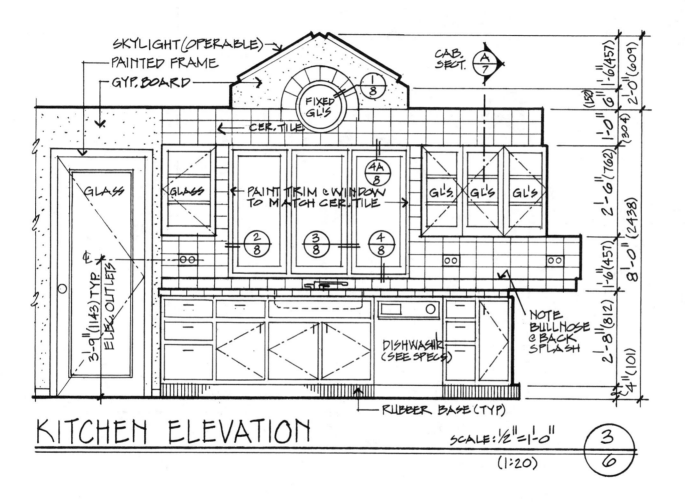

SKYLIGHT(OPERABLE)
PAINTED FRAME
GYP. BOARD
CAB. SECT. Ⓐ⁄7
FIXED GL'S
CER. TILE
GLASS
GLASS
GL'S GL'S GL'S
PAINT TRIM C WINDOW TO MATCH CER. TILE
3'-9" (1143) TYP. C ELEC. OUTLETS
DISHWASHR (SEE SPECS)
NOTE BULLNOSE C BACK SPLASH
RUBBER BASE (TYP)

KITCHEN ELEVATION   SCALE: ½"=1'-0"   ③⁄⑥
(1:20)

FIGURE 9-1 Elevations can provide detailed information about wall finishes, cabinetry, doors, windows, and other design features.

An elevation is a scaled drawing that shows a vertical surface or plane seen from a point of view perpendicular to the viewers' picture plane. An elevation is also a type of orthographic multiview drawing (discussed in Chapter 4). The various elevation views include the front, sides, and rear. Planes perpendicular to the picture plane are seen on edge, and other angles are seen foreshortened. Elevations are drawn as straight-on views, so there is no distortion as in a perspective or isometric drawing. Architectural

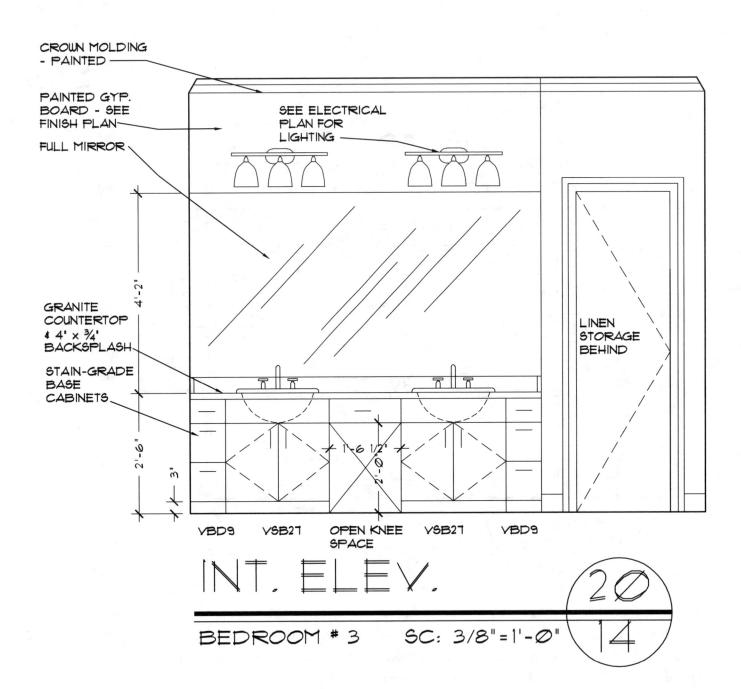

CROWN MOLDING
- PAINTED

PAINTED GYP.
BOARD - SEE
FINISH PLAN

FULL MIRROR

SEE ELECTRICAL
PLAN FOR
LIGHTING

GRANITE
COUNTERTOP
& 4' x ¾'
BACKSPLASH

STAIN-GRADE
BASE
CABINETS

LINEN
STORAGE
BEHIND

4'-2"

2'-6"

3"

1'-6 1/2"

2'-0"

VBD9   VSB27   OPEN KNEE   VSB27   VBD9
                        SPACE

INT. ELEV.

BEDROOM # 3   SC: 3/8"=1'-0"

20
14

FIGURE 9-2 This elevation shows details, such as the mirror above the vanity top and the open area below that cannot be shown in other drawings, such as the floor plan.

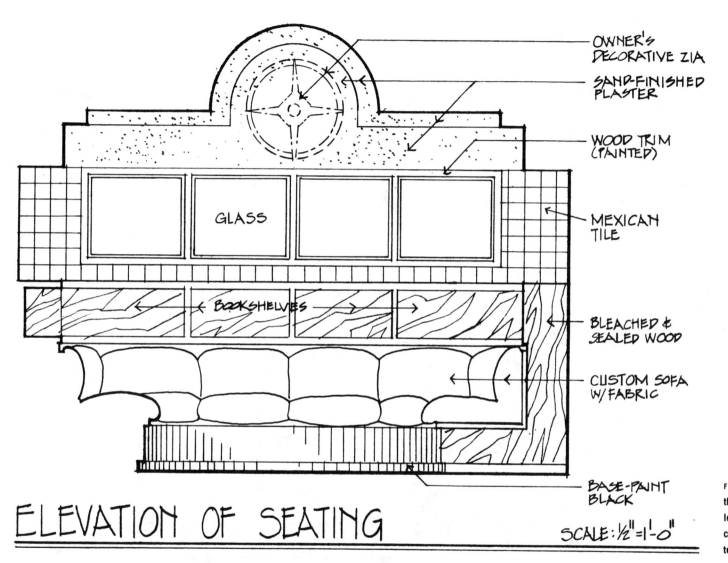

OWNER'S
DECORATIVE ZIA

SAND-FINISHED
PLASTER

WOOD TRIM
(PAINTED)

GLASS

MEXICAN
TILE

BOOKSHELVES

BLEACHED &
SEALED WOOD

CUSTOM SOFA
W/ FABRIC

BASE-PAINT
BLACK

ELEVATION OF SEATING

SCALE: ½"=1'-0"

FIGURE 9-3 In this elevation, the sofa is drawn in profile on the left, and the various materials are called out and delineated with a texture.

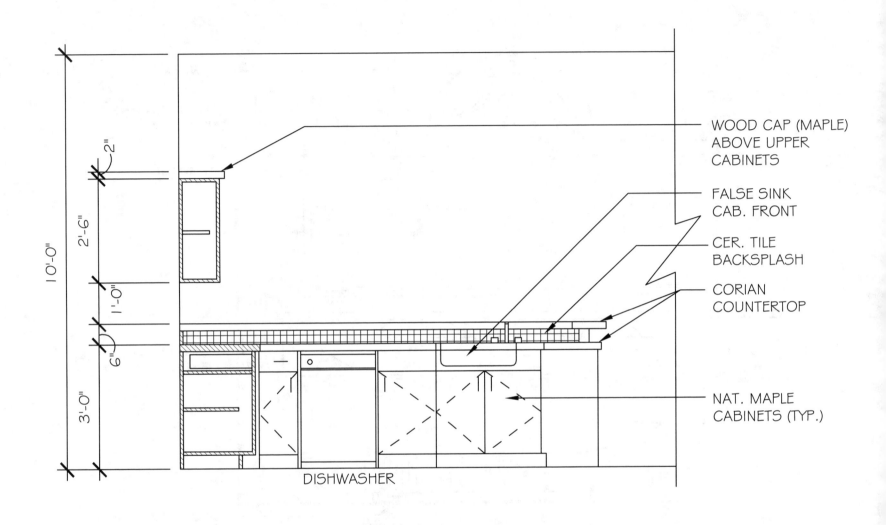

WOOD CAP (MAPLE)
ABOVE UPPER
CABINETS

FALSE SINK
CAB. FRONT

CER. TILE
BACKSPLASH

CORIAN
COUNTERTOP

NAT. MAPLE
CABINETS (TYP.)

DISHWASHER

2"

2'-6"

1'-0"

6"

3'-0"

10'-0"

KITCHEN ELEVATION

9
9

FIGURE 9-4 **A cabinet elevation can show heights, widths, and layout of doors, drawers, and items such as sinks and backsplashes.**

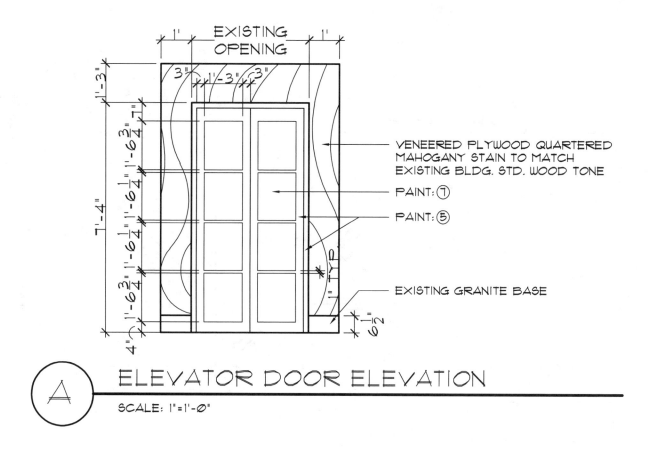

EXISTING OPENING

VENEERED PLYWOOD QUARTERED MAHOGANY STAIN TO MATCH EXISTING BLDG. STD. WOOD TONE

PAINT: ⑦

PAINT: ⑤

EXISTING GRANITE BASE

ELEVATOR DOOR ELEVATION

SCALE: 1"=1'-Ø"

FIGURE 9-5 Elevations are used to convey vertical dimensions of objects that can't be indicated in a plan view. Detailed horizontal dimensions can also be shown.

elevations illustrate the finished appearance of an exterior or interior wall of a building, as shown in Figure 9-1.

Elevations serve as a primary source to show heights, materials, and related information that cannot be seen in floor plans, sections, or other drawings. For example, a lavatory and vanity shown on a floor plan gives no information about what is located above or below the basin unit. An elevation is drawn to convey this information, as illustrated in Figure 9-2. Elevations are drawn as exterior or interior views of a building, or they might be specialized

views of objects such as furniture or free-standing cabinetry. Elevations generally show:

1. Object profiles and finish materials (Figure 9-3).

2. Relationships of different parts of objects such as doors, drawers, and top surfaces of a cabinet (Figure 9-4).

3. Vertical dimensions of an object that cannot be found in a plan view. In some cases, horizontal dimensions are also shown for clarity (Figure 9-5).

FIGURE 9-6 Exterior elevations convey the materials used and particulars about doors, windows, roofs, and footings, as well as important vertical dimensions.

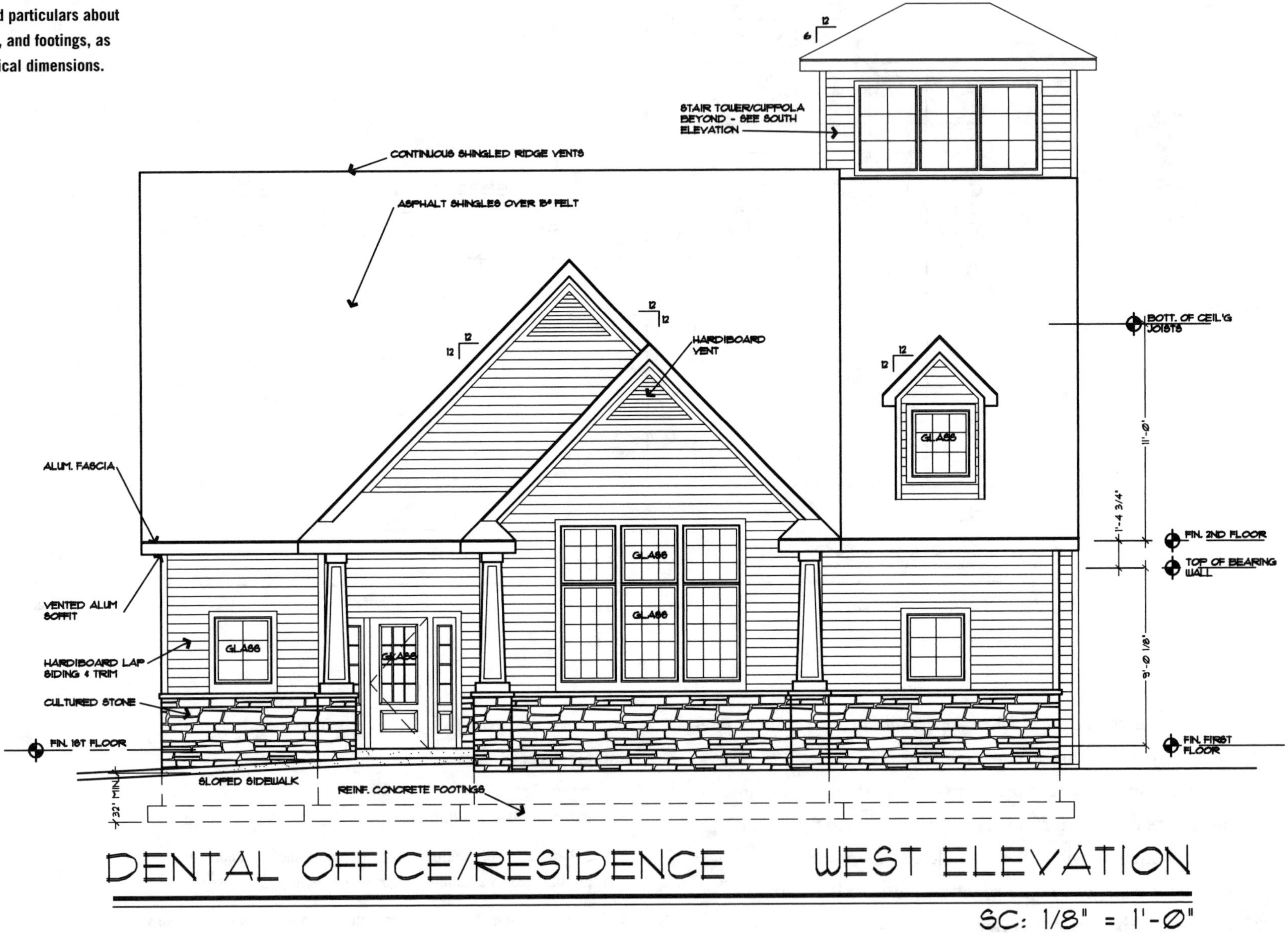

STAIR TOWER/CUPPOLA BEYOND - SEE SOUTH ELEVATION

CONTINUOUS SHINGLED RIDGE VENTS

ASPHALT SHINGLES OVER 15# FELT

HARDIBOARD VENT

BOTT. OF CEIL'G JOISTS

GLASS

ALUM. FASCIA

11'-0"

1'-4 3/4"

FIN. 2ND FLOOR

TOP OF BEARING WALL

VENTED ALUM SOFFIT

GLASS

GLASS

GLASS

9'-0 1/8"

HARDIBOARD LAP SIDING & TRIM

GLASS

CULTURED STONE

GLASS

FIN. 1ST FLOOR

FIN. FIRST FLOOR

32" MIN.

SLOPED SIDEWALK

REINF. CONCRETE FOOTINGS

DENTAL OFFICE/RESIDENCE   WEST ELEVATION

SC: 1/8" = 1'-0"

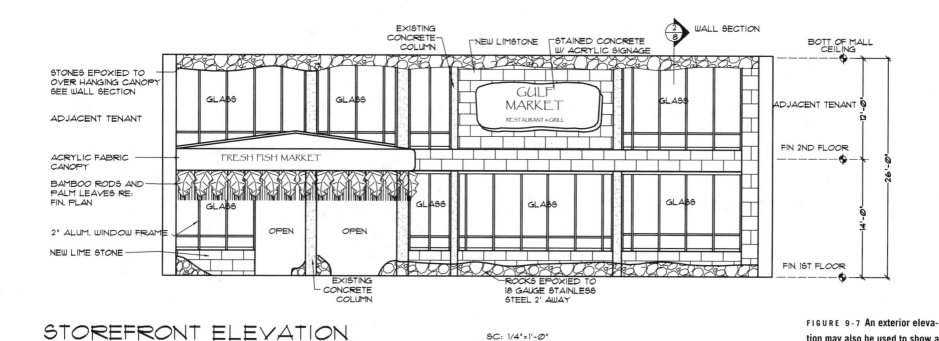

STORES EPOXIED TO
OVER HANGING CANOPY
SEE WALL SECTION

ADJACENT TENANT

ACRYLIC FABRIC
CANOPY

BAMBOO RODS AND
PALM LEAVES RE:
FIN. PLAN

2" ALUM. WINDOW FRAME

NEW LIME STONE

EXISTING
CONCRETE
COLUMN

EXISTING
CONCRETE
COLUMN

NEW LIMSTONE

STAINED CONCRETE
W/ ACRYLIC SIGNAGE

WALL SECTION

BOTT OF MALL
CEILING

ADJACENT TENANT

FIN 2ND FLOOR

FIN 1ST FLOOR

ROCKS EPOXIED TO
18 GAUGE STAINLESS
STEEL 2' AWAY

GLASS

GLASS

GULF
MARKET

RESTAURANT & GRILL

GLASS

FRESH FISH MARKET

GLASS

OPEN

OPEN

GLASS

GLASS

GLASS

STOREFRONT ELEVATION

SC: 1/4"=1'-0"

FIGURE 9-7 An exterior elevation may also be used to show a
store front in a shopping mall,
such as this façade for the Gulf
Markey Restaurant and Grill.

Exterior Elevations

Exterior elevations illustrate the finished appearance of an exterior wall of a building. They convey the type of materials proposed,
types of doors and windows, the finished grade, roof slope, foundation, footings, and selected vertical dimensions. Elevations assist
the designer in visualizing how proposed door and window types
and locations on the floor plan will influence the appearance and
style of the structure (Figure 9-6).

Exterior elevations are identified with a title and scale. Generally, exterior elevations are titled according to the compass direction they are facing, either North Elevation, East Elevation, South
Elevation, or West Elevation. If a building is not facing true north,
the side that is oriented the most nearly north is identified as such.
Then the other elevations are titled according to the compass
direction most closely related to them. In some cases, exterior elevations are titled as Front, Rear, Left, and Right.

In most cases, architects and engineers draw exterior elevations. However, interior designers may be required to draw exterior elevations for residential or small commercial projects, such as
retail store facades, as shown in Figure 9-7. When remodeling a
building or adding space to an existing structure, it may be necessary for the interior designer to draw partial exterior elevations for
clarity and understanding.

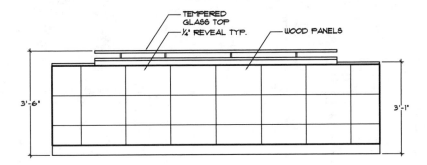

TEMPERED
GLASS TOP
¼' REVEAL TYP.   WOOD PANELS

3'-6'   3'-1'

① RECEPTION DESK - ELEVATION
SCALE: ¼'=1'-∅'

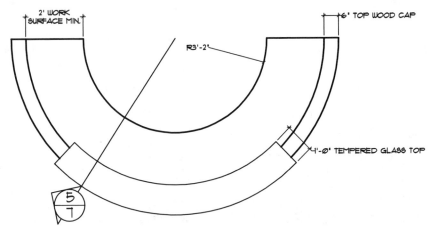

2' WORK
SURFACE MIN.   6' TOP WOOD CAP

R3'-2'

4'-∅' TEMPERED GLASS TOP

5
7

② RECEPTION DESK - PLAN
SCALE: ¼'=1'-∅'

FIGURE 9-8 A curved reception desk looks flat in the elevation. Its curved surface is only apparent in the floor plan.

Interior Elevations

An interior elevation is a vertical projection of a wall or other surface inside a building and shows the finished appearance of that wall or surface. It is seen as a straight-on view of the surface, as there is not a lot of need to show depth. Curves, spheres, and slanted surfaces disappear on the flat vertical plane of an elevation, as illustrated in Figure 9-8. However, depth can be indicated if desired by adding shading and shadowing.

In most cases, the real importance of an elevation is to show vertical elements, dimensions, and details that cannot be explained clearly in plan view. Interior elevations are particularly useful for showing the height of openings in a wall, materials and finishes of a wall, vertical dimensions, wall-mounted items (such as shelves and/or cabinets), location of switches, and special wall treatments. For example, an interior wall elevation might show the height of a grab bar and the location (height and cut-out size required) of a recessed tissue dispenser in a commercial bathroom, as illustrated in Figure 9-9.

Scale of Interior Elevations

The scale at which an interior elevation should be drawn will depend upon the complexity and detail of items, information, and finishes to be shown. Generally, interior elevations are drawn to the same scale as the floor plan(s). If the wall plane and other items are fairly simple, then a scale of ¼" = 1'-0" (1:50 metric) is acceptable. This is especially applicable in large public spaces. However, in very large commercial interior spaces a smaller scale of ⅛" = 1'0" (1:100 metric) might be required. In small projects or spaces, elevations might be drawn at a larger scale, such as ½" =1'-0" (1:20

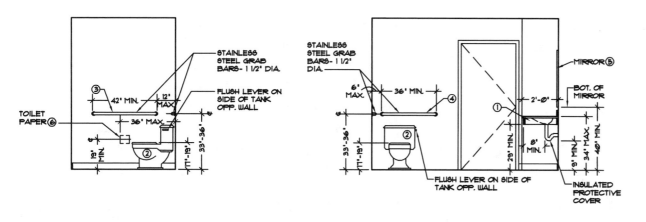

STAINLESS
STEEL GRAB
BARS- 1 1/2" DIA.

FLUSH LEVER ON
SIDE OF TANK
OPP. WALL

TOILET
PAPER ⑥

③ 42" MIN.   12"
MAX

36" MAX.

19"
MIN.

33"-36"

17"-19"

②

STAINLESS
STEEL GRAB
BARS- 1 1/2'
DIA.

MIRROR ⑤

BOT. OF
MIRROR

6'
MAX

36" MIN.   ④

①

33"-36'   17"-19'

②

2'-0"

28" MIN.   9" MIN.   34" MAX   40" MIN.

FLUSH LEVER ON SIDE OF
TANK OPP. WALL

INSULATED
PROTECTIVE
COVER

RESTROOM ADA COMPLIANCE LEGEND

① ADA CERAMIC WALL HUNG SINK

② ADA WATER CLOSET

③ GRAB BAR (WITH PEENED GRIP SURFACE)-
(SIDE WALL) MOUNT @ 33' CENTERLINE
MFG: BOBRICK OR APPROVED EQUAL
NO: 6206-42'

④ GRAB BAR (WITH PEENED GRIP SURFACE)-
(BACK WALL) MOUNT @ 33' CENTERLINE
MFG: BOBRICK OR APPROVED EQUAL
NO: 6206-36'

⑤ WALL MIRROR- MOUNT BOTTOM @ 40' AFF.

⑥ SINGLE ROLL TOILET TISSUE DISPENSER

RESTROOM   ④
③

SC: 3/8"=1'-0"

RESTROOM   ③
③

SC: 3/8'=1'-0'

FIGURE 9-9 Interior wall
elevations and legend convey
detailed information about
this restroom.

metric) or ⅜" = 1'-0" (1:30 metric) to show small details. The scale
of the drawing is noted directly beneath the drawing, as shown in
Figure 9-10, or elsewhere on the sheet if the same scale is used
throughout the entire sheet.

Drafting Standards for Interior Elevations

Interior elevations are drafted to clearly indicate surfaces, edges,
and the intersections of materials and forms. The elevation is
drawn to scale with the limits of the ceiling, floor, and adjacent
walls (or other forms) shown with a dark outline. There are two
basic methods that professional firms use to draw interior elevations. These methods are illustrated in Figure 9-11. The first
method is to outline all the elements (such as cabinets, beams, soffits, etc.) that project toward the viewer and establish the limits of

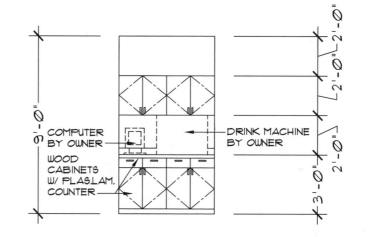

COMPUTER
BY OWNER

DRINK MACHINE
BY OWNER

WOOD
CABINETS
W/ PLAS.LAM.
COUNTER

9'-0"   2'-0"   2'-0"   2'-0"   2'-0"   3'-0"

WAIT STAT'N   W
12

SC: 1/4"=1'-0"   1ST FLOOR

FIGURE 9-10 The scale an
elevation is drawn to is
placed directly beneath the
drawing, along with the title
of the drawing.

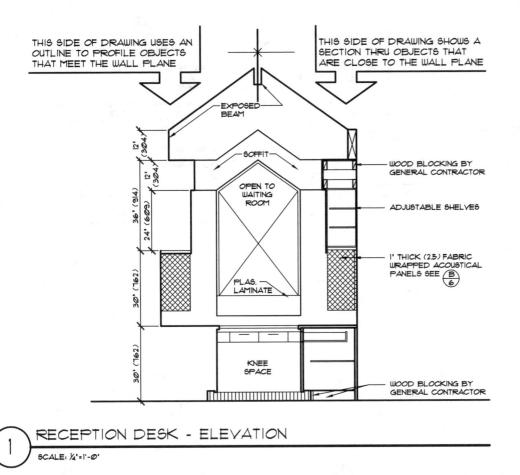

THIS SIDE OF DRAWING USES AN OUTLINE TO PROFILE OBJECTS THAT MEET THE WALL PLANE

THIS SIDE OF DRAWING SHOWS A SECTION THRU OBJECTS THAT ARE CLOSE TO THE WALL PLANE

EXPOSED BEAM

SOFFIT

OPEN TO WAITING ROOM

WOOD BLOCKING BY GENERAL CONTRACTOR

ADJUSTABLE SHELVES

1' THICK (25) FABRIC WRAPPED ACOUSTICAL PANELS SEE (B/6)

PLAS. LAMINATE

12' (304)
12' (304)
36' (914)
24' (609)
30' (762)
30' (762)

KNEE SPACE

WOOD BLOCKING BY GENERAL CONTRACTOR

① RECEPTION DESK - ELEVATION

SCALE: ¼"=1'-0"

FIGURE 9-11 This elevation drawing shows two methods for drawing the limits of an elevation. The left side traces the outline of a cabinet adjacent to the wall, whereas the right side cuts through the cabinet revealing its interior construction.

the wall elevation, as shown in Figure 9-12. The other method depicts these items in a cross-section, often showing construction details, materials, and other hidden items. This method is useful for explaining the details of an adjacent object (or cabinet interior, for example) without having to generate a separate drawing elsewhere. See Figure 9-13 for an example of this type of drawing. The choice between these techniques is dependent upon the complexity of the interior, the information that needs to be conveyed, and the established office standards.

Drawing interior elevations does not always follow a rigid set of architectural rules. Decorative elements or embellishment may need to be added to convey the character of the space. Many interior designers and architects take some liberty with elevations to convey important features, even if that means departing from "architecturally correct" drafting standards. For example, wall coverings, finishes, drapery treatments, or other decorative elements might be indicated on the drawing, as illustrated in Figure 9-14.

Generally, when drawing interior elevations of doors, windows, and built-in cabinetry, such as in a kitchen, bath, or office, dashed lines are used to indicate hinge location and door swings, as shown in Figure 9-15. The angled dashed line near the midpoint of the cabinet door points to the hinge side.

In theory, construction drawings include a sheet (or more) dedicated specifically to interior elevations. In practice however, this is not always the case. A small project with seven or eight interior elevations may not warrant a separate sheet, and so the elevations are drawn with other details in the construction set. Sometimes, on small projects that involve built-in cabinetry, it is advantageous to place the interior elevations on the same sheet as the floor plan if space permits. This way, the elevations can be studied without flipping sheets back and forth. The actual number of interior elevations is proportional to the complexity of the project. On large complex projects, interior elevations may be placed together on one or more sheets and referenced back to the floor plans, as illustrated in Figure 9-16.

Referencing and Naming Interior Elevations

Interior elevations can be named in several different ways. An interior elevation can be assigned a compass orientation according to the direction the viewer would be facing if looking at the surface

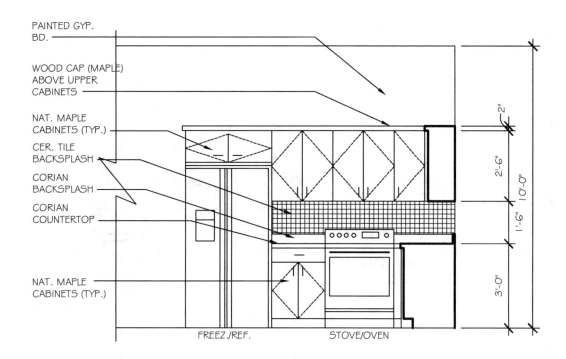

PAINTED GYP. BD.

WOOD CAP (MAPLE) ABOVE UPPER CABINETS

NAT. MAPLE CABINETS (TYP.)

CER. TILE BACKSPLASH

CORIAN BACKSPLASH

CORIAN COUNTERTOP

NAT. MAPLE CABINETS (TYP.)

FREEZ./REF.   STOVE/OVEN

2"

2'-6"

1'-6"

3'-0"

10'-0"

FIGURE 9-12 The cabinetry in this wall elevation is shown in outline form, rather than with its interior construction.

FIGURE 9-13 In this elevation, the adjacent cabinets are drawn showing their interior construction.

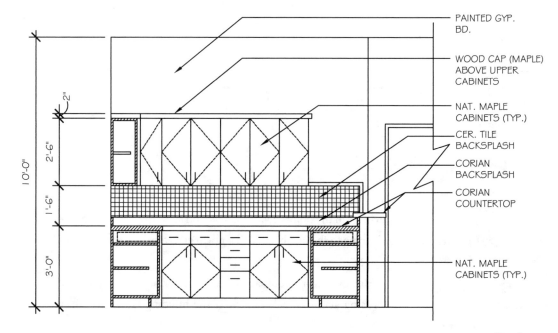

PAINTED GYP. BD.

WOOD CAP (MAPLE) ABOVE UPPER CABINETS

NAT. MAPLE CABINETS (TYP.)

CER. TILE BACKSPLASH

CORIAN BACKSPLASH

CORIAN COUNTERTOP

NAT. MAPLE CABINETS (TYP.)

2"

2'-6"

1'-6"

3'-0"

10'-0"

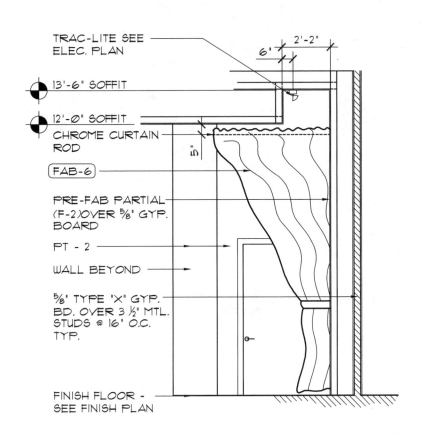

TRAC-LITE SEE ELEC. PLAN

6' 2'-2"

13'-6" SOFFIT

12'-0" SOFFIT

CHROME CURTAIN ROD

FAB-6

PRE-FAB PARTIAL (F-2) OVER ⅝' GYP. BOARD

PT - 2

WALL BEYOND

⅝" TYPE "X" GYP. BD. OVER 3 ½" MTL. STUDS @ 16' O.C. TYP.

FINISH FLOOR - SEE FINISH PLAN

② WALL SECTION @ DRAPERY
SCALE: ½" = 1'-0'

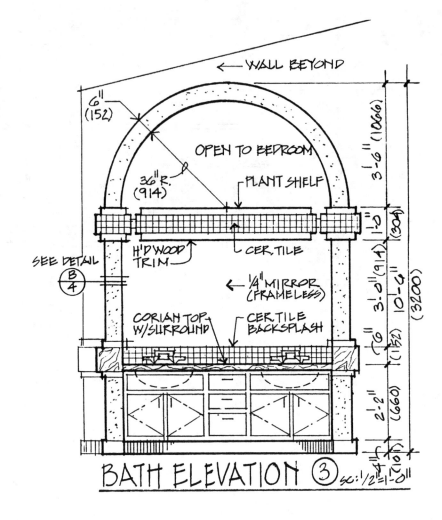

← WALL BEYOND

6" (152)

OPEN TO BEDROOM

PLANT SHELF

36" R. (914)

CER. TILE

SEE DETAIL
B/4

H'DWOOD TRIM

¼" MIRROR (FRAMELESS)

CORIAN TOP W/SURROUND

CER. TILE BACKSPLASH

3'-6 (1066)

1'-0" (304)

3'-0" (914)

10'-6" (3200)

6" (152)

2'-2" (660)

BATH ELEVATION ③ SC: ½"=1'-0"

FIGURE 9-14 **(left)** This wall section shows the drapery and wall beyond in elevation view.

FIGURE 9-15 **(right)** Dashed lines are drawn in an elevation to show the direction doors open. The dashed lines at the mid-point indicate the hinge side.

depicted—north, south, east, or west. For example, an elevation drawn from the point of view of a person standing inside an office and facing to the north is called a north elevation, as shown in Figure 9-17.

However, using compass names for interior elevations can be confusing at times, particularly if the building is oriented in a direction such as southwest or northeast. A wall might even run at a diagonal to others within a room, further confusing the assigned compass names.

Reference symbols are the preferred way to assign names to interior elevations. A reference symbol is shown on the floor plan and a number is assigned to the interior elevation view, as illus-

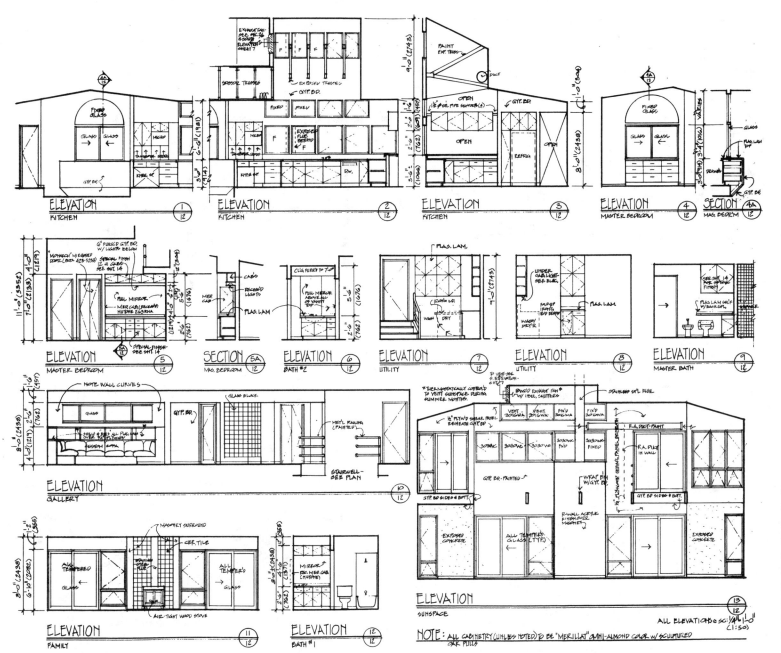

FIGURE 9-16 Interior elevations of a project are grouped together on one sheet and cross-referenced, below each drawing, to the floor plan. The scale is the same for all elevations and noted as such on the lower right side.

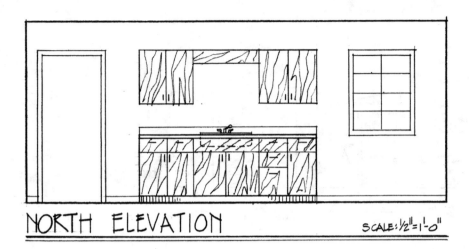

NORTH ELEVATION

SCALE: 1/2"=1'-0"

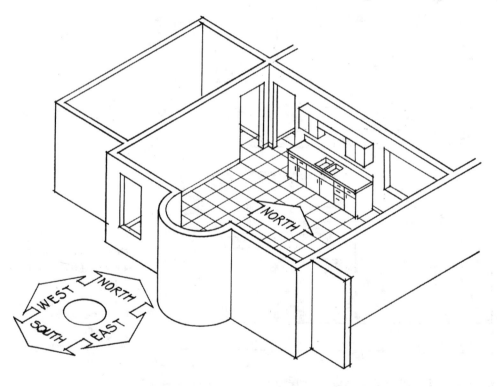

FIGURE 9-17 Interior elevations can be named according to the compass direction the viewer is facing.

WEST NORTH SOUTH EAST

NORTH

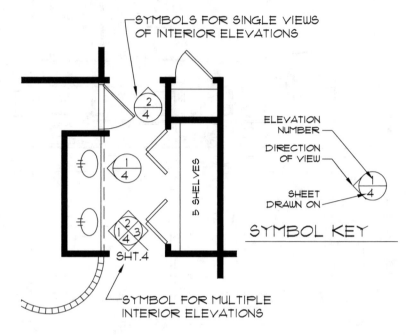

SYMBOLS FOR SINGLE VIEWS OF INTERIOR ELEVATIONS

5 SHELVES

SHT.4

SYMBOL FOR MULTIPLE INTERIOR ELEVATIONS

ELEVATION NUMBER

DIRECTION OF VIEW

SHEET DRAWN ON

SYMBOL KEY

PARTIAL PLAN OF BATH

FIGURE 9-18 Elevation reference symbols on a plan can indicate a single elevation view or be divided to indicate multiple views.

trated in Figure 9-18. An arrow is drawn around the elevation symbol on the plan to indicate the direction the viewer is looking, and another number is assigned to indicate on what sheet the interior elevation may be found. On the elevation sheet, these numbers are also repeated just below the elevation view.

The full title of an elevation often includes the room name or number by which it is referenced on the floor plan. Although it may seem obvious that the viewer is looking at an interior eleva-

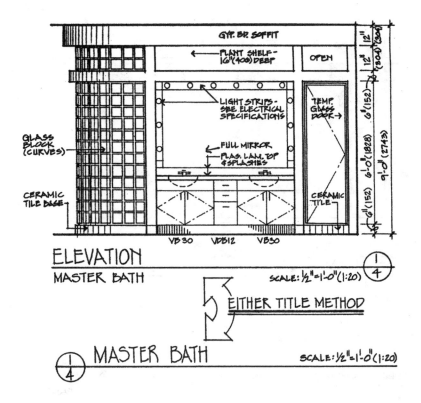

ELEVATION
MASTER BATH

EITHER TITLE METHOD

MASTER BATH

SCALE: ½"=1'-0" (1:20)

tion, most firms prefer to identify the drawing, as in "Master Bath Elevation." See Figure 9-19 for an example of this procedure.

Designation of Materials

Materials can be shown on interior elevations simplistically with notes only, or various line textures can be drawn to help visually convey differences in materials. This latter method is particularly helpful when an interior elevation is complex and needs to convey a lot of information—which can be difficult with just simple line drawings, as illustrated in Figure 9-20. In small-scaled elevation drawings, some liberty can be taken in simplifying an object or material that is complicated and cannot be accurately drawn at that scale. For example, a highly decorative raised wood panel on a kitchen cabinet may have to be blocked out in panel proportions rather than drawn in detail. One should remember that the purpose of a construction drawing is to delineate to others how things are to be constructed—not to produce a work of art. In some cases, to save on drafting time or to prevent a drawing from becoming overly complicated, material types are not delineated

FIGURE 9-19 It is preferable to title an elevation with the room name for easy identification.

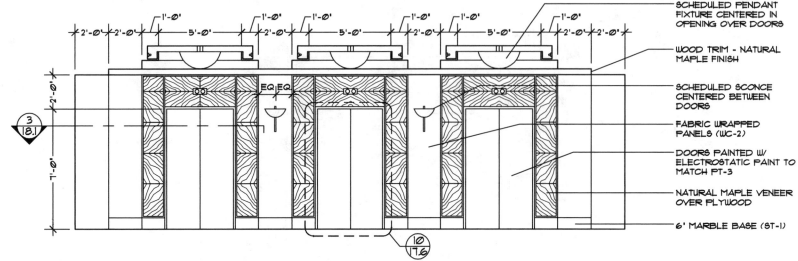

SCHEDULED PENDANT
FIXTURE CENTERED IN
OPENING OVER DOORS

WOOD TRIM - NATURAL
MAPLE FINISH

SCHEDULED SCONCE
CENTERED BETWEEN
DOORS

FABRIC WRAPPED
PANELS (WC-2)

DOORS PAINTED W/
ELECTROSTATIC PAINT TO
MATCH PT-3

NATURAL MAPLE VENEER
OVER PLYWOOD

6' MARBLE BASE (ST-1)

6 / 17.2 ELEVATION OF ELEVATOR LOBBY
SCALE: 1/4"=1'-0'

FIGURE 9-20 A wood-grain pattern is used to make the mahogany panels discernible from other surface materials.

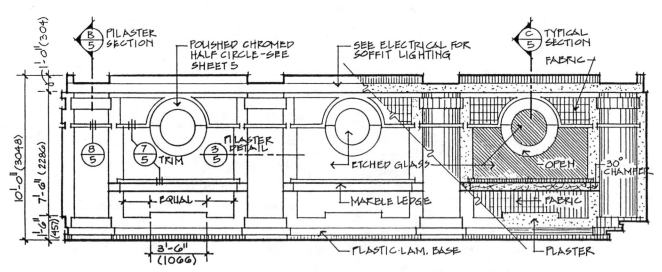

PILASTER SECTION B/5

POLISHED CHROMED
HALF CIRCLE-SEE
SHEET 5

SEE ELECTRICAL FOR
SOFFIT LIGHTING

TYPICAL SECTION C/5
FABRIC

8/5   7/5 TRIM   3/5 PILASTER DETAIL

ETCHED GLASS

OPEN

30° CHAMFER

EQUAL

MARBLE LEDGE

FABRIC

3'-6" (1066)

PLASTIC-LAM. BASE

PLASTER

LOBBY WALL ELEVATION SC:1/4"=1'-0" (1:50) 2/4
SEE SHEET 12 FOR PAINT/FABRIC FINISH SCHEDULE

FIGURE 9-21 The detailed textures on this elevation end with a diagonal break line rather than filling the entire drawing.

entire surfaces. A break line is used to stop the rendering of materials, or the material designation simply fades out, as illustrated in Figure 9-21.

Notes describing materials, such as ceramic tile, are kept generic in most cases. Specifics such as color, finishes, sizes, thickness, brand names, installation details, and other items are generally covered in the specifications that accompany the construction drawings. This allows changes to be made (such as the switch to an alternate manufacturer's products) without the need to revise the drawing. For example, an exhaust hood shown in a commercial kitchen elevation would simply be labeled as an "exhaust hood." The manufacturer's brand name, fan speed, color, and other particulars would be listed in an accompanying note or in the specifications.

Dimensioning Elevations

Interior elevations are the primary drawings that show correct vertical heights of walls and elements related to it, such as doors, windows, and millwork. For this reason, horizontal dimensioning of spaces and objects is better left to be represented elsewhere. For example, the width of a wall or room is best dimensioned on the floor plan. Cabinet depths and widths are also usually dimensioned on the floor plan. However, some professionals do place these dimensions on the elevations for more clarity and convenience for the cabinetmaker. Whichever method is used, dimensions should not be repeated in both places, as errors can be made when one drawing or the other is revised.

In construction drawings, dimensions are indicated in feet and inches (or metric). However, in specialized drawings (such as interior elevations in the kitchen and bath industry), cabinetry,

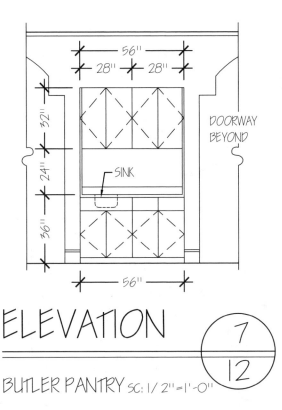

FIGURE 9-22 In specialized drawings, such as for this butler pantry in a kitchen, dimensions are indicated in inches only.

doors, windows, and other items are dimensioned only in inches (or metric), as shown in Figure 9-22. In laying out the dimensions, one should indicate overall heights and similar cumulative dimensions of important elements (Figure 9-23).

Checklist for Interior Elevations

General

■ **Title elevation and note the scale it is drawn at, either below title or in the sheet title block.**

■ **Cross-reference drawing (with correct symbols) to floor plans and/or other drawings.**

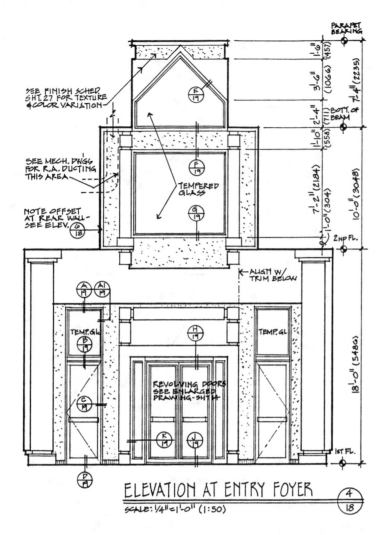

Inside the drawing, the following labels appear:

SEE FINISH SCHED SHT. 27 FOR TEXTURE & COLOR VARIATION

SEE MECH. DWGS FOR R.A. DUCTING THIS AREA

TEMPERED GLASS

NOTE OFFSET AT REAR WALL – SEE ELEV. 6/18

ALIGN W/ TRIM BELOW

2ND FL.

TEMP. GL

TEMP. GL

REVOLVING DOORS SEE ENLARGED DRAWING SHT 14

1ST FL.

PARAPET BEARING

BOTT. OF BEAM

ELEVATION AT ENTRY FOYER

SCALE: 1/4"=1'-0" (1:50)   4/18

FIGURE 9-23 Vertical dimensions can be shown on elevations to indicate overall heights and dimensions of other important elements.

- Draw doors, windows, and their frames. Show (with hidden/dotted lines) direction of door and cabinetry door swings and shelf locations. The angled dashed line near the midpoint of the door indicates the hinge side.

- Add notes to cross-reference items to other drawings where necessary (finish plan, electrical/lighting plan, etc.).

- Draw the outline (profile) of the elevation nice and dark, as it repre-

sents outermost limits of the drawing. Use a minimum of three line weights to represent outlines of spaces, contours, and textures.

- Use manufacturers' templates, or the computer "library of symbols," for drawing plumbing fixtures, such as water closets and lavatories.

- Check all elevations for code compliance and ADA requirements and clearances.

- Check elevations for LEED certification credits, if applicable.

- Are all the elevations and notes clear and readable when reproduced or printed? If not, correct as necessary.

Notations

- Draw and note appliances/equipment such as refrigerators, dishwasher, washer/dryer, microwave, trash compactor, etc. If item is not to be supplied by contractor, add note that it is N.I.C. (not in contract), or supplied by the owner.

- Call out (with generic names) wall and base cabinet materials, wainscot, moldings, chair rails, and shelves (adjustable or fixed).

- Call out generic wall finishes (vinyl, ceramic tile, brick, wood paneling, gypsum board, fabric, etc.) and refer to the finish plan for detailed information.

- Call out glass, mirrors, metal frames, and other related information.

- Key window or glazing wall details to the appropriate enlarged drawings.

- Note folding partitions, roll-down security, and fire doors.

Dimensions

- Dimension heights of important items such as base and wall cabinetry, countertops, backsplashes, toe spaces, soffits, and fixtures.

- Dimension miscellaneous trim, moldings, wall surface treatments such as wainscots, chair rails, and handrails.

- Dimension walls and other items to important building elements, such as existing walls, concrete walls, or columns.

- Dimension heights, lengths, and clearances of any ADA facility and equipment, such as grab bars, toilet stalls, plumbing fixtures, dispensers, and water fountains.

We have seen how elevations and floor plans show finish materials, heights, room layouts, and locations of doors and windows. However, many of the details and subsurface parts of a building or interior space cannot be completely understood through only these types of drawings. To gain more information as to how a building, interior space, or an object is to be constructed, one or more slices may have to be cut through the assembly in a vertical direction.

Section drawings take an imaginary slice through an object or building as illustrated in Figure 10-1. They give information on heights and relationships between floors, ceilings, spaces, walls, and in some instances details of the specific construction techniques used. Sections can be cut as a vertical (most common) or horizontal plane. In fact, a floor plan is really a horizontal section view drawing. Two or more sections are often cut at 90 degrees to one another to give additional information, unless the space or object is very simple. Section cuts should ideally be cut in a continuous, straight plane without too many jogs. This slice should be taken where it will best illustrate the relationships between significant components of an object or interior space, as shown in Figure 10-2. The location of this cut is indicated on the floor plan or elevation (whichever is the base drawing) with a graphical sym-

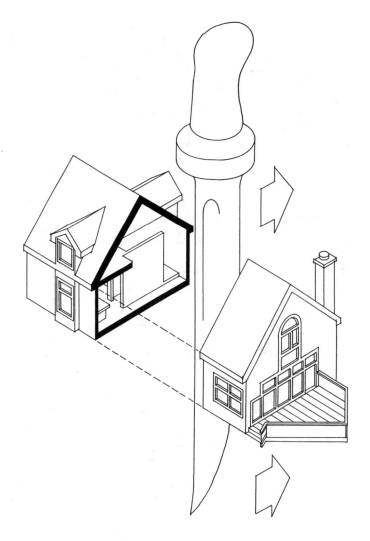

FIGURE 10-1 **A building section drawing takes an imaginary slice through a structure, showing its materials and components.**

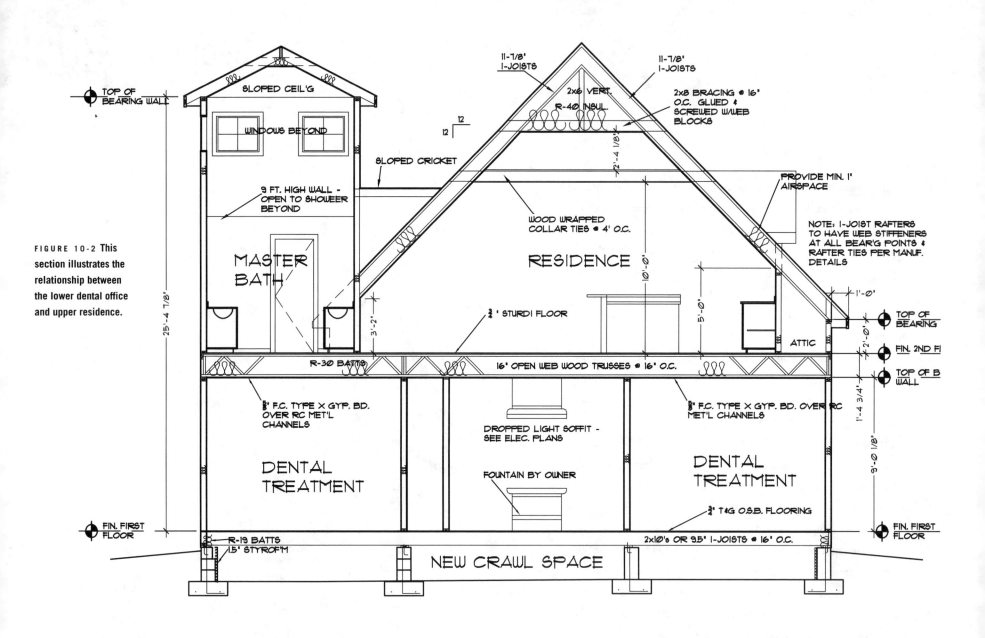

TOP OF
BEARING WALL

SLOPED CEIL'G

WINDOWS BEYOND

11-7/8"
I-JOISTS

11-7/8"
I-JOISTS

2x6 VERT.

R-40 INSUL.

2x8 BRACING @ 16"
O.C. GLUED &
SCREWED W/WEB
BLOCKS

12 ⌐12

SLOPED CRICKET

9 FT. HIGH WALL -
OPEN TO SHOWER
BEYOND

7'-4 1/8"

PROVIDE MIN. 1"
AIRSPACE

WOOD WRAPPED
COLLAR TIES @ 4' O.C.

NOTE: I-JOIST RAFTERS
TO HAVE WEB STIFFENERS
AT ALL BEAR'G POINTS &
RAFTER TIES PER MANUF.
DETAILS

MASTER
BATH

RESIDENCE

10'-0"

1'-0"

25'-4 1/8"

3'-2"

3/4' STURDI FLOOR

5'-0"

ATTIC

TOP OF
BEARING

FIN. 2ND Fl

R-30 BATTS

16" OPEN WEB WOOD TRUSSES @ 16" O.C.

TOP OF B
WALL

1'-4 3/4"

2'-0"

FIGURE 10-2 This
section illustrates the
relationship between
the lower dental office
and upper residence.

5/8" F.C. TYPE X GYP. BD.
OVER RC MET'L
CHANNELS

DROPPED LIGHT SOFFIT -
SEE ELEC. PLANS

5/8" F.C. TYPE X GYP. BD. OVER RC
MET'L CHANNELS

9'-0 1/8"

DENTAL
TREATMENT

FOUNTAIN BY OWNER

DENTAL
TREATMENT

3/4" T&G O.S.B. FLOORING

FIN. FIRST
FLOOR

R-19 BATTS

1.5" STYROF'M

2x10's OR 9.5" I-JOISTS @ 16" O.C.

FIN. FIRST
FLOOR

NEW CRAWL SPACE

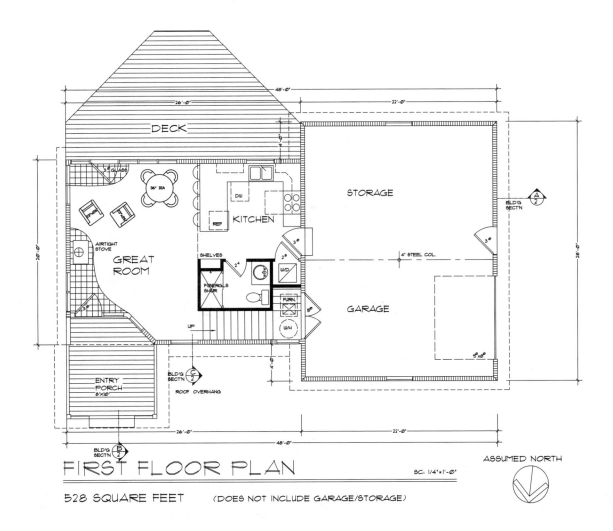

FIRST FLOOR PLAN

SC: 1/4"=1'-0'

528 SQUARE FEET   (DOES NOT INCLUDE GARAGE/STORAGE)

ASSUMED NORTH

FIGURE 10-3 The arrow on building section symbol shows the direction of the view. The top number is the section number, and the bottom one indicates the sheet it is drawn on.

bol as seen in Figure 10-3. This symbol gives the section an identification number with an arrow that shows the direction the person is looking when viewing the final sectional drawing. If there are a number of sheets in a designer's set of construction drawings, the indicator mark also shows which sheet the particular section is drawn on.

Types of Section Drawings

Sections can be drawn of a total building, interior space, or object. These are referred to as full sections. However, if only an isolated area needs to be illustrated, a partial section can also be drawn. Sections can be cut in a variety of ways to show more detailed information. A section might be cut all the way through a build-

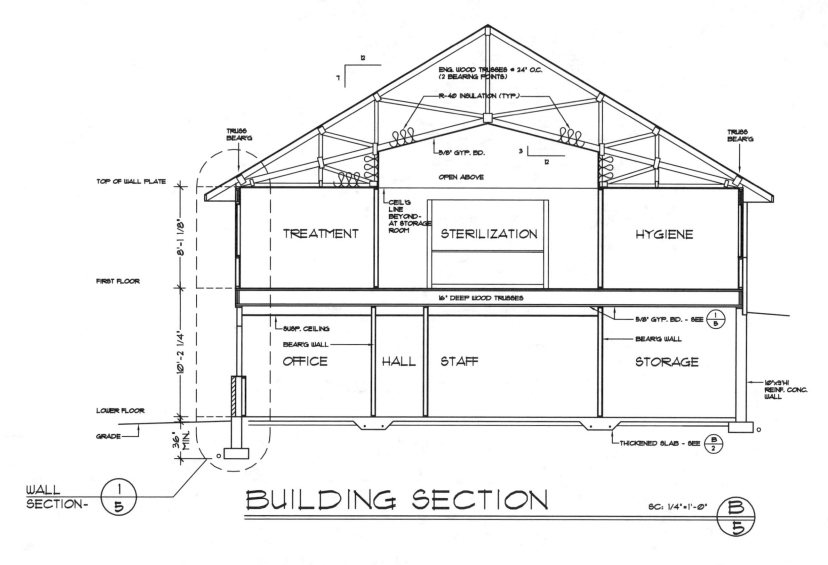

ENG. WOOD TRUSSES @ 24" O.C.
(2 BEARING POINTS)

R-40 INSULATION (TYP.)

TRUSS
BEAR'G

5/8" GYP. BD.

OPEN ABOVE

TRUSS
BEAR'G

TOP OF WALL PLATE

8'-1 1/8"

CEIL'G
LINE
BEYOND -
AT STORAGE
ROOM

TREATMENT

STERILIZATION

HYGIENE

FIRST FLOOR

16" DEEP WOOD TRUSSES

5/8" GYP. BD. - SEE 1/5

10'-2 1/4"

SUSP. CEILING

BEAR'G WALL

BEAR'G WALL

OFFICE

HALL

STAFF

STORAGE

10"x9'HI
REINF. CONC.
WALL

LOWER FLOOR

GRADE

36" MIN.

THICKENED SLAB - SEE B/2

WALL
SECTION- 1/5

BUILDING SECTION

SC: 1/4"=1'-0" B/5

FIGURE 10-4 **The wall section ballooned on the left side of this building section can be found enlarged on sheet 5.**

ing (called a building section), or only through a wall (wall section). Both may be needed, because the small scale and complexity of a building section generally means the materials and details related to the walls cannot be drawn there. A symbol on the building section shown in Figure 10-4 marks the wall area to be enlarged. The enlarged wall section (Figure 10-5) is drawn to accu-

rately show the many details and materials that are needed in the assembly.

In addition to building and wall sections, there may also be a need to draw a section through built-in or custom components within a space, such as shelving, reception desks, credenzas, bars, display cases, cabinets, and counters. Figure 10-6 illustrates a built-in cabinet section. These types of sections are discussed in more detail in Chapter 11.

In interior construction drawings, sometimes the terms *section* and *detail* are interchanged, thus causing some confusion. Section cuts through small portions of construction or objects are referred to as details. But details are not always drawn in section. They may also include enlarged portions of the floor plan or elevation.

The scale of section drawings may range from ⅛" to 3" (3.17 mm to 76 mm), depending upon the size of the drawing paper, the size of the building (or component), and the desired features to be shown. The specific information a section shows may vary, depending on whether it is a design or construction drawing. Construction drawings show only the items or components of a space that are built-in or attached to the structure. Movable furniture is not shown in this type of drawing.

Drafting Standards

Section drawings are shown as cut through solid elements and spaces (voids) within an object or building. To graphically represent these, certain accepted techniques are often employed. For example, solid materials cut through in the section slice are pouched with standard material designations, such as wood, brick, concrete, and so forth. There are some fairly common material designations as shown in Figure 3-11. Many offices use these, but variations on these graphic standards also occur. Legends or keys are used in the drawings to explain what the material designation stands for. The lines or outlines around these sliced materials are drawn with heavy thick lines to accent the cut. To differentiate these materials from adjacent construction or objects seen beyond

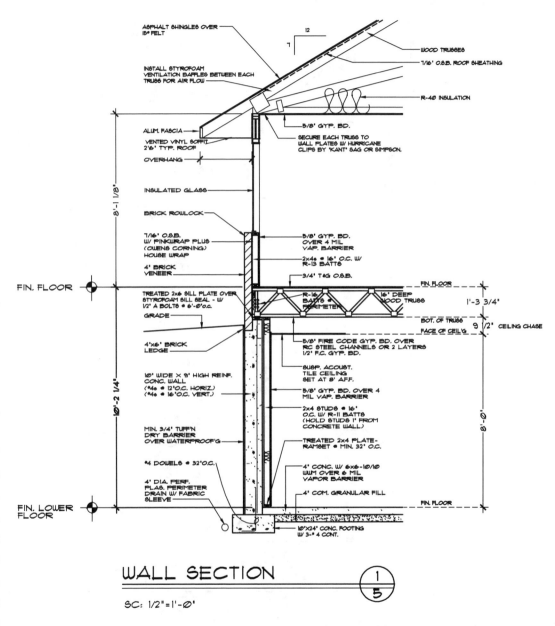

FIGURE 10-5 This is the enlarged wall section keyed on the building section in Figure 10-4.

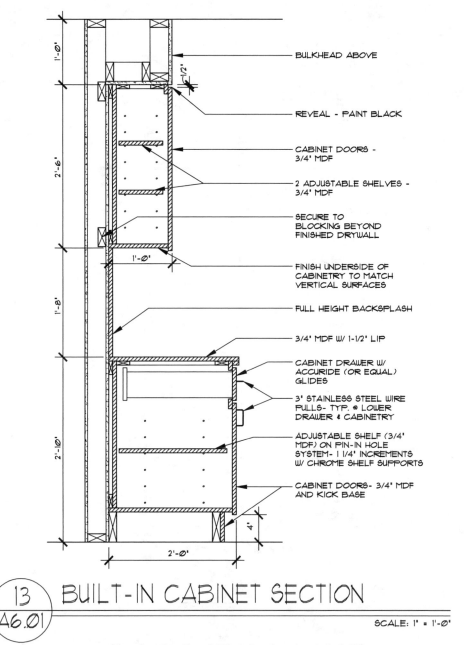

BULKHEAD ABOVE

REVEAL - PAINT BLACK

CABINET DOORS -
3/4" MDF

2 ADJUSTABLE SHELVES -
3/4" MDF

SECURE TO
BLOCKING BEYOND
FINISHED DRYWALL

FINISH UNDERSIDE OF
CABINETRY TO MATCH
VERTICAL SURFACES

FULL HEIGHT BACKSPLASH

3/4" MDF W/ 1-1/2" LIP

CABINET DRAWER W/
ACCURIDE (OR EQUAL)
GLIDES

3" STAINLESS STEEL WIRE
PULLS- TYP. @ LOWER
DRAWER & CABINETRY

ADJUSTABLE SHELF (3/4"
MDF) ON PIN-IN HOLE
SYSTEM- 1 1/4" INCREMENTS
W/ CHROME SHELF SUPPORTS

CABINET DOORS- 3/4" MDF
AND KICK BASE

(13 / A6.01) BUILT-IN CABINET SECTION

SCALE: 1" = 1'-0"

FIGURE 10-6 **An enlarged section might just show through part of a building assembly to depict specific details, such as this built-in cabinet construction.**

the construction drawings, lighter and thinner lines are used (Figure 10-7).

Building Sections

Building sections can effectively show the construction details of single or multilevel structures, including the floors, walls, and ceiling/roof. The location and number of building sections to be cut will depend upon the clarity and amount of information to be shown about the structure and its features (Figure 10-8). Building sections are typically drawn at a scale of $\frac{1}{8}$" = 1'-0" or $\frac{1}{4}$" = 1'-0" (1:100 or 1:50 metric). A section cut through the length of a building is called a longitudinal section and one cut 90 degrees to this, through the narrow width of a building is a transverse section. If

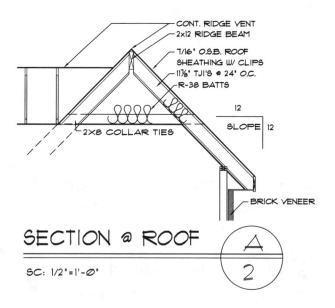

CONT. RIDGE VENT
2x12 RIDGE BEAM

7/16" O.S.B. ROOF
SHEATHING W/ CLIPS
11⅞" TJI'S @ 24" O.C.
R-38 BATTS

SLOPE 12 / 12

2X8 COLLAR TIES

BRICK VENEER

SECTION @ ROOF (A / 2)

SC: 1/2"=1'-0"

FIGURE 10-7 **Heavier line work is used to delineate materials that are "sliced" through, while lighter lines show objects beyond the cutting plane.**

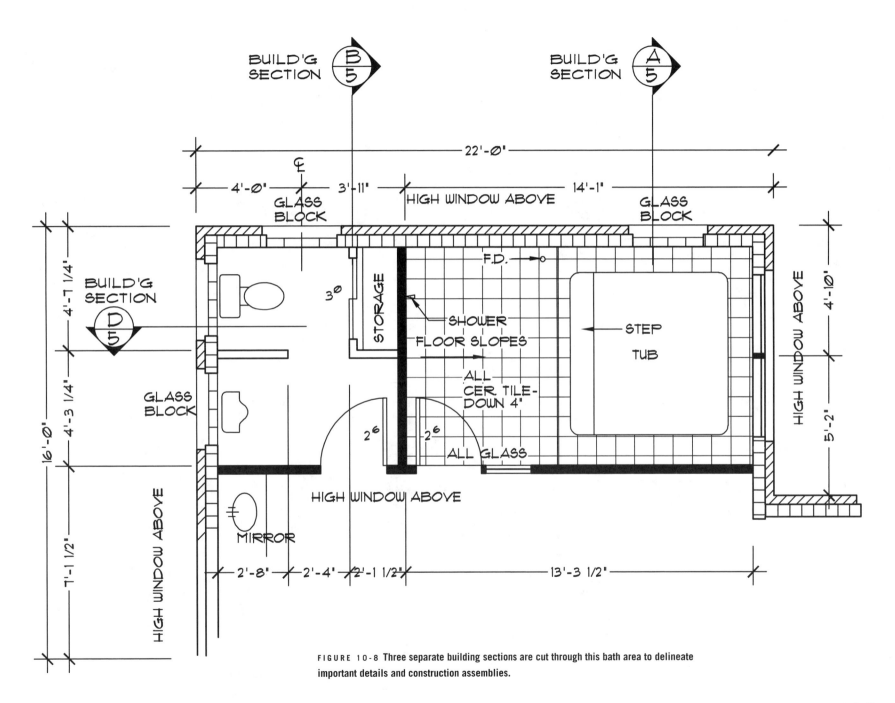

BUILD'G SECTION B/5

BUILD'G SECTION A/5

22'-0"

₵

4'-0" 3'-11" HIGH WINDOW ABOVE 14'-1"

GLASS BLOCK

GLASS BLOCK

4'-7 1/4"

BUILD'G SECTION D/5

F.D.

3⁰

STORAGE

SHOWER FLOOR SLOPES

STEP TUB

HIGH WINDOW ABOVE

4'-10"

16'-0"

4'-3 1/4"

GLASS BLOCK

ALL CER TILE- DOWN 4"

2⁶

2⁶

ALL GLASS

5'-2"

7'-1 1/2"

HIGH WINDOW ABOVE

HIGH WINDOW ABOVE

MIRROR

2'-8" 2'-4" 2'-1 1/2" 13'-3 1/2"

FIGURE 10-8 Three separate building sections are cut through this bath area to delineate important details and construction assemblies.

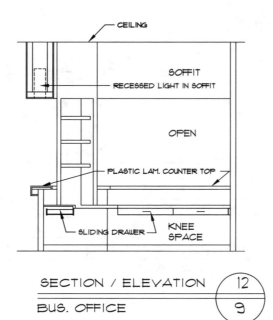

CEILING

SOFFIT

RECESSED LIGHT IN SOFFIT

OPEN

PLASTIC LAM. COUNTER TOP

SLIDING DRAWER

KNEE SPACE

SECTION / ELEVATION ⑫
BUS. OFFICE ⑨

FIGURE 10-9 The countertop, overhead soffit, and sliding drawer are shown cut in cross section on this interior elevation.

a detail or other assembly (such as a wall) needs to be presented in a way that conveys more information, indicator marks are drawn on the building section for cross-reference to another location where this detail is drawn at a larger scale.

Sections of Interior Spaces

When working with interior spaces, it may not be necessary to include a building section in its entirety. For example, if the extent of construction work is primarily limited to an interior remodel of an existing space, the section may not need to include all the structural details. Full assemblies such as the concrete floor thickness, granular fill, and below-ground footings do not really need to

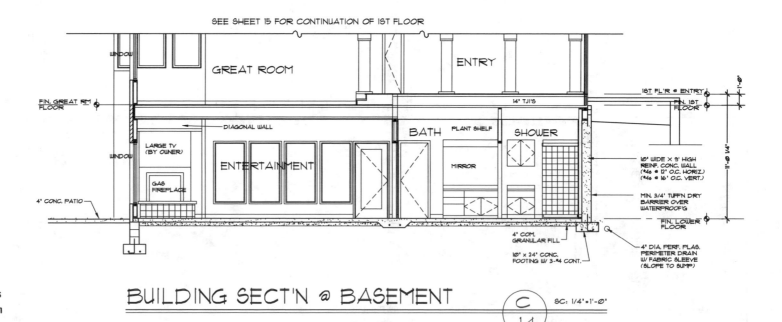

SEE SHEET 15 FOR CONTINUATION OF 1ST FLOOR

GREAT ROOM

ENTRY

FIN. GREAT RM. FLOOR

WINDOW

DIAGONAL WALL

LARGE TV (BY OWNER)

ENTERTAINMENT

GAS FIREPLACE

14" TJI'S

BATH

PLANT SHELF

MIRROR

SHOWER

1ST FL'R @ ENTRY

FIN. 1ST FLOOR

10" WIDE X 9' HIGH REINF. CONC. WALL (#4 @ 12" O.C. HORIZ.) (#4 @ 16" O.C. VERT.)

MIN. 3/4" TUFF'N DRY BARRIER OVER WATERPROOF'G

FIN. LOWER FLOOR

4' CONC. PATIO

4" CONC. GRANULAR FILL

10" x 24" CONC. FOOTING W/ 3-#4 CONT.

4" DIA. PERF. PLAS. PERIMETER DRAIN W/ FABRIC SLEEVE (SLOPE TO SUMP)

BUILDING SECT'N @ BASEMENT ⓒ ⑭ SC: 1/4" = 1'-0"

FIGURE 10-10 This partial section view of the basement level of a residence also shows the fireplace wall and bathroom in elevation.

be illustrated. In such cases, the intent of the section is cut through a portion of the structure to detail the features of one or more internal spaces and the related construction. These drawings might show cabinetwork, wall wainscots, suspended ceilings, dropped soffits, doors, wall openings, and other interior components. Objects such as cabinetry that are cut through in the section cut will be seen in a cross-sectional view, as illustrated in Figure 10-9. Sections through interior spaces often resemble a building section in their composition, but are more concerned with the interior aspects of the assembly and don't necessarily show floor thickness and other structural details (Figure 10-10). If objects or assemblies are too small to draw in detail, they are keyed with a symbol on a section drawing and enlarged elsewhere, as illustrated in Figure 10-11. Interior section drawings are usually drawn at a scale of ⅛" = 1'-0", ¼" = 1'-0", or even ½" = 1'-0" (1:100, 1:50, or 1:20 metric).

Wall Sections

A section that is drawn at a large scale to show the specifics of an interior or exterior building wall is called a wall section (Figure 10-12). The wall section is often keyed to the main building section and permits the designer to enlarge and show more clearly the details for that particular wall, such as the floor and ceiling systems. Again, more than one wall section is often required to delineate the uniqueness of a design or construction assembly. The scale of the drawing depends upon the details to be shown and the paper size. Generally, wall sections are drawn at a scale of ½" = 1'-0" to 1-½" = 1'-0" (1:20 to 1:10 metric). It is desirable to draw the wall section in its entirety from the bottom of the wall to the top. However, if the sheet size does not allow this, the section can

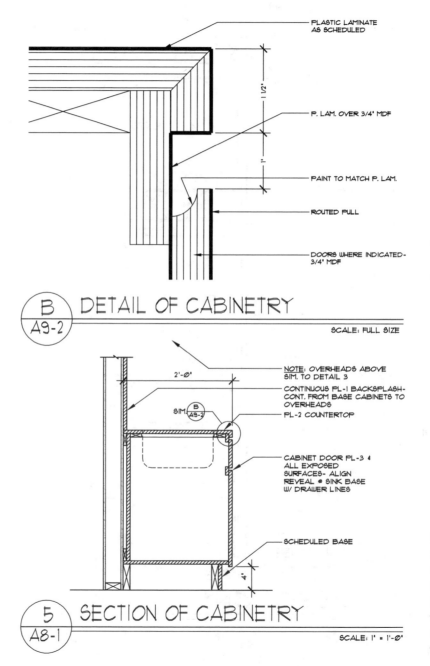

FIGURE 10-11 A detail of millwork is drawn at a very large scale for clarity and keyed by symbols to the corresponding part of a sectional view of the cabinetry.

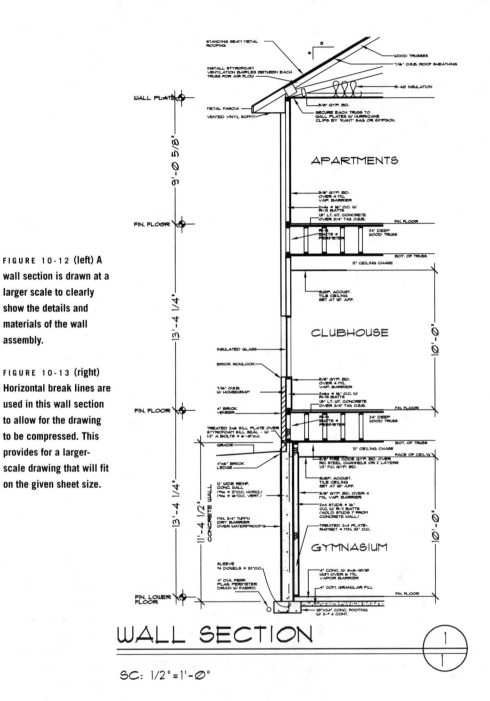

FIGURE 10-12 (left) A wall section is drawn at a larger scale to clearly show the details and materials of the wall assembly.

FIGURE 10-13 (right) Horizontal break lines are used in this wall section to allow for the drawing to be compressed. This provides for a larger-scale drawing that will fit on the given sheet size.

WALL SECTION

SC: 1/2"=1'-0"

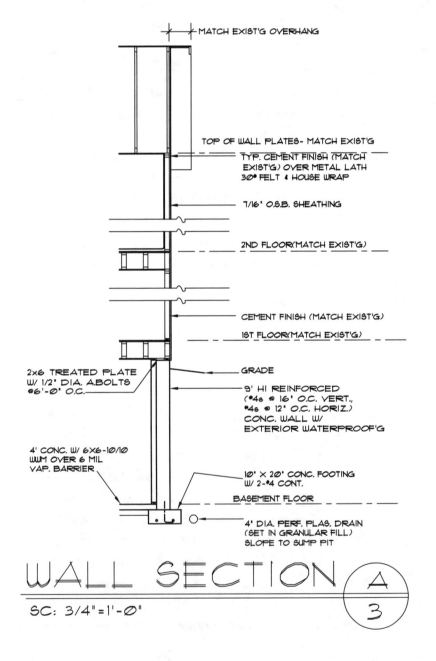

WALL SECTION A

SC: 3/4"=1'-0"

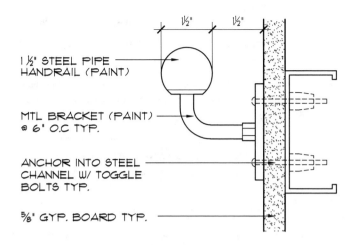

1 ½" STEEL PIPE
HANDRAIL (PAINT)

MTL BRACKET (PAINT)
@ 6' O.C TYP.

ANCHOR INTO STEEL
CHANNEL W/ TOGGLE
BOLTS TYP.

⅝" GYP. BOARD TYP.

② SECTION @ HANDRAIL
A4.6   SCALE: N.T.S.

FIGURE 10-14 A detailed handrail drawn at a large scale for clarity.

be cut in one or more areas (where large areas of the wall have the same construction) with break lines to compress the drawing to fit the paper size (Figure 10-13).

Detail and Object Sections

Sometimes, a complete building or wall section cannot be drawn large enough to fully explain a portion of the assembly. Or, there might be items that are not tied to the building structure in such a way that the wall section needs to be included in the drawing. These might include handrails, as shown in Figure 10-14, or objects such as cabinets and furniture. In these cases, a detailed

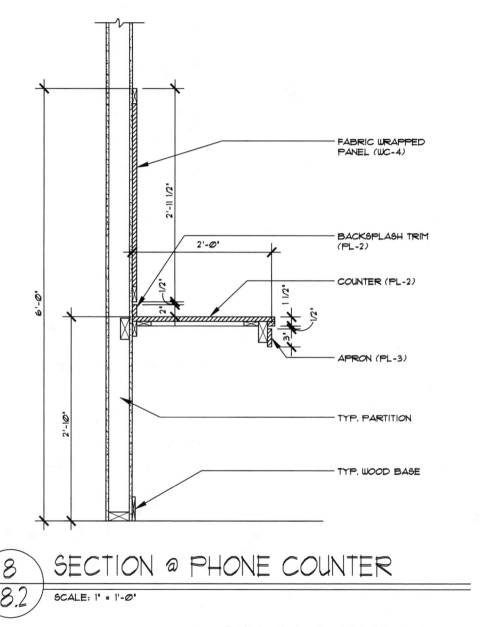

FABRIC WRAPPED
PANEL (WC-4)

BACKSPLASH TRIM
(PL-2)

COUNTER (PL-2)

APRON (PL-3)

TYP. PARTITION

TYP. WOOD BASE

⑧ SECTION @ PHONE COUNTER
18.2   SCALE: 1" = 1'-0"

FIGURE 10-15 Detailed sections can be cut through items such as cabinetry, and also show the adjacent building structure.

section or part of it is drawn at a large scale to clearly show the items, as seen in Figure 10-15. The scale of details and partial section drawings are usually at a minimum of ½" = 1'-0" (1:20 metric) and can range to a drawing scaled to full size. These detailed sections are cross-referenced to other drawings, indicating where the assembly is located within the whole.

Checklist for Section Drawings

General

- Title the drawing and note its scale.

- Key the drawing to other sections, plans, or related drawings.

- Pouche areas of the section that cut through a material, if the scale of the drawing permits.

- Make sure materials rendered in section view are commonly recognized graphical symbols, or place a nearby note or key and legend to their meaning.

- Use at least three graphical line weights to visually make the section clearly understandable as to materials shown in section, voids, and objects seen beyond the section cut.

- Check plan for code compliance and ADA requirements and clearances.

- Check plan for LEED certification credits, if applicable.

- Are the drawings clear and readable when reproduced or printed? If not, correct as necessary.

Notations

- Note special materials, features, clearances, alignments, and other important items.

- Call out room/space names or numbers that section refers to.

- Cross-reference the section drawing, carefully checking for accuracy and completeness of information.

- Use manufacturers' templates or CAD images for drawing plumbing fixtures such as water closets and lavatories in the sections where they might show.

- In building and interior sections, draw and note appliances/equipment such as refrigerators, dishwasher, washer/dryer, microwave, trash compactor, etc. If item is not to be supplied by contractor, add note that it is N.I.C. (not in contract).

- Specify or clearly show substitute construction materials.

- Call out (with generic names) wall and cabinet base materials, mirrors, wainscot, moldings, chair rails, and shelves (adjustable or fixed).

- In interior sections, call out generic wall finishes (vinyl, ceramic tile, brick, wood paneling, gypsum board, fabric, etc.), or cross-reference to the finish plans.

- Check for proper heights, lengths, and clearances required for ADA compliance.

Dimensions

- In building and interior sections, add vertical dimensions tying important elements, such as floor levels, together.

- Dimension important items in a horizontal direction where they are not shown on referenced plan views.

- Dimension clearances, alignments, and other controlling factors.

- Dimension ceiling heights, soffits, and other headers.

- Dimension any ADA-related items and clearances.

Purpose of Specialty Drawings

There are a number of components, assemblies, and other specialized items in buildings and interiors that do not fall neatly in commonly recognized groupings such as floor plans, elevations, sections, finish plans, and so on. These elements often require a more detailed drawing and even specialized graphic techniques to fully explain them. These pieces of construction and their details often require a series of views that may be done in plan, elevation, section, and even isometric drawings. In most cases, the designer draws the basic sizes, arrangements, materials, and overall details of these components. Then, many are redrawn in more detail and submitted back to the designer as "shop drawings" done by one of the subcontractors, such as the cabinetmaker or glazing subcontractor. These shop drawings are highly detailed with expanded views and descriptions of the designer's original design intent and construction drawings. An example is shown in Figure 11-1.

Stairs and Ramps

Stairs, ramps, elevators, and escalators provide the flow of traffic to different floor levels within or on the exterior of a structure. Stairs and ramps are often used in buildings three stories in height and less, where elevators and escalators are employed on buildings

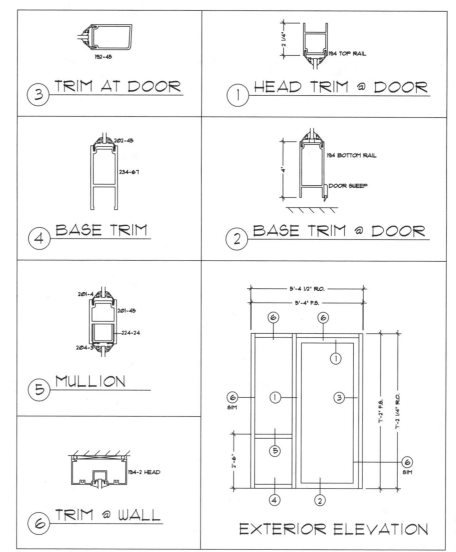

FIGURE 11-1
Shop drawings are highly detailed drawings done by a subcontractor. They show a designer's basic drawing with more detail and expanded views, descriptions, and construction details.

STAIRS

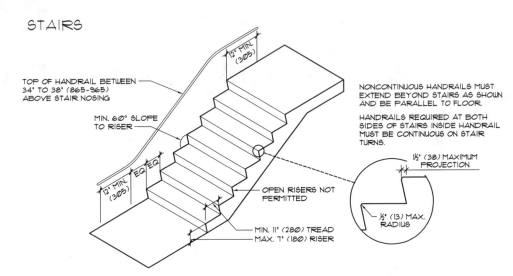

TOP OF HANDRAIL BETWEEN 34" TO 38" (865-965) ABOVE STAIR NOSING

MIN. 60° SLOPE TO RISER

12" MIN. (305)

EQ EQ

12" MIN. (305)

NONCONTINUOUS HANDRAILS MUST EXTEND BEYOND STAIRS AS SHOWN AND BE PARALLEL TO FLOOR

HANDRAILS REQUIRED AT BOTH SIDES OF STAIRS INSIDE HANDRAIL MUST BE CONTINUOUS ON STAIR TURNS.

1½" (38) MAXIMUM PROJECTION

OPEN RISERS NOT PERMITTED

MIN. 11" (280) TREAD
MAX. 7" (180) RISER

½" (13) MAX. RADIUS

FIGURE 11-2 Stair design and construction must meet building code and ADA requirements, including rules on configuration, width, risers, treads, landings, and handrails.

RAMPS

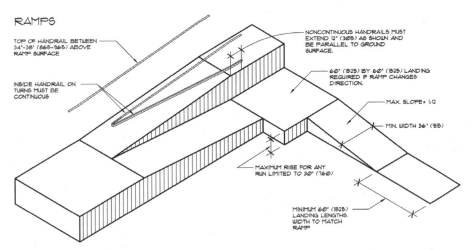

TOP OF HANDRAIL BETWEEN 34"-38" (865-965) ABOVE RAMP SURFACE

INSIDE HANDRAIL ON TURNS MUST BE CONTINUOUS

NONCONTINUOUS HANDRAILS MUST EXTEND 12" (305) AS SHOWN AND BE PARALLEL TO GROUND SURFACE.

60" (1525) BY 60" (1525) LANDING REQUIRED IF RAMP CHANGES DIRECTION.

MAX. SLOPE = 1:12

MIN. WIDTH 36" (915)

MAXIMUM RISE FOR ANY RUN LIMITED TO 30" (760)

MINIMUM 60" (1525) LANDING LENGTHS. WIDTH TO MATCH RAMP

HANDRAILS OMITTED FOR CLARITY, BUT REQUIRED ON BOTH SIDES OF RAMP RUNS WHEN RISE IS OVER 6" (150) OR HORIZONTAL LENGTH IS OVER 72" (1830).

FIGURE 11-3 Ramps must be constructed in accordance with ADA guidelines and building codes. They provide physically disabled individuals with access to different floors.

ings of four floors or more. However, in buildings such as shopping centers, that have high floor-to-floor dimensions and a greater number of people, escalators are commonly used. The design of stairs should provide the least amount of physical strain on people who use them, while reinforcing the design character of the space and structure of the building. Designs can range from major or monumental stairways to stairways that are strictly used for utilitarian purposes.

Stairs are usually constructed from wood, steel, or concrete. Their design and construction must meet a number of building code and ADA requirements for configuration, width, risers, treads, landings, and handrails (Figure 11-2). In many cases, a stair is augmented by a ramp that provides vertical transit for physically impaired individuals or ease of moving heavy objects (Figure 11-3). Interior design projects might involve the design and construction of a new stair or the remodel of an existing stair. Remodeling is often done to upgrade a stair in an older building to meet the current building codes or ADA requirements.

Stairway Configurations and Terms

Stairs may be designed in a number of configurations to suit the amount of space available, the geometry of its layout, and the vertical/horizontal distance they must transverse. The most common stair configurations are shown in Figure 11-4. Their basic arrangements can be described by the following categories: straight run, right-angle run, reversing run, and some form of circular run. Figure 11-5 illustrates some of the most commonly used stair terms, defined below:

Baluster: the vertical component that holds the handrail. These are spaced to prevent people from falling through. These are governed

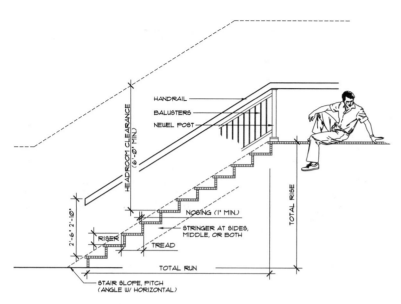

FIGURE 11-5 Typical parts of a stair.

by building codes and are usually a maximum clearance to prevent a 4-inch (101.6-mm) sphere from passing through.

Guardrail: a rail that is used on the landings or floor levels to prevent people from falling between floor levels. It is usually a minimum of 36 inches (.914 m) high in residential and 42 inches (1.066
m) high in commercial buildings.

Handrail: a continuous section of railing adjacent to a stair for a
person to grasp as an aid when ascending or descending the stair.
Building codes closely control whether the railing is on one or
both sides of the stair, its height above the floor, and other
specifics.

Headroom: the minimum clearance between the edge (or nose) of
the tread and any part of an obstruction above.

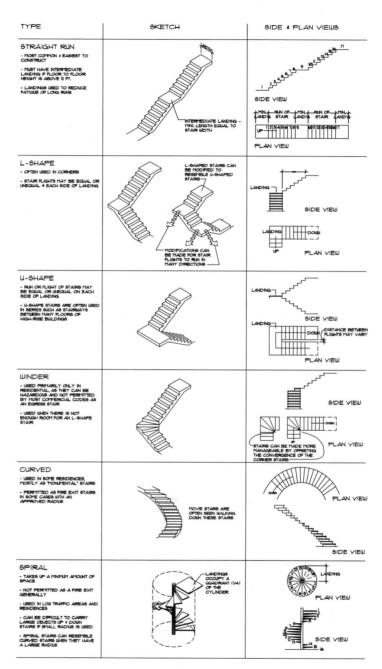

FIGURE 11-4 Stairs can be constructed in a number of different configurations, depending on the amount of space available and the distance between floors.

Landing: the floor or platform at the beginning or end of a stair, or between two or more stair runs.

Newel: the terminating baluster at the bottom or top of a stair, which is usually larger than the other balusters.

Nosing: the part of the tread that overhangs the riser, reducing the problem of a person accidentally kicking the riser as they ascend the stair.

Rise: the total vertical distance that is traveled on a stair. It is the perpendicular measurement between floor levels and is the sum of all the riser heights.

Riser: the vertical part of a stair between the treads.

Run: the total horizontal depth of a stair, which is the sum of the total treads.

Stringer: the structural support for the stair treads and risers. This is also referred to as a carriage. It might be exposed on a utilitarian stair, or hidden with various finishes on more decorative stairs.

Tread: the horizontal part of a stair that the foot bears down upon.

Winder: the wedge-shaped tread in a turn of the stairway run—found mostly in residential work, as commercial building codes restrict these.

Drafting Standards for Stairways

The design and drawing details needed to illustrate a stair are dependent upon the complexity of the stair and the basic structural material it is constructed of. Stair systems are made primarily of wood, steel, or concrete. Wood stairs are mostly used in residential construction and are generally the simplest to draw and

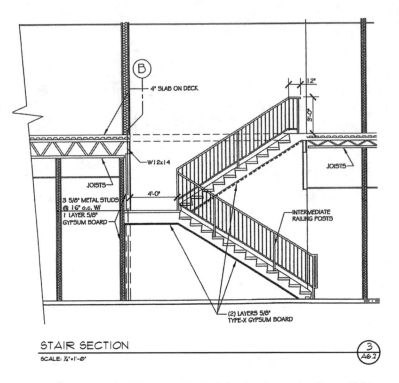

STAIR SECTION
SCALE: ¼"=1'-0"

FIGURE 11-6 Stair sections are often drawn to show the construction and finish details, that cannot be shown in plan views.

detail. Stairs are shown on the floor plans and called out as to their basic widths and number of treads and risers. The plan also shows the stairway with the run and an arrow indicating whether the stairs go up or down from that level. Floor-plan views of stairs often cannot show all the materials and cross-sectional parts of their assemblies. Special stair sections (Figure 11-6) are often drawn to show the construction and finish details. In most cases, the designer does not have to draw every detail of a stairway and its many components. The fabricators of metal, concrete, and some wood stairs often make shop drawings. These detailed drawings are submitted to the designer for review.

Scale of Drawings

The scale of stairway drawings are generally ⅛" = 1'-0" (1:100 metric) or ¼' = 1'-0" (1:50 metric), both in plan and elevation views. The number of treads and risers, as well as their dimensions, are called out here. Generic features such as the handrails and guardrails are also shown in both the plan and elevation views. Generally, handrails seen in elevation views are placed at a uniform height 30 to 34 inches (762 to 864 mm) above the stair nosing. In commercial projects with a steel or concrete stairs, a large-scale drawing and a stair section are required to fully explain these detailed stairs and handrail/guardrail specifics. These are drawn at a scale of at least ½" = 1'-0" (1:20 metric) and cross-referenced to the floor plans.

To determine the number of treads and risers a stair must have, the vertical dimension between each floor level must be known. This vertical dimension is divided by the maximum riser height allowed by the building codes. At this writing, most residential stairs are limited to a maximum riser height of 8 inches (203 mm) and a minimum tread depth width of 9 ¼ inches (235 mm). Commercial codes restrict the maximum height of a riser to 7 inches (178 mm), with a minimum tread depth of 11 inches (280 mm). In a residential building, the typical vertical dimension might be 9'-10" or 106 inches (2.69 m). The designer divides 106 by 8 to find the minimum number of risers needed, which is 13.2. If only 13 are used, each riser will be slightly over 8 inches (203 mm), which is not allowed according to the code. Rounding up to 14 will insure each riser is slightly below the allowed 8 inches (203 mm).

To find the total number of treads, remember that there is always one tread fewer than number of risers, as the floor levels at each stair end are not counted as treads. In our example, there

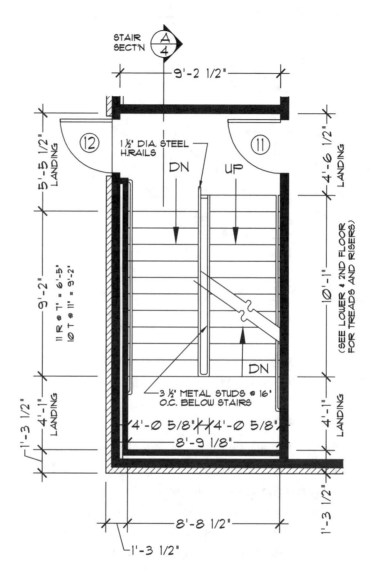

FIGURE 11-7 This enlarged plan of a stairway shows the dimensions of the landings, the widths and the run of each stair, risers, treads, and other details.

FIRST FLOOR STAIRWAY

SC: ½"=1'-0"

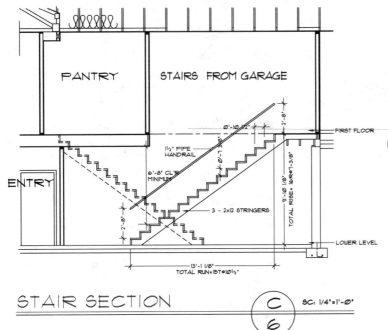

PANTRY   STAIRS FROM GARAGE

ENTRY

FIRST FLOOR

1½" PIPE HANDRAIL

6'-8" CL'R MINIMUM

3 - 2x12 STRINGERS

LOWER LEVEL

TOTAL RISE = 16R@7-3/8"

13'-1 1/8"
TOTAL RUN = 15T@10½"

STAIR SECTION   C / 6   SC: 1/4"=1'-0"

FIGURE 11-8 Stair sections show heights of the stair rise, handrails and other details, cross-referenced to the plan view.

would be 13 treads at 9 inches (229 mm) each, for a resulting stair run of 13 x 9" = 9 feet, 11 inches (3.02 m).

Dimensioning Stairways

Stairways are dimensioned on the floor plans as to their landing sizes, widths, and run of each stair as seen in Figure 11-7. The total number and dimensions of the risers and runs are also shown on the plan. Vertical heights of the stair rise, handrails, and other particulars are dimensioned on a separate section or elevation drawing that is cross-referenced to the plan view (Figure 11-8).

Designation of Materials

A stair's materials can be indicated in a number of different ways, depending upon how many materials there are and complexity of

the construction. Underlying structural materials might be called out with notes or shown in a sectional view. If the structural material is also the finished surface, this should be called out. If a separate finish material covers the stair, these might be called out in the section view, plan view, or on a separate finish plan.

Checklist for Stairways

General

■ If a separate enlarged drawing is done for the stairway, key it and cross-reference to the floor plans.

■ Show stairs in their entirety where possible, or use break lines where they continue on another floor level.

■ Check stair widths, riser heights, tread widths, landing widths, and other particulars against the appropriate building codes and ADA requirements. Verify required dimensions and clearances.

■ Call for submission of shop drawings for specialized stairs where required. This might include metal stairs and premanufactured units.

■ Check plan for code compliance and ADA requirements and clearances.

■ Are the drawings clear and readable when reproduced or printed? If not, correct as necessary.

Notations

■ Call out direction of travel (up or down) on each section of stairway and indicate with an arrow.

■ Note handrails and other trim. Key to where these can be found in more detail.

■ Call out materials where stairs are shown in section view, including structural and finish components.

■ Cross-reference to any structural plans where they are provided.

Dimensions

■ Call out number and widths of treads, as well as number and height of risers.

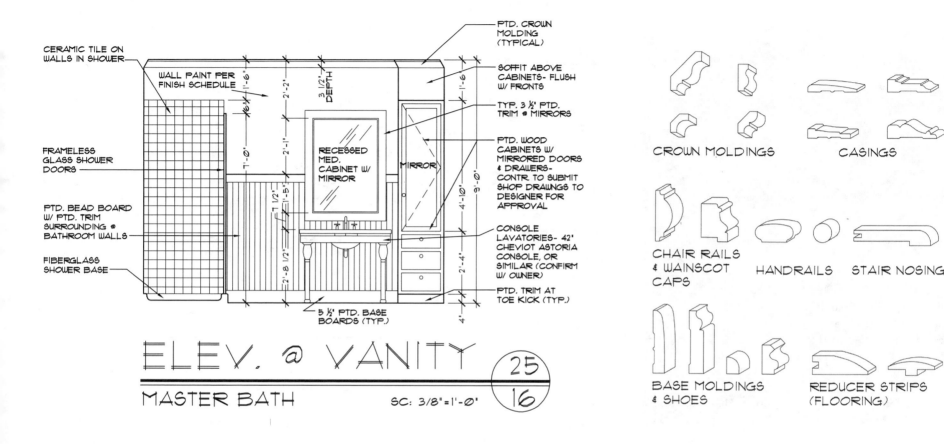

CERAMIC TILE ON WALLS IN SHOWER

WALL PAINT PER FINISH SCHEDULE

FRAMELESS GLASS SHOWER DOORS

PTD. BEAD BOARD W/ PTD. TRIM SURROUNDING @ BATHROOM WALLS

FIBERGLASS SHOWER BASE

PTD. CROWN MOLDING (TYPICAL)

SOFFIT ABOVE CABINETS- FLUSH W/ FRONTS

TYP. 3 ½' PTD. TRIM @ MIRRORS

PTD. WOOD CABINETS W/ MIRRORED DOORS & DRAWERS- CONTR. TO SUBMIT SHOP DRAWINGS TO DESIGNER FOR APPROVAL

CONSOLE LAVATORIES- 42' CHEVIOT ASTORIA CONSOLE, OR SIMILAR (CONFIRM W/ OWNER)

PTD. TRIM AT TOE KICK (TYP.)

5 ½' PTD. BASE BOARDS (TYP.)

RECESSED MED. CABINET W/ MIRROR

MIRROR

ELEV. @ VANITY
MASTER BATH
SC: 3/8"=1'-0"   25/16

CROWN MOLDINGS   CASINGS

CHAIR RAILS & WAINSCOT CAPS   HANDRAILS   STAIR NOSING

BASE MOLDINGS & SHOES   REDUCER STRIPS (FLOORING)

- **Dimension the total run of stairs in both plan and section views.**

- **Dimension the width of the stairs and any landings.**

- **Dimension treads, nosings, risers, landings, and handrail locations in sectional views of stairways.**

Millwork

Many interior designers have a commitment of designing millwork that is sensitive to the prevention of the deforestation of global rain forests. They specify appropriate woods for projects that will help old wood growth and encourage new wood harvesting from sustainable forests. Many alternative products are now made that use a fraction of the original forest wood, combining laminates, veneers, glues, and dyes to produce lumber products that can look and perform as well as the original wood species.

Architectural plans are often drawn at a scale too small to show adequate detail for cabinetry and millwork such as moldings, paneling, miscellaneous trim, and casings for doors and win-

FIGURE 11-9 (left) This large scale drawing shows the placement of stock manufactured base cabinets.

FIGURE 11-10 (right) Molding trim comes in a variety of styles, sizes, materials, and finishes depending on their application.

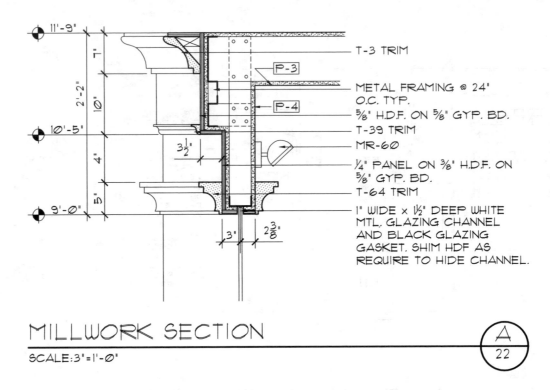

T-3 TRIM

P-3

METAL FRAMING @ 24"
O.C. TYP.

⅝" H.D.F. ON ⅝" GYP. BD.

P-4

T-39 TRIM

MR-60

¼" PANEL ON ⅜" H.D.F. ON
⅝" GYP. BD.

T-64 TRIM

1" WIDE × ½" DEEP WHITE
MTL. GLAZING CHANNEL
AND BLACK GLAZING
GASKET. SHIM HDF AS
REQUIRE TO HIDE CHANNEL.

11'-9"

7"

2'-2"

10'-5"

10"

4"

9'-0"

5"

3½"

3"   2⅜"

MILLWORK SECTION

SCALE: 3"=1'-0"

A
22

FIGURE 11-11 Molding trim is produced in standard shapes and wood species, as noted in this section detail.

dows. These components are drawn and detailed at a large scale and cross-referenced to the basic plans. Millwork and cabinetry, also referred to as architectural woodwork, can include both manufactured stock components, and custom woodwork that is assembled on the job site (Figure 11-9). Although some designers include cabinetry under the category of millwork, it will be treated here as a separate classification due to the specialized drawings needed to describe it.

A variety of styles, sizes, materials, and finishes are used in the construction of millwork, as shown in Figure 11-10. Molding trim is produced in standard shapes and wood species by a manufacturer, or milled and assembled on the job site as a custom fit (Figure 11-11). These include wall base, door and window casings,

cornices, chair rails, handrails, and a number of other applications. In custom work, a mill shop is responsible for the prefabrication of the assemblies in sections. Specialized drawings, called shop drawings, are made by the mill shop for the designer to review. These drawings show in detail how each component is constructed and how the various sections can be assembled on the job site.

Scale of Drawing

Millwork elements are drawn simplistically in small-scale drawings with reference to a large-scale rendering to show the exact details of the component (Figure 11-12). Particular attention should be paid in the drawing details to show both the desired aesthetic results and incorporate the methods of construction.

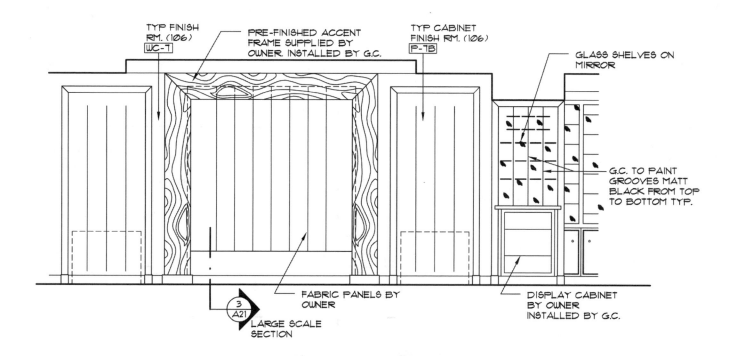

TYP FINISH
RM. (106)
WC-7

PRE-FINISHED ACCENT
FRAME SUPPLIED BY
OWNER. INSTALLED BY G.C.

TYP CABINET
FINISH RM. (106)
P-7B

GLASS SHELVES ON
MIRROR

G.C. TO PAINT
GROOVES MATT
BLACK FROM TOP
TO BOTTOM TYP.

3
A21
LARGE SCALE
SECTION

FABRIC PANELS BY
OWNER

DISPLAY CABINET
BY OWNER
INSTALLED BY G.C.

FIGURE 11-12 **Millwork is
drawn simplistically in small-
scale drawings to show overall
design, and then referenced to
an enlarged scale to show more
details.**

Millwork may include various types of paneling such as wood stile and rail paneling, wood flush paneling, and laminate-faced panels with various sorts of trim pieces, as shown in Figure 11-13. Stile and rail paneling is the traditional kind, where separate panels are contained by solid wood or synthetic-material rails, as illustrated in Figure 11-14. Historically, the panels were made from solid wood, but today they are mostly covered with a thin layer of wood called a veneer. Wood flush paneling consists of veneers glued to backing panels composed of plywood or particleboard. These panels can be glued end to end, producing a larger smooth surface with a minimum of wood trim at the edges or between panel joints. Laminate-faced panels are constructed similar to wood veneer panels and are also installed as a smooth flush system or detailed with trims of wood or plastic laminate.

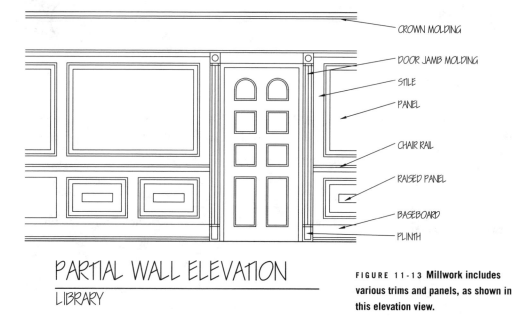

CROWN MOLDING

DOOR JAMB MOLDING

STILE

PANEL

CHAIR RAIL

RAISED PANEL

BASEBOARD

PLINTH

PARTIAL WALL ELEVATION
LIBRARY

FIGURE 11-13 **Millwork includes
various trims and panels, as shown in
this elevation view.**

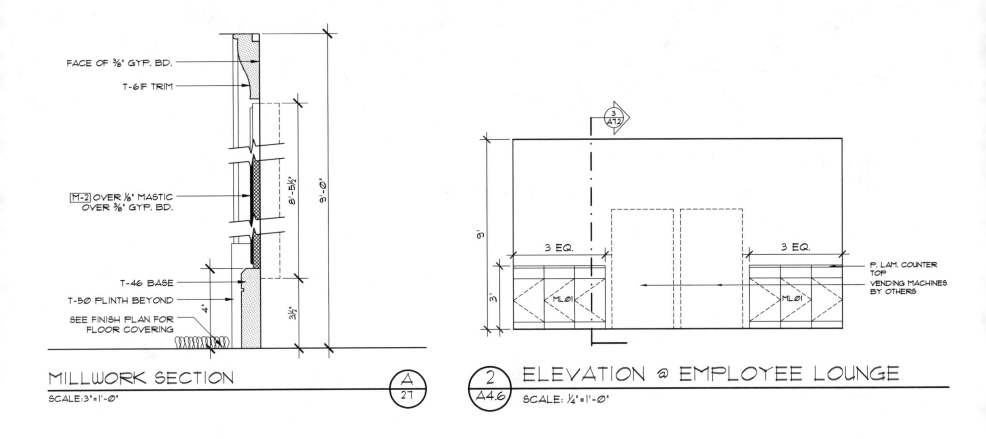

FACE OF ⅜" GYP. BD.

T-61F TRIM

M-2 OVER ⅛" MASTIC OVER ⅜" GYP. BD.

T-46 BASE

T-50 PLINTH BEYOND

SEE FINISH PLAN FOR FLOOR COVERING

8'-5½"

9'-0"

3½"

4"

MILLWORK SECTION

SCALE: 3"=1'-0"

Ⓐ 27

3 A1.2

9'

3'

3 EQ.

3 EQ.

P. LAM. COUNTER TOP

VENDING MACHINES BY OTHERS

MLØ1

MLØ1

② **ELEVATION @ EMPLOYEE LOUNGE**

A4.6

SCALE: ¼"=1'-0"

FIGURE 11-14 (left) Sections through a wall enable the designer to show exact dimensions, materials, and style of various types of paneling and trim pieces.

FIGURE 11-15 (right) Elevations of cabinetry millwork show the extent of the assemblies, and section marks are cross-referenced to section drawings of the millwork.

All of the panel systems are generally drawn in elevation views at ⅛", ¼", or ½" scales, (1:100, 1:50, 1:20 metric) depending upon the complexity and size of the assembly.

Drafting Standards

Millwork is generally drawn in plan view, and if the floor plan drawing scale is too small to effectively show the components of the millwork, the plan is also keyed to a large-scale plan view. Elevations are also drawn and keyed to the plan view to show the extent of the millwork. In some cases, wood grains may be indi-

cated on the elevation views, as well as panel shapes and joinery. Section marks are then added to the elevations (Figure 11-15) and cross-referenced to enlarged details of the panel trims and joints, as illustrated in Figure 11-16. Millwork sections show materials and tolerances needed.

Designation of Materials

Millwork can be drawn at a number of different scales, depending on the size and complexity of the installation. The rendering of the materials will depend upon the scale of the drawings and what material can be designated without complicating or over-rendering the drawing. Generally, outlines of assemblies are dark, changes in planes are lighter, and any textures that are rendered are done in the lightest line weights. The material features are not necessarily drawn to scale with the rest of the drawing. For example, a tight wood grain is suggested with a few lines, rather than drawn accurately, as attempting to render the material to scale could produce a muddy, unreadable drawing. In most cases, notes are added to describe materials that are too complex or small in scale to draw well.

Dimensioning Millwork

Millwork drawings are dimensioned both horizontally and vertically. Overall dimensions are provided to indicate the limits of the millwork. Then, detailed dimensions are added to fully explain sizes, clearances, and tolerances of the assemblies. In some cases, an enlarged detail or other drawing is needed to fully detail something that is too small to see in the basic drawing. Figures 11-14 and 11-15 illustrate basic dimensioning standards.

Checklist for Drawing Millwork

General

- Title the drawings and note scale drawn at below the assembly.

- Use symbols to cross-reference detailed drawings to the floor plans and other drawings.

- Draw the outline (profile) of the objects darker than the textures and minor plane changes. Try to use at least three line weights in the drawings.

- Call for the submission of shop drawings to designer for approval of specialized millwork assemblies.

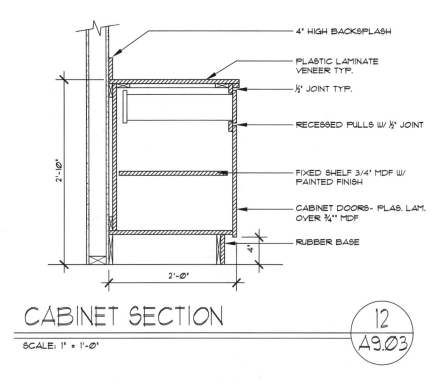

CABINET SECTION

SCALE: 1" = 1'-0"

12 / A9.03

- Pouche materials shown in cross-section, where the scale of the drawing allows this.

- Check plan for code compliance and ADA requirements and clearances.

- Check plan for LEED certification credits, if applicable.

- Are the drawings clear and readable when reproduced or printed? If not, correct as necessary.

Notations

- Note materials, clearances, and other items that need to be cross-referenced to these drawings. For example, the cabinet width might be dimensioned and a note added to verify with the floor plan dimensions.

- Call out related objects that fit within or adjacent to the millwork. These might include doorframes, mirrors, wall bases, hardware, etc.

- Call out generic sizes of manufactured millwork or list the model numbers.

FIGURE 11-16 Millwork sections show details such as materials and tolerances needed, as well as panel trims and joints.

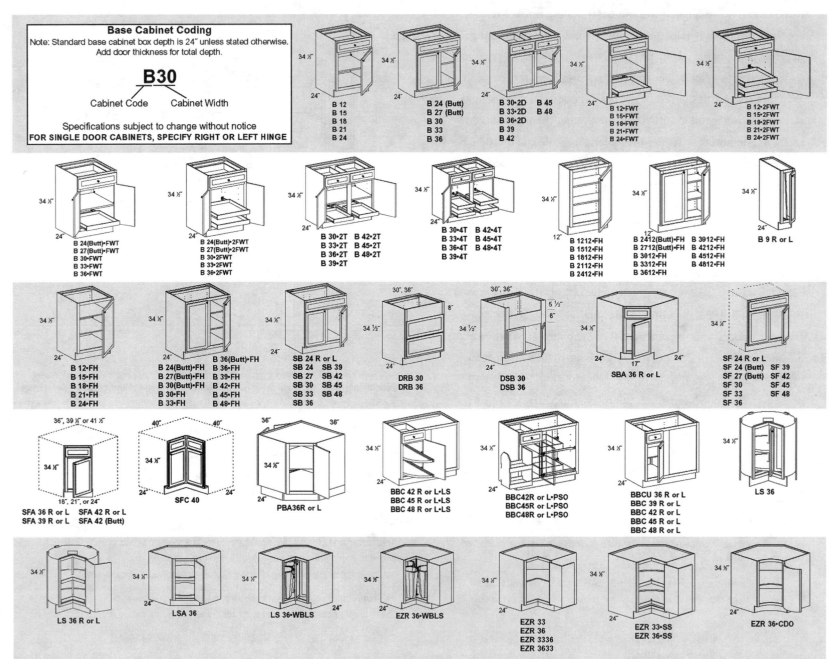

Base Cabinet Coding

Note: Standard base cabinet box depth is 24″ unless stated otherwise.
Add door thickness for total depth.

B30

Cabinet Code   Cabinet Width

Specifications subject to change without notice
FOR SINGLE DOOR CABINETS, SPECIFY RIGHT OR LEFT HINGE

B 12
B 15
B 18
B 21
B 24

B 24 (Butt)
B 27 (Butt)
B 30
B 33
B 36

B 30•2D   B 45
B 33•2D   B 48
B 36•2D
B 39
B 42

B 12•FWT
B 15•FWT
B 18•FWT
B 21•FWT
B 24•FWT

B 12•2FWT
B 15•2FWT
B 18•2FWT
B 21•2FWT
B 24•2FWT

B 24(Butt)•FWT
B 27(Butt)•FWT
B 30•FWT
B 33•FWT
B 36•FWT

B 24(Butt)•2FWT
B 27(Butt)•2FWT
B 30•2FWT
B 33•2FWT
B 36•2FWT

B 30•2T   B 42•2T
B 33•2T   B 45•2T
B 36•2T   B 48•2T
B 39•2T

B 30•4T   B 42•4T
B 33•4T   B 45•4T
B 36•4T   B 48•4T
B 39•4T

B 1212•FH
B 1512•FH
B 1812•FH
B 2112•FH
B 2412•FH

B 2412(Butt)•FH   B 3912•FH
B 2712(Butt)•FH   B 4212•FH
B 3012•FH   B 4512•FH
B 3312•FH   B 4812•FH
B 3612•FH

B 9 R or L

B 12•FH
B 15•FH
B 18•FH
B 21•FH
B 24•FH

B 24(Butt)•FH   B 36•FH
B 27(Butt)•FH   B 39•FH
B 30(Butt)•FH   B 42•FH
B 30•FH   B 45•FH
B 33•FH   B 48•FH
B 36(Butt)•FH

SB 24 R or L
SB 24   SB 39
SB 27   SB 42
SB 30   SB 45
SB 33   SB 48
SB 36

DRB 30
DRB 36

DSB 30
DSB 36

SBA 36 R or L

SF 24 R or L
SF 24 (Butt)   SF 39
SF 27 (Butt)   SF 42
SF 30   SF 45
SF 33   SF 48
SF 36

SFA 36 R or L   SFA 42 R or L
SFA 39 R or L   SFA 42 (Butt)

SFC 40

PBA36R or L

BBC 42 R or L•LS
BBC 45 R or L•LS
BBC 48 R or L•LS

BBC42R or L•PSO
BBC45R or L•PSO
BBC48R or L•PSO

BBCU 36 R or L
BBC 39 R or L
BBC 42 R or L
BBC 45 R or L
BBC 48 R or L

LS 36

LS 36 R or L

LSA 36

LS 36•WBLS

EZR 36•WBLS

EZR 33
EZR 36
EZR 3336
EZR 3633

EZR 33•SS
EZR 36•SS

EZR 36•CDO

FIGURE 11-17
Manufactured cabinets are made in standard sizes and styles, which are listed in catalogs.

Dimensions

- **Dimension important heights, widths, and limits of the millwork.**

- **Dimension radii, thickness, and clearances of all millwork assemblies.**

- **Dimension millwork in relation to built-in features of the building, such as window sizes, door openings, etc.**

Cabinetry

Cabinetry includes base and wall cabinets, shelving, desks, planters, mantles, dividers, and many other special items. Cabinetry might be manufactured as a prebuilt unit, partially made at the factory and site-finished, or totally custom-built on site. Manufactured cabinets are made in standard sizes and styles. These are listed in catalogs (often available on the Internet), so the designers and builders can coordinate them into their plans (Figure 11-17). Manufactured cabinetry is available in both stock configurations and finishes, and as semi-custom units with options on door and drawer types, configurations, and other details.

Cabinetry can be designed and built in a variety of ways. However, two standard methods of construction are rail and stile and solid construction, as illustrated in Figure 11-18. Cabinetry materials and construction methods are further classified as grades, consisting of Economy, Custom, and Premium, as defined in detail by the Architectural Woodwork Institute (AWI). Economy is the lowest grade in materials and manufacturing, while Premium is the highest and most expensive. The quality and durability of the finishes, joints, fasteners, and hardware also vary greatly according to the grade.

Cabinets are generally manufactured and placed at the job site without a countertop. The countertop is then field-fitted to the

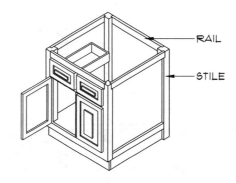

RAIL AND STILE

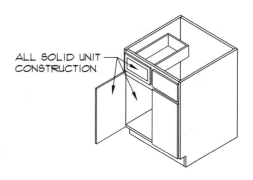

SOLID CONSTRUCTION

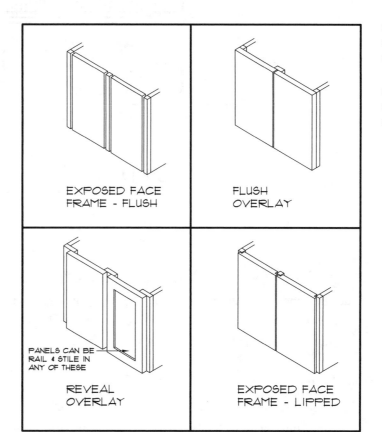

EXPOSED FACE FRAME - FLUSH

FLUSH OVERLAY

REVEAL OVERLAY

EXPOSED FACE FRAME - LIPPED

FIGURE 11-18 (above) There are two basic methods of constructing cabinetry.

FIGURE 11-19 (left) Cabinetry uses four basic types of door and drawer fronts.

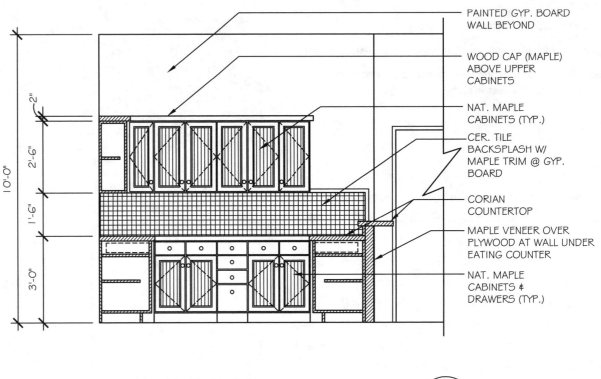

PAINTED GYP. BOARD
WALL BEYOND

WOOD CAP (MAPLE)
ABOVE UPPER
CABINETS

NAT. MAPLE
CABINETS (TYP.)

CER. TILE
BACKSPLASH W/
MAPLE TRIM @ GYP.
BOARD

CORIAN
COUNTERTOP

MAPLE VENEER OVER
PLYWOOD AT WALL UNDER
EATING COUNTER

NAT. MAPLE
CABINETS &
DRAWERS (TYP.)

KITCHEN ELEVATION

SCALE: 3/8" = 1'-0"

10
17.2

FIGURE 11-20 Cabinet door and drawer designs can be shown in an elevation view.

cabinet and adjoining surfaces, such as walls. Cabinets are designed and constructed with four basic types of door and drawer fronts. These are flush, flush overlay, reveal overlay, and lipped overlay, as shown in Figure 11-19.

Scale of Drawing

The floor-plan and elevation drawings only show the outline and major features of cabinetry. Large-scale drawings are then made

showing detailed construction and installation requirements. These are cross-referenced to the basic drawings. Cabinetry that is factory-built is closely referenced to major placement dimensions on the floor plan or elevation.

Drafting Standards

Detailed cabinetry drawings include plan, elevation, sectional, and pictorial views, which are often included with factory-produced components to show their proper placement. When a manufacturer's standard cabinetry is placed on the job site, the floor plan and elevation generally show the cabinet's positioning dimensions. Alternately, these might be shown only in one drawing and referenced to the manufacturer's detailed identification units. In some cases, additional drawings might be needed to fully explain other site-built components that interface with the standard cabinetry.

Custom cabinetry and other important woodwork is described in a separate set of drawings specifying basic features and dimensions. Then, an architectural woodworking contractor will take field measurements and produce shop drawings showing every specific detail and condition. These are often drawn at full scale. These drawings are submitted to the designer and contractor to check against the intent of the construction drawings.

Designation of Materials

Cabinetry is drawn in plan view, elevation view, sectional views, and any other details needed to fully describe the units and their particulars. In plan view, the tops of cabinetry are generally shown if they are less than about 4 feet (122 cm) from the finished floor. In small-scale drawings, the materials for the tops are generally not shown, unless the tops are ceramic tile or stone that needs rendering designations.

In elevation views of cabinetry, material designations will depend primarily on the scale of the drawing and how items such as door and drawer designs can be effectively shown, as illustrated in Figure 11-20. Textures and wood grain designations are possible in large-scale drawings; drawing them can be time-consuming. Most cabinetry elevations are treated simplistically with line varieties and are held to a minimum of detailing to designate materials and shapes of doors, drawers, and other decorative items.

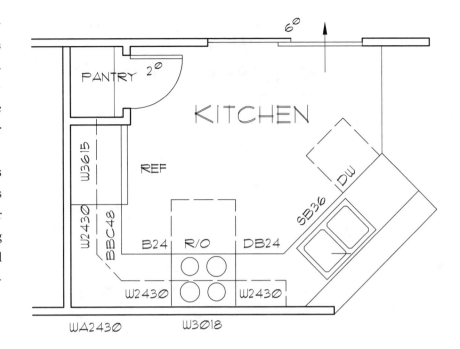

FIGURE 11-21 Sizes of wall and base cabinets may be designated with the common manufactured component sizes.

Notes can be added to call out materials and features versus drawing exact items, such as paneled doors and decorative handles.

In sectional views of cabinetry, material designation is done in a manner discussed in Chapter 10. Again, the scale of the drawing will dictate to what extent it is possible to delineate materials.

Dimensioning Cabinetry

Cabinetry can be dimensioned in a number of different ways. First, if the cabinetry is built in, it is shown on the floor plan. Overall dimensions are given here to match the size of the unit to its location in the building. In turn, symbols or notes might be used to

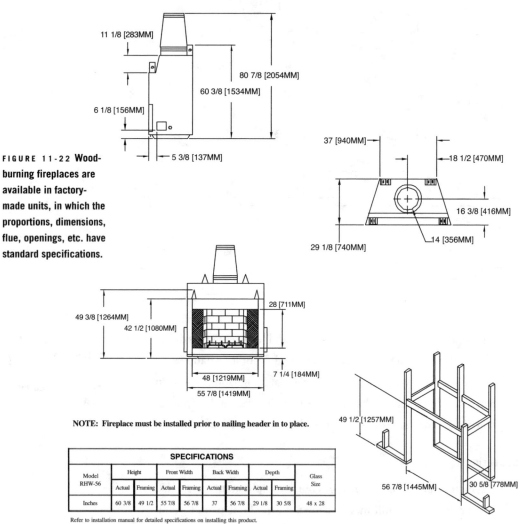

RHW-56
56" ROYAL HEARTH FIREPLACE

11 1/8 [283MM]

80 7/8 [2054MM]

60 3/8 [1534MM]

6 1/8 [156MM]

5 3/8 [137MM]

FIGURE 11-22 Wood-burning fireplaces are available in factory-made units, in which the proportions, dimensions, flue, openings, etc. have standard specifications.

37 [940MM]

18 1/2 [470MM]

16 3/8 [416MM]

14 [356MM]

29 1/8 [740MM]

49 3/8 [1264MM]

42 1/2 [1080MM]

28 [711MM]

48 [1219MM]

7 1/4 [184MM]

55 7/8 [1419MM]

49 1/2 [1257MM]

56 7/8 [1445MM]

30 5/8 [778MM]

NOTE: Fireplace must be installed prior to nailing header in to place.

SPECIFICATIONS									
Model RHW-56	Height		Front Width		Back Width		Depth		Glass Size
	Actual	Framing	Actual	Framing	Actual	Framing	Actual	Framing	
Inches	60 3/8	49 1/2	55 7/8	56 7/8	37	56 7/8	29 1/8	30 5/8	48 x 28

Refer to installation manual for detailed specifications on installing this product.

cross-reference this small-scale plan view to a larger and more detailed plan view. Also, an elevation or section symbol is drawn on the floor plan and referenced to a large-scale elevation or section view of each exposed cabinet face. In a large-scale elevation drawing, important vertical heights are dimensioned. Horizontal dimensions might be also added if necessary for clarity. This depends primarily on the office standards that are adopted by the firm or individual. Some firms designate the cabinet widths with short-hand for the common manufactured component sizes (Figure 11-21). For example, a 24-inch-wide base cabinet might be designated B24, an 18-inch-wide drawer base cabinet would be DB18, and a 24-inch-wide wall cabinet that is 30 inches high would be a W2430.

Checklist for Cabinetry

General

■ Title the drawings and note their scale.

■ Cross-reference the drawings (with correct symbols) to floor plans and other related drawings.

■ Adopt commonly accepted designations of materials and their rendering techniques.

■ Vary graphical line weights to visually make the plan, elevation, and sectional drawings clearly understandable. Draw the outline (profile) of elevation or plan nice and dark, as it represents the boundaries of the cabinet.

■ Show direction of cabinet door swings (with dashed line) in elevation views.

■ Differentiate between drawers and fixed panels.

■ Check cabinetry for adherence to required code compliances and/or ADA requirements. This includes dimensions, clearances, and materials.

- Check plan for **LEED** certification credits, if applicable.
- Are the drawings clear and readable when reproduced or printed? If not, correct as necessary.

Notations

- Use notes to describe special materials, features, clearances, alignments, and other important items.
- In elevation views, call out tops, bases, toe kicks, backsplashes, end splashes, and other features of the cabinetry.
- Note shelves, brackets, and other items related to the cabinetry.
- Call out generic sizes of manufactured wall and base cabinets.
- Where necessary, add notes to the drawings for the contractor to field measure and verify existing dimensions and clearances of cabinetry (before ordering or installing them).

Dimensions

- Dimension important heights of major items such as base and wall cabinets.
- Dimension toe spaces and height of space between base cabinets and wall cabinets, and other important clearances.
- Dimension miscellaneous items such as grab bars, clearances, and spacing of shelving.

Fireplaces

Traditionally, fireplaces have been constructed to burn wood as a heat source and for the cooking of meals. Today, we still use fireplaces for some heat, but modern mechanical systems have taken over the need to warm ourselves totally by an open flame. However, many people still like the look and feel of the heat from a roaring fire. We now find fireplaces being constructed primarily as a visual element rather than for heating. To this end, the gas fireplace was invented to produce a flame similar to the wood-burning units, but without the need to collect and burn wood, and

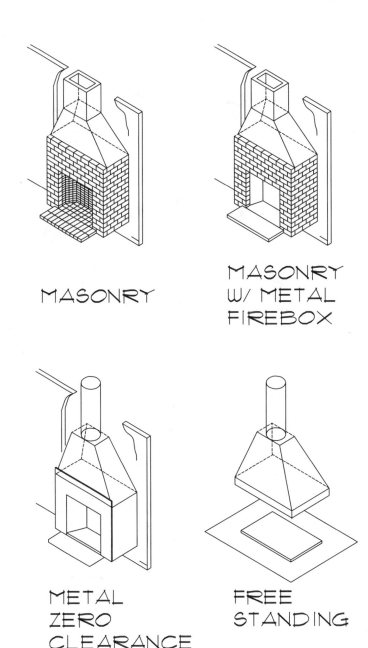

MASONRY

MASONRY W/ METAL FIREBOX

METAL ZERO CLEARANCE

FREE STANDING

FIGURE 11-23 The four types of wood-burning fireplaces.

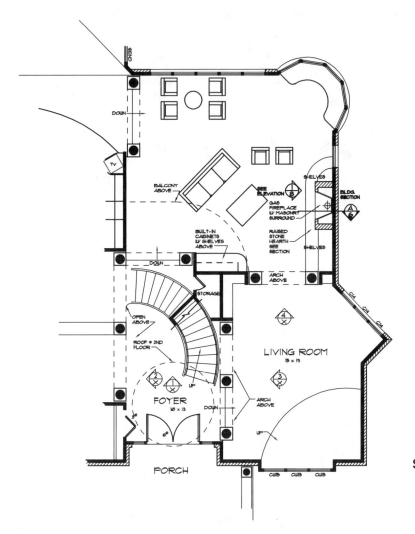

FIGURE 11-24 **Fireplace in floor-plan view.**

sions of such fireplaces and their various parts, such as the flue and openings, are based upon the laws of nature of heat transfer, and the various building codes. These features have been developed over the years. Their dimensions are tabulated for site-built units and are provided by the manufacturers for their factory-made units (Figure 11-22).

Today, wood-burning fireplaces are of four basic types: those completely constructed on-site; those consisting of a manufactured firebox that is covered with masonry on the job site, prebuilt metal units (commonly called zero-clearance models); and free-standing units (Figure 11-23), including both fireplaces and wood-burning stoves. Site-constructed units and some of the heavier types require a structural support or foundation to rest on. Most such foundations are of concrete construction.

Gas fireplaces are manufactured as modular units and are offered with a variety of openings, similar to the wood-burning units. Vented units are sealed from the interior space and have a small round pipe that vents the fumes to the exterior, either vertically or horizontally through an exterior wall. Nonvented models are completely sealed, with no exhausting of fumes.

Scale of Drawing

The floor plans usually show the location of the fireplace, its hearth, and basic dimensions at a scale of $\frac{1}{8}" = 1'-0"$ (1:100 metric) or $\frac{1}{4}"=1'-0"$ (1:50 metric). These plan views are simplistic, as shown in Figure 11-24, and usually cross-referenced to more detailed drawings done at a larger scale . For example, if the fireplace is a wood-burning masonry unit, large-scale drawings are needed to more fully describe the dimensions and materials of the assembly.

remove ashes of the wood fuel. In fact, there is now more of an emphasis on using gas fireplaces versus wood-burning units for both convenience and reduction of air pollution.

Wood-burning fireplaces have been constructed for centuries by skilled masons and bricklayers. The proportions and dimen-

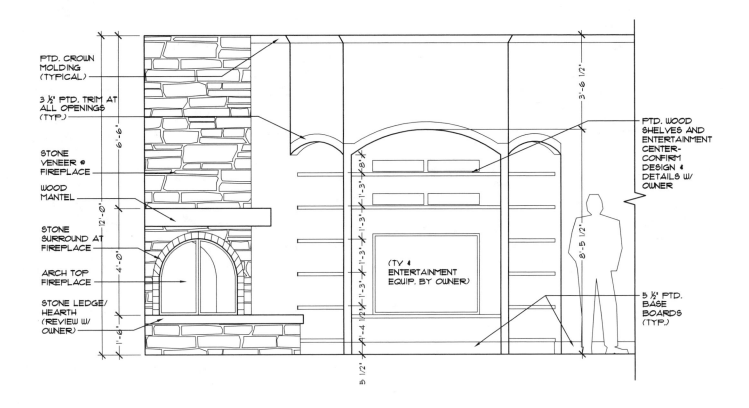

PTD. CROWN
MOLDING
(TYPICAL)

3 ½' PTD. TRIM AT
ALL OPENINGS
(TYP.)

STONE
VENEER @
FIREPLACE

WOOD
MANTEL

STONE
SURROUND AT
FIREPLACE

ARCH TOP
FIREPLACE

STONE LEDGE/
HEARTH
(REVIEW W/
OWNER)

PTD. WOOD
SHELVES AND
ENTERTAINMENT
CENTER-
CONFIRM
DESIGN &
DETAILS W/
OWNER

(TV &
ENTERTAINMENT
EQUIP. BY OWNER)

5 ½' PTD.
BASE
BOARDS
(TYP.)

FIGURE 11-25 **The fireplace, hearth, and mantle are shown in the great room as well as in the entertainment area of the basement in this building section.**

Drafting Standards

The design of a fireplace often requires a series of drawings that show the plan views, elevation views, and sections through the firebox. Materials are noted in these drawings, as well as the size of the openings, hearths, chimneys, and other particulars. The plan drawings are referenced to an elevation of the fireplace and are further cross-referenced to more detailed large-scale drawings.

For wood-burning, built-in masonry fireplaces, the drawings are placed in the construction set. Many zero-clearance wood-burning units and gas fireplaces are predrawn by the manufacturer and are just referred to and included with the designer's drawings. There is no need to redraw all of these details.

Designation of Materials

The materials a fireplace is made of might be shown in a number of different places, as one drawing is generally not enough to accurately describe the unit. The floor plan might show the hearth material and fireplace wall construction, using cross-hatching to represent masonry and firebrick liners. Hearth sizes should be noted for wood-burning units, and further notations added for noncombustible trim work around the fireplace. Building sections and/or interior elevations would show the design and materials of the front of the fireplace as well as the mantle, such as in Figure 11-25.

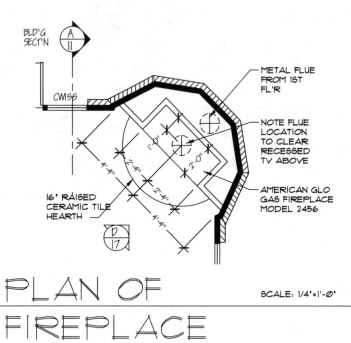

BLD'G SECT'N A/11

CW155

METAL FLUE FROM IST FL'R

NOTE FLUE LOCATION TO CLEAR RECESSED TV ABOVE

AMERICAN GLO GAS FIREPLACE MODEL 2456

16' RAISED CERAMIC TILE HEARTH

D/17

PLAN OF FIREPLACE

SCALE: 1/4"=1'-∅'

FIGURE 11-26 Plan view of fireplace showing flues and vertical chases.

Dimensioning Fireplaces

The floor plan is dimensioned as to the exact size and location of the exterior surface of the fireplace unit, whether it is of masonry or prefabricated metal. Flues and their vertical chase spaces are dimensioned on floor plans that are above the fireplace, as illustrated in Figure 11-26. Other dimensions would include hearth sizes and minimum clearances to adjacent combustible materials.

Checklist for Fireplace Drawings

General

- Draw the firebox to scale in the plan view and cross-reference to other drawings that show more detail.

- Draw or note the flue (if required) and where it is routed through the building structure.

- Draw and note the size of the hearth.

- Check plan for code compliance and ADA requirements and clearances.

- Check plan for LEED certification credits, if applicable.

- Are the drawings clear and readable when reproduced or printed? If not, correct as necessary.

Notations

- Call out the basic materials of the fireplace and the hearth. Note if the hearth is raised or flush with the floor.

- Key the plan view with appropriate elevation and section views where other drawings are used to fully delineate the fireplace particulars.

- In elevation views, call out the surrounding materials and features adjacent to the basic fireplace. This could include mantles, trim work, cabinetry, or other features.

- Cross-reference to finish plans and other details, as necessary.

Dimensions

- Dimension the fireplace general firebox opening size, or designate the manufacturer's model number (for premanufactured units), which in turn gives the proper dimensions.

- In elevation views, dimension the size and location of any mantles over the fireplace opening.

- Dimension or call out the size of the hearth.

- Dimension the firebox to any required clearances to wood or other combustible materials.

Doors

Doors perform a variety of operating and aesthetic features in a building. They can serve as a link between interior spaces; controlling physical access and influencing movement from space to space. Designing the door and its parts requires a systematic series of decisions that address the functional and aesthetic needs of assembly to meet the users' needs, including fire and safety requirements. The door size should be appropriately scaled to permit passage of people and any furnishings or equipment. The location of the door along a wall is also a design decision that must address the traffic patterns of the users, placement of objects (such as desks) near the door, visual impact of the door assembly, and consideration of possible confliction of the door operation. Aesthetically, the door, its frame, and hardware can also augment the design features of the interiors.

Doors and their frames are standardized for interior usage, although they can be made to meet customized details as a designer creates a unique solution for a project.

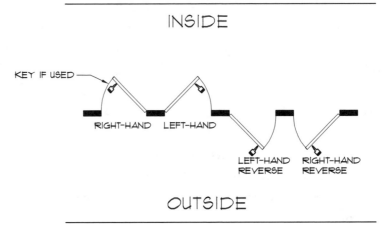

FIGURE 12-1 **There are four ways or hands that doors are beveled and hardware is made to match that particular configuration.**

Door Classifications: Operation, Types, and Materials

Doors are classified by their operation, which is the unique way a door opens and closes (see Figure 7-17). Each type allows the designer to select the most appropriate door for the project solution. These issues encompass how the door controls passage, how much use the door will receive, and other acoustical, visual, weather tightness requirements. In addition to these requirements, the door assembly can be designed to provide ventilation, security, and fire/smoke resistance from space to space.

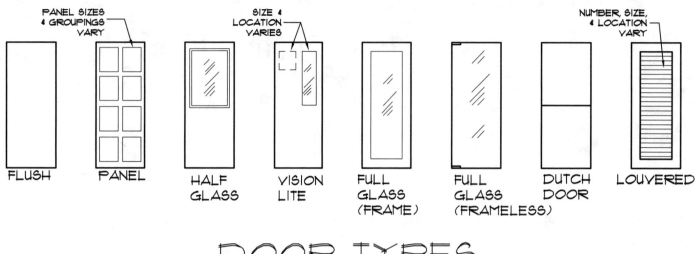

FIGURE 12-2 Door styles are made as variations from these eight basic types.

PANEL SIZES & GROUPINGS VARY

SIZE & LOCATION VARIES

NUMBER, SIZE, & LOCATION VARY

FLUSH   PANEL   HALF GLASS   VISION LITE   FULL GLASS (FRAME)   FULL GLASS (FRAMELESS)   DUTCH DOOR   LOUVERED

DOOR TYPES

Swinging doors are referred to as either right or left handed, depending upon the direction of the door swing. This nomenclature helps the designer work with the hardware suppliers in determining the specific hardware that must be supplied for a specific door's directional swing. However, some hardware can work on any hand of door and is considered *nonhanded* or *reversible.* Door hand is determined by standing on the exterior of the building or the side from which security is desired. In a corridor leading to a room or series of rooms, the door hand is viewed from the corridor side. Handing for a closet or storage door is viewed from the room side. There are four distinct "hands" of doors—right handed, left handed, right-hand reverse, and left-hand reverse (Figure 12-1). If the distinction cannot be readily apparent between two spaces, the rule of thumb is the outside is considered the side of the door where the hinge pin cannot be seen.

Door Types and Materials

The type and materials of which they are constructed also define doors. The types or styles range from panel, flush, sash (full or partial), and louvered (Figure 12-2). Materials typically are wood, various metals, glass, plastic laminate, and various combinations of these.

Wood is the most prominent material used for door subsurfaces and finishes, but they are also made with metal, glass, and facings such as plastic laminate or other materials (such as aluminum, grass, bronze, and stainless steel). These materials can also be combined in many ways to produce doors with unique features such as metal laminated to wood doors.

Selecting, Designing, and Specifying the Door Assembly

A door assembly is composed of four distinct parts: the door, its frame, the hardware, and the wall or partition in which it is installed. Each part must be carefully coordinated with the others for a proper functioning and aesthetic attribute of the whole assembly. The primary steps in selecting the door assembly parts are:

1. **OPERATION:** Determine the function of the door and how it will open/close. Does it need to meet building code, ADA compliance, and security parameters? How often is it opened and closed, and by whom? Does it need to withstand a lot of abuse not common to most doors?

2. **TYPE AND MATERIAL:** Select the aesthetic/visual look of the door and its features, such as vision panels, louvers, etc. Determine the most appropriate material for this door. How much maintenance will be required for the door over its lifetime?

3. **SIZE AND DOOR THICKNESS:** Determine the door size based on the function and code requirements. Select the door thickness based on whether the door construction is solid, hollow, or made of other composite materials. Generally, hollow core doors are used in the interiors of residential settings, and solid core doors are used in commercial projects.

4. **DOOR FRAME AND WALL INTERFACE:** Decide on the material of the door frame and how it will be installed with the wall substrate and finish. Coordinate the frame for appearance, maintenance, code (fire) requirements, and security needs.

5. **HARDWARE:** Select the appropriate hardware based on use, function, and appearance. Verify if the hardware needs to have fire ratings or security needs to match the door and frame.

Fire-rated door assemblies

Fire protection in buildings can be achieved by completely enclosing spaces with fire barriers, which include firewalls, ceilings, floors, and doors. The fire door is essential to the integrity of the fire barrier, as it presents an access portal to a space that temporarily breaks the fire barrier. To minimize this break in fire protection, fire doors must be self-closing and have proper latching devices to contain the possible spread of fire, smoke, and toxic gases. In cases where the fire door serves as an exit route, a specific type of hardware is used—primarily in Assembly and Educational occupancies. Commonly called a "panic bar," it is a door-latching assembly consisting of a horizontal bar spanning at least half of the door leaf, at waist height. However, not all panic bars are fire rated, and only those specifically labeled should be used on a fire-rated exit.

Fire-rated doors are designed as an entire assembly for the protection of openings in fire-rated walls. The fire rating of the wall dictates the minimum fire-rating classification of the fire door assembly. However, not all doors are fire doors, as they must be certified by a recognized testing laboratory and display the laboratory's certification label. Standards are set by the National Fire Protection Agency (NFPA) to establish minimum standards for each fire-door assembly in a particular rated wall. These standards set the minimum test duration (in hours) a door can withstand exposure to fire test conditions. These standards are listed in a fire door classifications system, which sets the class of the opening (designated by a letter) as seen in Figure 12-3. These ratings are a result of testing in fire conditions established by the Underwriters' Laboratories, Inc., and doors are commonly called "U.L. labeled doors." In general, door assemblies are rated at three-fourths of the rating of the surrounding wall. For example, a 3-hour fire door is used in a 4-hour rated wall, and a 1-½-hour fire door is used in a 2-hour rated wall. However, it is acceptable to use a door with a higher fire rating than the opening requires. For example, a Class "B" fire door can be used in a Class "C" fire door—as long as the glazing restriction is not exceeded.

The maximum size and number of vision lights in a door are controlled by the hourly rating of the door. The vision lights and

U.L. LABEL CLASSIFICATION		WALL FIRE RATING	USAGE OF WALL IN BUILIDNG	MAX. GLASS AREA ALLOWED IN DOOR
A	3 Hour (180 minutes)	4 Hour	Doors dividing fire walls with openings not to exceed 1,299 sq. ft. in area	No glass permitted
B	1 ½ Hour (90 minutes)	2 Hour	Door in vertical shafts with openings not to exceed 1, 200 sq. ft. in area	100 sq. in. per door leaf
C	¾ Hour (45 minutes)	1 Hour	Doors in corridor and room partitions not to exceed 1,200 sq. ft. in area	1,296 sq. in. per door leaf, 54" max. dimension
D	1 ½ Hour (90 minutes)	2 Hour	Doors in exterior walls where potential for severe exterior fire hazard - not to exceed 1,200 sq. ft. in area	No glass permitted
	20 Minute or 1/3 Hour	1Hour	No classification as doors are used primarily in openings of corridors for smoke and draft control	1,296 sq. in. per door leaf, 54" max. dimension

The above requirements must be approved by the code having juridisdiction of the project, as codes vary.

FIGURE 12-3 Fire doors are rated according the fire rating of the wall they are placed in and have restrictions in glass sizes and areas.

their frames must be approved for their use in the appropriate labeled fire door assembly. Glass in fire doors is primarily either ¼ inch wire glass or ceramic glass.

Door Hardware

Interior designers work with hardware consultants or suppliers to select the proper hardware for each door and its function, as well as its aesthetics. Hardware is available in many metals such as aluminum, steel, stainless steel, brass, and bronze. These can also be the finish look of the units, or the finishes can be applied over the base material in many ways. Hardware is selected on five basic requirements: function, accessibility, code requirements, security, and appearance. Door hardware consists of the operating device (latches and locks), the hinges, closers, silencers, pulls, and many other parts that make up a complete hardware group. Door hardware is handed in three ways; handed, reversible, and universal. Handed hardware can only be used on those doors that the hand matches the beveled locks, and cannot be reversed for an opposite-handed door. Reversible hardware can be changed from left to right (or vice versa) by turning the unit upside down or reversing part of the mechanism. Universal hardware, such as a doorstop, can be used on any handed door.

Operating Devices

Operating devices are primarily the latch set or the lockset, although there are a few other specialized devices, such as pull handles and push plates. The latch set holds the door in a closed position and can be either a knob or lever, depending on the style, function, and accessibility required. A lockset can have an angled face similar to the latch set and do the same function, but it physically locks the door in position until opened with a key or other method. There are four types of locksets: mortise (latch bolt-style or deadlock), bored, and unit (preassembled). The American National Standards Institute (ANSI) has set standards for each of these four series of locksets. These locks are provided in three grades as defined for their operation and security desired.

The mortise lock is named for the complete assembly that is installed in a door recess (mortise), thus making it one of the most secure locking units. Mortise locks are installed in a door as a deadbolt and a latch bolt, which can both be retracted with a single operation. They provide a much stronger locking operation than the bored lock and are used in high security areas.

The bored lock is also called a cylindrical lock or latch set, as it is installed by boring holes from the edge and face of the door to receive hardware. Bored locks are the most common of the locksets and are generally the easiest to install. However, they are not as strong as the mortise unit and are often limited to residential or light commercial projects.

The preassembled lock is also referred to as a unit lock, as it is a factory unit that is installed in a reinforced rectangular notch cut into the door edge. It is not commonly used much anymore, however.

Hinges

There are three basic types of door hinges (Figure 12-4): full mortise, half mortise or half surfaced, and full surface. In addition to these, there are specialized hinges such as the spring hinge, which is used on double acting doors such as those in a commercial kitchen. An invisible hinge is mortised (concealed) completely

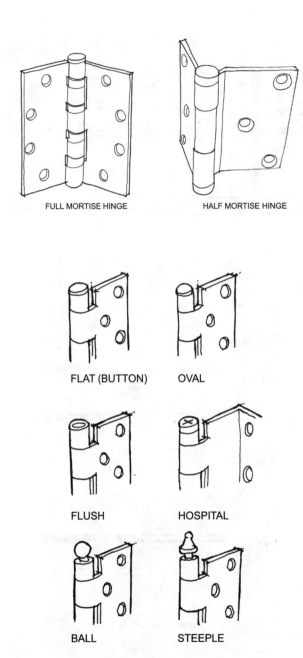

FULL MORTISE HINGE   HALF MORTISE HINGE   FULL SURFACE HINGE

FLAT (BUTTON)   OVAL

FLUSH   HOSPITAL

BALL   STEEPLE

COMMON HINGE PIN TIPS

FIGURE 12-4 (above) Door hinges are manufactured as three basic types, according to how they are mounted to the door and frame.

FIGURE 12-5 (left) Door hinge pins are capped in various ways in relation to their function and style.

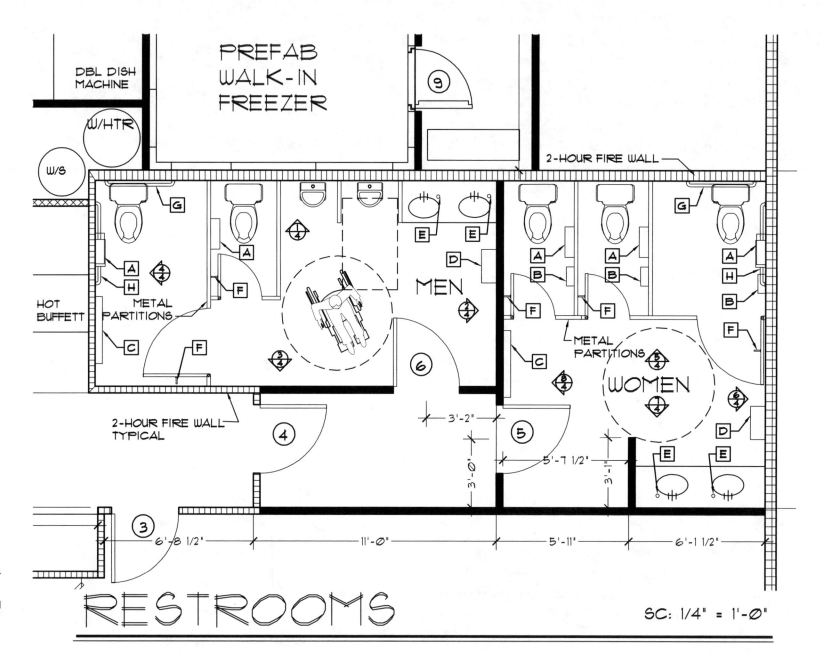

PREFAB
WALK-IN
FREEZER

DBL DISH
MACHINE

W/HTR

W/S

2-HOUR FIRE WALL

MEN

WOMEN

HOT
BUFFETT

METAL
PARTITIONS

METAL
PARTITIONS

2-HOUR FIRE WALL
TYPICAL

3'-2"

3'-0"

5'-7 1/2"

3'-1"

6'-8 1/2"

11'-0"

5'-11"

6'-1 1/2"

RESTROOMS

SC: 1/4" = 1'-0"

FIGURE 12-6 **Doors in a floor plan are numbered or identified by some other designation, which is referenced to a door schedule that includes more detailed information about each door.**

DOOR SCHEDULE

DOOR#	DOOR TYPE	DOOR				FRAME		HARDWARE
		WIDTH	HEIGHT	THICKN'S	MATERIAL	MATERIAL	FINISH	
①	A	6'-0'	6'-8'	1 3/4'	W'D/GLASS	W'D	SS	LOCKSET/CLOSER
②	A	6'-0'	6'-8'	1 3/4'	W'D/GLASS	W'D	SS	LOCKSET/CLOSER
③	B	3'-0'	6'-8'	1 3/4'	W'D	W'D	SS	LATCHSET
④	B	2'-8'	6'-8'	1 3/4'	W'D	W'D	SS	LATCHSET
⑤	B	2'-6'	6'-8'	1 3/4'	W'D	W'D	SS	PRIVACY LOCK
⑥	B	2'-8'	6'-8'	1 3/4'	WD	WD	SS	LATCHSET
⑦	B	2'-4'	6'-8'	1 3/4'	WD	WD	SS	LATCHSET
⑧	B	2'-6'	6'-8'	1 3/4'	WD	WD	SS	LATCHSET/CLOSER
⑨	B	3'-0'	6'-8'	1 3/4'	WD	WD	SS	LATCHSET/CLOSER
⑩	B	2'-4'	6'-8'	1 3/4'	WD	WD	SS	PRIVACY LOCK
⑪	B	2'-8'	6'-8'	1 3/4'	WD	WD	PT	LOCKSET
⑫	B	2'-4'	6'-8'	1 3/4'	WD	WD	SS	PRIVACY
⑬	C	3'-0'	6'-8'	1 3/4'	MT'L/PT	MT'L	PT	LOCKSET
⑭	C	2'-8'	6'-8'	1 3/4'	MT'L/PT	MT'L	PT	LOCKSET
⑮	D	3'-0'	6'-8'	1 3/4'	MT'L/PT	MT'L	PT	LOCKSET/CLOSER
⑯	D	3'-0'	6'-8'	1 3/4'	MT'L/PT	MT'L	PT	LOCKSET

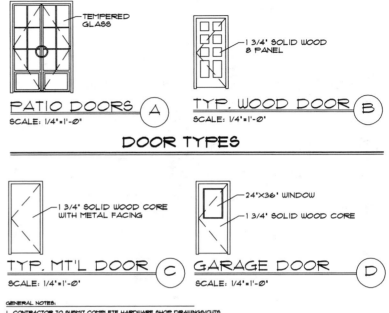

PATIO DOORS Ⓐ — TEMPERED GLASS
SCALE: 1/4"=1'-0'

TYP. WOOD DOOR Ⓑ — 1 3/4' SOLID WOOD 8 PANEL
SCALE: 1/4"=1'-0'

DOOR TYPES

TYP. MT'L DOOR Ⓒ — 1 3/4' SOLID WOOD CORE WITH METAL FACING
SCALE: 1/4"=1'-0'

GARAGE DOOR Ⓓ — 24'X36' WINDOW / 1 3/4' SOLID WOOD CORE
SCALE: 1/4"=1'-0'

GENERAL NOTES:
1. CONTRACTOR TO SUBMIT COMPLETE HARDWARE SHOP DRAWINGS/CUTS AND KEYING SCHEDULE FOR DESIGNERS APPROVAL.

2. SS= STAIN PER DESIGNER'S SAMPLE AND SEAL (TWO COATS MINIMUM)

within the door and frame so that it can't be seen when the door is closed. The specific selection of the hinge type depends on its mounting to the door and frame, the weight of the door, its width, its frequency of use, and the appearance of the hinges. Most hinges are standard pivoting units, whereas heavier doors or usage may require ball bearings in the hinge units. The pin in the hinge can be the most common flat or button, oval, flush, hospital, or decorative (steeple, ball, etc.) as seen in Figure 12-5. The size and number of hinges on a door leaf is dependent not only on the weight of the door, but its height. Generally, a minimum of three hinges (or pairs of hinges, as they are often referred to) are recommended per door leaf. However, some lightweight doors up to 5 feet (1500 mm)

in height might require only two hinges (two pairs). One additional hinge is selected for each 30 inches (750 mm) of additional door height.

Large, heavy doors might also be mounted with continuous "piano" type hinges which provide full support along the entire door edge and frame. Hinges are not the only way to support and operate swinging doors. Pivoting devices are used when a frameless door is used or the door is made to pivot around its center, allowing the door to swing in either direction of a 180 degree (or more) arc. In addition to hinges and pivots, sliding doors and pocket (recessed) doors are provided with tracks and rollers at the top and often the bottom.

FIGURE 12-7 Door schedules, for residential projects, contain information such as the door number, quantity required, size, type of door, material and remarks.

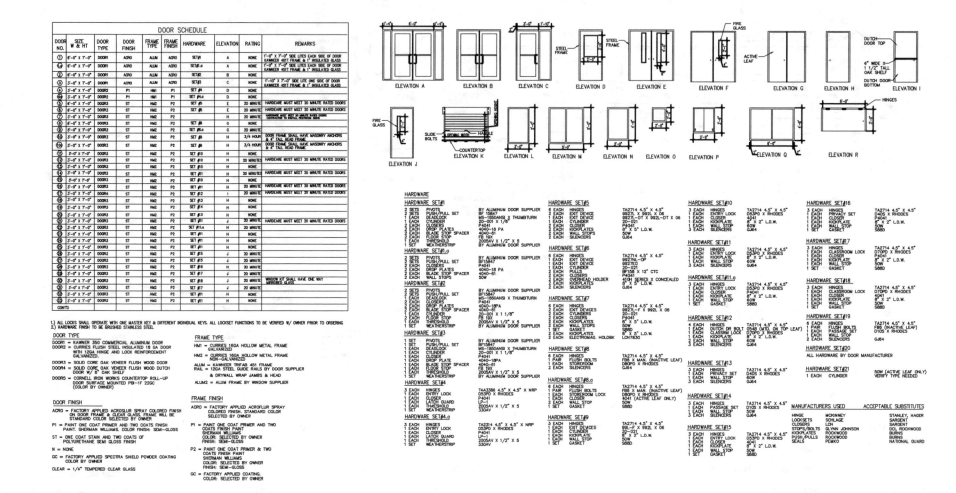

FIGURE 12-8 For commercial projects, more detailed information is required, such as specific door types and finishes, frames, and hardware.

Closers

Doors can be automatically closed and regulated in the amount of opening they provide by utilizing a variety of closer devices. They can be surface mounted on either side of the door and frame, providing either a "pull" or "push" operation. In turn, they can also be specified to be a concealed unit, either cut into the door edge (head) or doorframe. Closers are manufactured in three grade classifications depending on their frequency of use and weight of the door. They can also be specified in a number of materials and finishes. Closers can be used in conjunction with smoke detectors and alarms, to hold a door open for normal usage and be released to close and latch the door in a fire emergency.

DOOR SCHEDULE

DOOR*	DOOR TYPE	DOOR OPENING				FRAME				HARDWARE	HARDWARE GROUP	REMARKS
		WIDTH	HEIGHT	THICKN'S	MATERIAL	HEAD	JAMB	MATERIAL	FINISH			
①	A	6'-0"	9'-0"	1 3/4"	W'D/GLASS	2	2	W'D	SS	LOCKSET/CLOSER	1	
②	A	6'-0"	9'-0"	1 3/4"	W'D/GLASS	2	2	W'D	SS	LOCKSET/CLOSER	1	
③	B	3'-0"	7'-0"	1 3/4"	W'D	1	1	W'D	SS	LATCHSET	2	SOLID CORE/1-HR ASSEMBLY
④	C	6'-0"	7'-0"	1 3/4"	W'D/GL'S/MT'L	2	2	MT'L	PT	CLOSER	3	SOLID CORE WOOD DOOR W/ STAINLESS STEEL FACING
⑤	D	3'-0"	7'-0"	1 3/4"	W'D/GL'S/MT'L	2	2	MT'L	PT	CLOSER/DB'L ACTION SPRING	3	PAINT 1 (FRAME)
⑥	B	3'-0"	7'-0"	1 3/4"	W'D	1	1	W'D	SS	CLOSER	4	SOLID CORE/1-HR ASSEMBLY
⑦	B	3'-0"	7'-0"	1 3/4"	W'D	1	1	W'D	SS	CLOSER	4	SOLID CORE/1-HR ASSEMBLY
⑧	E	3'-0"	7'-0"	1 3/4"	MT'L/PT	2	2	MT'L	PT	LOCKSET	5	

HARDWARE GROUPS:

1. HIAWATHA SPHERICAL DOOR PULLS - POLISHED STAINLESS STEEL, POLISHED STAINLESS STEEL PUSHPLATE, & SCHLAGE HEAVY DUTY DEADBOLT - BRIGHT CHROMIUM PLATED

2. SCHLAGE MEDITERRANEAN ELITE/TREVI LEVER - BRIGHT CHROMIUM PLATED

3. NEWMARK SPRING LOADED/DOUBLE ACTION HINGES

4. HIAWATHA POLISHED STAINLESS STEEL PUSHPLATE AND PULLPLATE WITH DOUBLE ACTION SPRING ON DOOR #5

5. SCHLAGE HEAVY DUTY TULIP KNOB - BRIGHT CHROMIUM PLATED

6. SCHLAGE GRIP HANDLE ENTRANCE LOCK/TREVI PLYMOUTH- BRIGHT CHROMIUM PLATED

GENERAL NOTES:

1. CONTRACTOR TO SUBMIT COMPLETE HARDWARE SHOP DRAWINGS/CUTS AND KEYING SCHEDULE FOR DESIGNERS APPROVAL.

2. SS= STAIN PER DESIGNER'S SAMPLE AND SEAL WITH VARNISH (TWO COATS MINIMUM)

FIGURE 12-9 Door schedules are used to give information about doors being used in a project, such as their type, frame, width, height, thickness, material and other details such as hardware types and fire rating.

Miscellaneous Hardware

The edges surrounding the door and its frame can be made tight for acoustic and light penetration by using various types of seals, as manufactured in a variety of materials and configurations. Fire doors use a special fire-rated seal to prevent the passage of possible smoke and drafts between spaces.

Door bumpers and stops are used to keep the door operation from damaging adjacent surfaces, such as walls, equipment, and other construction. These can be either wall, floor, or frame mounted depending on the frequency of the door use and type of traffic anticipated, such as heavy classroom use. In some cases, closers can be used to provide similar controls, but the bumpers and stops are more reliable and lasting.

Door and Hardware Schedules

Door schedules identify each door by a number of other designations that is shown on the floor plan. See Figure 12-6 for an example. Depending on the complexity of a project, door schedules differ in the amount of information required. Door schedules for residential projects usually contain the number of the door, quantity required, size, type of door, material, and remarks (Figure 12-7). More detailed information, such as frame type, hardware, and fire rating, is generally required for large commercial projects (Figure 12-8). Door schedules are generally longer than window schedules, as most projects have many more different types of sizes of doors than windows.

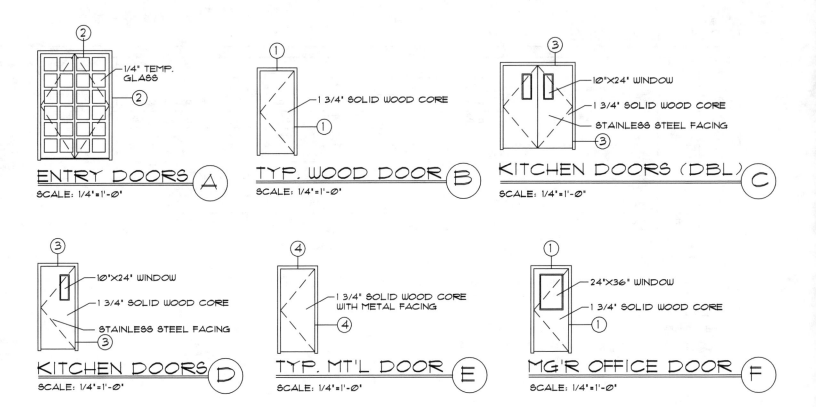

FIGURE 12-10 Door elevations make up one section of a door schedule; they are graphic representations of each type of door to be used in a project.

In general, door schedules are laid out in a grid format with lines preferably spaced at ¼ inch (6.35 mm), but no less than ³⁄₁₆ inch (4.76 mm), for ease of viewing. Lettering or font sizes should preferably be ⅛ inch (3.17 mm), but no smaller than ³⁄₃₂ inch (2.4 mm) in height, as sizes less than this can be difficult to read. As many schedules are read during construction or in the field, where temporary lighting is dim, information must be clearly readable. The schedule should be organized logically, with titles larger and bolder than the information below them. Heavier borders can also be used to set the sched-

ule apart from other drawings and information on the same sheet.

Generally, in more complex projects, the door numbers are the same as the room number into which they open. When more than one door opens into a room, a letter can be added to the number, such as 101 for the first door and 101A for the second, 101B for the third, and so on.

The purpose of a door schedule is to show the type of door being used in a given opening, the type of frame, the size (including width, height, and thickness), the material, and any other pertinent details, such as the type of hardware or fire rating as seen in Figure 12-9. Door schedules are generally presented in two parts. The first part is a graphic representation or legend of each type of door that exists in the particular project, as seen in Figure 12-10. The door elevations are typically drawn at a ¼" = 1'-0" (1:50 metric) scale; however, this scale is not a rigid standard. Any special features, such as glazing or wood louvers should also be drafted, noted, and dimensionally located, for clarity. Each door elevation should be identified with a letter that keys it to other parts of the door schedule.

The other part of the door schedule is in tabular form and includes the bulk of the information about the given assembly, such as the type of door, material, frame type and material, and the type of hardware. Every schedule should also include an area for remarks for general information not covered in the other columns (Figure 12-11). The door type, such as solid core flush, sliding, pocket door, etc., is identified by the letter used in the first section of the door schedule. Door materials might include wood, aluminum, or hollow metal. The information might include head and jamb details of each specific door, if necessary. These details are keyed in the door schedule and are drafted nearby or referenced to another sheet, as illustrated in Figure 12-12. The door hardware is either called out here or referenced to a more specific hardware group that includes items such as hinges, closers, locksets, and other detailed information. In hand-drafted projects, the door schedule can be easily created by using a spreadsheet or word processing program. It can then be reproduced on clear plastic film with an adhesive back and adhered to a drawing for copying. In CAD programs, the entire schedule and related drawings can be created simultaneously directly on the sheet.

DOOR SCHEDULE

DOOR#	DOOR TYPE	DOOR				FRAME		HARDWARE	HARDWARE GROUP	REMARKS
		WIDTH	HEIGHT	THICKN'S	MATERIAL	MATERIAL	FINISH			
1	A	3'-0"	7'-0"	1 3/4"	W'D/GLASS/SS	STL	PT	CLOSER	1	
2	B	3'-0"	7'-0"	1 3/4"	WOOD	STL	PT	LATCHSET, CLOSER	2	1 HR. RATED
3	B	3'-0"	7'-0"	1 3/4"	WOOD	STL	PT	LATCHSET, CLOSER	2	1 HR. RATED
4	B	3'-0"	7'-0"	1 3/4"	WOOD	STL	PT	LATCHSET, CLOSER	2	1 HR. RATED
5	B	3'-0"	7'-0"	1 3/4"	WOOD	STL	PT	CLOSER	3	PUSH/PULL HARDWARE
6	B	3'-0"	7'-0"	1 3/4"	WOOD	STL	PT	CLOSER	3	PUSH/PULL HARDWARE
7	B	3'-0"	7'-0"	1 3/4"	WOOD	STL	PT	LATCHSET	4	
8	D	3'-0"	7'-0"	1 3/4"	WOOD	STL	PT	LOCKSET	5	VIEW WINDOW
9	C	3'-0"	7'-0"	1 3/4"	W'D/GLASS/SS	STL	PT	DOUBLE ACT'N HINGE	6	PUSH/KICK PLATES
10	C	3'-0"	7'-0"	1 3/4"	W'D/GLASS/SS	STL	PT	DOUBLE ACT'N HINGE	6	PUSH/KICK PLATES
11	E	15'-2"	10'-0"	3"	PLAS LAM	STL	PT	LEVER		UNISPAN SELF-SUPPORTING SYSTEM: FIELD VERIFY SIZE BEFORE ORDERING

HARDWARE GROUP 1
3 EACH HINGES
1 EACH PUSH PLATE
1 EACH PULL
2 EACH KICK PLATES
1 EACH CLOSER
3 EACH SILENCERS

HARDWARE GROUP 2 (1 HR. RATED)
3 EACH HINGES
1 EACH PASSAGE LOCK
1 EACH CLOSER
3 EACH SILENCERS
1 EACH ELECTROMAGNETIC HOLD-OPEN DEVICE

HARDWARE GROUP 3
3 EACH HINGES
1 EACH PUSH PLATE
1 EACH PULL
1 EACH CLOSER
3 EACH SILENCERS

HARDWARE GROUP 4
3 EACH HINGES
1 EACH PASSAGE LOCK
3 EACH SILENCERS
1 EACH WALL STOP

HARDWARE GROUP 4
3 EACH HINGES
1 EACH PASSAGE LOCK
3 EACH SILENCERS
1 EACH WALL STOP

HARDWARE GROUP 5
3 EACH HINGES
1 EACH LOCKSET
3 EACH SILENCERS
1 EACH WALL STOP

HARDWARE GROUP 6
TOP & BOTTOM PIVOT/SPRING HINGES
2 EACH PUSH PLATES
2 EACH KICK PLATES

GENERAL NOTES:
1. CONTRACTOR TO SUBMIT COMPLETE HARDWARE SHOP DRAWINGS/CUTS AND KEYING SCHEDULE FOR OWNERS APPROVAL.

2. SS. STAIN PER DESIGNERS SAMPLE AND SEAL WITH POLYESTER (TWO COATS MINIMUM).

ABBREVIATIONS:
1. PT = PAINT
2. W'D = WOOD
3. STL. = STEEL

Checklist for Door and Hardware Schedules

General

■ Start numbering door assignments in a logical sequence on the floor plans. Most systems start with the entry of the building, or work from one side of the plan to the other, trying to place consecutive numbers or symbols where they can easily be followed.

■ Title the schedule and cross-reference it to all the plans that it might be used for. Usually only one schedule is included for multiple floors, with a note on each floor plan to see the proper sheet number to find the location of the schedule.

■ Make sure lettering, symbols, and line work is clear, concise, and easy to read.

FIGURE 12-11 The other section of a door schedule is a table listing the bulk of information about the doors used. It includes an area for remarks.

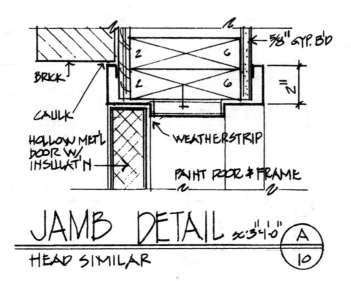

JAMB DETAIL x:3"-1'0" (A/10)
HEAD SIMILAR

Labels: 5/8" GYP. B'D, BRICK, CAULK, HOLLOW MET'L DOOR W/ INSULAT'N, WEATHERSTRIP, PAINT DOOR & FRAME

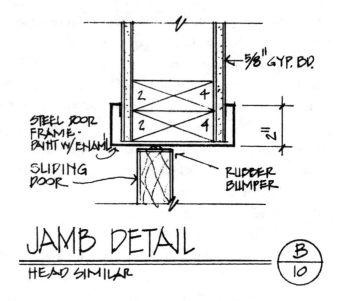

JAMB DETAIL (B/10)
HEAD SIMILAR

Labels: 5/8" GYP. BD., STEEL DOOR FRAME - PAINT W/ ENAMEL, SLIDING DOOR, RUBBER BUMPER

FIGURE 12-12 This enlarged detail of a door jamb is cross-referenced to the door schedule.

- Verify for proper door sizes, swing direction, and hardware requirements.

- Determine if any doors will need to be fire-rated assemblies and specify as such.

- Verify if the door and clearances around it need to meet ADA requirements.

- Check plan for LEED certification credits, if applicable.

- Are the drawings clear and readable when reproduced or printed? If not, correct as necessary.

Notations

- Include an abbreviation key near the schedule (or reference to the sheet that contains common abbreviation explanations).

- Cross-reference the schedule to any other drawing that might need clarification.

- Call out for submittal of door and/or hardware shop drawings where required on commercial projects.

Dimensions

- Door dimensions can be placed directly on the floor plan in small residential projects.

- Most door sizes and thicknesses are indicated in the door schedule or an elevation view of the door type.

- Dimension major features in the door of glass panels and attached plates (such as kick or push plates).

Windows

Windows are selected to provide protection from the natural elements, thermal control, air, light, privacy, security, and sometimes escape during an emergency. These decisions are also concerned with a number of external factors, such as building orientation, climate, views, and architectural style. Interior selection of windows include availability of natural light, view to the exterior, ventilation, safety factors, and the occupants' use of the room. Selection of the type of glass in a window depends on the use, location, and aesthetics of the window assembly.

Windows are selected for function and style. These can be either as fixed or operable units. Fixed windows are selected when opening capability is not required, such as large store windows. Operable windows can also provide a view, but are selected primarily to provide ventilation and a means of escape during an emergency. Operable windows are manufactured as sliding (double-hung and horizontal sliders), swinging (casement, awning, hopper, and jalousie), and pivotal (center or edge fulcrums). In addition to the fixed and operable, windows are made in groupings, such as bay or bow windows.

Windows are manufactured with a frame surround, which has the subparts of sill, head, and jamb. These frames are made of a variety of materials such as wood, steel, aluminum, plastic, and a combination of all. Exterior windows are often made with a weather-resistive outer coat (such as aluminum), and the interior trim can be most anything, such as wood or plastic. The placement of an exterior window involves four areas of measurement. These are the unit size of the window assembly, the rough opening (r.o.) in the wall to receive the unit, the sash (size of the glass and material that grips it), and the glass size (measurement of the glass alone). Similar to doors, the width of the window is called out first, followed by the height.

Windows are placed on the wall in relation to ceiling heights and adjacent door head height. For example, in residential work, the top of the window generally aligns with the door frame top. The height of the window sill is then selected, based on the room use, privacy, view, adjacent furniture, and if the window is used for egress (such as in a sleeping room). In this latter case, not only

is the sill height set to a maximum limit, but the minimum size of glazing is set, as well as the clear opening width. Manufacturers provide detailed charts and details for the windows they produce. Many of these can be found on the Internet, and generally both the elevation of the window as well as its details can be directly downloaded into the construction drawings.

Window Schedules

A window schedule typically includes such information as the window number or identification mark by each window on the floor plan, the quantity required, manufacturer, type, unit size, rough opening, materials, type of glass, and finish (Figure 12-13). A "remarks" column is also useful for special information pertaining to the windows. Window schedules are set up similar to the door schedule in that they may require two separate parts, depending on the complexity of the project. If there are a wide variety of windows within a project, then elevations and sections may be required to explain how they are to be installed or any special features (Figure 12-14). Interior designers may have to specify exterior windows, or what are commonly referred to as interior glass partitions, depending on the scope of the project, and whether it is a building addition or interior tenant build-out.

Window elevations and sections should be located beside the tabular window schedule so they can refer to one another and be keyed accordingly. Window elevations and sections are typically drawn at a $\frac{1}{4}$" = 1'-0" scale (1:50 metric); however, $\frac{1}{8}$" = 1'-0" (1:100 metric) or $\frac{1}{2}$" = 1'-0" (1:20 metric) may be more appropriate for some projects.

Window types are generally referenced on the floor plan and elevations by the means of a polygon-shaped symbol and a num-

WINDOW SCHEDULE

WINDOW SYMBOL	QUANTITY	MANF. / STYLE	MODEL NO.	UNIT SIZE	ROUGH OPENING	TYPE	FINISH	TYPE OF GLASS	REMARKS
A	7	PELLA / ARCHITECT. SERIES	CM3553	2'-11" x 4'-5"	2'-11 3/4" x 4'-5 3/4"	CLAD CASEMENT	WHITE	CLEAR	
B	3	PELLA / ARCHITECT. SERIES	CCH35531	5'-10" x 4'-5"	5'-10 3/4" x 4'-5 3/4"	CLAD CASEMENT	WHITE	CLEAR	3 PAIRS ARCH-TOP WINDOWS
C	5	PELLA / ARCHITECT. SERIES	CCM35539	2'-11" x 4'-5"	2'-11 3/4" x 4'-5 3/4"	CLAD CASEMENT	WHITE	CLEAR	ARCHED WINDOWS
D	2	PELLA / ARCHITECT. SERIES	CM1771	1'-5" x 5'-11"	1'-5 3/4" x 5'-11 3/4"	CLAD CASEMENT	WHITE	CLEAR TEMPERED	
E	1	PELLA / ARCHITECT. SERIES	CM3535	2'-11" x 2'-11"	2'-11 3/4" x 2'-11 3/4"	CLAD CASEMENT	WHITE	CLEAR	

NOTES:

1. CONTRACTOR TO FIELD MEASURE FOR CUSTOM WINDOW SIZES. VERIFY ANY DISCREPENCIES WITH DESIGNER.
2. SUBMIT SHOP DRAWINGS TO DESIGNER FOR APPROVAL BEFORE ORDERING & INSTALLATION.
3. SEE WINDOW TYPES FOR LOCATION OF MULLIONS.

FIGURE 12-13 Window schedules include information about the windows being used, such as the identification mark, quantity, type, size, rough opening, materials, type of glass, and finish.

ber inside it, as illustrated in Figure 12-15. The same symbol and number should also be drafted under the window elevation that is shown. Every window that is different should have a number; if two or more windows are the same they may share the same number. However, make sure that identical windows have the exact same head, sill, and jamb conditions because details are referenced from these elevations. The glazing system and glass must also be identical for each window.

Checklist for Window Schedules

General

- Identify the windows and their appropriate symbols in a logical sequence on the floor plans.

- Add a note on the floor plan(s) or sheet index (for a set of drawings) where window schedule can be found.

- In elevation views of windows, show the operable window unit's swing.

- Title the schedule and cross-reference it to all the plans that it might be used for. Usually only one schedule is included for multiple floors, with a note on each floor plan to see the proper sheet number to find the location of the schedule.

- Make sure lettering, symbols, and line work are clear, concise, and easy to read.

- Draw the window elevations and details where necessary and cross-reference to the window schedule.

- Check plan for code compliance and ADA requirements and clearances.

- Check plan for **LEED** certification credits, if applicable.

- Are the drawings clear and readable when reproduced or printed? If not, correct as necessary.

Notations

- Include an abbreviation key near the schedule (or reference to the sheet that contains common abbreviation explanations).

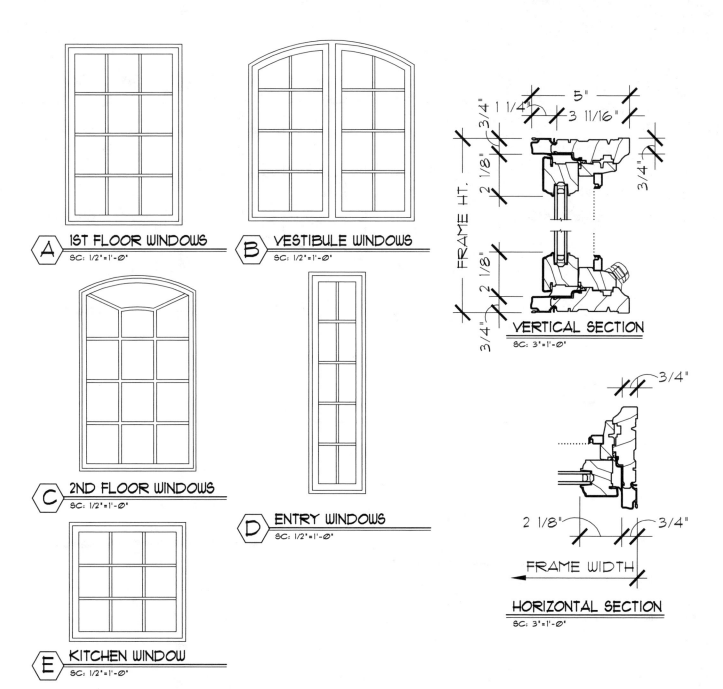

A ⬡ 1ST FLOOR WINDOWS
SC: 1/2"=1'-∅'

B ⬡ VESTIBULE WINDOWS
SC: 1/2"=1'-∅'

C ⬡ 2ND FLOOR WINDOWS
SC: 1/2"=1'-∅'

D ⬡ ENTRY WINDOWS
SC: 1/2"=1'-∅'

E ⬡ KITCHEN WINDOW
SC: 1/2"=1'-∅'

VERTICAL SECTION
SC: 3"=1'-∅'

FRAME HT.

5"
1 1/4"
3 11/16"
3/4"
2 1/8"
2 1/8"
3/4"
3/4"

HORIZONTAL SECTION
SC: 3"=1'-∅'

3/4"
2 1/8"
3/4"

FRAME WIDTH

FIGURE 12-14 **Windows can be further explained with elevations and details showing installation methods or special features.**

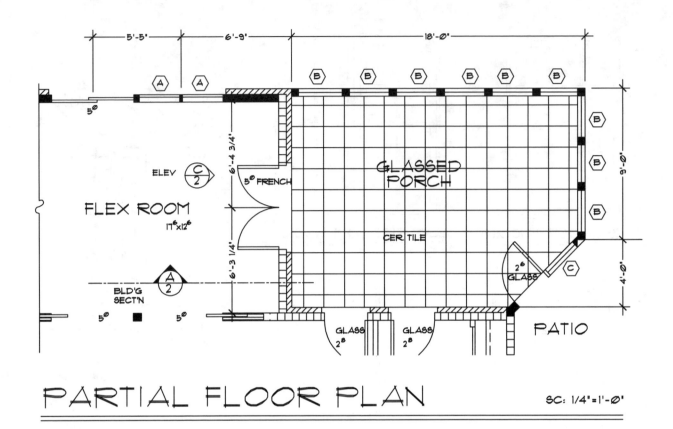

FIGURE 12-15 Windows are generally noted on a floor plan or elevation with a number or letter inside a polygon-shaped symbol.

PARTIAL FLOOR PLAN

SC: 1/4"=1'-0"

- Cross-reference the schedule to any other drawing that might need clarification.

- Note where windows might have special materials, such as tempered glass.

- Check for windows that might require tempered glass, as those adjacent to doors often have this requirement.

- Check the windows against code requirements that might specify minimum sizes for health/light and egress.

Dimensions

- Window dimensions can be placed directly on the floor plan in small residential projects.

- Most window sizes are indicated in the window schedule or an elevation view of the window type.

There are a variety of ways to communicate what interior finishes are required for a project. Traditionally, a finish schedule is developed in a tabular form that lists each room or space and the specific types of finishes that are to be applied to the floors, walls, bases, and ceilings (Figure 13-1). In residential or small commercial projects where only a single finish is applied on each wall and one or two different floor finishes are used, a finish schedule works fairly well. In some interior projects, however, rooms have more than four walls that correspond to the compass direction keyed on the plan as north, south, east, or west. In these cases, it can be difficult to use only a finish schedule to accurately locate the corresponding finishes in the space. A room might have complex shapes of angles and curves that cannot be effectively communicated by the use of a finish schedule. In these cases, a finish plan is developed to more accurately spell out these complex situations. This will be addressed following our discussion of room finish schedules.

Room Finish Schedules

Room finish schedules are created to show, in tabular form, the finish materials to be applied to each wall and floor surface of a

ROOM FINISH SCHEDULE

ROOM	FLOOR			BASE			WALLS			CEILING			NOTES
	CARPET	HARDWOOD	CERAMIC TILE	WOOD	VINYL	CERAMIC TILE	WALLPAPER	PAINT	CERAMIC TILE	PTD. GYP. BD.	WOOD	ACOUS. TILE	
FOYER		●	●				●				●		COFFERED CEILING
LIVING ROOM		●	●				●	.		●			
DINING ROOM		●	●				●			●			
KITCHEN			●			●		●		●			
BREAKFAST NOOK			●			●		●		●			
GREAT ROOM	●		●					●		●			
OFFICE	●		●					●				●	
LAUNDRY/ MUD ROOM			●	●				●		●			
MASTER BEDROOM	●		●				●			●			
MASTER BATH			●			●		●		●			
POWDER ROOM			●			●	●		●	●			CERAMIC TILE WAINSCOT
BEDROOM 1	●		●				●			●			
BEDROOM 2	●		●					●		●			
BATHROOM (2ND FLR)			●			●		●		●			
BONUS ROOM	●		●					●		●			

FIGURE 13-1 Room-finish schedules are commonly used in interior construction plans.

ROOM FINISHES SCHEDULE

ROOM NO.	ROOM NAME	FLOOR	BASE	WALLS				CEILING		NOTES
				NORTH	EAST	SOUTH	WEST	HEIGHT	MATERIAL / FINISH	
201	RECEPTION	SEE PLAN	WB-1	WC-1	SEE PLAN	WC-1	WC-1	9'-0"	GYP. BD. / PT-3	SEE DRAWINGS FOR SIGNAGE ON EAST WALL
202	SALES	CPT-1	WB-1	WC-2	WC-2	WC-2	WC-2	9'-0"	GYP. BD. / PT-3	
203	CONFERENCE A	CPT-2	WB-1	WC-2	WC-3	WC-2	WC-3	10'-0"	ACOUSTICAL TILE	PT-3 FOR GYP. BD. CEILING AT BORDERS
204	CONFERENCE B	CPT-2	WB-1	WC-2	WC-4	WC-2	WC-4	10'-0"	ACOUSTICAL TILE	PT-3 FOR GYP. BD. CEILING AT BORDERS
205	KITCHEN	VCT-1	RB-1	PT-1	PT-2	PT-1	PT-1	10'-0"	ACOUSTICAL TILE	
206	CLOSET	VCT-1	RB-1	WC-2	WC-4	WC-2	WC-4	10'-0"	ACOUSTICAL TILE	
207	STORAGE	VCT-1	RB-1	PT-1	PT-1	PT-1	PT-1	10'-0"	ACOUSTICAL TILE	
208	OPEN OFFICE	CPT-3	RB-1	PT-2	PT-2	PT-2	PT-2	10'-0"	ACOUSTICAL TILE	
209	CORRIDOR	CPT-3	RB-1	PT-2	PT-2	PT-2	PT-2	10'-0"	ACOUSTICAL TILE	
210	OFFICE	CPT-1	RB-1	PT-1	PT-1	PT-1	PT-1	9'-0"	ACOUSTICAL TILE	
211	OFFICE	CPT-1	RB-1	PT-1	PT-1	PT-1	PT-1	9'-0"	ACOUSTICAL TILE	
212	WOMENS RESTROOM	CT-1	CT-1	CT-2	CT-2	CT-2	SEE PLAN	9'-0"	GYP. BD. / PT-3	
213	MENS RESTROOM	CT-1	CT-1	CT-2	SEE PLAN	CT-2	CT-2	9'-0"	GYP. BD. / PT-3	

FIGURE 13-2 Room-finish schedules show the finish materials to be applied to each surface in a room; they should also include a section for notes.

project. The schedule is generally set up showing each room by name or number along the left side of a sheet. Column heads are then drawn across the top for each wall surface, floor, base, ceiling, and any other special features of a room. A "notes" column is also a helpful addition for any miscellaneous comments that might be needed to clarify the design intent, as shown in Figure 13-2. Sometimes the walls in a room will have different finishes. For example, three walls may be painted and the fourth wall finished in a wood paneling. In order to clarify which wall receives the proper treatment, each wall of each room is noted on the finish schedule. The most common way to record this information is to relate each wall to its orientation, such as the north, east, south, and west compass directions. In individual rooms or single walls with complex fin-

ishes, it may be necessary to supplement the finish schedule with wall elevations for further clarity, as shown in Figure 13-3.

The room finish schedule consists of two different sections: the main section, which is in tabular form, and the second section which is called the legend or materials key. The first part is used primarily to indicate which floor and wall will receive what type of finish. Therefore, the information provided in the schedule should be generic. Trade or manufacturers' names are indicated in the legend. For example, a P may be used in the schedule to indicate that a particular wall will be finished with paint. The P will then be repeated in the "materials key" which will indicate what paint manufacturer will be used as well as what type of paint and what color. If several different types or colors of paint are to be used within the same project, each type and/or color would get a different symbol, such as P-1, P-2, P-3, and so on. This keying system saves a tremendous amount of time and space in preparing the finish schedule. Interior room finish schedules will vary in complexity and presentation, depending upon the amount of information required. For example, in a residential project where all walls of each room will have a common interior finish, the schedule can be rather brief. Commercial projects generally have a much wider range of interior finishes, with wall treatments ranging from simple painted drywall to expensive custom-made paneling. In these situations, the interior room finish schedule must also be coordinated with the floor plan, or drawn as a separate finish plan. A variety of symbols are used on the floor plan to identify interior finishes in each room with the interior finish schedule.

Checklist for Room Finish Schedules

General

- Identify the rooms and finishes and their appropriate symbols in a clear manner in the schedule.

- Title the schedule and cross-reference it to all the plans that it might be used for.

- Usually only one schedule is included for multiple floors, with a note on each floor plan to see the proper sheet number to find the location of the schedule.

- Make sure lettering, symbols, and line work are clear, concise, and easy to read.

- Check plan for code compliance and ADA requirements and clearances.

- Check plan for LEED certification credits, if applicable.

- Are the drawings clear and readable when reproduced or printed? If not, correct as necessary.

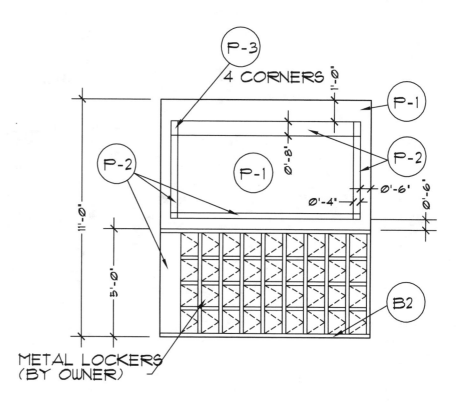

Notations

- Include an abbreviation key near the schedule (or reference to the sheet that contains common abbreviation explanations).

Dimensions

- Dimensions are generally not needed on a finish schedule, unless a finish has a specific size, such as a 4-inch (101 mm) vinyl base or a 2-foot by 4-foot (60.9- by 122-cm) suspended acoustical tile ceiling.

FIGURE 13-3 An elevation may accompany the finish schedule to show where selected finishes are to be placed.

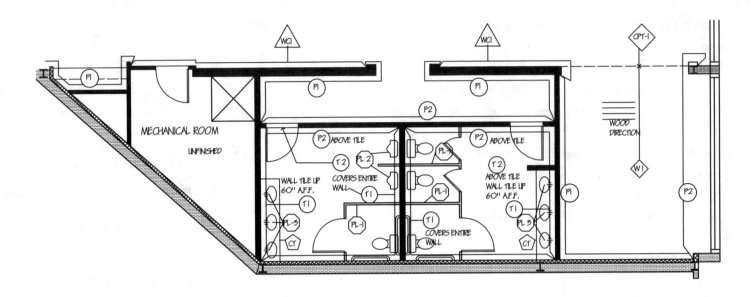

PARTIAL FINISH PLAN AT 3RD FLOOR   SCALE: 1/ 4"=1'-0"

Finish Plans

In large or more complex interiors when there is more than one type of finish on each wall, or when there are complex finish configurations, such as a tile design on a floor, a finish plan is more appropriate. A finish plan, as shown in Figure 13-4 shows the finish material to be applied to wall and floor surfaces graphically, with a corresponding legend (Figure 13-5).

The finish plan codes and graphically indicates where each surface treatment goes. The code is then keyed to a legend and is cross-referenced to written specifications, if necessary. The legend specifies the exact material, manufacturer, catalog number, color, fire rating, and any other specific information necessary for a successful application, as illustrated in Figure 13-6. A number or a combination of alphabetical letters and a number generally forms the code. For example, all carpet floor notations could be preceded with a "C" or "FC" for floor covering, and then given numerical designations such as FC-1, FC-2, and so on, as shown in Figure 13-7. The code for a wall treatment may indicate a single wall finish, such as "P" for paint, or a combination of treatments, such as WC-1/WB-2 for wainscot and wall base. Some common abbreviations are shown in Table 13-1. If the wall base finish or the trim is the same throughout the project, a general note will be sufficient. Also, if the majority of the walls are finished the same, this could be indicated in a general note and only the exceptions graphically drawn on the plan or in an accompanying schedule (Figure 13-8).

FINISH SCHEDULE

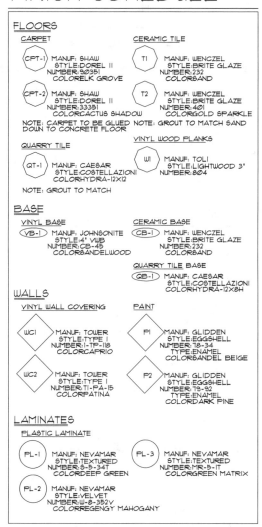

FLOORS

CARPET

CPT-1 MANUF: SHAW
STYLE:DOREL II
NUMBER:90351
COLOR:ELK GROVE

CPT-2 MANUF: SHAW
STYLE:DOREL II
NUMBER:33351
COLOR:CACTUS SHADOW

NOTE: CARPET TO BE GLUED
DOWN TO CONCRETE FLOOR

CERAMIC TILE

T1 MANUF: WENCZEL
STYLE:BRITE GLAZE
NUMBER:232
COLOR:SAND

T2 MANUF: WENCZEL
STYLE:BRITE GLAZE
NUMBER:401
COLOR:GOLD SPARKLE

NOTE: GROUT TO MATCH SAND

QUARRY TILE

QT-1 MANUF: CAESAR
STYLE:COSTELLAZIONI
COLOR:HYDRA-12X12

NOTE: GROUT TO MATCH

VINYL WOOD PLANKS

W1 MANUF: TOLI
STYLE:LIGHTWOOD 3'
NUMBER:804

BASE

VINYL BASE

VB-1 MANUF: JOHNSONITE
STYLE:4' VWB
NUMBER:CB-45
COLOR:SANDELWOOD

CERAMIC BASE

CB-1 MANUF: WENCZEL
STYLE:BRITE GLAZE
NUMBER:232
COLOR:SAND

QUARRY TILE BASE

QB-1 MANUF: CAESAR
STYLE:COSTELLAZIONI
COLOR:HYDRA-12X8H

WALLS

VINYL WALL COVERING

WC1 MANUF: TOWER
STYLE:TYPE I
NUMBER:1-TP-118
COLOR:CAFRIO

WC2 MANUF: TOWER
STYLE:TYPE I
NUMBER:T1-PA-15
COLOR:PATINA

PAINT

P1 MANUF: GLIDDEN
STYLE:EGGSHELL
NUMBER:78-34
TYPE:ENAMEL
COLOR:SANDEL BEIGE

P2 MANUF: GLIDDEN
STYLE:EGGSHELL
NUMBER:79-92
TYPE:ENAMEL
COLOR:DARK PINE

LAMINATES

PLASTIC LAMINATE

PL-1 MANUF: NEVAMAR
STYLE:TEXTURED
NUMBER:S-5-34T
COLOR:DEEP GREEN

PL-2 MANUF: NEVAMAR
STYLE:VELVET
NUMBER:W-8-352V
COLOR:REGENCY MAHOGANY

PL-3 MANUF: NEVAMAR
STYLE:TEXTURED
NUMBER:MR-5-1T
COLOR:GREEN MATRIX

FIGURE 13-5 (above) A finish legend that accompanies a finish plan.

FIGURE 13-6 (right) The symbols on the finish plan are keyed to a legend that specifies the material, manufacturer, catalog number, color, fire rating, and any other specific information necessary for successful installation.

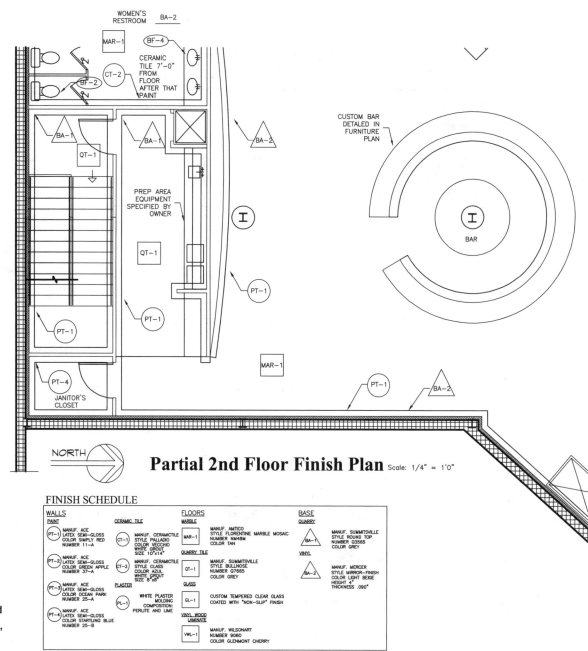

Partial 2nd Floor Finish Plan Scale: 1/4" = 1'0"

WOMEN'S RESTROOM BA-2

CERAMIC TILE 7'-0" FROM FLOOR AFTER THAT PAINT

CUSTOM BAR DETAILED IN FURNITURE PLAN

PREP AREA EQUIPMENT SPECIFIED BY OWNER

JANITOR'S CLOSET

BAR

NORTH

FINISH SCHEDULE

WALLS

PAINT

PT-1 MANUF. ACE
LATEX SEMI-GLOSS
COLOR SIMPLY RED
NUMBER 11-A

PT-2 MANUF. ACE
LATEX SEMI-GLOSS
COLOR GREEN APPLE
NUMBER 37-A

PT-3 MANUF. ACE
LATEX SEMI-GLOSS
COLOR OCEAN PARK
NUMBER 25-A

PT-4 MANUF. ACE
LATEX SEMI-GLOSS
COLOR STARTLING BLUE
NUMBER 25-B

CERAMIC TILE

CT-1 MANUF. CERAMICTILE
STYLE PALLADIO
COLOR VECCHIO
WHITE GROUT
SIZE 10"x14"

CT-2 MANUF. CERAMICTILE
STYLE CLASS
COLOR AZUL
WHITE GROUT
SIZE 8"x8"

PLASTER

PL-1 WHITE PLASTER
MOLDING
COMPOSITION:
PERLITE AND LIME

FLOORS

MARBLE

MAR-1 MANUF. AMTICO
STYLE FLORENTINE MARBLE MOSAIC
NUMBER NM48M
COLOR TAN

QUARRY TILE

QT-1 MANUF. SUMMITSVILLE
STYLE BULLNOSE
NUMBER Q7865
COLOR GREY

GLASS

GL-1 CUSTOM TEMPERED CLEAR GLASS
COATED WITH "NON-SLIP" FINISH

VINYL WOOD LAMINATE

VWL-1 MANUF. WILSONART
NUMBER 9060
COLOR GLENMONT CHERRY

BASE

QUARRY

BA-1 MANUF. SUMMITSVILLE
STYLE ROUND TOP
NUMBER Q3565
COLOR GREY

VINYL

BA-2 MANUF. MERCER
STYLE MIRROR-FINISH
COLOR LIGHT BEIGE
HEIGHT 4"
THICKNESS .090"

FLOOR COVERING SCHEDULE

FLOOR COVERING

FC-1	CARPET MANF: WINFIELD STYLE: CIRCUS COLOR: GREEN APPLE WIDTH: 12'-0'	
FC-2	RESILIENT FLOORING MANF: JOHNSTON STYLE: METRO (VINYL) COLOR: ELECTRIC BLUE SIZE: 12' X 12' TILES	*BASE: 2 1/2' VINYL COVE BASE - JOHNSTON/ OCEAN #621
FC-3	MARBLE MANF: IGRL STYLE: REGENCY COLOR: ROYAL CREAM SIZE: 18' X 18' X 3/8'	* GROUT: GRISSOM/ BEIGE #422-1
FC-4	CERAMIC TILE MANF: FLORIDIAN TILE STYLE: SEABREEZE COLOR: TANGERINE SIZE: 12' X 12' X 3/8'	* GROUT: GRISSOM/ BEIGE #422-1

FLOOR COVERING NOTES

1. GROUT TO BE SUPPLIED & INSTALLED BY G.C. TILES TO BE INSTALLED WITH CONSISTENT GROUT WIDTH THROUGHOUT - APPROX. 1/16' GROUT JOINT WIDTH.

2. CERAMIC TILE TO BE SUPPLIED BY OWNER, INSTALLED BY G.C. TILES TO BE INSTALLED WITH CONSISTENT GROUT WIDTH THROUGHOUT - APPROX. 1/4' GROUT JOINT WIDTH.

PAINT SCHEDULE

SUPPLIED AND APPLIED BY THE GENERAL CONTRACTOR, UNLESS NOTED OTHERWISE.
NOTES:

1. PAINT MANUFACTURER IS SPECIFIED AS GLIDDEN PAINTS. SUBSTITUTIONS ALLOWED ARE BENJAMIN MOORE AND SHERWIN-WILLIAMS.

2. PREFERRED METHOD OF PAINT APPLICATION IS BY SPRAY APPLICATION.

P-1	GLIDDEN 1067 - SEMI-GLOSS LATEX - LT. BEIGE
P-2	GLIDDEN 1064 - FLAT FINISH LATEX - IVORY
P-3	GLIDDEN 2364 - SEMI-GLOSS LATEX - LT. PINK
P-4	GLIDDEN 1254 - SEMI-GLOSS FINISH LATEX - MEDIUM PINK

PAINT NOTES

1. CONTRACTOR TO REVIEW DETAIL SHEETS, FINISH PLANS, AND ELEVATIONS FOR PAINTED SURFACES.

2. ALL FACTORY WHITE SPEAKER PLATES TO BE SPRAY PAINTED TO MATCH ADJACENT SURFACES.

3. ALL WOOD SURFACES ARE TO BE PRIMED WITH OIL-BASED PRIMER AND FINISHED W/OIL-BASE SEMI-GLOSS PAINT.

4. ALL METAL SURFACES TO BE PAINTED SHALL FIRST BE PRIMED WITH METAL PRIMER AND FINISHED WITH SEMI-GLOSS OIL-BASED PAINT.

5. FINISH COATS MUST NOT SHOW BRUSH MARKS, IF THIS METHOD IS USED VS. SPRAYING OF ANY MISCELLANEOUS ITEM.

FIGURE 13-7 (left) An example of a floor covering schedule for a commercial project.

FIGURE 13-8 (right) A detailed paint schedule is helpful in commercial projects where several walls and details are to be painted.

Scale of Finish Plans

Finish plans are drawn at as small of a scale as possible, yet large enough to accurately convey information critical for placing finishes. The finishes are drawn in plan view simplistically, preventing clutter for ease of recognition. As there is often not a lot of detailed information that needs to be drawn in the floor-plan view, a scale of 1/8" = 1'-0" (1:100 metric) is generally used. However, if sufficient detail is needed to clarify exact configurations or details of the pieces, a scale of ¼" = 1'-0" (1:50 metric) or larger can be used.

Drafting Standards for Finish Plans

The advantage to the dedicated finish plan is that more detailed information can be given to the workers for locations on specific finish treatments. A finish plan helps to eliminate questions and

Table 13-1: Common Abbreviations for Interior Finishes

FLOORS

FC - FLOORCOVERING
C - CARPET
CPT - CARPET
CT - CERAMIC TILE
VCT - VINYL COMPOSITION TILE
W - WOOD
VWP - VINYL WOOD PLANKS
SV - SHEET VINYL
ST - STONE

BASES

VB - VINYL BASE
RB - RUBBER BASE
CB - CERAMIC BASE
QB - QUARRY TILE BASE
WB - WOOD BASE
STB - STONE BASE

WALLS

WT - WALL TREATMENT
WC - WALLCOVERING
P or PT - PAINT
VWC - VINYL WALL COVERING
CT - CERAMIC TILE

LAMINATES (OR COUNTERTOPS)

PL - PLASTIC LAMINATE
SS - SOLID SURFACE

PLUMBING

PF - PLUMBING FIXTURES

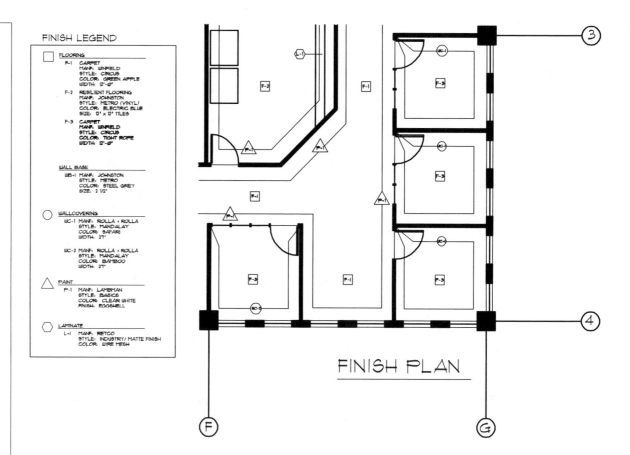

FINISH PLAN

mistakes that might arise if a finish schedule alone were used. However, remember that items such as installation preparations and instructions, are not included on the finish plan, but in the written specifications.

When drawing the finish plan, the designer uses lines to show the extent and location of each finish, as shown in Figure 13-9. When the finish lines are drawn, door openings are generally ignored to insure that the surfaces above the doors, in corners, and between doors are also covered. Finishes on the doors and frames

FIGURE 13-9 Lines are used to show the exact location and extent of each finish.

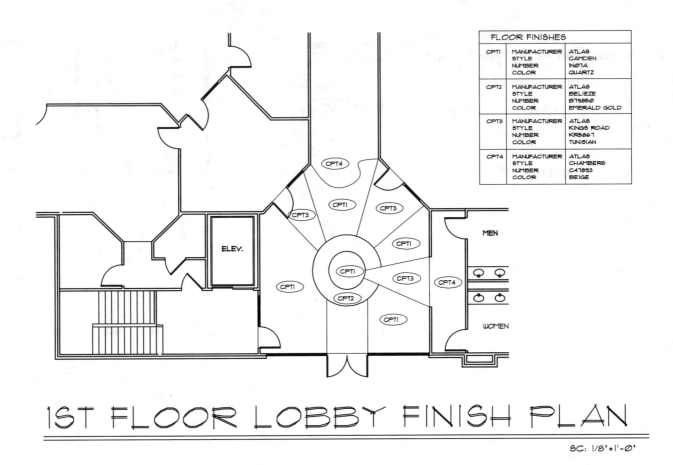

FLOOR FINISHES		
CPT1	MANUFACTURER STYLE NUMBER COLOR	ATLAS CAMDEN IN071A QUARTZ
CPT2	MANUFACTURER STYLE NUMBER COLOR	ATLAS BELIEZE B19850 EMERALD GOLD
CPT3	MANUFACTURER STYLE NUMBER COLOR	ATLAS KINGS ROAD KR8867 TUNISIAN
CPT4	MANUFACTURER STYLE NUMBER COLOR	ATLAS CHAMBERS C47893 BEIGE

1ST FLOOR LOBBY FINISH PLAN

SC: 1/8"=1'-0"

FIGURE 13-10 Floor and wall finishes can generally be indicated on the same drawing for a project depending on the complexity of the finishes.

are either specified in a note or referred to on the door schedule; they are not generally a part of the finish plan. However, some designers prefer to list their colors here on this sheet to coordinate with other finish and color selections. Floor finishes and wall finishes can generally be indicated on one drawing. However, if complex floor patterns are designed, a separate large-scale floor-finish drawing may be needed for clarity, as illustrated in Figure 13-10.

Designation of Materials in Finish Plans

If the plan or detail of a particular area is drawn at a scale of ½" = 1'-0" (1:20 metric), material sizes might be shown in the plan view. However, the plans are generally too small to accurately represent the size of most materials. For example, 4 x 4 inch (101.6 mm) is too small to draw at the ⅛" (1:100 metric) or ¼" (1:50 metric) scales. Likewise, the attempt at drawing wood grain in floors or even the widths and lengths of random floor planks is not necessary in these small-scale drawings. The most critical item to

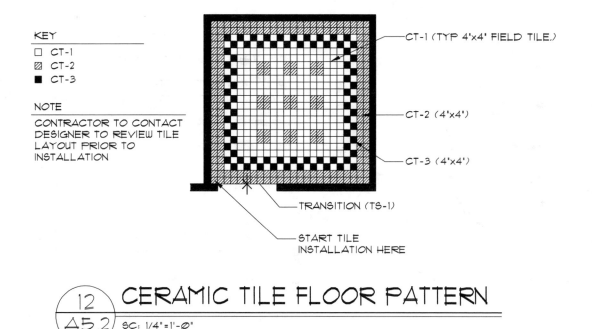

KEY

☐ CT-1
▨ CT-2
■ CT-3

NOTE

CONTRACTOR TO CONTACT
DESIGNER TO REVIEW TILE
LAYOUT PRIOR TO
INSTALLATION

CT-1 (TYP 4'x4' FIELD TILE.)

CT-2 (4'x4')

CT-3 (4'x4')

TRANSITION (TS-1)

START TILE
INSTALLATION HERE

12
A5.2 CERAMIC TILE FLOOR PATTERN
SC: 1/4"=1'-0"

WC-1 Vinyl Wallcovering

Man: Lanark
Pattern: Kyosi
Color: Fresco
Number: L2-KY-05
Repeat: Random Match
Type: II
Width: 54"

include in such cases is the start and stop of the flooring, and the direction of the pattern if it has one. In many CAD programs, the software for rendering finish materials is available, but the readability of the drawing should take precedence over drawing them to scale. A different scale is selected and assigned to the patterns, for ease of visibility. As mentioned before, this can be done on a large blow-up drawing of the finish material and cross-referenced to the main plan. See Figure 13-11 for a detail of a tile floor pattern.

Sometimes a texture, color, fabric, or other feature cannot be accurately specified in the finish schedule. In these instances, a swatch of material or paint color chip is often attached to the drawing or put in the specification booklet. Or a material can be

scanned and placed digitally in the schedule, as illustrated in Figure 13-12.

Dimensioning Finish Plans

Generally, there is not a lot of dimensioning placed on the finish plan. As long as the plan is drawn to scale and the dimensions of the spaces and structure are indicated on the floor plan(s), the finishes can be estimated from these or other drawings. However, in some cases, dimensions are needed to describe limits of finishes or start and stop points occurring in areas that are not easily referenced in the plan view. Alignment and direction of patterns might need to be dimensioned directly on the plan, as illustrated in Fig-

FIGURE 13-11 (left) Enlarged detail of a custom tile floor pattern.

FIGURE 13-12 (right) A specification using an actual material swatch that has been digitally scanned for insertion.

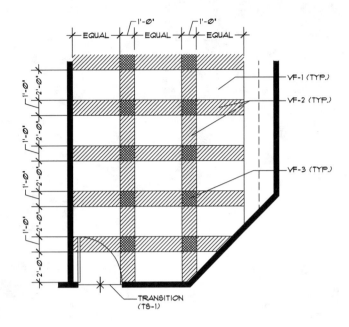

⑦ / A5.1   **BREAKROOM FLOOR PATTERN**   SC: 1/4"=1'-0"

FIGURE 13-13 **A detail for a custom floor pattern with dimensions.**

ure 13-13. In these instances, references should be given that are easily obtainable in the field. Dimensions should be referenced from the face of a wall, column, or imaginary centerline of a room.

Checklist for Finish Plans

General

- Title the drawing, note its scale, and identify north (or reference direction).
- Title the accompanying finish schedule and key it to the plan.
- Place finish schedule on the same sheet as the finish plan (if possible) or on a sheet immediately preceding or following the plan.

- Clean up the plan (or in **CAD**, turn of superfluous information) so the walls, spaces, and key codes are clear, dark, and very legible.
- Number or name all applicable rooms/spaces where necessary.
- Note all flooring transitions to be centered under doors unless otherwise drawn. Show or key all transitional details in the floor finishes.
- Check plan for code compliance and ADA requirements and clearances.
- Check plan for **LEED** certification credits, if applicable.
- Are the drawings clear and readable when reproduced or printed? If not, correct as necessary.

Notations

- Cross-reference the plan (and schedule if applicable) to other drawings that might contain pertinent information critical to the finish plan.
- Note special features, clearances, alignments, and other important items.
- Cross-reference the finish plan and finish schedule, carefully checking for accuracy and completeness of information.
- Add notes on issues for the installer to be alerted to when placing the finishes.
- Show or call out directions of linear patterns, such as strip wood flooring.
- If the designer is to approve a trial layout (such as floor or wall tile) in the field, add a note to this effect.
- Add notes to refer to reflected ceiling plan if that drawing specifies ceiling finishes.

Dimensions

- Dimension clearances, alignments, and other controlling factors.
- Call out for installer or contractor to verify existing dimensions of the space/structure with those shown on the finish, and verify these with the designer before installation.
- If floor material transitions are not readily apparent as to location, provide dimensions to locate them from walls, columns, or other reference points.

Furniture Installation Plans

The selection of furniture is an integral phase in the design of interior spaces as it affects human functions and desires. Spaces can also be personalized by furniture, which reflects individual preferences, activities, and needs. This chapter will discuss furniture in both residential and commercial buildings. In commercial spaces, furniture generally reflects the concept, theme, or image an establishment wants to convey to the public or their clients. The selection of furniture in residential spaces often reflects the personal tastes and lifestyles of the individuals who occupy them.

Furniture is often included as a part of what interior designers call the furniture, furnishings, and equipment (FF&E) package. (This terminology can be found in many printed documents available through many of the professional design societies, such as ASID, IIDA, and AIA.) Furniture provides for the users' daily needs and completes the humanization of the environment. Furniture is often planned for early in an interior design project. It may even be a design generator. For example, space can be organized by the placement of furniture to define traffic patterns or provide conversation areas.

Most interior projects involve the reuse of existing furniture. Depending on the budget for the project and the condition of the existing furniture, such pieces might be reused in their original condition or refurbished for coordination with the designer's new concepts.

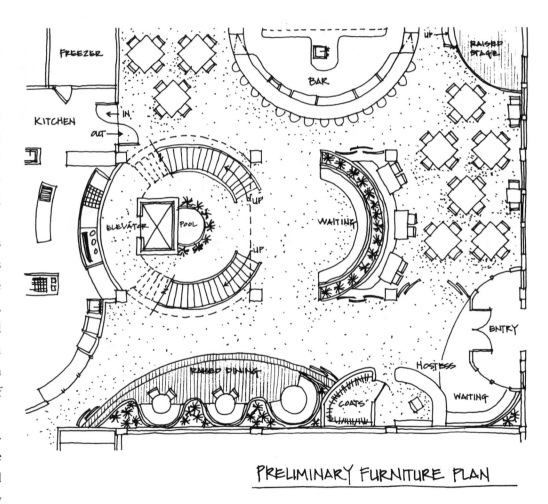

PRELIMINARY FURNITURE PLAN

FIGURE 14-1 A preliminary furniture plan for a proposed restaurant.

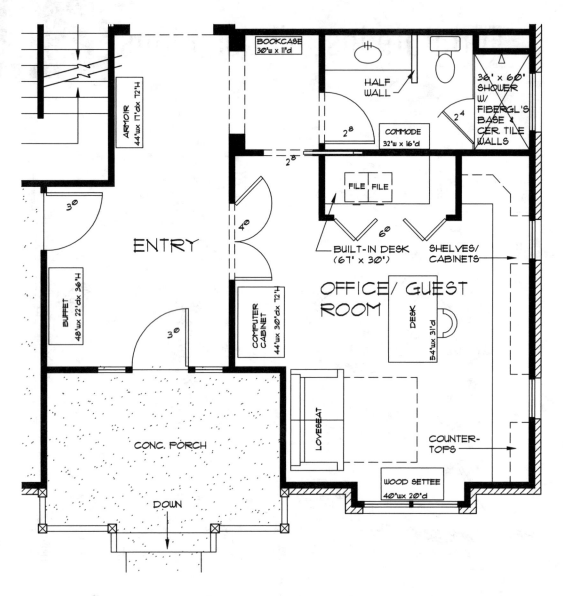

FIGURE 14-2 In small projects, selections can be noted directly on the plan view.

The design of interior environments with furniture often begins in the programming and space planning. These initial steps define furniture needs in terminology of type, size, and quantity. It continues throughout the project, with the exact placement and selection of individual characteristics often occurring after the initial programming and planning.

For specifying, ordering, and placing furniture, several steps are needed. The first step is to ascertain the client's activities in a space and what furniture is needed to perform these. During this phase, the furniture selection is often generic, which means the exact furniture pieces are not selected. For example, a conference table might be specified as required seating for eight people. At this time, the designer might not even determine if the table is round, rectangular, or oval. However, this selection in form will occur soon, as it could have a major impact on the space planning and clearances around the table for seating and circulation. The next step is the creation of a preliminary furniture plan to determine furniture number, groups, and orientation to support user activities, as illustrated in Figure 14-1. Next, a scaled furniture plan is drawn using the actual dimensions of the furniture pieces and an accompanying schedule is made. The next process is the creation of what is referred to as a job or control book or catalog, listing the specifications of each piece of furniture and furnishings involved in the project. These are cross-referenced to the written specifications as to the standards to be met in the performance of the work for the materials and the installation. The written specifications have the same contractual weight as the construction drawings and are part of the contract documents.

The exact placement of furniture is important in interior design projects. In many projects, a separate drawing is created to show the final placement and orientation of the selected furniture.

FURNITURE SCHEDULE (PARTIAL EXAMPLE)

MARK	QUANTITY	MANUFACTURER	DESCRIPTION	FABRIC/ FINISH	REMARKS	MARK	QUANTITY	MANUFACTURER	DESCRIPTION	FABRIC/ FINISH	REMARKS
C-1	90	MIKE INDUSTRIES, INC.	20-483 NELSON CHAIR 20W, 22D, 35H	SEAT: NUANCE, LIZ JORDON-HILL, MAHOGANY FRAME: POLISHED CHROME	CLASS A FLAME SPREAD FABRIC	T-3	11	FALCON PRODUCTS	CUSTOM WOOD TABLE TOP 30"X36"	SOLID OAK TOPS W/ NATURAL MAPLE STAIN	FIELD FINISH TO MATCH DESIGNER'S EXAMPLE
C-2	30	MIKE INDUSTRIES, INC.	35-670 SONAR BARSTOOL 19W, 19D, 45H - 30"SH	SEAT: 2057-701 TALISMAN DESIGNTEX FRAME: NATURAL MAPLE CAPS: BRUSHED CROME	CLASS A FLAME SPREAD FABRIC	T-4	6	FALCON PRODUCTS	CUSTOM WOOD TABLE TOP 36" DIA. ROUND	SOLID OAK TOPS W/ NATURAL MAPLE STAIN	TOP WITH STAINLESS STL INSET STRIP - SEE DETAIL, SHT 22
T-1	16	FALCON PRODUCTS	CUSTOM WOOD TABLE TOP 48" DIA. ROUND	SOLID OAK TOPS W/ NATURAL MAPLE STAIN	BASE TB BRUSHED CHROME - SEE LISTING UNDER TB	T-5	5	FALCON PRODUCTS	CUSTOM WOOD TABLE TOP 42" DIA. ROUND	SOLID OAK TOPS W/ NATURAL MAPLE STAIN	FIELD FINISH TO MATCH DESIGNER'S EXAMPLE
T-2	12	FALCON PRODUCTS	CUSTOM WOOD TABLE TOP 42"X42"	SOLID OAK TOPS W/ NATURAL MAPLE STAIN		T-6	7	BROWN JORDON	2901-4800 DINING TABLE 42" DIA. ROUND	FRAME: POLISHED STAINLESS STEEL W/ VENEERED TOP	

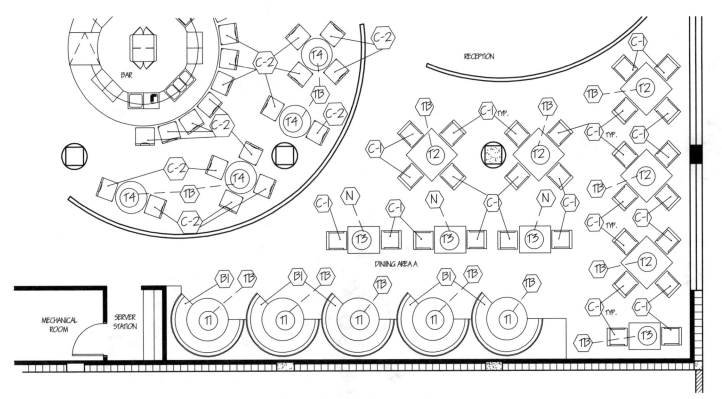

PARTIAL FIRST FLOOR FURNITURE PLAN

FIGURE 14-3 A furniture plan shows the placement of each piece of furniture. It is referenced by a symbol to an accompanying furniture schedule that details the specifications of the component.

PROJECT:	JOHNSON & KLINKER, INC.
ITEM #:	T11
QUANTITY:	4
MANF:	VECTA
MODEL:	GINKGO BILOBA - 606902
DESCRIPTION:	ROUND CONFERENCE TABLE WITH WOOD VENEER TOP AND ALUMINUM TUBE BASE
	W: 48" DIA. H: 29"
FINISH:	NATURAL CHERRY
LOCATION:	CONFERENCE ROOM 2004
ILLUSTRATION:	

PROJECT:	JOHNSON & KLINKER, INC.
ITEM #:	C3
QUANTITY:	16
MANF:	KNOLL
MODEL:	BULLDOG MANAGEMENT (7A1-1-B5G-H-K722/2)
DESCRIPTION:	MEDIUM BACK UPHOLSTERED CONFERENCE CHAIR WITH ARMS
	W: 25 ½" D: 21 ¼" SEAT H: 16" – 21" ARM H: 23 ¾" – 28 ¾" OVERALL H: 30" - 39"
FINISH:	DARK GREY
UPHOLSTERY:	KNOLL TEXTILES/ CHOPSTICKS/ JADE
LOCATION:	CONFERENCE ROOM 2004
ILLUSTRATION:	

FIGURE 14-4 (left) A job book details each piece of furniture, such as this table, T11, and references it to the furniture installation plan.

FIGURE 14-5 (right) The job book often includes a piece of the fabric and a drawing of the item, such as this chair C3.

This is the furniture plan or what is commonly called the furniture installation plan. It may include new, existing, and future pieces of furniture and related items. The selected pieces of furniture might be keyed directly on the plan view, as illustrated in Figure 14-2. However, most furniture plans in commercial projects include an accompanying key or schedule that is referenced to the plan view (Figure 14-3). Code numbers identify each piece of furniture. Information on pricing and ordering, as well as the final placement of the furniture, will generally be included in the job or control book.

The schedule, which is located adjacent to the furniture plan, may simply be in the form of a legend indicating codes and the generic types of furniture they refer to, such as C for chair or TA for table, and not specific product information. The codes must then be explained in more detail in the job or control book, as seen in the example in Figure 14-4. In the job or control book, trade names, product numbers, color names, and other specific information is given. A photograph or line drawing may be included as well as an actual piece of the finish or upholstery fabric. Figure 14-5 shows an example of a page from a job book in which a chair is specified for a project.

For a more complex project, the code may consist of a combination of letters and numbers, such as C14/409, whereas the C stands for chair, 14 stands for the fourteenth type of chair, and the 409 following the slash refers to the room number where the chair is to be located. These codes must further be explained in the control book and specifications.

On large, office-building projects, with open-plan workstations, each workstation and panel cluster may be coded as a unit and keyed to the "systems" furniture division of the furnishings specifications. That is, instead of identifying each piece of furniture

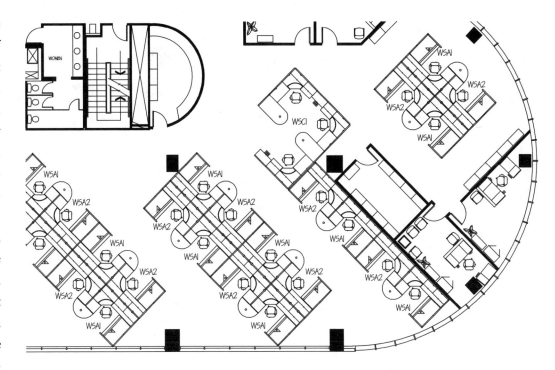

and component on the plan, each workstation may be designated by a code. The code may be a simple designator such as S1 or S5, meaning merely systems furniture group one or five. Codes may also be more complex and have designators that relate to the size and/or job function of the workstation, such as A being the largest, for executives; B for middle management; C for assistants, and so on. These may be further broken down as A1, A2, etc., depending on the number of different configurations and/or components. Other prefixes such as WS for open-plan workstations or PO for private offices, may also be added to the code for clarity as to the specific type of workspace and location. Thus, a code such as POA1 or WSC3 may appear on the plan and in the schedule (see Figure 14-6).

FIGURE 14-6 In this furniture plan, workstations are coded WSA1, WSC1, etc. – then specified in detail in the job book or schedule.

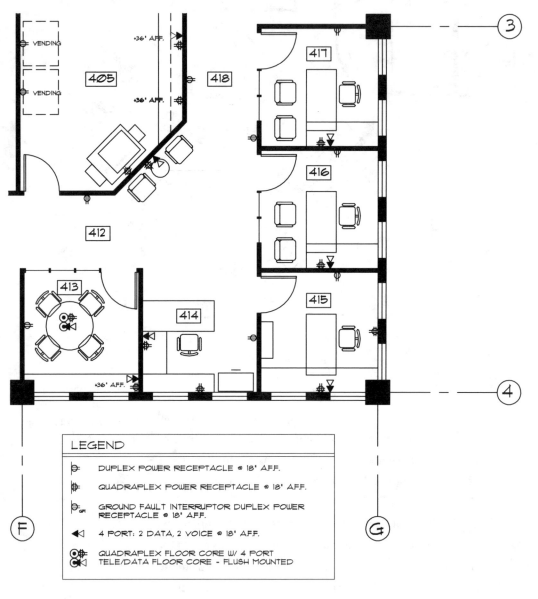

405 VENDING VENDING •36' A.F.F. •36' A.F.F.

418

417

412

416

413 414

415

•36' A.F.F.

3

4

F

G

LEGEND

⊕ DUPLEX POWER RECEPTACLE @ 18' A.F.F.

⊕ QUADRAPLEX POWER RECEPTACLE @ 18' A.F.F.

⊕ GFI GROUND FAULT INTERRUPTER DUPLEX POWER RECEPTACLE @ 18' A.F.F.

◄ 4 PORT: 2 DATA, 2 VOICE @ 18' A.F.F.

QUADRAPLEX FLOOR CORE W/ 4 PORT TELE/DATA FLOOR CORE - FLUSH MOUNTED

FIGURE 14-7 This plan combines the power/communication and furniture plans in order to accurately locate electrical devices in relation to furniture and other cabinetry.

Furniture plans are also used to itemize the furnishings for pricing and ordering as well as to show the installers the exact location and orientation of each piece during move-in. The furniture plan is sometimes aligned with the electrical and power/communication plans, because the exact location of many of these outlets is directly related to the location and orientation of the furniture. See Figure 14-7 for an example of a combined power/communication and furniture plan.

Scale of Furniture Installation Plans

Furniture installation plans are drawn at as small of a scale as possible to reduce the amount of space they take up on the sheet. The furniture drawn in plan view may be simplistic in form to prevent clutter. For example, a chair could be drawn as a rectangle, with no back or arms depicted. However, most designers prefer to visually portray the furniture shape in more detail. Today, this is particularly easy as many manufacturers supply furniture templates that can be directly transferred into the designer's CAD program. As there is often not a lot of detailed information that needs to be drawn in the floor-plan view, a scale of $\frac{1}{8}$" = 1'-0" (1:100 metric) is generally used. However, if more detail is needed to clarify exact configurations or elements of pieces, a scale of $\frac{1}{4}$" = 1'-0" (1:50 metric), or larger can be used.

Drafting Standards for Furniture Installation Plans

Furniture can be identified on plans using numerical codes, graphic depictions of the object, or a combination of these, depending on the complexity and size of the project. Most design firms prefer a simple drawing convention that labels furniture

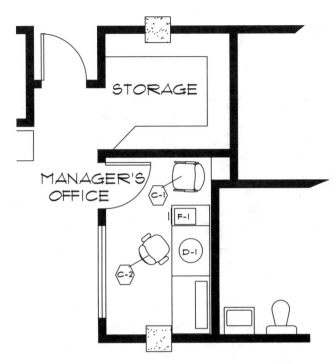

FIGURE 14-8 Furniture is keyed on the floor plan with a symbol, such as this hexagon, for identification in the furniture schedule.

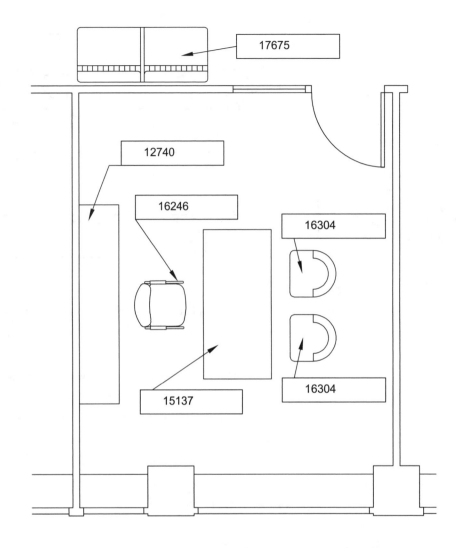

based on their generic category. For example, a chair is designated C-1, C-2, C-3, etc. Sofas are called S-1, S-2, S-3, and tables are T-1, T-2, and T-3. An identifying symbol is drawn around the designation on the floor plan to isolate the key clearly from other information on the drawing (Figure 14-8). In some cases, symbols can be used to identify generic groups of furniture. For example, hexagons might be used for chairs, rectangles for desks, and circles for tables. In all of these methods, it is imperative that the coded information be clear, concise, and legible.

Another method of encoding furniture on an installation plan is to use the coding system on the specifications or accompanying schedule for easy cross-referencing. This convention assigns a ref-

erence number to each item. For example, all tables are indexed as belonging to the 15,000 series. Specific tables could then be itemized as 15100, 15200, and so forth, as illustrated in Figure 14-9. The first two digits reference all tables to the specifications and the last four digits could be used to describe the specific table.

A variety of information can be included in a schedule accom-

FIGURE 14-9 In this example, the furniture is coded with a series of numbers. The chairs are all in the 160000 series. Their specific characteristics are reflected in the numbers following the 16 in each code.

FURNITURE SCHEDULE

KEY	QUANTITY	ITEM	MFG'R / CATALOG NO.	FABRIC / FINISH	REMARKS
C1	12	CHAIR	BROWN JORDAN± 4320-2001	WALL-PRIDE, INC. KL 1267 KALEIDOSCOPE WIDTH:54'± NO REPEAT	FINISH: NATURAL± CLASS A FLAME SPREAD
B1	7	BOOTH	SHELBY WILLIAMS 81-564 LOUNGE SETTEE-CUSTOM SIZE PER PLANS	A. BACK: WAVERLY FABRICS 6071, WIDTH 54' B. SEAT: MAHARAM FABRICS 4538 WOOL #28 FOREST± WIDTH 54' REPEAT Ø.	FLAME PROOF PER CHICAGO BUILDING CODE
T1	4	TABLE	ICF: CARIBE TABLE± L1 MARI	A. BASE: POLISHED BRASS (SMOOTH SURFACE #458) B. TOP: PLASTIC LAMINATE FORMICA NATURAL ALMONDD361. ONE INCH BRASS BAND INSET INTO TOP PERIMETER 2" FROM TABLE EDGE	36 INCHES SQUARE, WITH DROP LEAVES TO 54 INCHES
S1	5	SOFA	KRIES, INC / SHOWPLACE SERIES 9507	BODY: SCHUMACHER AMETHYST PALLADIO TEXTURE, WIDTH 54', REPEAT Ø PILLOWS: MADDEN DESIGNS, JADE SERIES A713	YARDAGE: 17 YARDS FLAMEPROOF PER CHICAGO BUILDING CODE

FIGURE 14-10 The furniture schedule lists the specifics represented by the symbol in the floor plan. Other columns might be added for the quantity, size, manufacturer, fabric/finish, room location, and other information needed to order and install the furniture.

panying a furniture installation plan. Figure 14-10 shows the basic information included in the furniture schedule. Design firms may augment this basic information as necessary for the scope, size, and complexity of the project. Firms vary as to whether the "quantity" column is to be included in this schedule. Some firms prefer to leave the exact count of the pieces up to the furniture representative supplying the items, whereas other firms want to make sure of the exact count before the final order is placed. In such cases, the furniture items can be cross-checked between the purchase orders and the location on the floor plan.

Dimensioning Furniture Installation Plans

Generally, there is not a lot of dimensioning placed on the furniture installation plan. As long as the plan is drawn to scale and the exact sizes are known, the pieces should fit into their assigned spaces and arrangements. However, in some cases, such as with systems furniture, critical clearances and alignment with other items might need to be dimensioned directly on the plan. In these instances, references should be given that are easily obtainable in the field. For example, a dimension might be from the face of a wall, column, or imaginary centerline of a room, as illustrated in Figure 14-11.

Designation of Materials

If the furniture installation plan is drawn at a scale of ½" = 1'-0" (1:20 metric), material designations might be included on the piece shown in the plan view. However, this designation of materials is often reserved for presentation drawings rather than included in the construction drawings. Designers must use their discretion or the office standard when deciding to include material designations. In many CAD libraries, the software for rendering the material is available, but the scale of the drawing and the clear placement of the furniture should take precedence over making the drawing a visual delight.

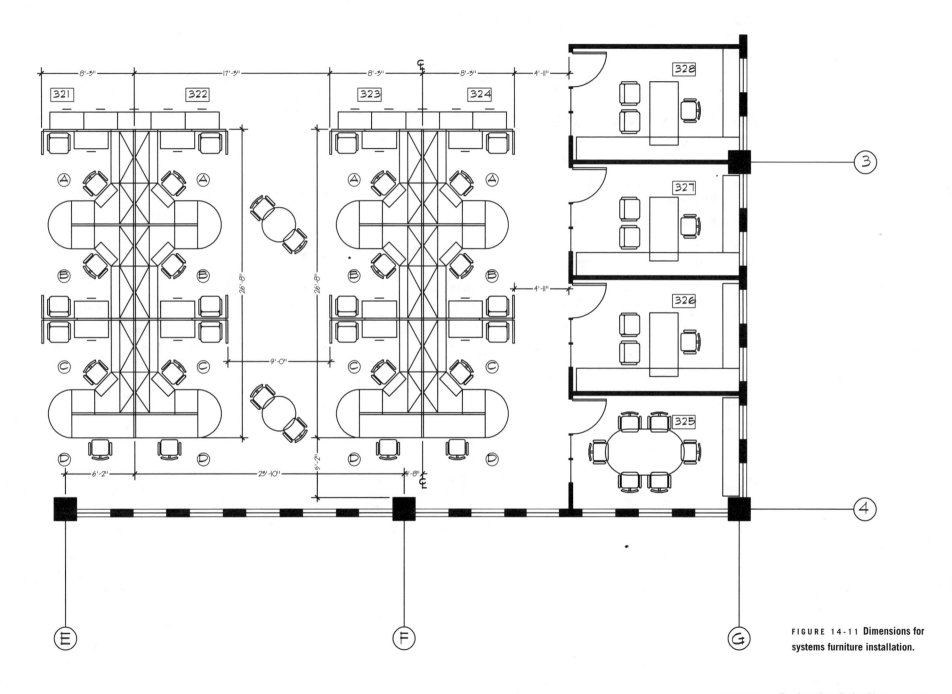

FIGURE 14-11 Dimensions for systems furniture installation.

Checklist for Furniture Installation Plans

General

- Title the drawing, note its scale, and identify north (or reference direction).

- Title the accompanying furniture schedule and key it to the plan.

- Place furniture schedule on the same sheet as furniture plan (preferred) or on a sheet immediately preceding or following the plan.

- Clean up the plan (or in CAD, turn off superfluous information) so the furniture and key codes are clear, dark, and legible.

- Number or name all applicable rooms/spaces.

- Dot in wheelchair access circles and other special furniture items to show compliance with ADA standards (where applicable).

- Carefully check placement of furniture with the electrical and lighting plans for coordination with electrical and luminaire devices.

- Check plan for code compliance and ADA requirements and clearances.

- Check plan for LEED certification credits, if applicable.

- Are the drawings clear and readable when reproduced or printed? If not, correct as necessary.

Notations

- Cross-reference the plan (and schedule if applicable) to other drawings that might contain pertinent information critical to the furniture installation plan.

- Note special features, clearances, alignments, and other important items.

- Cross-reference the furniture installation plan and furniture schedule, carefully checking for accuracy and completeness of information.

- Add notes about issues the installer should be alerted to when placing the furniture.

- Call for submissions of shop drawings where applicable.

Dimensions

- Dimension clearances, alignments, and other controlling factors.

- Call out for installer or contractor to verify existing dimensions of the space/structure against those shown on the installation plan, and to verify these with the designer before furniture installation.

15

Interior spaces are comprised of more than just floors, walls, ceilings, and furniture. Other elements are often needed to enrich and support a space to make it more "completed" and habitable. Furniture, furnishings, and equipment comprise what is commonly referred to as the FF&E program. Furniture was discussed in Chapter 14. The last two areas of the FF&E program, furnishings and equipment, are discussed in this chapter. Furnishings and equipment are an integral part of the total interior environment and are generally selected by the interior designer. They are not items that are just "thrown together" and placed in the interiors. Sometimes, interior designers, when referring to furnishings and some specialized equipment, such as for retail spaces, use the term *fixtures*.

Furnishings are those items that add the finishing touches to the spaces. Furnishings can be utilitarian or decorative, and serve to enhance the architectural features of the space as well as meet the user needs and aspirations. The selection and display of furnishings can impart a person's individual character to a space. Generally, furnishings include accessories, artwork, plants, graphics, and special free-standing or constructed items, as illustrated in Figure 15-1. Accessories could include baskets, figurines, collections, clocks, pottery, or many other items. Accessories might provide a sense of uniqueness or freshness, or be in a serious vein.

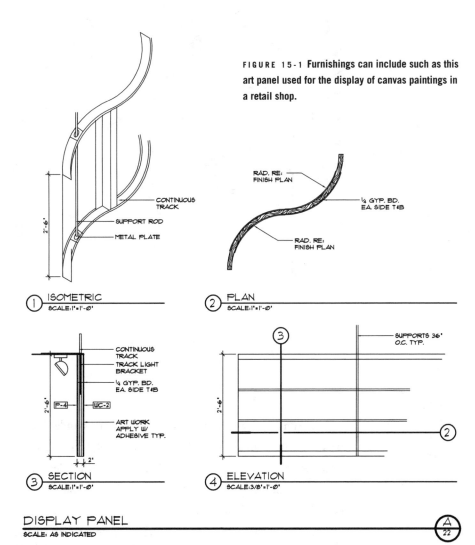

FIGURE 15-1 **Furnishings can include such as this art panel used for the display of canvas paintings in a retail shop.**

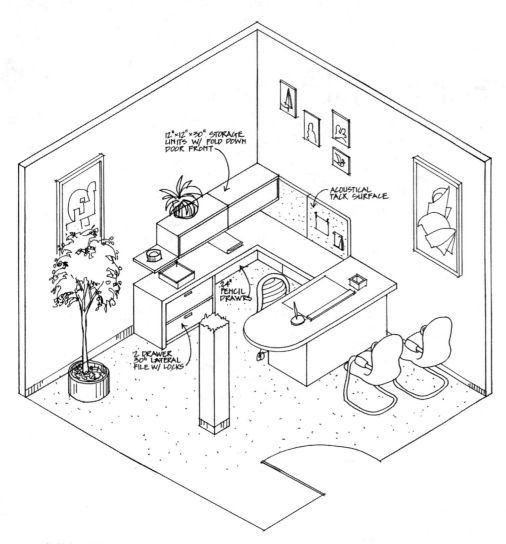

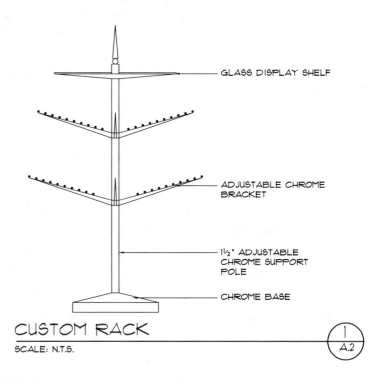

CUSTOM RACK
SCALE: N.T.S.

GLASS DISPLAY SHELF

ADJUSTABLE CHROME BRACKET

1½" ADJUSTABLE CHROME SUPPORT POLE

CHROME BASE

12"×12"×30" STORAGE UNITS W/ FOLD DOWN DOOR FRONT

ACOUSTICAL TACK SURFACE

24" PENCIL DRAWRS

2 DRAWER 30" LATERAL FILE W/ LOCKS

FIGURE 15-2 (left) Artwork and plants help to personalize work environments. Tack surfaces allow the worker to display photographs and other personal items.

FIGURE 15-3 (right) Commercial furnishings can include custom display racks used in a retail-clothing store.

The selection and display of furnishings follows the standard principals with attention to their suitability for the total environment.

Most people like to surround themselves with objects that have special meaning. Items such as personal collections or cherished photographs elicit fond memories and create the sense of continuity in our lives. Placing these items can be difficult for the

interior designer, as their intrinsic aesthetic qualities may not be as strong as the personal connection the client feels for them. However, it is best to coordinate these items and their placement with the client, rather than have the client misplace them later.

Nonresidential or commercial furnishings might be keyed to a theme, for example, a Mexican or seaside motif in a restaurant. In work environments, people also like to surround themselves with personal items, just as they do in their residences. This often gives them a feeling of territoriality and supports them emotionally. Office workers often use elements such as pictures and other personal mementos to personalize their work environment, as illustrated in Figure 15-2. It is generally perceived that these items can add to the worker's feelings of self-worth and perhaps even increase productivity. The interior designer should strive to coor-

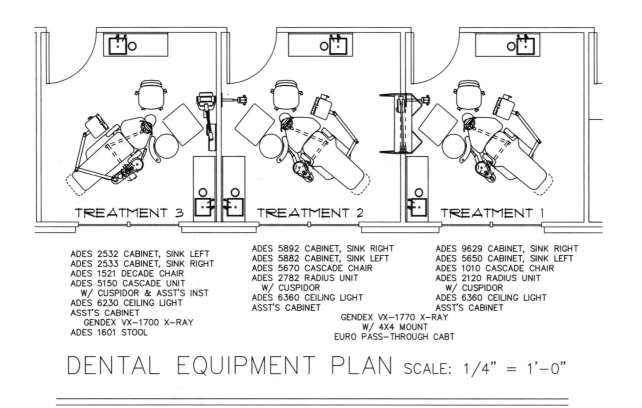

ADES 2532 CABINET, SINK LEFT
ADES 2533 CABINET, SINK RIGHT
ADES 1521 DECADE CHAIR
ADES 5150 CASCADE UNIT
   W/ CUSPIDOR & ASST'S INST
ADES 6230 CEILING LIGHT
ASST'S CABINET
   GENDEX VX-1700 X-RAY
ADES 1601 STOOL

ADES 5892 CABINET, SINK RIGHT
ADES 5882 CABINET, SINK LEFT
ADES 5670 CASCADE CHAIR
ADES 2782 RADIUS UNIT
   W/ CUSPIDOR
ADES 6360 CEILING LIGHT
ASST'S CABINET

ADES 9629 CABINET, SINK RIGHT
ADES 5650 CABINET, SINK LEFT
ADES 1010 CASCADE CHAIR
ADES 2120 RADIUS UNIT
   W/ CUSPIDOR
ADES 6360 CEILING LIGHT
ASST'S CABINET

GENDEX VX-1770 X-RAY
   W/ 4X4 MOUNT
EURO PASS-THROUGH CABT

DENTAL EQUIPMENT PLAN SCALE: 1/4" = 1'-0"

FIGURE 15-4 The dental chairs and related equipment in this office are provided and installed by a dental equipment company following specialty equipment layout plans.

dinate the whole environment while providing for the significant humanization of the spaces the people who will occupy them as part of their daily routine. In some situations, special display equipment must be designed to show accessories, whether they belong to an individual or are for sale (Figure 15-3).

Equipment consists primarily of those specialized items that are necessary for an occupant to carry out their activities. For example, equipment might include tools used in commercial kitchens, or teller equipment needed in banking facilities. Equipment is not generally recognized as a part of the building systems, furniture, or furnishings. However, in some cases, equipment might be physically attached to the building, as with retail display equipment or specialized chairs and other equipment in dental treatment rooms, as shown in Figure 15-4.

Equipment information, guidelines, and location of electrical and plumbing interfaces are often supplied by the manufacturer or supplier, and coordinated by the interior designer. He or she works with the manufacturer, installer, and user when selecting this equipment. In residential work, equipment might include appliances, security systems, or built-in ironing boards. Office equipment in the nonresidential area might include computers, printers, copiers, and other work-related devices. In some situa-

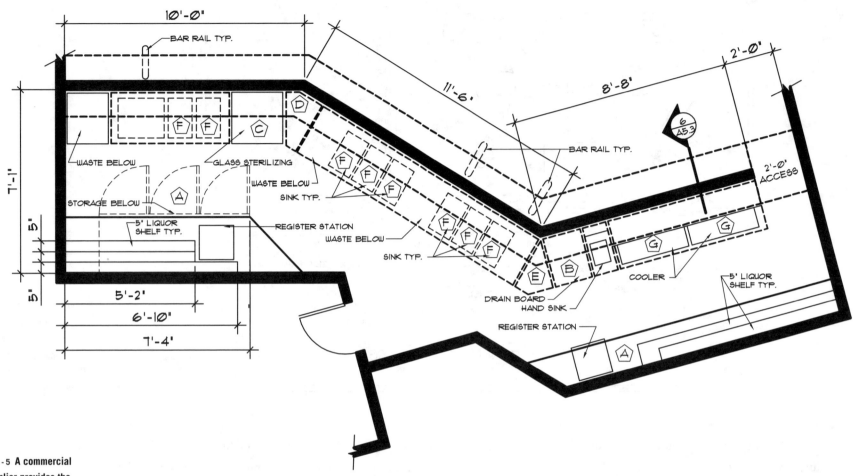

FIGURE 15-5 **A commercial kitchen supplier provides the equipment, specification schedule, and installation plans for this small bar area.**

KEY	QUANTITY	DESCRIPTION	DIMENSIONS	COMMENTS
Ⓐ	2	36" UNDER BAR #CJ5150	36"Hx23½"D	SELF CONT. / S.S. DOORS
Ⓑ	1	DRAIN BOARD # CJ1500	30"Hx24"Dx18W	30"Hx24"Dx18W
Ⓒ	1	GLASS STERILIZER #CJ0804	30"Hx24"Dx24W	S.S. FRONT
Ⓓ	1	CUSTOM CORNER	V.I.F.	S.S. TOP / CUSTOM
Ⓔ	1	CUSTOM CORNER	V.I.F.	S.S. TOP / CUSTOM
Ⓕ	8	SINK	30"Hx24"Dx16W	S.S.
Ⓖ	2	COOLER	33"Hx24"Dx72W	S.S. FRONT

tions, consultants such as commercial kitchen specialists do the actual equipment installation plan if it is complex, as illustrated in Figure 15-5. In many of these cases, the manufacturers supply their equipment templates and detailed information on CD files, or make them available on the Internet. They can often be downloaded directly into the designer's CAD drawings.

Scale of Drawings

The placing of furnishings in small commercial or residential projects might not need any drawings. The interior designer might locate many of the furnishings after the spaces are almost complete, either alone or with the owner. When drawings are needed for specifying and locating furnishings, a variety of scales can be used, depending on the complexity of the project. In some cases, partial sections of the floor plan or interior elevations might be drawn at a large scale, such as ½" = 1'-0" (1:20 metric) to convey the information for locating items.

Equipment is often best located with the help of drawings, as much of it is related to the electrical, communication, and other architectural features of the building. Most of these drawings are in a plan view and drawn at a scale of ⅛" = 1'-0" (1:100 metric), or ¼" = 1'-0" (1:50 metric). However, if more detail is needed to clarify exact configurations or elements of equipment, a larger scale such as ½" = 1'-0" (1:20 metric) can be used, as shown in Figure 15-6.

Drafting Standards

Many of the furnishings for interior spaces are small in scale. The drawing of these items is often simplified in plan or elevation view, as their exact appearance is often too complicated to represent in

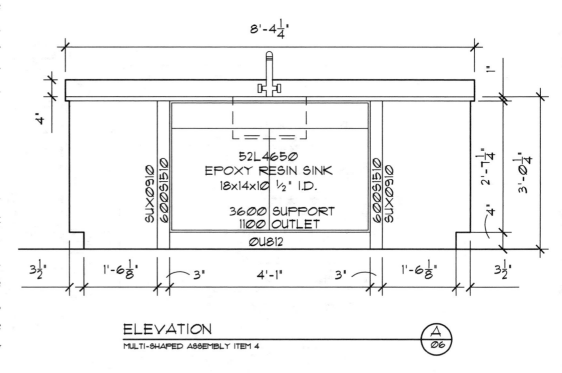

ELEVATION
MULTI-SHAPED ASSEMBLY ITEM 4

(A/06)

a small-scale drawing. In such cases, the basic outline shape and important surface qualities might only be shown. Some items may be left undrawn, and will have to be physically located in the space by the interior designer in conjunction with the client. However, it is best to portray in at least a general way, to provide drawings that can be the governing principal for the price and location of the installation. This can prevent confusion and relocation costs if the items are difficult to move.

Equipment plans should be drawn accurately, with the size and configuration of the items shown in a scaled plan or elevation view, as illustrated in Figure 15-7. Drawings can be produced in CAD using templates provided by the manufacturers or in a soft-

FIGURE 15-6 Some equipment drawings, such as this scientific workstation elevation are drawn at a large scale to detail out the components of the assembly.

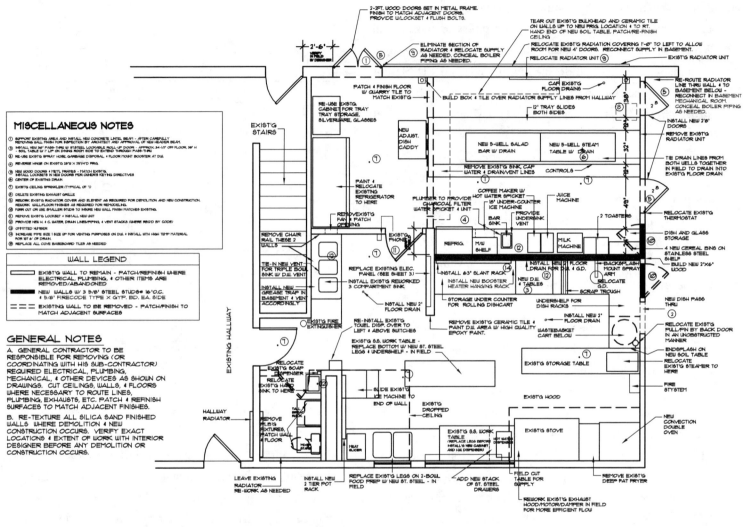

FIRST FLOOR KITCHEN PLAN

SC: 1/2" = 1'-∅"

FIGURE 15-7 A plan view is needed to indicate equipment and remodeling work needed in this small commercial kitchen.

ware library in the designer's office. The drawings should be produced in sufficient detail to accurately portray the item, with a key to cross-reference it to a nearby legend that gives more specific information. Some equipment legends not only show specific items, but also list whose responsibility it is to furnish or install them, as shown in Figure 15-8.

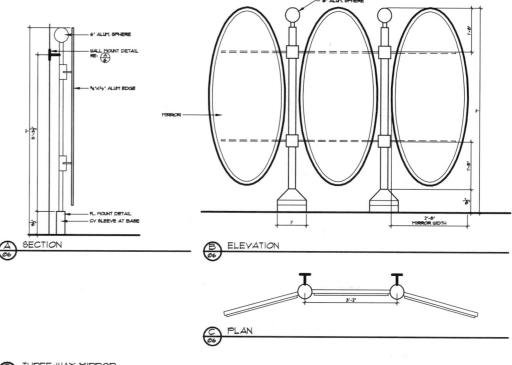

FIXTURE / RESPONSIBILITY SCHEDULE

		QUANTITY	FURNISHED			INSTALLED			REMARKS
			OWNER	GENERAL CONTRACTOR	FIXTURE CONTRACTOR	OWNER	GENERAL CONTRACTOR	FIXTURE CONTRACTOR	
	MISCELLANEOUS CONT								
MS-1	SECURITY KEY PAD		●				●		
MS-2	FIRE EXTINGUISHER			●			●		
MS-3	HAT RACKS		●			●			
	HARDWARE								
R-1	2'x48' U-RAIL				●		●		
R-2	3'x48' U-RAIL				●		●		LINGERIE FIXTURES
R-3	8'x36' U-RAIL				●		●		LINGERIE WALL
R-4	12'x42' U-RAIL				●		●		
R-5	14'x36' U-RAIL SHELF				●		●		
R-6	U-RAIL BRACKET				●		●		FOR SHELF @ HANDBAG DEPT.
R-7	3' FACEOUT				●		●		
R-8	3' SLIP OVER FACEOUT				●		●		
R-9	6' SLIP OVER FACEOUT				●		●		
R-10	14' FACEOUT				●		●		
F-1	14' SLIP OVER FACEOUT				●		●		
B-1	BOW RAIL				●		●		
H-1	SINGLE HAT FACEOUT				●		●		

FIGURE 15-8 Schedules can help coordinate the work of equipment suppliers and installers.

6' ALUM. SPHERE
WALL MOUNT DETAIL RE: △
¾'x½' ALUM EDGE
MIRROR
FL. MOUNT DETAIL
CV SLEEVE AT BASE

(A) SECTION
06

(B) ELEVATION
06

6' ALUM. SPHERE
2'-8" MIRROR WIDTH

(C) PLAN
06
3'-2"

(C) THREE-WAY MIRROR
06   SCALE: ½'=1'-0'

FIGURE 15-9 These drawings show the dimensions of a three-way mirror, as well as its location to the floor and adjacent wall.

Designation of Materials

As mentioned earlier, many materials cannot be accurately drawn in a small-scale plan or elevation view. However, some materials can be delineated or described in drawings if they are not overly complicated, as seen in the three-way mirror design in Figure 15-9. Designers should use their discretion as to how much detail is really needed to convey the material qualities in an architectural drawing. Most of the material information that cannot be drawn clearly is placed in the accompanying schedule or cross-referenced to the specifications, which are often located elsewhere in the drawings or in a separate booklet. In some cases, photographs or scanned images can be placed on the drawing sheets, both in two- and three-dimensional work.

Dimensioning Furnishings and Equipment Plans

Furnishing installation plans, equipment plans, and other drawings are dimensioned as needed. Generally, the most important dimensions are those used to accurately locate the items in relation

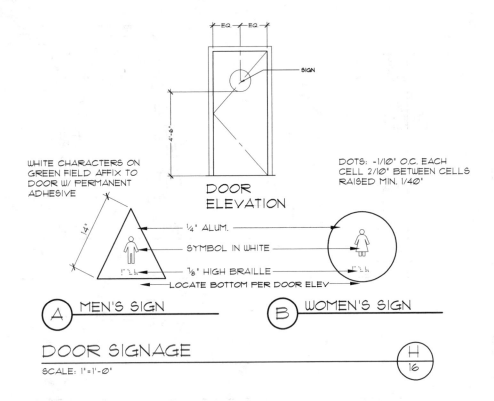

WHITE CHARACTERS ON GREEN FIELD AFFIX TO DOOR W/ PERMANENT ADHESIVE

DOOR ELEVATION

EQ — EQ

SIGN

4'-6"

DOTS: -1/10" O.C. EACH CELL 2/10" BETWEEN CELLS RAISED MIN. 1/40"

1/4" ALUM.

SYMBOL IN WHITE

1/8" HIGH BRAILLE

LOCATE BOTTOM PER DOOR ELEV

(A) MEN'S SIGN

(B) WOMEN'S SIGN

DOOR SIGNAGE

SCALE: 1"=1'-0"

(H 16)

FIGURE 15-10 A combination of notes and drawings are used to present the specifics of the door signage in this dressing area.

to physical objects such as walls, ceilings, and columns. Heights above finish floor, in elevation viewsare often referenced, as seen in the example in Figure 15-10.

Checklist for Furnishings and Equipment Plans

General

- Title the drawing, note its scale, and identify north (or reference direction).

- Title the accompanying furnishings or equipment schedule and key it to the plan.

- Place furnishings and equipment schedule on the same sheet as the

furnishings or equipment plan (preferred) or on a sheet immediately preceding or following the plan.

- Clean up the plan (or in CAD, turn off superfluous information) so the furnishings or equipment key codes are clear, dark, and very legible.

- Number or name all applicable rooms/spaces.

- Dot in wheelchair access circles and other special items to show compliance with ADA standards (where applicable).

- Check plan for code compliance and ADA requirements and clearances.

- Check plan for LEED certification credits, if applicable.

- Are the drawings clear and readable when reproduced or printed? If not, correct as necessary.

Notations

- Note special features, clearances, alignments, and other important items.

- Cross-reference the plan (and schedule if applicable) to other drawings that might contain pertinent information critical to the furnishings or equipment installation plan.

- Cross-reference the furnishings and equipment plans and related schedules, carefully checking for accuracy and completeness of information.

- Add notes on issues of importance the installer should be alerted to when placing the furnishings or equipment.

- Add notes to refer to other consultant drawings that might have input on the furnishing or equipment plans.

- Call for the submission of shop drawings where applicable, either on these sheets or cross-referenced to the general specifications.

Dimensions

- Dimension clearances, alignments, and other controlling factors. Refer to manufacturers', suppliers', or installers' dimensional standards.

- Call out for installer or contractor to verify existing dimensions of the space/structure against those shown on the installation plan, and verify these with the designer before installation of any items or equipment.

Reflected Ceiling, Lighting, and Electrical Plans

Electrical systems in a building includes lighting, electrical outlets, telephone lines, and other communication systems such as computer networks. A designer's objective is to communicate the nature and location of these systems in a clear, uncluttered manner. Several approaches are commonly used to do this. The particular method and type of drawing selected will depend on the size and complexity of the project and the office drafting standards. This chapter will discuss electrical system drawings in both residential and commercial projects, both small and large in scale.

The interior designer is responsible for developing the lighting design that is drawn and then documented as a reflected ceiling plan. The reflected ceiling plan is part of the overall architectural drawings and shows the construction of the ceiling, the location of all the lighting, as well as the location of sprinklers, smoke detectors, and any other objects in or on the ceiling, such as the mechanical (HVAC) air diffusers and grilles. In residential projects and some small commercial projects, the switching and electrical outlets may also be indicated, as illustrated in Figure 16-1.

In larger projects, primarily in commercial work, after the interior designer develops the reflected ceiling plan, an electrical engineering consultant is contacted to prepare a separate plan, called the lighting plan, which includes switching and circuitry. A separate electrical plan, which is sometimes referred to as the

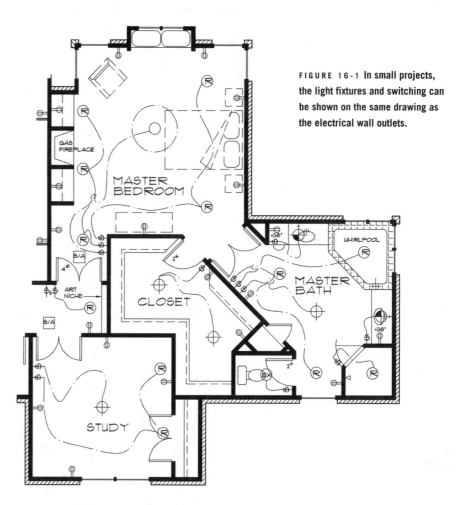

FIGURE 16-1 **In small projects, the light fixtures and switching can be shown on the same drawing as the electrical wall outlets.**

PARTIAL LIGHTING/ELECTRICAL PLAN
SC: 1/4"=1'-0" LIGHT FIXTURES SHOWN AS REFLECTED CEILING PLAN

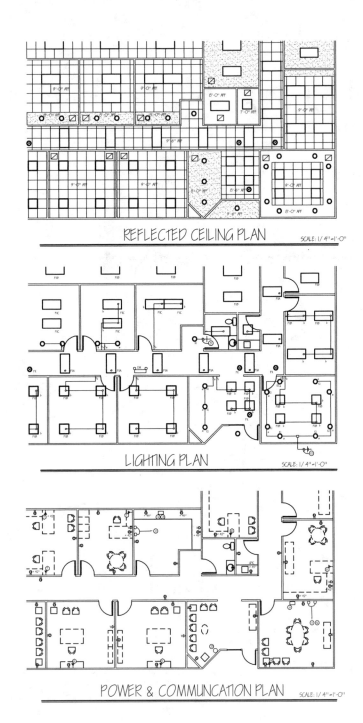

REFLECTED CEILING PLAN SCALE: 1/4"=1'-0"

LIGHTING PLAN SCALE: 1/4"=1'-0"

POWER & COMMUNCATION PLAN SCALE: 1/4"=1'-0"

FIGURE 16-2 In large commercial projects, electrical drawings often include a reflected ceiling plan that shows elements on the ceiling, a lighting plan for fixtures and switching, and a power plan for electrical supply devices.

power and signal plan or power and communication plan, specifies the exact type of circuiting, wire sizes, and other aspects of the systems needed for lighting, convenient outlets, and other fixed equipment. All three types of plans are shown in Figure 16-2. As the electrical requirements vary a great deal from project to project, a careful analysis of equipment needs will help to determine what type(s) of drawings will be necessary.

Note that the electrical lighting plan and the reflected ceiling plan appear similar, but differ in some important ways. The reflected ceiling plan is often drawn first by the interior designer, showing the various ceiling materials and other particulars. The light fixture types and locations are planned on this drawing to coordinate with other items such as mechanical ceiling diffusers, dropped soffits, a suspended ceiling, sprinklers, and other items that appear on the ceiling plane, as illustrated in Figure 16-3. Since the lighting fixtures, referred to as luminaries, are shown on the reflected ceiling plan in a schematic form, a legend is used to cross-reference this drawing to the lighting plan for the exact specifications of the luminaries' wattages, sizes, wall switches, and the various circuits and wiring for these fixtures, as shown in Figure 16-4.

Lighting

The process of illuminating commercial interior spaces from the original design intent to the actual installation of the lighting system involves a number of people as well as different types of drawings. During the design development phase of a project, the interior designer sets the design intent of the project and focuses on aesthetics, finishes, and quality of light, as well as the shapes and materials of the ceiling plane as illustrated in Figure 16-5. The

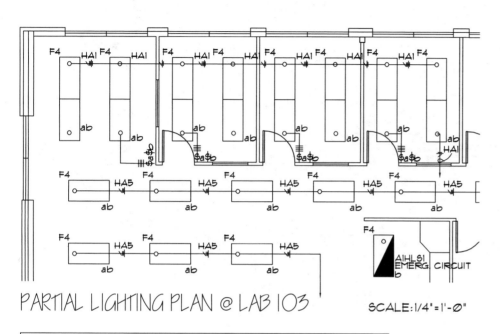

PARTIAL LIGHTING PLAN @ LAB 103

SCALE:1/4"=1'-0"

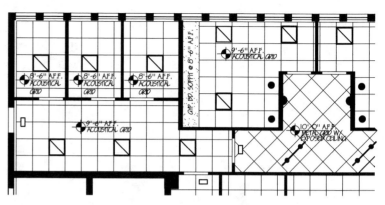

PARTIAL REFLECTED CEILING PLAN

LIGHT FIXTURE LEGEND

◩ 2' x 2' RECESSED FLUORESCENT LIGHT FIXTURE

● RECESSED INCANDESCENT DOWNLIGHT

●—● SURFACE MOUNTED TRACK LIGHT

FIGURE 16-3 This reflected ceiling plan shows light fixture locations in reference to other items. Details about lamps, housing, trim, and switching for the fixtures are provided separately in a legend or in written specifications.

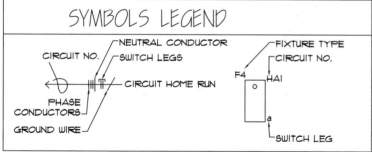

SYMBOLS LEGEND

FIGURE 16-4 A lighting plan indicates the luminaires' wattage and sizes and the location of wall switches and circuits.

LIGHT FIXTURE SCHEDULE

TYPE	DESCRIPTION	VOLTAGE	LAMPS	MOUNT'G	LENS	MANUFACTURER
F4	2'x4' TROFFER, BAKED WHITE ENAMEL, RETURN AIR SLOTS	277	(4) 32W F32T8 3500K	RECESSED CEILING	PATTERN #12, 0.125 NOMINAL PRISMATIC (ACRYLIC)	HE WILLIAMS

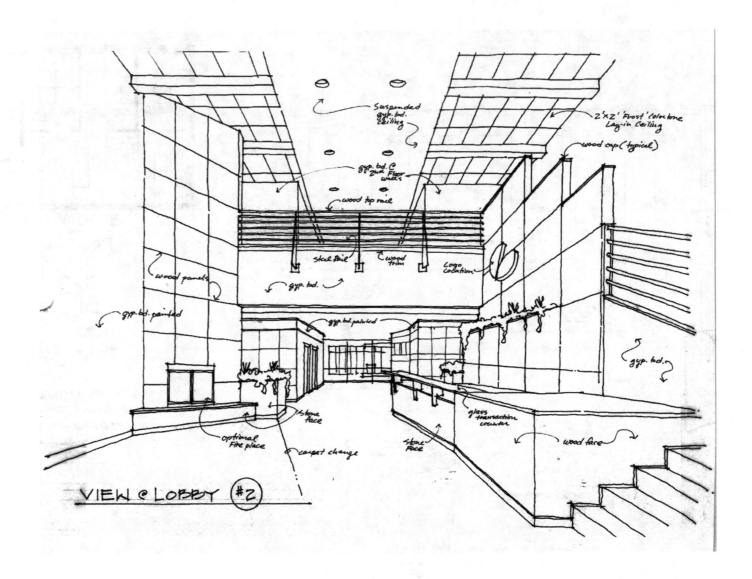

Figure labels (as annotated on sketch):

suspended gyp. bd. ceiling

2'x2' 'Frost' Colortone Lay-in Ceiling

wood cap (typical)

gyp. bd. @ 2nd floor walls

wood top rail

steel rail

wood trim

logo location

wood panels

gyp. bd.

gyp. bd. painted

gyp. bd. painted

gyp. bd.

stone face

glass transaction counter

optional fire place

carpet change

stone face

wood face

VIEW @ LOBBY #2

FIGURE 16-5 This hand sketch explores the relationships of the various ceiling treatments and features with the overall design intent of the space.

client and/or users of the space are primarily concerned with the comfort level of the lighting system as it affects productivity or sales, as well as the initial and operating costs. The third person or group of people involved in commercial lighting is the electrical engineer, whose primary focus is on identifying the appropri-

ate amount of light, power, and electrical circuits needed, energy conservation, and maintenance requirements.

In order to accomplish a well-designed lighting environment several factors must first be considered:

1. **Establish the design intent**

2. **Identify visual tasks and determine the appropriate illumination levels**

3. **Determine amount of daylight available and sustainability issues**

4. **Consider energy efficiency and conservation**

5. **Determine initial and operating costs/budgets**

Types of Drawings

The interior designer is generally responsible for setting the overall design concepts, as well as preparing the reflected ceiling plan (RCP) and schedule that indicates any changes in ceiling height, fixture locations and selections, as shown in Figure 16-6. Lighting is one of the major uses of electrical energy in most commercial buildings and is part of the electrical system of a building. These electrical systems include the lighting, electrical outlets, telephone lines and other communication systems, as well as computer power and networks. The lighting design for a large building must be coordinated with the electrical and mechanical engineers, as well as the architect. The reflected ceiling plan will include everything that interfaces with the ceiling, such as the location of all the lighting, sprinklers, smoke detectors, and heating, ventilating, and air-conditioning (HVAC) air diffusers and grilles, as shown in Figure 16-7.

Types of Ceiling Systems

The ceiling provides the finish surface for a space and defines the upper limits of it. Ceilings form a system that accommodates lighting, supply- and return-air grilles and diffusers, speakers, partition attachments and other structural components, such as thermal barriers, acoustical barriers, and fireproofing. Because

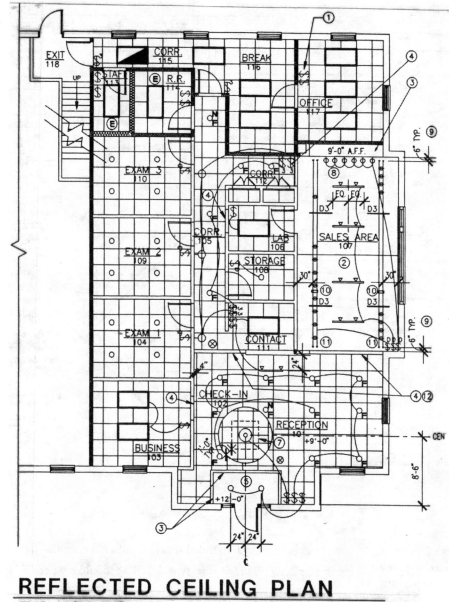

REFLECTED CEILING PLAN

SCALE: 1/8 = 1'-0"

FIGURE 16-6 The interior designer is responsible for setting the overall design concepts as well as drawing the reflected ceiling plan that indicates any changes in ceiling height, fixture locations and selections.

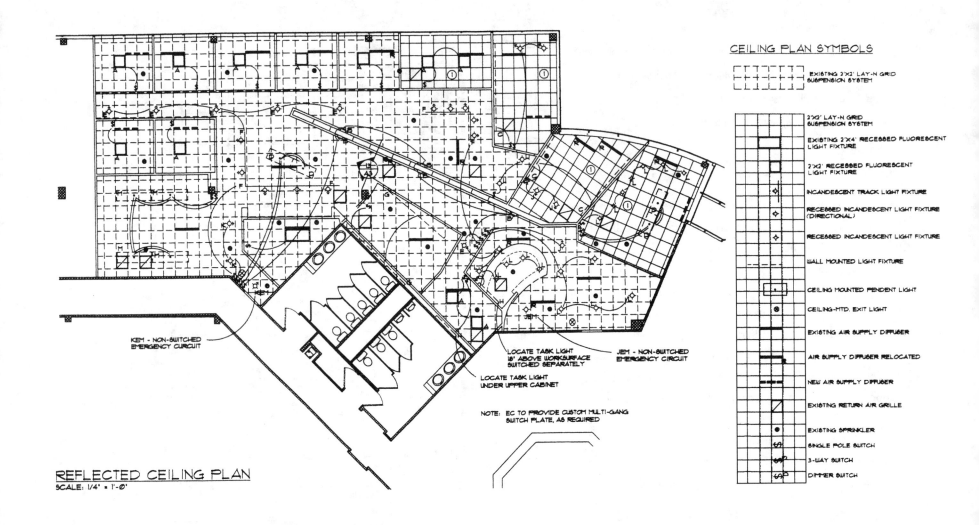

CEILING PLAN SYMBOLS

⬚⬚⬚⬚⬚	EXISTING 2'X2' LAY-IN GRID SUSPENSION SYSTEM
⬜	2'X2' LAY-IN GRID SUSPENSION SYSTEM
▭	EXISTING 2'X4' RECESSED FLUORESCENT LIGHT FIXTURE
▭	2'X2' RECESSED FLUORESCENT LIGHT FIXTURE
◇	INCANDESCENT TRACK LIGHT FIXTURE
◇	RECESSED INCANDESCENT LIGHT FIXTURE (DIRECTIONAL)
◇	RECESSED INCANDESCENT LIGHT FIXTURE
	WALL MOUNTED LIGHT FIXTURE
▭	CEILING MOUNTED PENDENT LIGHT
⊗	CEILING-MTD. EXIT LIGHT
▭	EXISTING AIR SUPPLY DIFFUSER
▬	AIR SUPPLY DIFFUSER RELOCATED
▬▬▬	NEW AIR SUPPLY DIFFUSER
⟋	EXISTING RETURN AIR GRILLE
●	EXISTING SPRINKLER
$	SINGLE POLE SWITCH
$₃	3-WAY SWITCH
$ᴰ	DIMMER SWITCH

KEM - NON-SWITCHED EMERGENCY CURCUIT

LOCATE TASK LIGHT 18' ABOVE WORKSURFACE SWITCHED SEPARATELY

JEM - NON-SWITCHED EMERGENCY CIRCUIT

LOCATE TASK LIGHT UNDER UPPER CABINET

NOTE: EC TO PROVIDE CUSTOM MULTI-GANG SWITCH PLATE, AS REQUIRED

REFLECTED CEILING PLAN
SCALE: 1/4" = 1'-0'

FIGURE 16-7 This reflected ceiling plan includes the HVAC, lighting, sprinklers, and ceiling finish treatments.

ceilings have many functional requirements, it is essential that the interior designer know what type of ceiling should be specified in a commercial project and what functions it must perform. Proper selections and locations for lighting fixtures must also include the overall depth and appropriate flange for recessed luminaries.

Ceiling systems can be divided into three basic groups,

depending on how they are attached to the structure of a building. They can be attached directly to the structure, suspended from the structure, or the finish ceiling and the structure form the same component, sometimes referred to as an "exposed" ceiling, as illustrated in Figure 16-8.

Attached Ceiling Systems

Attached ceilings are generally made of gypsum wallboard or wood and can be attached to the bottom of floor or ceiling joists using screws or nails. For most commercial spaces, gypsum wallboard for ceilings must be at least ⅝ inch (16 mm) thick, which is used for typical framing of 24 inches (600 mm) on center. The gypsum wallboard is finished using tape and joint compound to produce a continuous plane. In commercial construction, screws are the preferred fastener for both ceiling and partitions because they hold stronger than nails. Depending on the occupancy classification, fire ratings of ceiling assemblies may vary from none to 4 hours. In attached ceiling systems, surface-mounted lighting fixtures need UL-approved mechanical hangers to bear the fixtures' weight. If recessed fixtures are used, their hangers must have the same fire rating of the ceiling system, as they are attached to the building's structure.

Suspended Ceiling Systems

Suspended ceilings are hung from a building's structure to provide space above the ceiling, called the plenum, for concealment of mechanical and electrical components, and other services. The most common type of suspended ceilings in commercial interior construction is the acoustical panels. This type of system consists of thin panels of wood, mineral or glass fiber, or fabric-covered acoustical batts set in a grid of metal framing that is suspended by wires from the structure above (Figure 16-9). The fiber panels are fissured in various ways to absorb sound to reduce noise levels with a space while providing easy plenum access. Specific sound transmission data for various panel types can be seen in manufacturers' specifications. Suspended acoustical ceilings are used in commercial interiors for low cost, fast installation, sound control,

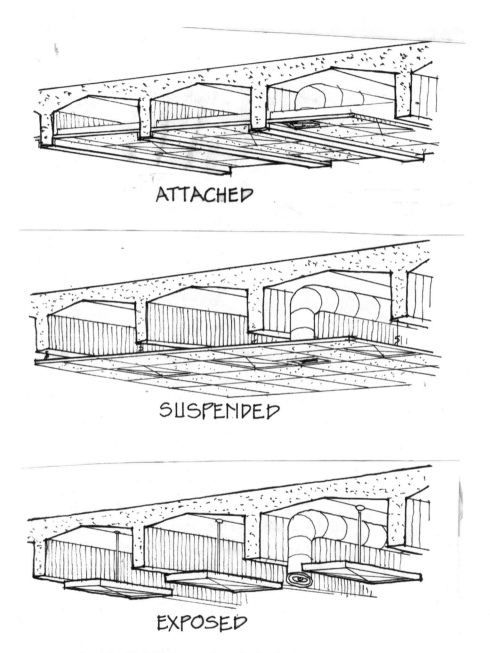

FIGURE 16-8 In relationship to the structure above, the three basic ceiling system types are attached, suspended, and exposed.

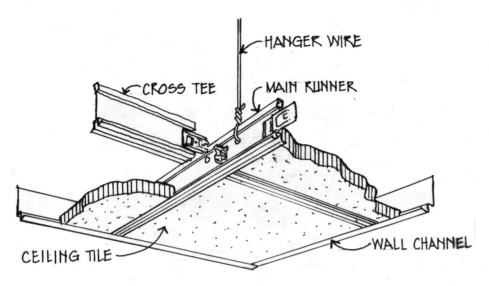

CROSS TEE — MAIN RUNNER

HANGER WIRE

CEILING TILE — WALL CHANNEL

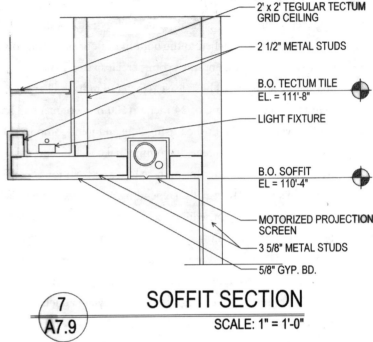

2' x 2' TEGULAR TECTUM
GRID CEILING

2 1/2" METAL STUDS

B.O. TECTUM TILE
EL. = 111'-8"

LIGHT FIXTURE

B.O. SOFFIT
EL = 110'-4"

MOTORIZED PROJECTION
SCREEN

3 5/8" METAL STUDS

5/8" GYP. BD.

SOFFIT SECTION

7
A7.9

SCALE: 1" = 1'-0"

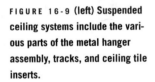

FIGURE 16-9 (left) Suspended ceiling systems include the various parts of the metal hanger assembly, tracks, and ceiling tile inserts.

FIGURE 16-10 (right) This detail in a conference room features Tegular ceiling tile that is placed in a gridded ceiling, that terminates into a cove lighting and adjacent drop down projection screen.

flexibility, adaptability to lighting and mechanical services, and easy accessibility to the plenum. In most commercial interiors, the ceiling system must also be fire rated. In turn, lighting fixtures that penetrate a fire-rated ceiling, such as a recessed fixture, must be UL-labeled for the same hour rating as the ceiling.

Suspended Ceiling Assemblies and Components

Suspended ceilings are installed with hanger wires attached to the structural floor or roof joists above, which hold the metal supporting grid. The most common type of the suspended system is the lay-in system where the panels are simply laid on top of an exposed metal T-shaped grid system. Manufacturers offer many types of grid shapes and sizes, which can be seen in manufacturers' catalogs or web sites on the Internet. These include both acoustical tiles and support systems. Other systems are also avail-

able in which the grid is completely concealed or where the system uses panels with rabbeted edges, referred to as the tegular system as illustrated in Figure 16-10. A ceiling grid system at the perimeter walls is supported by a ceiling angle that is attached directly to the wall.

Acoustical ceiling systems come in a variety of sizes with the 2 x 2 foot (600 mm x 600 mm) and 2 x 4 foot (600 mm x 1200 mm) being the most common. However, if a building shell has a 5-foot working module, a 20 x 60-inch (500 x 1500-mm) size is also available so that three panels fit within one 60-inch (1500-mm) grid. This allows special 20 x 48-inches (508 x 1219-mm) light fixtures

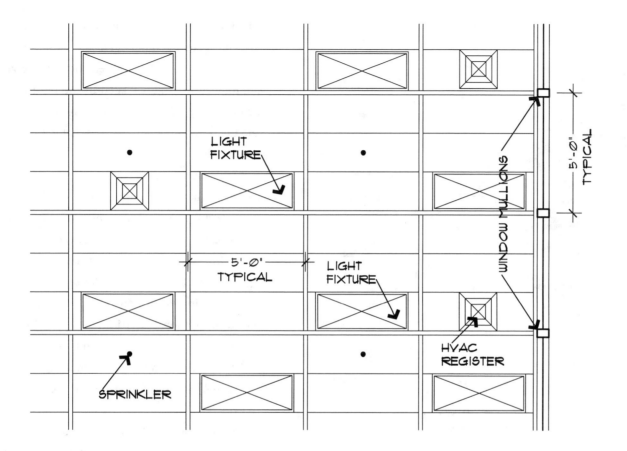

LIGHT
FIXTURE

LIGHT
FIXTURE

5'-0"
TYPICAL

WINDOW MULLIONS

5'-0"
TYPICAL

HVAC
REGISTER

SPRINKLER

FIGURE 16-11 **This acoustical ceiling system is set in a 5 foot (1500 mm) grid to match the building's architectural spacing.**

to be located in the center of a module and office partitions to be laid out on the 5-foot module without interfering with HVAC registers (Figure 16-11).

Exposed Ceiling Systems

Another common type of exposed ceiling is the exposed beam type. Its beams are structural members and support planking and a layer of sheathing, as illustrated in Figure 16-12. Before this sys-

tem is complete any electrical circuits or lighting outlets have to be positioned before the final stage is finished. This type of ceiling requires special considerations for the designer as the beams are structural, and any drilling, notching, or cutting of them requires coordination with the engineer or architect. If a large pendant fixture or chandelier is desired in this type of system, its weight must be supported with adequate bracing beneath the surface of the final sheathing. Exposed beam ceilings can also be of timber or

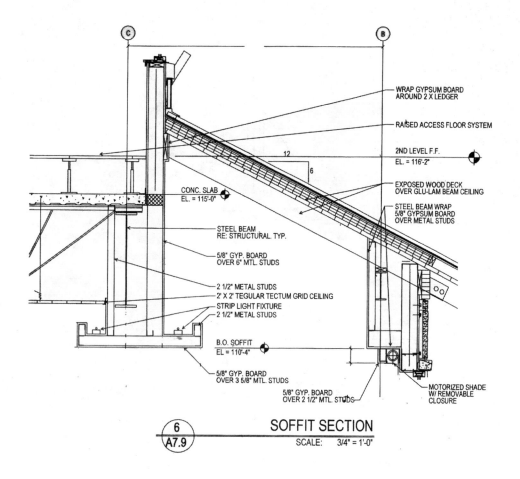

WRAP GYPSUM BOARD
AROUND 2 X LEDGER

RAISED ACCESS FLOOR SYSTEM

2ND LEVEL F.F.
EL. = 116'-2"

EXPOSED WOOD DECK
OVER GLU-LAM BEAM CEILING

STEEL BEAM WRAP
5/8" GYPSUM BOARD
OVER METAL STUDS

CONC. SLAB
EL. = 115'-0"

STEEL BEAM
RE: STRUCTURAL. TYP.

5/8" GYP. BOARD
OVER 6" MTL. STUDS

2 1/2" METAL STUDS
2' X 2' TEGULAR TECTUM GRID CEILING
STRIP LIGHT FIXTURE
2 1/2" METAL STUDS

B.O. SOFFIT
EL = 110'-4"

5/8" GYP. BOARD
OVER 3 5/8" MTL. STUDS

5/8" GYP. BOARD
OVER 2 1/2" MTL. STUDS

MOTORIZED SHADE
W/ REMOVABLE
CLOSURE

SOFFIT SECTION

6 / A7.9

SCALE: 3/4" = 1'-0"

FIGURE 16-12 **This soffit section illustrates a detail of an exposed wood deck over a Glu-Lam beam ceiling and steel beams wrapped with 5/8" gypsum board over metal studs.**

concrete in residential or commercial buildings (Figure 16-13). The beams can be left exposed, painted, or have an acoustical material sprayed on them, if concrete.

Code Issues Affecting Lighting

Building codes are designed to protect the health, safety, and welfare of the public. Interior designers must be aware how these codes apply to the lighting systems of their project and comply with them. There are three main areas of codes that relate to lighting. One is energy conservation and the power-budget limitations. The second area is the requirements for emergency lighting and illuminated exit signs related to the means of egress from the building. The third area is related to the fire rating of a building and the selection of light fixtures that may penetrate a rated ceiling or wall.

Lighting standards and codes are set by various authorities, based on where the building is located, the type of building, and whether it is government owned or built. Two federal agencies are the U.S. Department of Energy (DOE) and the General Services Administration (GSA) that have specific requirements for lighting. Lighting standards and regulations are also set by the National Fire Protection Association (NFPA) codes, which include the National Electrical Code as well as the American Society of Heating, Refrigeration, and Air-Conditioning Engineers (ASHRAE), the Illuminating Engineering Society of North America (IESNA), and the National Institute of Science and Technology (NIST).

As lighting uses 20 to 30 percent of a commercial building's electrical energy usage, good lighting design can save up to one-half of the electrical power used for lighting. The ASHRAE/IESNA Standard 90.1, Energy Efficient Design of New Buildings, developed a set of standards for lighting power credits for lighting control systems designed with energy conserving controls.

Lighting levels and energy power budgets set by these standards affect the type of lighting source, the luminaire selection, the lighting system, furniture placement, and maintenance schedules. The International Code provides power-level criteria based upon the use of the building. For office buildings, the overall building is allowed to use 1.3 watts per square foot to power the interior light-

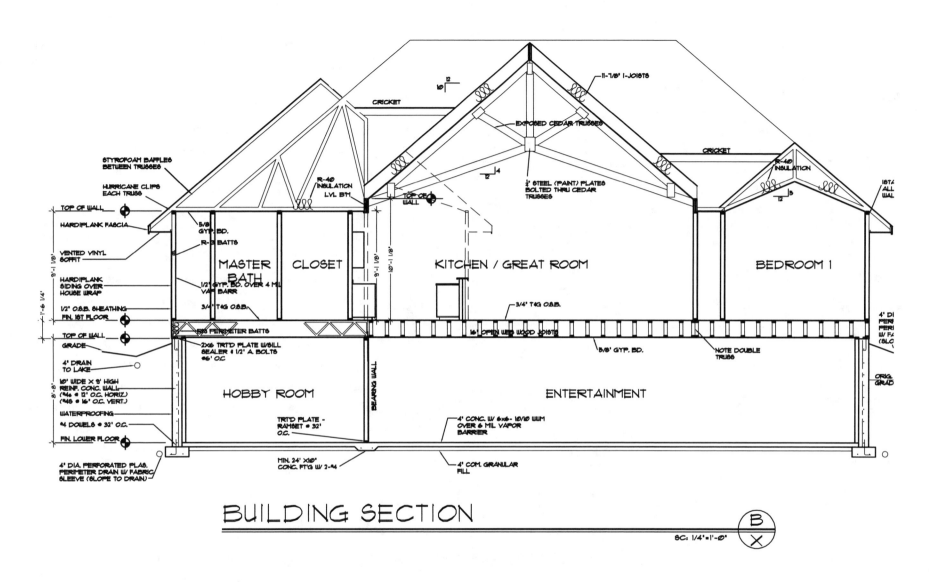

STYROFOAM BAFFLES
BETWEEN TRUSSES

HURRICANE CLIPS
EACH TRUSS

16 | 12

11-7/8" I-JOISTS

CRICKET

EXPOSED CEDAR TRUSSES

CRICKET

R-40
INSULATION

R-40
INSULATION
LVL BTM

12 | 4

12 | 3

1" STEEL (PAINT) PLATES
BOLTED THRU CEDAR
TRUSSES

TOP OF WALL

HARDIPLANK FASCIA

VENTED VINYL
SOFFIT

HARDIPLANK
SIDING OVER
HOUSE WRAP

1/2" O.S.B. SHEATHING

FIN. 1ST FLOOR

5/8"
GYP. BD.

R-3 BATTS

1/2" GYP. BD. OVER 4 MIL
VAP. BARR

3/4" T&G O.S.B.

MASTER
BATH

CLOSET

9'-1 1/8"

10'-1 1/8"

TOP OF
WALL

KITCHEN / GREAT ROOM

3/4" T&G O.S.B.

BEDROOM 1

18T/A
ALL
WAL

9'-1 1/8"

1'-6 1/4"

TOP OF WALL

GRADE

4" DRAIN
TO LAKE

10' WIDE X 9' HIGH
REINF. CONC. WALL
(#4 @ 12" O.C. HORIZ)
(#4 @ 16" O.C. VERT.)

WATERPROOFING

#4 DOWELS @ 32" O.C.

FIN. LOWER FLOOR

4" DIA. PERFORATED PLAS.
PERIMETER DRAIN W/ FABRIC
SLEEVE (SLOPE TO DRAIN)

R-8 PERIMETER BATTS

2X6 TRT'D PLATE W/SILL
SEALER & 1/2" A. BOLTS
@ 6' O.C.

HOBBY ROOM

BEARING WALL

8'-8"

TRT'D PLATE -
RAMSET @ 32"
O.C.

MIN. 24" X10"
CONC. FT'G W/ 2-#4

16" OPEN WEB WOOD JOISTS

5/8" GYP. BD.

NOTE DOUBLE
TRUSS

4" D
PERI
PERI
W/ F/
(SLC

4" DI
PERI
PERI
W/ F/
(SLC

ENTERTAINMENT

4" CONC. W/ 6x6- 10/10 WWM
OVER 6 MIL VAPOR
BARRIER

4" COM. GRANULAR
FILL

ORIG.
GRAD

BUILDING SECTION

SC: 1/4"=1'-0"

Ⓑ
Ⓧ

ing for the entire building. Each tenant portion of the building may use up to 1.5 watts per square foot, assuming that light power levels will be lower elsewhere to allow the entire building to meet the lower overall building criteria.

Lighting-control criteria for commercial buildings is based on the assumption that most commercial office use occurs primarily in the daytime, or during defined periods of a 24-hour day. Therefore, lighting is required to be switchable to be able to reduce the connected lighting load by approximately 50 percent while maintaining a reasonably uniform illumination pattern. Exterior light-

FIGURE 16-13 This building section illustrates how exposed cedar trusses can add a dramatic effect in the ceiling of this kitchen/great room.

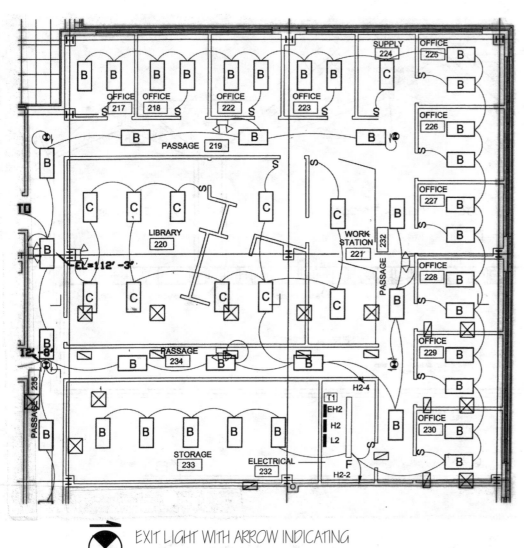

EXIT LIGHT WITH ARROW INDICATING
DIRECTION OF EXIT

FIGURE 16-14 Illuminated exit lights are drawn in this lighting plan, pointing the way to the exit-ways outside of the tenant space.

ing, not intended for 24-hour use, is to have automatic switches or time-clock controls.

Exit and Emergency Lighting

Typically, commercial codes require that in the event of a power failure, sufficient lighting must be available to safely evacuate building occupants. Emergency lighting is required in exit stairs, corridors, and in places of assembly, educational facilities, hazardous locations, and other places where occupancy loads require this. Emergency lights must have the capability to remain illuminated for up to 90 minutes either by battery, internal illumination, or connection to an emergency power source. Emergency lighting requirements for means of egress require a minimum lighting level of 1 footcandle (11 lux) at the floor level upon initial operation.

Illuminated exit signs are required in most commercial buildings at each exit door and at each door leading to an exit-way. Exit signs must be directional at corridor intersections and where a corridor changes direction, as illustrated in Figure 16-14. Emergency lighting circuits and exit lights are usually a part of the original architectural design of a building but must be added to any new tenant build-out.

Sustainability Issues in Lighting and Daylighting

Sustainable design is a means of encouraging conservation in daily life and is one of the major issues in the building industry. Energy conservation in commercial buildings and interiors is a complex issue that involves the building site, choice of appropriate construction methods, use and control of daylight, selection of finishes and colors, and the design of artificial lighting. The choice of heating, ventilating, and air-conditioning (HVAC) and other

SOUTH ELEVATION

3/10
NOT TO SCALE

equipment can also have a major effect on energy conservation. An interior designer must be environmentally conscious and create indoor environments that are healthy and sustainable for their occupants. The choices interior designers make impact the global environment; therefore, their choices must provide comfort for the users of the commercial space as well as benefit the environment. By designing with natural light where possible, natural ventilation, and adequate insulation, overall energy consumption can be reduced. Interior designers can further help to limit greenhouse gas production by specifying energy-efficient lighting fixtures.

Daylighting

Daylight can reduce the amount of energy required for artificial lighting in parts of a building when daylight is available for illumination. The success of daylighting as a sustainable practice depends on the integration and interaction of the various building

FIGURE 16-15 Appropriately placed windows, clerestory windows, and skylights allow natural daylight to penetrate deep into the building's interior spaces, thus reducing artificial lighting and energy needs.

TYPE	LIGHT DISTRIBUTION	CHARACTERISTICS
DIRECT-WIDE BEAM	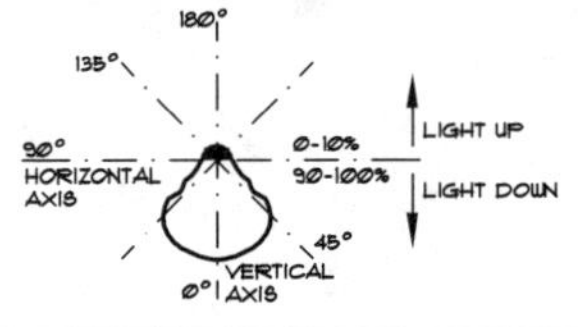	90-100% OF LIGHT OUTPUT IS DIRECTED DOWN. WIDE BEAM DIRECT LIGHTING CAN BE USED FOR EMPHASIS AND HIGHLIGHTING.
DIRECT-NARROW BEAM	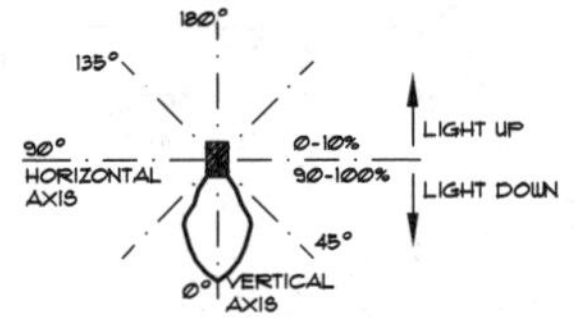	90-100% OF LIGHT OUTPUT IS DIRECTED DOWN. NARROW BEAM DIRECT LIGHTING CAN BE USED FOR EMPHASIS AND HIGHLIGHTING.
INDIRECT	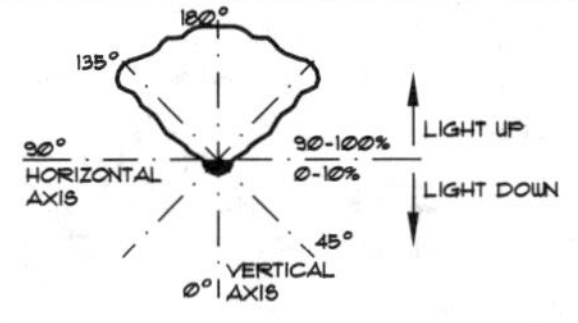	90-100% OF LIGHT OUTPUT IS DIRECTED UP TOWARD THE CEILING. CAN CREATE A FEELING OF HEIGHT AND PREVENT DARK CEILINGS.
DIRECT / INDIRECT	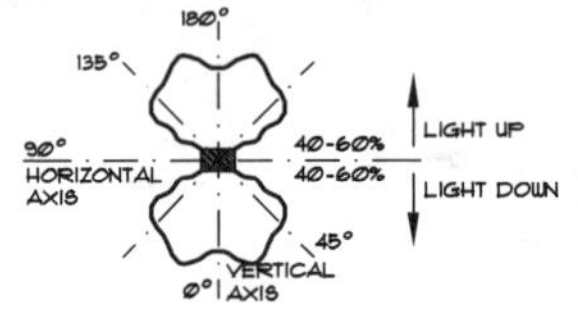	EQUAL AMOUNT OF LIGHT DIRECTED DOWN AS WELL AS UP WITH LITTLE PROVIDED TO THE SIDES. DIRECT GLARE IS REDUCED.
DIFFUSE	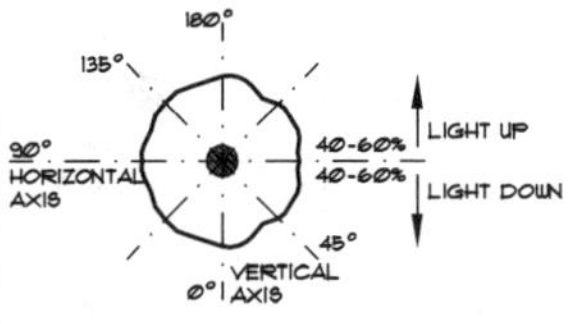	LIGHT OUTPUT IS DIRECTED IN ALL DIRECTIONS. DIRECT GLARE CAN BE PREVENTED BY DIFFUSE ENCLOSURES.
SEMI-DIRECT	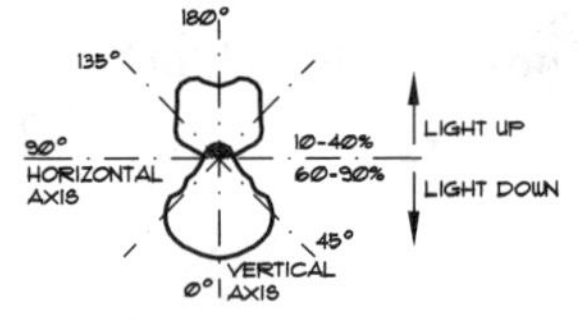	10-40% OF LIGHT OUTPUT IS DIRECTED UPWARD, WHILE 60-90% OF LIGHT IS DIRECTED DOWN. SHADOWS ARE NOT AS HARSH.
SEMI-INDIRECT	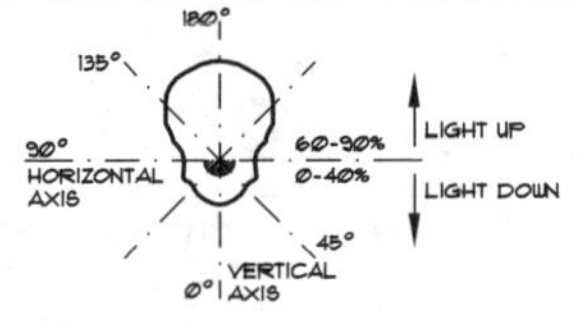	60-90% OF LIGHT IS DIRECTED UPWARD. SOME LIGHT IS DIRECTED DOWN, WHICH SOFTENS HARSH SHADOWS.

FIGURE 16-16 This chart illustrates luminaire beam spread patterns and the percentage of light directed upward or downward.

materials and systems. Successful design using daylighting requires the use of windows with appropriate orientation, clerestory windows, skylights, shading controls, monitors, and room surface finishes along with proper energy-efficient electric lighting (Figure 16-15). Designing a lighting plan with the use of daylight can be another energy-saving control system that works by automatic dimming. These dimmers, triggered by photocells, reduce energy use in perimeter areas of commercial interiors by up to 60 percent, if correctly installed and maintained.

Lighting and the Reflected Ceiling Plan

By creatively controlling natural and artificial light, the interior designer can create striking designs while providing for the visual needs of the user. Lighting design is a combination of art and applied science. It guides our vision and can affect our attitudes and behavior. The designer can also insure the conservation of energy by employing efficient luminaries. The switching of lighting controls and systematic maintenance programs can also affect the energy conservation.

The type of lighting system the interior designer selects determines the amount of detail the construction drawings need. Lighting systems can refer to the individual types of luminaries or to the total installation. They are described as direct, indirect, direct-indirect, diffuse, semi-direct, and semi-indirect, as illustrated in Figure 16-16. The reflected ceiling plan shows the ceiling in plan view and anything that is attached to it, such as light fixtures, sprinkler heads, visible HVAC devices, and soffits. Materials indications and any change in ceiling heights are also shown. It is referred to as a reflected ceiling plan because it is the view that one would see if looking down at a mirrored floor, reflecting what is on the ceil-

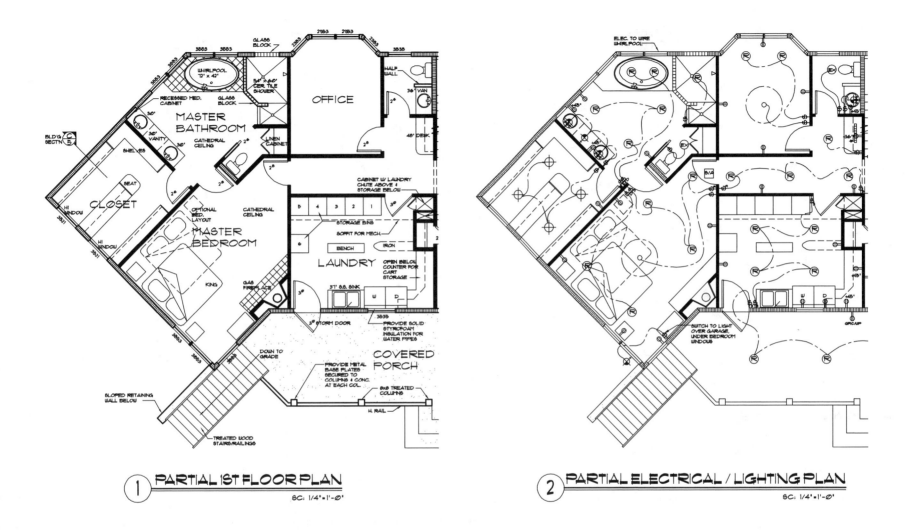

1 PARTIAL 1ST FLOOR PLAN
SC: 1/4"=1'-0"

2 PARTIAL ELECTRICAL / LIGHTING PLAN
SC: 1/4"=1'-0"

ing. Note, however, that the ceiling plan is not a mirrored or reversed image of the floor plan. This "reflected" view is in the same orientation as the floor plan and objects on it. It is drawn as if the ceiling was a clear glass sheet and one were looking downward through this at the floor plan. If the floor plan is oriented with north toward the top of the sheet, then the reflected ceiling plan should also be oriented with north toward the top of the sheet, as shown in Figure 16-17. This provides consistency in the construction documents.

The reflected ceiling plan is particularly useful to coordinate all ceiling-mounted building systems and for checking on the ceiling appearance and finished ceiling heights above the finish floor.

FIGURE 16-17 **The reflected ceiling plan is oriented in the same direction as the floor plan.**

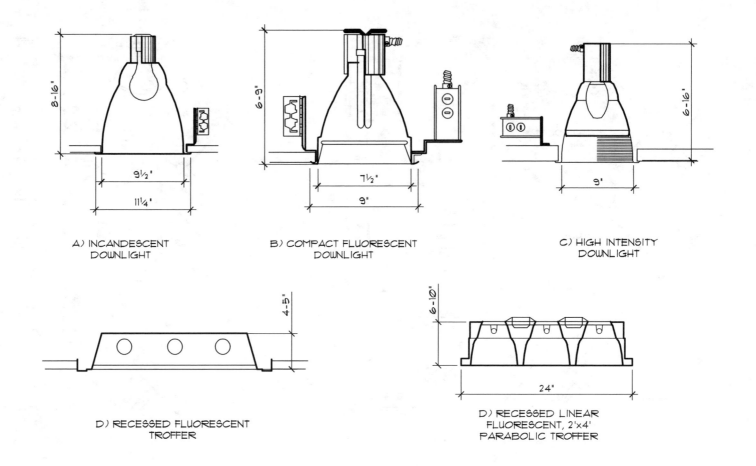

A) INCANDESCENT
DOWNLIGHT

B) COMPACT FLUORESCENT
DOWNLIGHT

C) HIGH INTENSITY
DOWNLIGHT

D) RECESSED FLUORESCENT
TROFFER

D) RECESSED LINEAR
FLUORESCENT, 2'x4'
PARABOLIC TROFFER

FIGURE 16-18 Typical sizes and clearances needed for recessed luminaires.

Before the design of the lighting system begins, the clearance above the finished ceiling must be verified by reviewing the architectural building sections and mechanical drawings. For recessed lighting systems, there must be enough space above the ceiling to install the fixtures. Most recessed fluorescent troffers used in commercial projects are only 4 to 10 inches (101 to 254 mm) in depth and are usually not a problem. However, recessed downlights can be as deep as 16 inches (406 mm), which may cause problems with other above-ceiling construction such as HVAC ductwork, elec-

trical conduit, or plumbing pipes. See Figure 16-18 for some typical sizes of various recessed luminaries.

Scale of Reflected Ceiling Plans

Reflected ceiling plans should be drawn at the same scale as the floor plans. Depending on the complexity of the project and ceiling treatment, the most common scale for residential and small commercial projects is ¼" = 1'-0" (1:50 metric) and ⅛" = 1'-0" (1:100 metric) for large commercial projects. The scale the ceiling

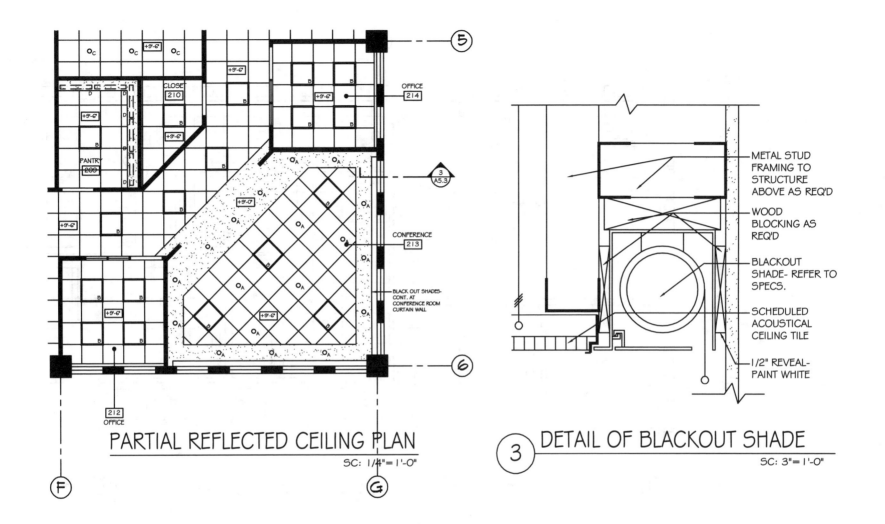

PARTIAL REFLECTED CEILING PLAN
SC: 1/4"=1'-0"

OFFICE 214

3 A5.3

CONFERENCE 213

BLACK OUT SHADES- CONT. AT CONFERENCE ROOM CURTAIN WALL

CLOSE 210

PANTRY 209

212 OFFICE

3 DETAIL OF BLACKOUT SHADE
SC: 3"=1'-0"

METAL STUD FRAMING TO STRUCTURE ABOVE AS REQ'D

WOOD BLOCKING AS REQ'D

BLACKOUT SHADE- REFER TO SPECS.

SCHEDULED ACOUSTICAL CEILING TILE

1/2" REVEAL- PAINT WHITE

plan is drawn at should be noted and placed directly below the drawing, either adjacent to or directly below the title. If an enlarged detail is needed to explain a feature in the ceiling, it is keyed with a note or symbol to a separate larger-scale drawing (Figure 16-19).

The luminaries should be drawn as simple rectangles, squares, or circles that depict the actual fixture as closely as possible (Fig-

ure 16-20). Simplistic forms prevent clutter in the view for ease of recognition. In most cases, the lighting fixture is drawn to the scale of the actual fixtures. However, in some cases such as miniature spotlights, a properly scaled unit is too small to show up on the plan view.

FIGURE 16-19 An enlarged detail of a blackout shade is drawn in section view and keyed to its location in the small-scale reflected ceiling plan.

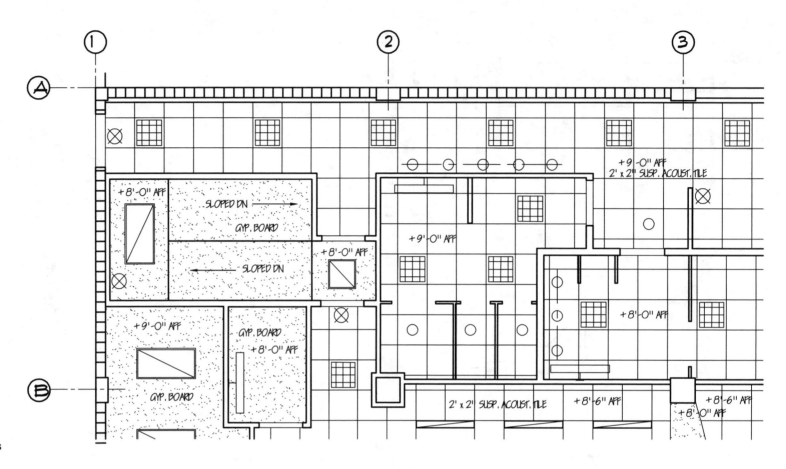

PARTIAL REFLECTED CEILING PLAN - 2ND FL'R

Drafting Standards for the Reflected Ceiling Plan

A reflected ceiling plan must clearly show all walls, partitions, and soffits that intersect with the ceiling. It should also specify changes in ceiling elevations and materials, such as lights, sprinklers, smoke detectors, and HVAC diffusers that attach to or penetrate the ceiling. In drafting reflected ceiling plans, the designer should repro-

duce the floor plan walls and openings such as doors and windows, but without showing items such as built-in cabinetry, plumbing fixtures, etc.

The lighting fixtures and other electrical features shown on the reflected ceiling plan are given symbols that are then keyed to a legend (Figure 16-21). It is advisable to draw in all the electrical

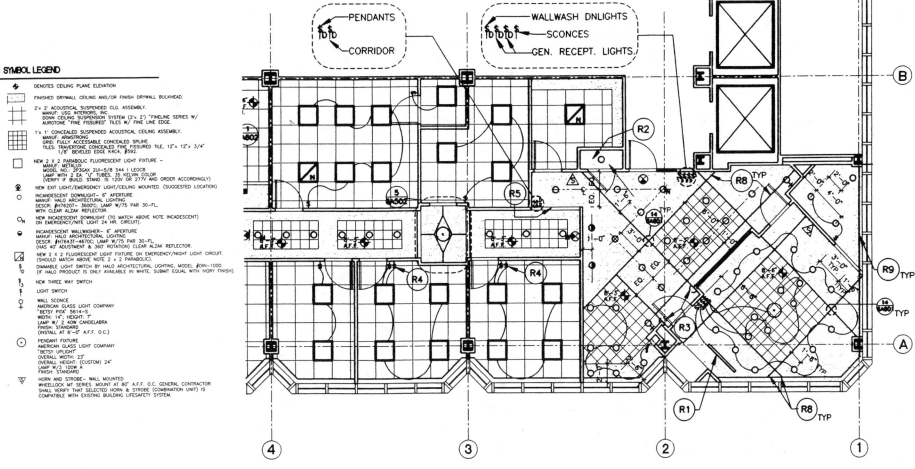

SYMBOL LEGEND

Symbol	Description
	DENOTES CEILING PLANE ELEVATION
	FINISHED DRYWALL CEILING AND/OR FINISH DRYWALL BULKHEAD.
	2'x 2' ACOUSTICAL SUSPENDED CLG. ASSEMBLY. MANUF: USG INTERIORS, INC. DONN CEILING SUSPENSION SYSTEM (2'x 2') "FINELINE SERIES W/ AUROTONE "FINE FISSURED" TILES W/ FINE LINE EDGE.
	1'x 1' CONCEALED SUSPENDED ACOUSTICAL CEILING ASSEMBLY. MANUF: ARMSTRONG GRID: FULLY ACCESSIBLE CONCEALED SPLINE TILES: TRAVERTONE CONCEALED FINE FISSURED TILE, 12"x 12"x 3/4" 1/8" BEVELED EDGE K4C4, #592.
	NEW 2 X 2 PARABOLIC FLUORESCENT LIGHT FIXTURE – MANUF: METALUX MODEL NO.: 2P3GAX 2U1-5/8 S44 I LEOC8 LAMP WITH 2 EA. "U" TUBES, 35 KELVIN COLOR (VERIFY IF BUILD. STAND. IS 120V OR 277V AND ORDER ACCORDINGLY)
	NEW EXIT LIGHT/EMERGENCY LIGHT/CEILING MOUNTED. (SUGGESTED LOCATION)
	INCANDESCENT DOWNLIGHT– 6" APERTURE MANUF: HALO ARCHITECTURAL LIGHTING DESCR: #H7620T– 3600'C; LAMP W/75 PAR 30–FL, WITH CLEAR ALZAK REFLECTOR.
	NEW INCANDESCENT DOWNLIGHT (TO MATCH ABOVE NOTE INCANDESCENT) ON EMERGENCY/NITE LIGHT 24 HR. CIRCUIT).
	INCANDESCENT WALLWASHER– 6" APERTURE MANUF: HALO ARCHITECTURAL LIGHTING DESCR: #H7643T–4670C; LAMP W/75 PAR 30–FL, (HAS 40' ADJUSTMENT & 360' ROTATION) CLEAR ALZAK REFLECTOR.
	NEW 2 X 2 FLUORESCENT LIGHT FIXTURE ON EMERGENCY/NIGHT LIGHT CIRCUIT. (SHOULD MATCH ABOVE NOTE 2 x 2 PARABOLIC).
	DIMMABLE LIGHT SWITCH BY HALO ARCHITECTURAL LIGHTING, MODEL #DIN-1000. (IF HALO PRODUCT IS ONLY AVAILABLE IN WHITE, SUBMIT EQUAL WITH IVORY FINISH).
	NEW THREE WAY SWITCH
	LIGHT SWITCH
	WALL SCONCE AMERICAN GLASS LIGHT COMPANY "BETSY PITA" 5614–S WIDTH: 14"; HEIGHT: 7" LAMP W/ 2 40W CANDELABRA FINISH: STANDARD (INSTALL AT 6'–0" A.F.F. O.C.)
	PENDANT FIXTURE AMERICAN GLASS LIGHT COMPANY "BETSY UPLIGHT" OVERALL WIDTH: 23" OVERALL HEIGHT: (CUSTOM) 24" LAMP W/3 100W A FINISH: STANDARD
	HORN AND STROBE– WALL MOUNTED WHEELLOCK MT SERIES. MOUNT AT 80" A.F.F. O.C. GENERAL CONTRACTOR SHALL VERIFY THAT SELECTED HORN & STROBE (COMBINATION UNIT) IS COMPATIBLE WITH EXISTING BUILDING LIFESAFETY SYSTEM.

FIGURE 16-21 Lighting fixtures are represented with symbols in the reflected ceiling plan and keyed to a legend showing specifications.

REFLECTED CEILING PLAN
SCALE: 1/8 = 1'–0"

NORTH

COMMON LIGHT SYMBOLS

⊕ CEILING MOUNTED LIGHT FIXTURE

⊕P CEILING MOUNTED PENDANT LIGHT FIXTURE

® RECESSED LIGHT FIXTURE

⊕ WALL MOUNTED LIGHT FIXTURE

├─○─┤ CEILING OR WALL MOUNTED TRACK LIGHTING -LENGTH & NO. OF FIXTURE ON PLAN

● RECESSED WALL WASHER LIGHT FIXTURE

(EX) EXHAUST FAN / LIGHT COMBINATION (VENT TO OUTDOORS)

▭ 2'x4' SURFACE MOUNTED FLUORESCENT LIGHT FIXTURE

▱ 2'x4' RECESSED FLUORESCENT LIGHT FIXTURE

□ 2'x2' RECESSED FLUORESCENT LIGHT FIXTURE

▭ 1'x4' SUSPENDED FLUORESCENT LIGHT FIXTURE (CERTAIN FIXTURES MAY BE ABLE TO CONNECT TO FORM CONTINUOUS ROW)

⊙ CEILING FAN W/ INTEGRAL LIGHT(S) - PROVIDE SEPARATE SWITCHING FOR FAN & LIGHT(S)

▭ UNDERCABINET FLUORESCENT LIGHT FIXTURE W/ INTEGRAL SWITCH (WIRE DIRECT)

⊗ EXIT LIGHT W/ STANDBY BATTERY

▽ EMERGENCY LIGHTS PACK

FIGURE 16-22
Standard lighting and electrical symbols.

symbols on the plan before it is dimensioned or notes are added. If not, a symbol may fall on top of a dimension, thus requiring the dimension to be moved. Locate the light fixtures in the ceiling plan in accordance with the lighting design concept. Common types of light fixtures on the lighting plan include surface-mounted, recessed, pendant, and track-mounted. See Figure 16-22 for a list of standard lighting and electrical symbols.

On commercial projects where there is a suspended ceiling, the reflected ceiling plans would show any partitions that extend through the ceiling plane as well. The ceiling grid lines (called "T" bars) should also be shown (Figure 16-23). Other information included in the reflected ceiling plan are the ceiling materials, ceiling heights, ceiling slopes, changes in ceiling heights, locations of all lighting fixtures (including exit and emergency lights), air diffusers and vents, access panels, speakers, sprinkler heads (if used), and other items that touch or are part of the ceiling plane.

Next, the interior designer should determine how the lights in a space are to be switched. For residential or small commercial projects, the switching can either be shown on the reflected ceiling plan or on the electrical lighting plan. The switching design is based on how much individual control is needed and the function of the lighting. Energy conservation needs and maximum circuit loads within the circuits will also determine the number and location of the switches. Generally, switches are located near the door or opening leading into the space. Large spaces that have more than one entry may require multiple switching locations.

After locating the switches, determine which luminaries they should control and delineate it on the plan. This can be done in two ways, depending on the size and complexity of the lighting plan.

The first method is to draw a line from the wall switch to the

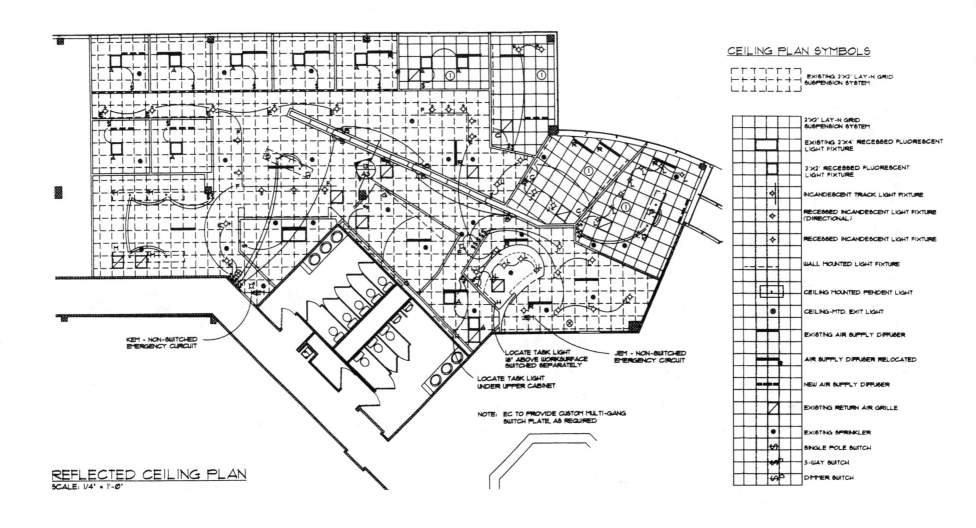

REFLECTED CEILING PLAN
SCALE: 1/4" = 1'-0"

KEM - NON-SWITCHED
EMERGENCY CIRCUIT

LOCATE TASK LIGHT
18" ABOVE WORKSURFACE
SWITCHED SEPARATELY

LOCATE TASK LIGHT
UNDER UPPER CABINET

NOTE: EC TO PROVIDE CUSTOM MULTI-GANG
SWITCH PLATE, AS REQUIRED

JEM - NON-SWITCHED
EMERGENCY CIRCUIT

CEILING PLAN SYMBOLS

EXISTING 2'X2' LAY-IN GRID
SUSPENSION SYSTEM

2'X2' LAY-IN GRID
SUSPENSION SYSTEM

EXISTING 2'X4' RECESSED FLUORESCENT
LIGHT FIXTURE

2'X2' RECESSED FLUORESCENT
LIGHT FIXTURE

INCANDESCENT TRACK LIGHT FIXTURE

RECESSED INCANDESCENT LIGHT FIXTURE
(DIRECTIONAL)

RECESSED INCANDESCENT LIGHT FIXTURE

WALL MOUNTED LIGHT FIXTURE

CEILING MOUNTED PENDENT LIGHT

CEILING-MTD. EXIT LIGHT

EXISTING AIR SUPPLY DIFFUSER

AIR SUPPLY DIFFUSER RELOCATED

NEW AIR SUPPLY DIFFUSER

EXISTING RETURN AIR GRILLE

EXISTING SPRINKLER

SINGLE POLE SWITCH

3-WAY SWITCH

DIMMER SWITCH

fixture(s) it controls. This connecting line should be dashed and curved to distinguish it from other objects and items on the drawing. Curved lines are preferred, as straight lines may get mixed up with wall lines or other items that are drawn in the plan. The connecting curved line should touch the outlet or fixture symbol, as illustrated in Figure 16-24. The symbols for switches can be a simple S. If a particular lighting fixture is switched from two locations, the symbols will be S_3 to indicate that three items (two switches and one lighting fixture) are connected electrically. Common switch symbols are shown in Figure 16-25.

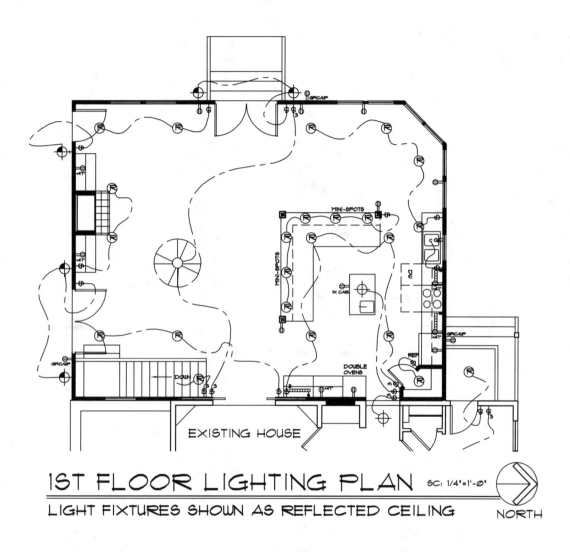

1ST FLOOR LIGHTING PLAN   SC: 1/4"=1'-0'

LIGHT FIXTURES SHOWN AS REFLECTED CEILING

NORTH

EXISTING HOUSE

FIGURE 16-24 In residential projects, curved, dashed lines are used to show which lights a wall switch controls.

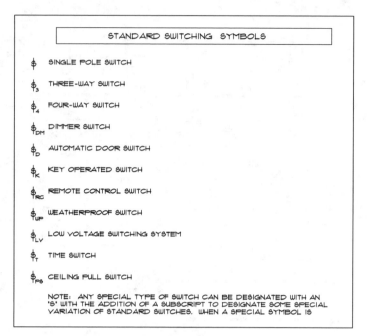

FIGURE 16-25 Common switch symbols for light controls.

The second method of showing light-fixture switching is to assign a number or letter to the switch and place this same number in or near the light fixture shown in the ceiling plan (Figure 16-26). This method is used primarily in commercial spaces, where there might be a lot of multiple switching and other items placed on the ceiling plan, so that the use of lines (the first method) could complicate the drawing.

After the interior designer lays out the lighting and switching, the drawing is given to an electrical engineer who indicates the exact circuitry, wire sizes, and other specifications required for the electrical system. In residential spaces, the drawing might be given

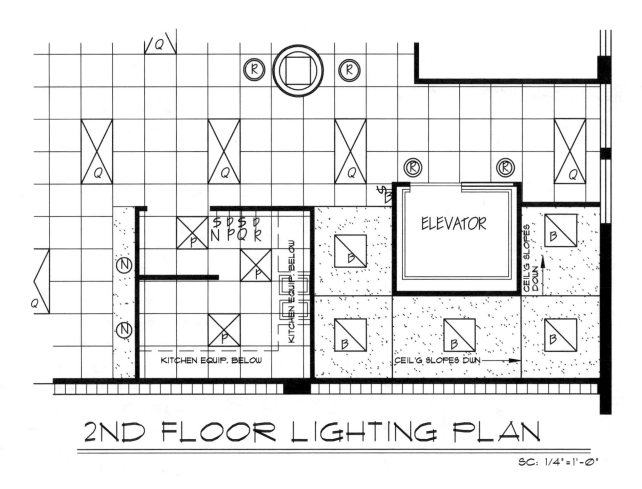

2ND FLOOR LIGHTING PLAN

SC: 1/4"=1'-0"

directly to the electrical contractor, as the circuitry and requirements here are not as complex as those in commercial work.

Designation of Materials

When preparing the reflected ceiling plan, the designer must call out the types and locations of specific ceiling materials. This can be done by placing notes on the plan, or symbols that are referenced to a ceiling material legend. Although the two most common ceiling systems used are gypsum board ceilings and suspended acoustical ceilings, other ceiling finishes might also include wood facing, linear metal, or even exposed wood joists and beams (Figure 16-27).

Dimensioning Reflected Ceiling Plans

As the reflected ceiling plans are generally drawn to a scale that matches the floor plans, there is no need for a lot of dimensioning

FIGURE 16-26 Another method of denoting light-switch controls in large commercial projects is by the use of subscript letters that match the light fixture to the proper wall switch.

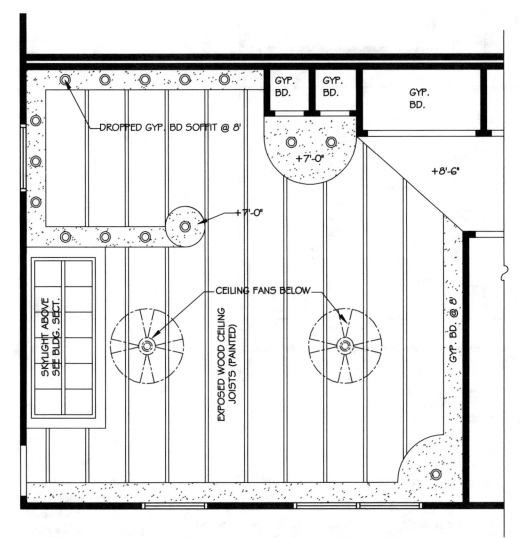

PARTIAL REFLECTED CEILING PLAN

SC: 1/4"= 1'-0"

Labels within the figure:
- DROPPED GYP. BD SOFFIT @ 8'
- GYP. BD.
- GYP. BD.
- GYP. BD.
- +7'-0"
- +7'-0"
- +8'-6"
- CEILING FANS BELOW
- SKYLIGHT ABOVE SEE BLDG. SECT.
- EXPOSED WOOD CEILING JOISTS (PAINTED)
- GYP. BD. @ 8'

FIGURE 16-27 A variety of textures and notes can be used to designate ceiling types, such as this exposed wood ceiling with gypsum board soffits.

placed on the plan, unless ceiling breaks or changes of materials occur where they are not obviously located at a door, wall, or column location. As long as the reflected plan is drawn to scale, the dimensions of the spaces and structure are known, the reflected ceiling plan can be reserved for the floor plan. However, in some cases, the sizes of the units and the fixture locations do need to be dimensioned. This is particularly true in large expanses of gypsum board ceiling, where the scale cannot be easily determined as in a gridded suspended ceiling assembly where, for example, one can count units to locate the light fixture.

When dimensioning the reflected ceiling plan, either "finish" dimensions or "framing" dimensions can be used, but must be noted on the plans. Elements such as recessed light troffers can be precisely located in the finished space. If a downlight in a gypsum wallboard ceiling is to be used, it generally is dimensioned to its center point so the electrical contractor knows where to install it. Alignment and direction of patterns might need to be dimensioned directly on the plan. In these instances, references should be given that are easily obtainable in the field. Dimensions should be referenced from the face of a wall, column, or imaginary centerline of a room, as illustrated in Figure 16-28.

Checklist for Reflected Ceiling Plans

General

- Title the drawing, note its scale, and identify north (or reference direction).

- If needed, develop a ceiling type material schedule and key it to the plan.

- Develop a lighting symbol legend and locate it on the same sheet as the first reflected ceiling plan (if more than one is required), or on a nearby sheet.

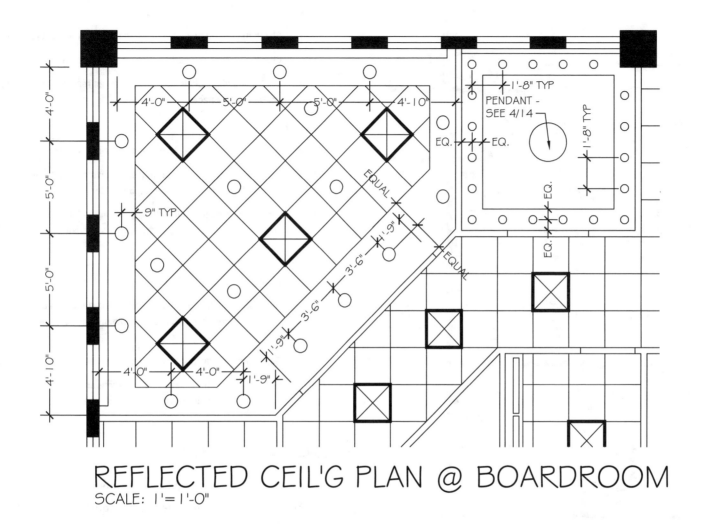

REFLECTED CEIL'G PLAN @ BOARDROOM
SCALE: 1"=1'-0"

FIGURE 16-28 The recessed down lights in this reflected ceiling plan are dimensioned in relation to each other and various wall elements and soffits.

- Clean up the plan (or in CAD, turn off superfluous information) so the walls, spaces, and key codes are clear, dark, and very legible. Don't show items unless they are on the ceiling plane or intersecting it.

- Draw in (with dashed lines) major soffits, coves, drapery pockets, attic access panels, or openings above and call them out in notes.

- Pouche walls, if applicable.

- Show HVAC grilles, light fixtures, sprinkler heads, emergency lighting, illuminated exit signs, and other items that may intersect or be attached to the ceiling planes.

- Decide on the switching patterns of the light fixtures if the reflected ceiling plan also serves as the lighting plan (residential interiors). Show by the curved-line method or use of numbers/letters.

- Cross-reference the reflected ceiling plan to other drawings (if applicable), carefully checking for accuracy and completeness of information.

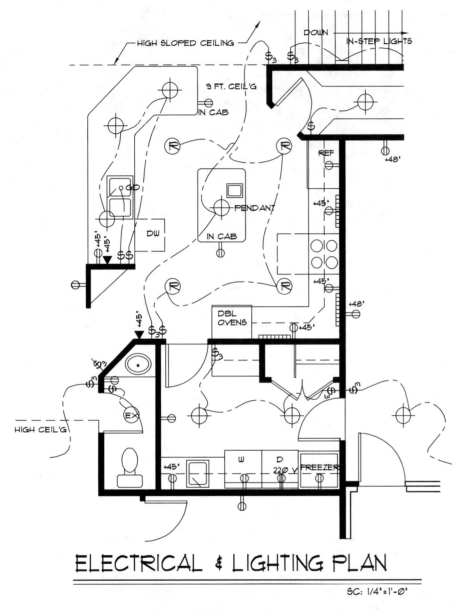

ELECTRICAL & LIGHTING PLAN

SC: 1/4"=1'-0'

- Check plan for code compliance and ADA requirements and clearances.

- Check plan for LEED certification credits, if applicable.

- Are the drawings clear and readable when reproduced or printed? If not, correct as necessary.

Notations

- Note where the ceiling level changes or has slopes.

- Note special features, clearances, finished ceiling heights above finish floors, alignments, and other important items.

- Cross-reference the plan with symbols and reference to the lighting schedule, details, and other drawings as needed.

Dimensions

- Dimension controlling factors, such as ceiling grid start points.

- Dimension location of light fixtures and changes in ceiling types that are not readily apparent. Locate to such items as columns or existing walls.

- Dimension clearances, alignments, and other controlling factors.

- Dimension lighting coves or other structural lighting, or create large-scale drawings of these and cross-reference.

Electrical or Power Plans

Electrical plans can include electrical outlets, telephones, communication devices, and other items requiring electrical power. In small projects, these items can be shown together with the lighting plan. An example of this type of drawing is illustrated in Figure 16-29. On large commercial projects, the electrical plan, often referred to as a power or power/communication plan, shows the outlets and related electrical devices separately (Figure 16-30). In most cases, the plumbing fixtures and items such as cabinetry and other built-in items are shown in order to more closely coordinate the location of electrical power devices. In some instances, such as in open office situations, designers also prefer to show the furniture, as many times it relates directly to the electrical outlet locations (Figure 16-31). The interior designer prepares the power plan and then forwards it to the electrical engineer to detail the circuitry, wire sizes, panel boxes, and other electrical specifications. On small residential plans, the drawing is given directly to the electrical contractor to install the work according to accepted practices.

The telephone and other communication systems are also generally shown on the electrical plan (Figure 16-32). Locations of telephones, public address systems, computer terminals, intercommunication devices, and security systems are the responsibility of the interior designer in conjunction with consultants. The designer draws a power/communications plan that schematically shows where power is needed for special equipment. Symbols for electrical devices are generally keyed to a legend that is on the same sheet as the plan. The electrical engineer or other system specialists do most of the detailed specifications for these devices.

Scale of Electrical Plans

Electrical plans in commercial spaces are generally drawn at the same scale as the floor plans. The most common scale for commercial projects is ⅛" = 1'-0" (1:100 metric). However, in complex installations, the scale might be increased to ¼" = 1'-0" (1:50 metric). The scale the plan is drawn at should be noted and placed either adjacent to or directly below the title.

Drafting Standards for Electrical Plans

Electrical plans must show all interior and exterior walls, stairs, and large devices, such as furnaces, water heaters, etc., that require

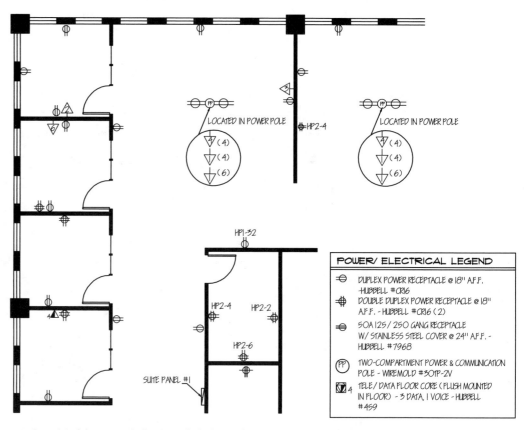

PARTIAL POWER/ ELECTRICAL PLAN
SCALE: 1/4"=1'-0"

power. Built-in fixtures and cabinetry, such as in bathrooms and kitchens, should also be drawn to better locate the electrical outlets and other devices. The walls should be drawn with lighter line weights so they do not dominate the drawing. Locate the convenience outlets on the walls where they are to be mounted, and call out the dimension above the finished floor (A.F.F.). Remember to

FIGURE 16-30 In large commercial projects, a separate electrical/power plan with a legend specifies outlets and circuitry. Many architectural features and other systems are left our so that the electrical plan can be easily read.

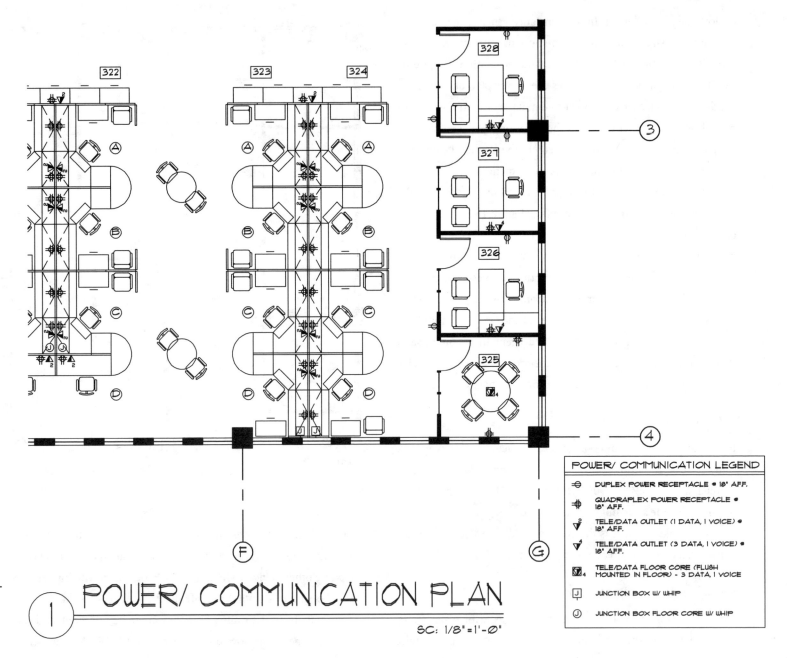

FIGURE 16-31 In commercial spaces with open-office workstations, designers prefer to show the furniture as it relates to the electrical outlets.

322   323   324   328   327   326   325

③   ④

POWER/ COMMUNICATION PLAN

①

SC: 1/8" = 1'-0"

F   G

POWER/ COMMUNICATION LEGEND

⊖	DUPLEX POWER RECEPTACLE @ 18" AFF.
⊕	QUADRAPLEX POWER RECEPTACLE @ 18" AFF.
▽²	TELE/DATA OUTLET (1 DATA, 1 VOICE) @ 18" AFF.
▽⁴	TELE/DATA OUTLET (3 DATA, 1 VOICE) @ 18" AFF.
⊠₄	TELE/DATA FLOOR CORE (FLUSH MOUNTED IN FLOOR) - 3 DATA, 1 VOICE
J	JUNCTION BOX W/ WHIP
J	JUNCTION BOX FLOOR CORE W/ WHIP

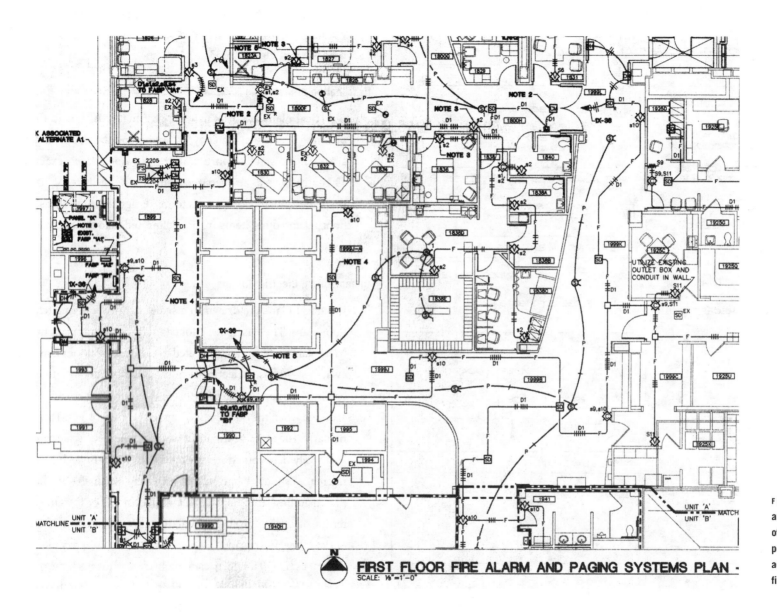

FIRST FLOOR FIRE ALARM AND PAGING SYSTEMS PLAN -
SCALE: ⅛"=1'-0"

FIGURE 16-32 The electrical and power plan can also include other specialty devices where power is needed, such as public address and paging systems and fire alarm systems.

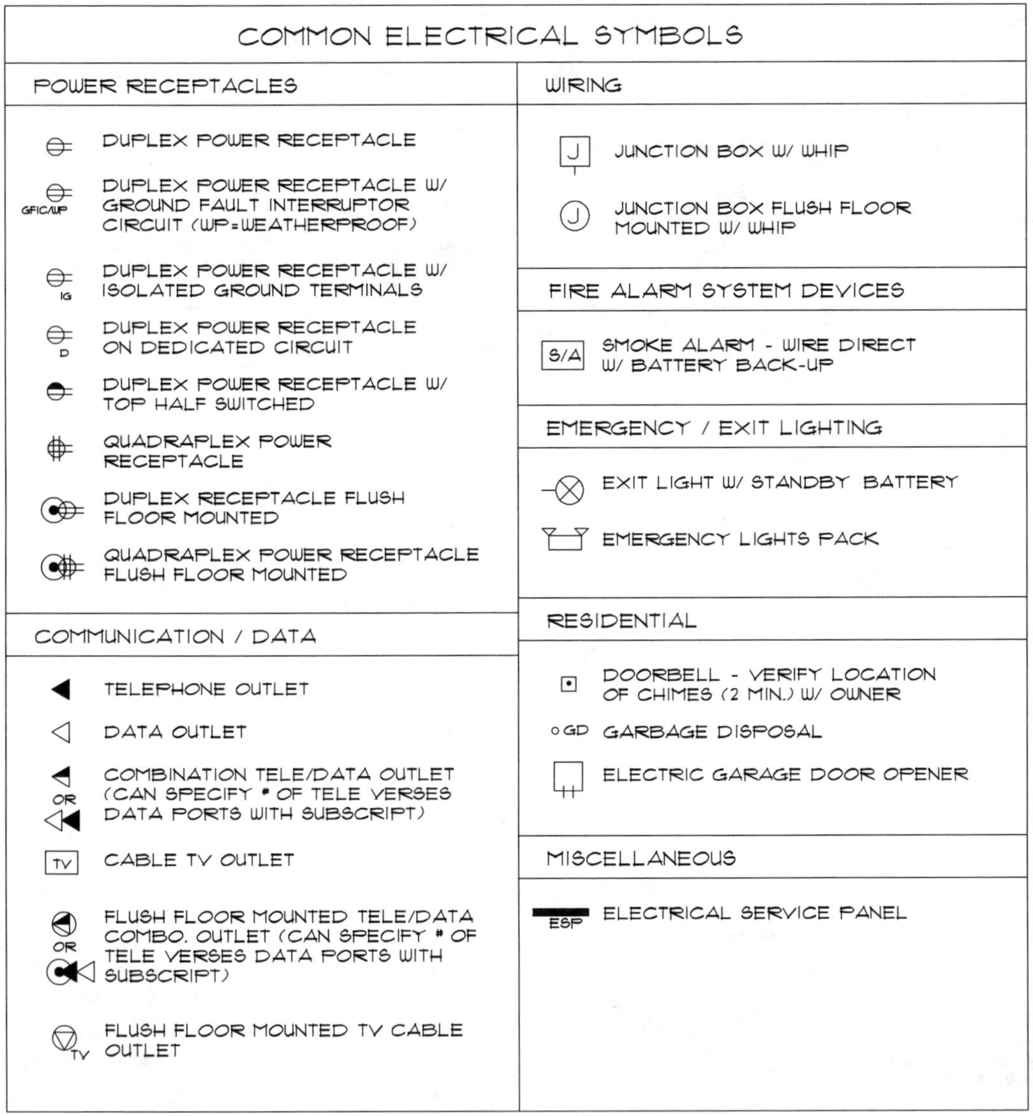

COMMON ELECTRICAL SYMBOLS

POWER RECEPTACLES

DUPLEX POWER RECEPTACLE

DUPLEX POWER RECEPTACLE W/ GROUND FAULT INTERRUPTOR CIRCUIT (WP=WEATHERPROOF)
GFIC/WP

DUPLEX POWER RECEPTACLE W/ ISOLATED GROUND TERMINALS
IG

DUPLEX POWER RECEPTACLE ON DEDICATED CIRCUIT
D

DUPLEX POWER RECEPTACLE W/ TOP HALF SWITCHED

QUADRAPLEX POWER RECEPTACLE

DUPLEX RECEPTACLE FLUSH FLOOR MOUNTED

QUADRAPLEX POWER RECEPTACLE FLUSH FLOOR MOUNTED

COMMUNICATION / DATA

TELEPHONE OUTLET

DATA OUTLET

COMBINATION TELE/DATA OUTLET (CAN SPECIFY # OF TELE VERSES DATA PORTS WITH SUBSCRIPT)
OR

CABLE TV OUTLET
TV

FLUSH FLOOR MOUNTED TELE/DATA COMBO. OUTLET (CAN SPECIFY # OF TELE VERSES DATA PORTS WITH SUBSCRIPT)
OR

FLUSH FLOOR MOUNTED TV CABLE OUTLET
TV

WIRING

JUNCTION BOX W/ WHIP
J

JUNCTION BOX FLUSH FLOOR MOUNTED W/ WHIP
J

FIRE ALARM SYSTEM DEVICES

SMOKE ALARM - WIRE DIRECT W/ BATTERY BACK-UP
S/A

EMERGENCY / EXIT LIGHTING

EXIT LIGHT W/ STANDBY BATTERY

EMERGENCY LIGHTS PACK

RESIDENTIAL

DOORBELL - VERIFY LOCATION OF CHIMES (2 MIN.) W/ OWNER

GARBAGE DISPOSAL
GD

ELECTRIC GARAGE DOOR OPENER

MISCELLANEOUS

ELECTRICAL SERVICE PANEL
ESP

FIGURE 16-33 Common electrical symbols.

note any special requirements such as weatherproof (WP), split-wired, or special purpose connection. Common electrical symbols are shown in Figure 16-33.

Designation of Materials

Electrical plans are primarily diagrammatic. Although they are drawn to a scale that matches the floor plans, the electrical devices are often too small to portray in the drawing at their exact scale. They are drawn as an oversized symbol to be easily recognized. To keep the drawing simple, material designations such as finish flooring and other items are not delineated as to their actual materials.

Dimensioning Electrical Plans

Electrical plans are drawn to a scale that generally matches the floor plans. There is no need for a lot of dimensioning on the electrical plan, as items can be located to scale on the floor plans. However, in some cases, electrical outlets and other devices do need to be dimensioned to accurately place them where they can be easily accessed when the building is occupied (Figure 16-34). This is particularly true for large expanses of walls, where the scale cannot be accurately determined by scaling the drawing. In such instances, references should be given that are easily obtainable in the field, dimensioning from the face of a wall, column, or imaginary centerline of a room. If a horizontal dimension is not given for a wall outlet, the electrician will place it as close as possible to the designer's plan. The electrician might choose to attach the outlet to a wall stud rather than locating it between two studs if the designer has not dimensioned a specific location.

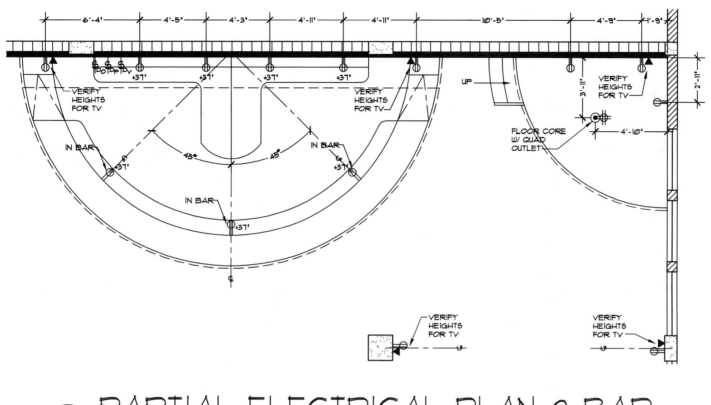

① PARTIAL ELECTRICAL PLAN @ BAR

SC: 1/4"=1'-∅'

FIGURE 16-34 Although most electrical outlets do not need to be exactly located, there are some exceptions, such as in this bar area, where outlets must coordinate with the equipment.

Checklist for Electrical Plans

General

- Title the drawing, note its scale, and identify north (or reference direction).

- Title the accompanying electrical schedule and key it to the plan.

- Add notes to clarify any abbreviations that are not commonly recognized.

- Clean up the plan (or in CAD, turn off superfluous information) so the walls, spaces, and key electrical codes are clear, dark, and very legible.

- Cross-reference the electrical plan to other drawings and schedules, carefully checking for accuracy and completeness of information.

- Check plan for code compliance and ADA requirements and clearances.

- Check plan for LEED certification credits, if applicable.

- Are the drawings clear and readable when reproduced or printed? If not, correct as necessary.

Notations

- Note special situations, such as devices supplied by owner or others.

- Note special features, clearances, outlet locations above finish floors, cabinetry, and other items.

- Note alignments and other important items that affect the electrical plan.

Dimensions

- Dimension location of outlets and changes in floor or wall types that affect the outlet installation.

- Dimension outlets to walls, wall corners, or intersections, and other items such as columns.

- Dimension the appropriate outlets to the proper distance above the finished floor (A.F.F.).

- Dimension clearances, alignments, and other controlling factors.

Mechanical and Plumbing Plans

The mechanical systems of a building are commonly referred to collectively as the HVAC (heating, ventilating and air-conditioning) systems. The HVAC system insures that occupants of a building are provided with a comfortable environment. The system does more than provide heating for winter and cooling for summer. It brings in fresh air, circulates it through the interiors, and exhausts stale air and odors. It can also treat air to control humidity, dust, pollen, and other undesirable conditions.

The plumbing system in a building serves a number of different functions, such as delivering water to people and machines through pressurization (water supply), and ejecting water to be removed through gravity (drainage). Plumbing serves three basic needs: it It provides water for human consumption, sanitary drainage of wastes, and mechanical systems. Water might be used for equipment or serve an automated sprinkler system as discussed later in this chapter in the undersection on plumbing plans. Some commercial buildings might also have a storm drainage system that rids the roof or other areas of rainfall or flooding. Such systems are separate from the sanitary sewage piping and collect into a storm sewer or are routed to a curbside drainage. A building might also have a waterfall feature, fountain, pond, or other decorative element that has a specialized, re-circulating water system.

Mechanical and plumbing drawings involve a lot of communication, coordination, and teamwork among the various design professionals and the contractors. The professional offices that produce the HVAC and plumbing drawings must be aware of one another's responsibilities to avoid conflicts, such as the location of a light fixture and air diffuser in the same position. At the same time, both of these types of drawings are schematic in nature, allowing the contractor some latitude in the exact placement of the parts during field installations. Great care and forethought should go into the engineered drawings, but existing conditions and the many variables present during the construction process may cause small deviations in the exact placement and installation of these systems.

Mechanical (HVAC) Plans

Engineers, architects, and mechanical contractors are the primary designers of HVAC plans (Figure 17-1). However, interior designers are often called on to coordinate the way the HVAC is installed and to monitor how it will affect the interiors of a building. A designer needs to be able to interpret the basic HVAC plans (particularly the reflected ceiling plan) for coordination of light fixtures, registers, grilles, thermostats, and other items that interface with the system (Figure 17-2). For example, an air diffuser in a

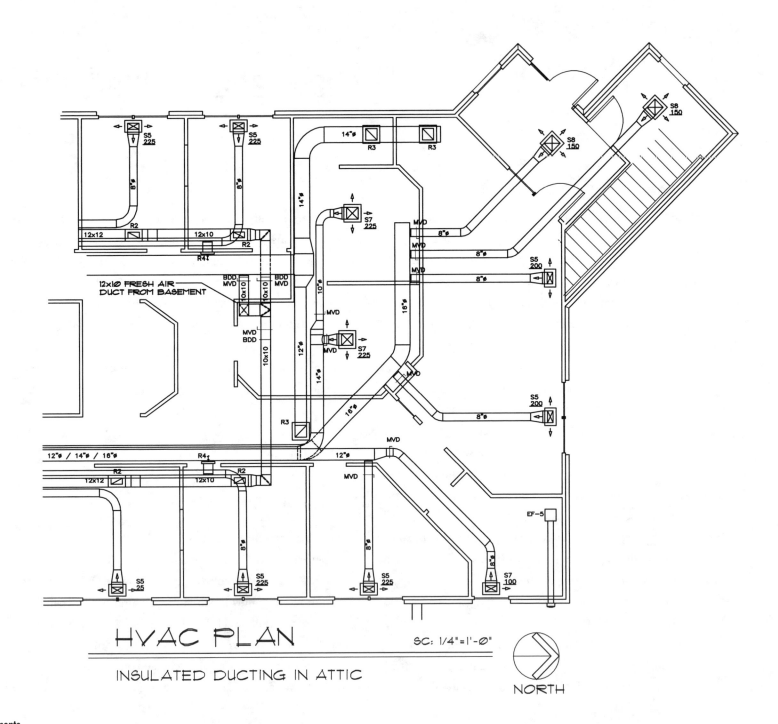

HVAC PLAN

SC: 1/4"=1'-0"

INSULATED DUCTING IN ATTIC

NORTH

FIGURE 17-1 Heating, ventilating, and air conditioning ductwork and related ceiling grilles are designed and drawn over the floor plan.

wood-paneled ceiling needs to be carefully dimensioned to fall in the center of a panel, rather than at a joint or other haphazard position. The interior designer should understand the basic layout of the HVAC system and take care that furniture, furnishings, and miscellaneous equipment does not obstruct the operation of the system.

HVAC systems utilize a number of different mediums to regulate the environment in a building. The two most common methods are air and liquid. These carry energy produced by electricity, oil, or renewable sources such as solar and wind power. Liquid systems primarily use water as a transport medium; however, other fluids, such as refrigerants and oils, are also used. In the water system, a boiler is used to create steam. The steam is circulated throught piping to radiators placed in the building spaces, creating a heating mode. In the cooling mode, water is chilled at the central plant and is circulated to individual radiator units that cool the surrounding air and absorb heat, which is piped back to the central plant. In the air system, heated or cooled air is transported to the interior spaces with supply and return ducts. In residential projects, these ducts are generally run below floor joists, above the ceiling, or even in an attic space. In commercial work, the ducting is run in the space between a suspended ceiling and the structure above, such as the next floor, as shown in Figure 17-3. When this space is also used as a return air space or plenum, building codes limit the use of combustible and other hazardous materials in the plenum. In other cases, raised floor systems can be placed above the structural floor, and ducting runs in this accessible system. In both residential and commercial work, ducting is also run in wall cavities, although the space is generally limited in large systems due to the larger sizes of ductwork required for moving great amounts of air.

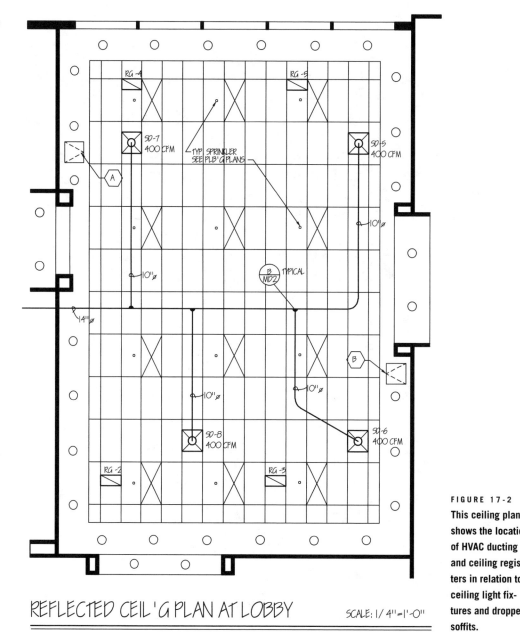

REFLECTED CEIL'G PLAN AT LOBBY   SCALE: 1/4"=1'-0"

FIGURE 17-2
This ceiling plan shows the location of HVAC ducting and ceiling registers in relation to ceiling light fixtures and dropped soffits.

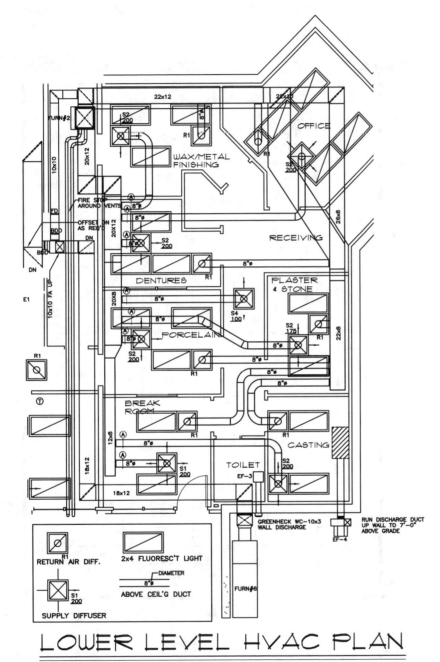

FIGURE 17-3 The HVAC ductwork is located between the lower and first floors of this dental lab. The drawing shows the coordination of the light fixtures and the HVAC ceiling grilles.

LOWER LEVEL HVAC PLAN

SC: 1/4"=1'-0"

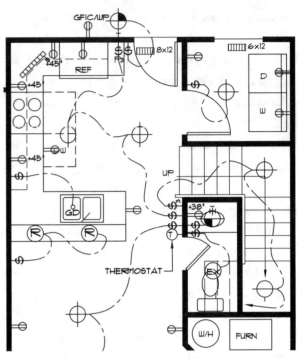

NOTE: LIGHT FIXTURES & CEIL'G HVAC SHOWN AS REFLECTED CEIL'G PLAN

ELECTRICAL PLAN

FIGURE 17-4 The thermostat for the first floor of this apartment is located on an inside wall, next to the light switches.

Access is needed to the HVAC system's components such as fire dampers, valves, and adjustable dampers. In suspended acoustical ceilings, a tile or two can be removed to gain access to the necessary parts. In gypsum board ceilings, special access doors are installed in strategically located areas. The interior designer should be able to read the plans and take note where these items

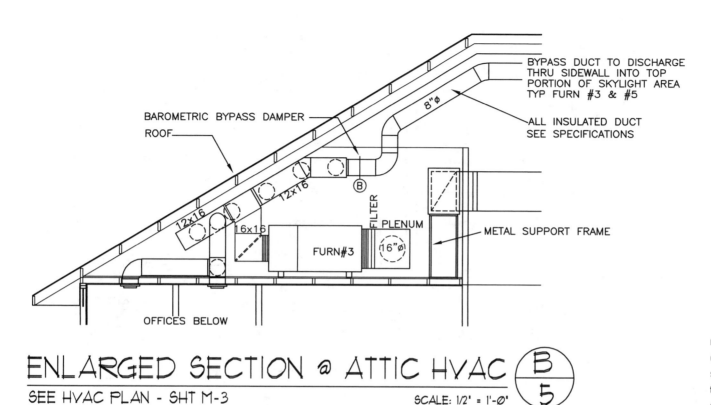

BAROMETRIC BYPASS DAMPER

ROOF

BYPASS DUCT TO DISCHARGE
THRU SIDEWALL INTO TOP
PORTION OF SKYLIGHT AREA
TYP FURN #3 & #5

8"φ

ALL INSULATED DUCT
SEE SPECIFICATIONS

12x16

12x16

16x16

Ⓑ

FILTER

PLENUM

(16"φ)

FURN#3

METAL SUPPORT FRAME

OFFICES BELOW

ENLARGED SECTION @ ATTIC HVAC Ⓑ/5

SEE HVAC PLAN - SHT M-3   SCALE: 1/2' = 1'-0'

FIGURE 17-5 **Furnaces and ducting are drawn at a large scale in this sectional view of the attic for this small commercial building.**

might cause physical conflicts or aesthetic problems with the ceiling design.

The HVAC system also includes the installation of various controls such as thermostats and other monitoring equipment. The position of the thermostats is generally specified by the mechanical engineer. They are placed away from heat sources such as fireplaces, exterior walls, large expanses of exterior glass, and other features that may hinder their operation. Generally, they are located on the walls, and must be coordinated with other interior finishes and equipment such as wall switches, wall sconces, etc.,

as illustrated in Figure 17-4. In large projects, there may be several thermostats to control heating and cooling in multiple zones of a building.

Scale of HVAC Plans

HVAC plans are generally drawn at the same scale as the floor plans. The most common scale is ¼" = 1'-0" (1:50 metric) for residential and small commercial projects and ⅛" = 1'-0" (1:100 metric) for large commercial ones. The scale the HVAC plan is drawn

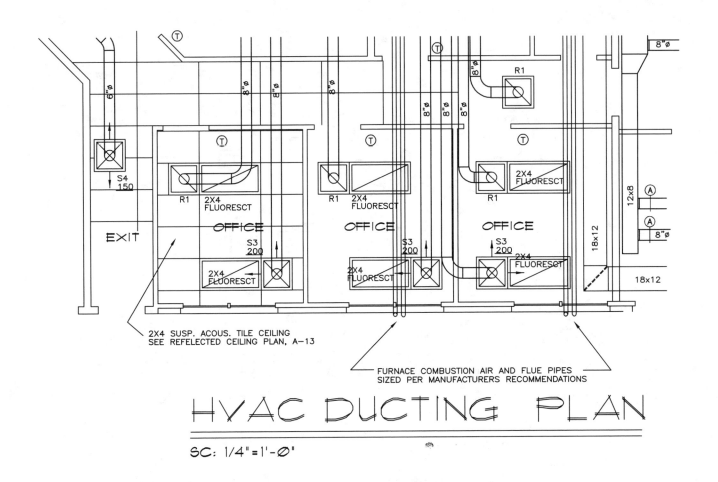

S4
150

EXIT

R1 2X4
FLUORESCT

OFFICE

2X4
FLUORESCT

S3
200

R1 2X4
FLUORESCT

OFFICE

2X4
FLUORESCT

S3
200

2X4
FLUORESCT

R1

OFFICE

S3
200

2X4
FLUORESCT

18x12

12x8

8"ø

8"ø

18x12

2X4 SUSP. ACOUS. TILE CEILING
SEE REFELECTED CEILING PLAN, A—13

FURNACE COMBUSTION AIR AND FLUE PIPES
SIZED PER MANUFACTURERS RECOMMENDATIONS

HVAC DUCTING PLAN

SC: 1/4"=1'-Ø"

FIGURE 17-6 This reflected ceiling plan shows the HVAC duct sizes and location of the supply and return registers where they penetrate the ceiling.

at should be noted and placed directly below the drawing title. Other detailed and related equipment drawings might be enlarged with their respective scales shown on the drawing and referenced to the HVAC plan (Figure 17-5).

Drafting Standards for HVAC Plans

As HVAC systems carry water, air, electrical currents, or a combination of these, detailed drawings are made to show the layout of each system and its operation. The drawings for HVAC air supply equipment reflect the ductwork system and sizes needed to deliver and return the proper amount of air to each space, as shown in Figure 17-6. HVAC systems that carry water use drawings to indicate the boiler equipment, piping sizes, and layouts.

In all of these systems, the equipment, piping, ducts, and other features are shown in a plan view. These floor plans should not be cluttered with notes, dimensions, room names, and other notations that might make the HVAC part of the plan difficult to read.

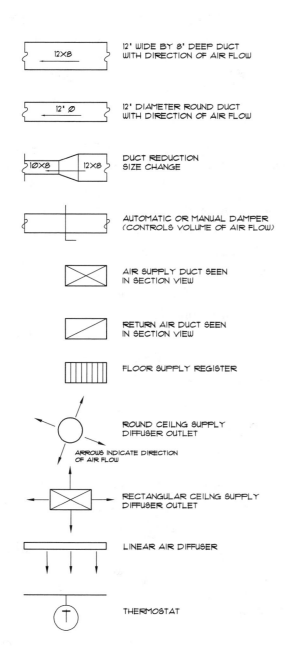

HEATING AND AIR CONDITIONING SYMBOLS

12" WIDE BY 8" DEEP DUCT WITH DIRECTION OF AIR FLOW — 12X8

12" DIAMETER ROUND DUCT WITH DIRECTION OF AIR FLOW — 12' Ø

DUCT REDUCTION SIZE CHANGE — 10X8 / 12X8

AUTOMATIC OR MANUAL DAMPER (CONTROLS VOLUME OF AIR FLOW)

AIR SUPPLY DUCT SEEN IN SECTION VIEW

RETURN AIR DUCT SEEN IN SECTION VIEW

FLOOR SUPPLY REGISTER

ROUND CEILNG SUPPLY DIFFUSER OUTLET / ARROWS INDICATE DIRECTION OF AIR FLOW

RECTANGULAR CEILNG SUPPLY DIFFUSER OUTLET

LINEAR AIR DIFFUSER

THERMOSTAT

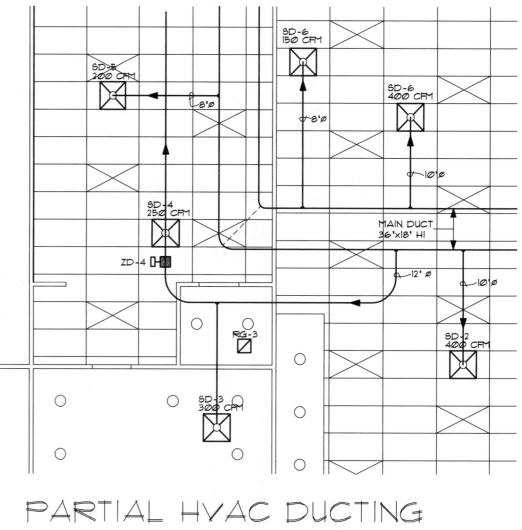

PARTIAL HVAC DUCTING

SD-6 150 CFM
SD-5 200 CFM
SD-6 400 CFM
8'ø
8'ø
10'ø
SD-4 250 CFM
MAIN DUCT 36"x18" HI
ZD-4
12' ø
10'ø
RG-3
SD-2 400 CFM
SD-3 300 CFM

FIGURE 17-8 In this office building, the above ceiling ductwork that radiates from a central main supply is shown as a single line, with size noted next to each duct.

FIGURE 17-7 HVAC drawings employ basic and common symbols to illustrate the various components of the system.

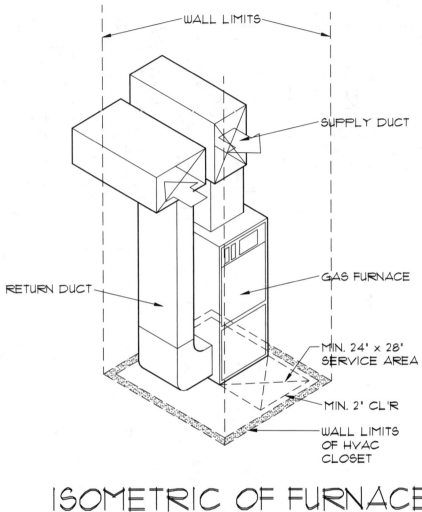

WALL LIMITS

SUPPLY DUCT

GAS FURNACE

RETURN DUCT

MIN. 24" x 28"
SERVICE AREA

MIN. 2' CL'R

WALL LIMITS
OF HVAC
CLOSET

ISOMETRIC OF FURNACE INSTALLATION

NO SCALE

FIGURE 17-9 An isometric is an effective way to illustrate certain equipment and ducting in the HVAC system, as seen in this furnace room.

Wall lines are often drawn lighter and thinner than the HVAC system lines in order to make the system stand out clearly. In some instances, the ductwork might even be shaded for easier identification. The HVAC plans are schematic, using symbols to denote the various parts such as furnaces, ducts, control devices, and piping. Although professional firms might vary in the symbols they use, some are fairly standard, as seen in Figure 17-7. The symbols are cross-referenced to a schedule that fully describes the piece of equipment or assembly. In some cases, a single line is used to represent the ductwork or piping (Figure 17-8). A note is then added next to the run indicating the size of the duct or pipe. In ducting, the first number generally refers to the width and the second number to the height of the assembly. In air systems, arrows are used to indicate the direction of flow through the ducting and at the diffusers. Isometric drawings are also used to explain HVAC assemblies or particulars of the system, as illustrated in Figure 17-9. These are prepared by the mechanical engineer to more clearly show the components of the system.

Designation of HVAC Materials

HVAC materials are generally not indicated on the plan drawings. They are primarily indicated by a note or referenced to the specifications. The notes might specify a duct as 1-inch (25 mm) fiberboard or 20-gauge sheet metal. In a water system, copper piping or other materials might be called out in a note as to their diameter and grade of copper. Elbows, tees, and other connector assemblies are drawn simplistically as they are commonly shown in HVAC standards.

Checklist for Mechanical Plans

General

- Title the drawing, note its scale, and reference it to north or another plan locator.

- Completely fill out the symbol legend for a clear understanding by the reader.

- Cross-reference equipment on the plans to schedules or specifications.

- Show thermostat locations. Check these locations against the floor plans for coordination with electrical receptacles, counters, cabinets, and other built-ins.

- Show the exterior location for air-conditioning equipment, such as compressors and coils.

- Call out access panels and controls as required by the equipment and building codes.

- Cross-reference the drawing with the reflected ceiling plan and other drawings for coordination to avoid conflicts in installation of lights, etc.

- Check plan for code compliance and ADA requirements and clearances.

- Check plan for LEED certification credits, if applicable.

- Are the drawings clear and readable when reproduced or printed? If not, correct as necessary.

Notations

- Call out exhaust vents (bathroom and kitchen equipment) to exterior or note if they are re-circulating.

- Call out domestic dryer vents to the exterior.

- Note furnaces and boilers and cross-reference to specifications.

- Note proper clearances and access to equipment for adjustments, repair, etc.

- Note fresh-air intakes where applicable.

- Note piping sizes, whether they are supply and return, and the type of fluid they carry (chilled water, hot water, etc.).

- Note (and coordinate with mechanical engineer) when air diffusers are to be specified a particular color or painted to match adjacent surfaces.

Dimensions

- Dimension the sizes of ducts by calling them out on the plan by width and height or diameter. With water systems, call out the pipe sizes and transitions.

- Call out the sizes of grilles and diffusers.

Plumbing Plans

Plumbing plans are prepared to show how pressurized fresh water and gravity-drained wastes are routed through the building. These two separate systems are called the fresh water supply system and the drain (sanitary), waste, and vent (DWV) system. These system plans are coordinated with the other structural and architectural plans to insure proper location, operation, and protection of the plumbing systems. Small residential buildings do not often require plumbing plans, leaving the plumbing contractor to design and install the system to meet the minimum building codes. On the other hand, commercial buildings always require the preparation of detailed plumbing plans. Plumbing drawings are often done in plan view (Figure 17-10) and elevation views, and sometimes an isometric drawing is provided. A number of plumbing materials are used in both residential and commercial projects, such as cast iron, copper, steel, and plastic pipe. Although the materials might vary, the drawing techniques and symbols used are primarily the same in all systems.

Fresh water is brought into a building from a public water system or well. It generally first passes through a meter (public systems) that records how much water is used and the resulting costs

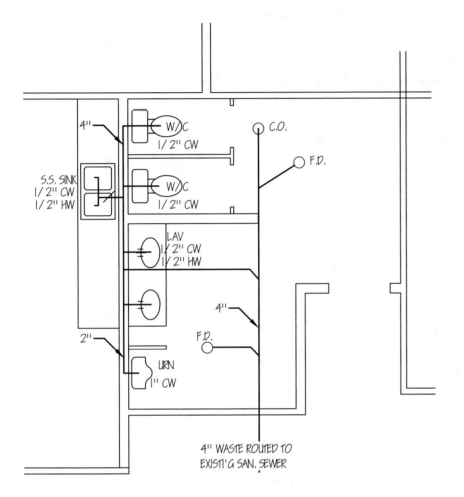

PLUMBING PLAN @ MEN'S RM 302

SCALE: 1/4"=1'-0"

FIGURE 17-10 The sanitary sewer system in this small apartment is drawn as heavy lines over the base floor plan, with sizes noted. Domestic waterline sizes are also specified.

of the water service. Water is then routed under pressure throughout the building in copper or plastic pipes. The pipe sizes for the water supply system in a building are designed by an engineer who sets the rate of flow at which the pipe will transport water to the fixture where it is needed. In this water supply network, pipes tend to start out large and get smaller as they get closer to the point of use and farther away from the water source. The actual pipe size depends on a number of variables: the pressure of the water supply system at its source; the type of fixture and its water discharge rate; the number of fixtures connected to the whole system; vertical travel of the water; and the pressure losses due to friction as the water flows through the piping. The process involves assigning a numerical score of fixture units to the corresponding fixture, such as a lavatory, shower, or water closet. The flow rate of the water in gallons per minute (gpm) is calculated based on the total number of fixtures and the pressure the water is supplied at the source.

The fire-protection system, which is considered separate from the plumbing, is usually a sprinkler system utilizing its own separate water system. This system is fed from dedicated water mains that in turn connect through piping to the individual sprinkler heads. In the case of a fire, heat sensor devices activate these heads to open and allow the directionally controlled flow of water to the fire's source. In most buildings, these sprinkler heads are visible, and they can be located on ceilings and walls, depending on the amount of coverage needed. However, recessed sprinkler heads that have a smooth flush cover with the ceiling are available at a higher cost. The cover is dropped away when the head activates and lowers below the ceiling to spray the water.

Although interior designers do not design these sprinkler systems, it is important to recognize the location of the heads in a drawing and coordinate them with other ceiling-mounted items. For example, the designer should consider how individual heads will fit with the design scheme of the reflected ceiling plan, as well as check for interference with light fixtures, ceiling treatments, and other features.

Scale of Plumbing Drawings

A variety of scales may be used to draw plumbing systems, depending on whether the drawings are depicted in plan view, isometric, or enlarged details. The most common scale is ¼" = 1'-0" (1:50 metric) for residential and small commercial projects and

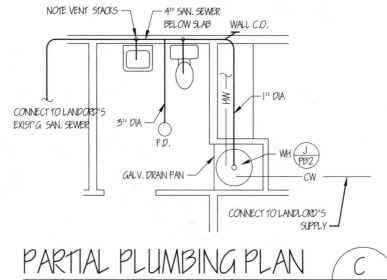

PARTIAL PLUMBING PLAN

SCALE: 1/2"=1'-0"

FIGURE 17-11 A large-scale drawing is made of this restroom to indicate pipe sizes and related information that could not be shown on a small-scale floor plan.

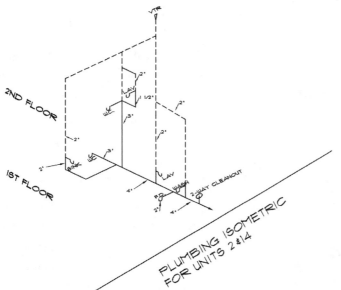

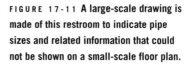

PLUMBING ISOMETRIC FOR FOR UNITS 2 & 14

FIGURE 17-12 An isometric drawing is often made to show the complete layout and piping sizes of the sanitary sewer system in a building.

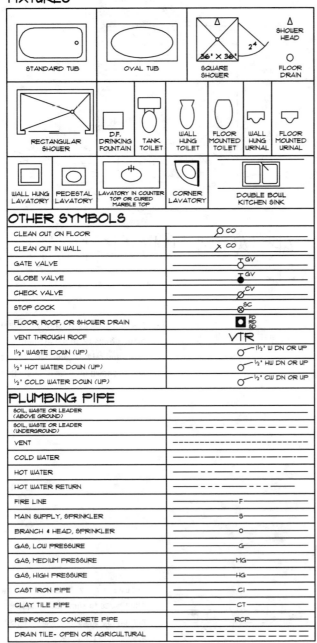

FIXTURES

STANDARD TUB	OVAL TUB	SQUARE SHOWER (36' X 36')	SHOWER HEAD / FLOOR DRAIN
RECTANGULAR SHOWER	D.F. DRINKING FOUNTAIN / TANK TOILET	WALL HUNG TOILET / FLOOR MOUNTED TOILET	WALL HUNG URINAL / FLOOR MOUNTED URINAL
WALL HUNG LAVATORY / PEDESTAL LAVATORY	LAVATORY IN COUNTER TOP OR CURED MARBLE TOP	CORNER LAVATORY	DOUBLE BOWL KITCHEN SINK

OTHER SYMBOLS

CLEAN OUT ON FLOOR	CO
CLEAN OUT IN WALL	CO
GATE VALVE	GV
GLOBE VALVE	GV
CHECK VALVE	CV
STOP COCK	SC
FLOOR, ROOF, OR SHOWER DRAIN	FD RD SD
VENT THROUGH ROOF	VTR
1½' WASTE DOWN (UP)	1½' W DN OR UP
½' HOT WATER DOWN (UP)	½' HW DN OR UP
½' COLD WATER DOWN (UP)	½' CW DN OR UP

PLUMBING PIPE

SOIL, WASTE OR LEADER (ABOVE GROUND)	
SOIL, WASTE OR LEADER (UNDERGROUND)	
VENT	
COLD WATER	
HOT WATER	
HOT WATER RETURN	
FIRE LINE	F
MAIN SUPPLY, SPRINKLER	S
BRANCH & HEAD, SPRINKLER	O
GAS, LOW PRESSURE	G
GAS, MEDIUM PRESSURE	MG
GAS, HIGH PRESSURE	HG
CAST IRON PIPE	CI
CLAY TILE PIPE	CT
REINFORCED CONCRETE PIPE	RCP
DRAIN TILE- OPEN OR AGRICULTURAL	

FIGURE 17-13 Standard plumbing symbols used in construction drawings.

⅛" = 1'-0" (1:100 metric) for large commercial ones. Floor plans serve as the base drawing and are turned into plumbing plans by the addition of piping, controls, and other devices. Domestic water lines and sanitary sewer lines are drawn as an overlay on the floor plans. It can be difficult to show a lot of piping details and other components that are close together in a space, such as a boiler room and other heavy water-usage equipment. In these instances, a portion of this area is enlarged to a larger scale and referenced to the plans (Figure 17-11). As most plumbing plans show only the horizontal positions of pipes and fixtures, a schematic is drawn to show the vertical elements of the system. This is often done with an isometric and generally is not drawn to a scale to conserve space on the drawings, as illustrated in Figure 17-12.

Drafting Standards for Plumbing Drawings

In small projects, domestic water supply and sanitary sewer systems are drawn on the same plan, as they are not often overly complicated. Solid, dashed, and other line types are developed to distinguish between the systems. In the sewage system, the waste line is shown as well as the various required vent lines as dictated by the building codes.

Lines are drawn to depict the various sizes of piping in vertical risers and vents as well as the horizontal runs. However, a plumbing system consists of more than runs of piping. Pipe elbows, fittings, valves, traps, faucets, and numerous other items are sized to work with the piping system and must be accurately called out. In addition to adding notes to the drawings, standard symbols have been developed and are placed on the sheet to coincide with the proper item, as shown in Figure 17-13. A legend is included to accurately identify the type of pipe, and other specific elements that must be connected. A schedule or legend is also developed to indicate a fixture's type, manufacturer, size, color, and other special features, such as a lavatory and faucet set, as illustrated in Figure 17-14. Special plumbing systems such as the automatic fire extinguishing system are generally drawn by a fire-protection engineer and coordinated into the designer or architect's drawings.

Designation of Materials for Plumbing Plans

Plumbing materials are basically shown in a simplistic manner. Double lines are primarily used to indicate sizes of air ducting, and water-piping systems are indicated mostly with single lines. The actual material might be called out in the plan, although it is usually found in the accompanying schedule or specifications.

Dimensioning Plumbing Plans

Plumbing plans are basically diagrammatic. Although they are scaled to the floor plans, exact dimensions are generally not noted, except in special cases. For example, the scale of the floor plan and building section will indicate fairly accurately the length of piping, but an exact measurement can only be made in the field during installation. For this reason, a note is added to most plans noting, "Piping shown is diagrammatic and must be accurately measured in the field." Many designers, architects, and engineers dimension the centerlines of important elements such as sinks, water closets, lavatories, and drains. But, in small residential projects, it is often left up to the builder or plumber to locate their exact placement.

PLUMBING FIXTURES

PF-1	TOILET PARTITIONS GENERAL PARTITIONS SERIES 30 STAINLESS STEEL	PF-4	URINAL ELGER 164-2457 256 BONE
PF-2	URINAL SCREENS GENERAL PARTITIONS SERIES 30 STAINLESS STEEL	PF-5	BOWL UNIT DUPONT CORIAN 387-2 BONE WHITE
PF-3	WATER CLOSET ELGER 111-8675 256 BONE	PF-6	GRAB BARS GENERAL PARTITIONS FF STAINLESS STEEL

FIGURE 17-14 An example of a plumbing legend that accompanies a plumbing plan drawing.

Checklist for Plumbing Plans

General

- Title the drawing, note its scale, and indicate north (or reference direction). Cross-reference this drawing to other related drawings.

- Title any accompanying schedules and key them to the plan.

- Place schedules on the same sheet as the plumbing plan (preferred) or on a sheet immediately preceding or following the plan.

- Clean up the plan (or in CAD, turn off superfluous information) so the plumbing information and key codes are clear, dark, and very legible.

- Clearly show the directional run of each pipe and draw its line weight and style to match that shown in the accompanying legend.

- Indicate special features such as valves, faucets, sinks, etc., with a standard symbol on the plan. Cross-reference to the specifications or a legend that details information such as manufacturer and model.

- Include an abbreviations legend on this sheet or cross-reference to the title sheet (where all the abbreviations are listed).

- Check plan for code compliance and ADA requirements and clearances.

- Check plan for LEED certification credits, if applicable.

- Are the drawings clear and readable when reproduced or printed? If not, correct as necessary.

Notations

- Note the minimum fall required for the gravity sanitary sewer (often ¼ inch per foot of horizontal run).

- Call out pipe sizes on the plan and their use (hot water, cold water, sanitary sewer, vents, etc.).

- Label the plumbing fixtures and cross-reference to a schedule or the specifications.

- Call out special devices such as vents through the roof (VTR), floor drains, clean-outs, and hose bibs where applicable.

- Note where existing and new plumbing lines are to be extended, removed, or connected.

Dimensions

- Dimension to centerlines of sink, lavatories, drains, faucets, supply lines, and other items where required.

- Dimension maximum runs, lengths, and sanitary sewer line fall.

Reproduction Methods and Computers

Once the construction drawings are complete, the designer must decide how to distribute them to the various parties involved in a project. This might be done by making multiple copies through a reproduction process or by sending them electronically through a computer system, such as the Internet.

Along with the discussion on reproduction processes, the use of computers in the design schools and professional offices is an everyday occurrence. Designers still sketch and design by hand, but we see the use of the computer taking over many of the repetitive and labor-intensive parts of the process. Designers also use CAD to do more of their creations, explorations, and presentations through various software programs (Figure 18-1). Most designers now see CAD as a tool, similar to the pencil and pen, but a much more powerful and dynamic tool.

This chapter will not attempt to describe the most popular models of computers and their peripherals (hardware) and programs (software), as there is a wide variety on the market today, and the technology changes rapidly. Also, preferences for particular software programs differ among professional firms, depending on their needs. The reader is encouraged to research the many computers and programs that are available to find those suited to their specific needs.

2ND FLOOR PLAN

1ST FLOOR PLAN

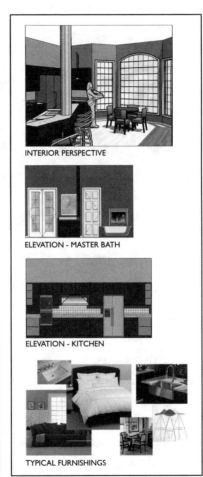

INTERIOR PERSPECTIVE

ELEVATION - MASTER BATH

ELEVATION - KITCHEN

TYPICAL FURNISHINGS

LKA DESIGNS

FITCH HOUSE REMODEL
INDIANAPOLIS, INDIANA

one
BOARD 1 OF 2

FIGURE 18-1 Designers use a variety of software programs to design and present their projects visually, such as this remodel to a house.

FIGURE 18-2 Electrostatic copiers can be multi-function machines that include additional features such as a scanner, and fax machine.

Reproduction of Drawings

Multiple copies are often made of drawings and are used for presentations and as check prints for construction drawings. Copies are also used for competitive bidding and are generally distributed to parties such as owners, contractors, subcontractors, and material suppliers during the construction of the project.

Blueprints

For over a hundred years, the prime method of coping drawings was through the use of the blueprint process, which produced a blue background (the white space on the original) with lettering and lines converted to white. From this process, the name "blueprint" was derived. However, the historic method of white print on blue ink is no longer utilized.

Whiteprint Reproduction

The next step in the blueprint process was the development of the whiteprint, produced through a diazo process. For a whiteprint, the original copy, which must be on translucent vellum or plastic film, was fed through a machine and the image was transferred to a piece of yellow diazo paper. The machine used an ultraviolet light that was directed through the original, bleaching out the diazo dye, except where the pencil or pen lines were. The sheet was then fed through a developer system that fixed the lines permanently in blue, black, or brown, depending on the type of diazo paper used. As with the historic blueprint process, this method of printing is hardly used anymore.

Electrostatic Reproduction

Today, the xerographic process is the preferred method of making reproductions of drawings. It is fast, very accurate in reproduction quality, and becoming more economical each year. This system produces multiple copies in black lines on white paper. Variations can include colored lines on a variety of colored papers, copies made on bond, vellum, plastic, and other surfaces. These copiers can handle a number of paper sizes, multiple copies, collating, and even reducing and enlarging images. Today, the machines are offered with other features, such as scanning images directly into a computer, serving as a copier, and a facsimile transmitter/receiver (Figure 18-2).

Facsimile Copies

A facsimile machine (fax) can be used to copy and transmit drawings over a telephone line to a receiver that reproduces the original drawing. The fax process is fairly fast and convenient, but in most cases, they are limited to the size of the original that can be placed in the machine. Also, most fax copies on the receiving end do not match the exact size and visual quality of the original. However, the process still makes it a handy tool in the design office.

Digital Printers and Plotters

With the advent of the large format plotters and plain paper copiers, multiple copies can be made conveniently. Today, high-speed digital printers are making copying even more economical and improving the quality of the images. Even the photographic process used in the photocopier machines is being replaced with digital and laser technology. This has brought down the costs of printing and copying even further. Digital technology and Internet use has also reduced the time to physically deliver the designer's originals to the printing company for reproductions, and then return the originals to the designer office. Now, CAD plans can be electronically transferred as print-ready format to a remote print station or separate print company, while retaining the original file in the design office. Drawings can be electronically sent in many forms (JPEG, TIFF, PDF, AutoCAD, etc.), depending on what software the recipient has and the quality needed of the digital format.

When printing out a drawing from a CAD file, the designer has several basic ways to create the image. The most basic is the use of a small-scale, ink-jet plotter that can do multiple copies at 8-½ x 11 inch (216 mm x 279 mm) formats, either in black and white or color. Fairly economical machines can also increase these sizes up to 11 x 17 inch (279 mm x 432 mm) formats (Figure 18-3). For oversized drawings, the large-scale plotter can reproduce the large sheet sizes commonly used in architectural and engineering offices. These can also print in black and white or color, (Figure

FIGURE 18-3 **LaserJet and inkjet printers are economical ways to make small black-and-white or color prints of plans, drawings, and other images.**

FIGURE 18-4 **For large-format printing, this Hewlett Packard DesignJet plotter can produce black-and-white or color plots.**

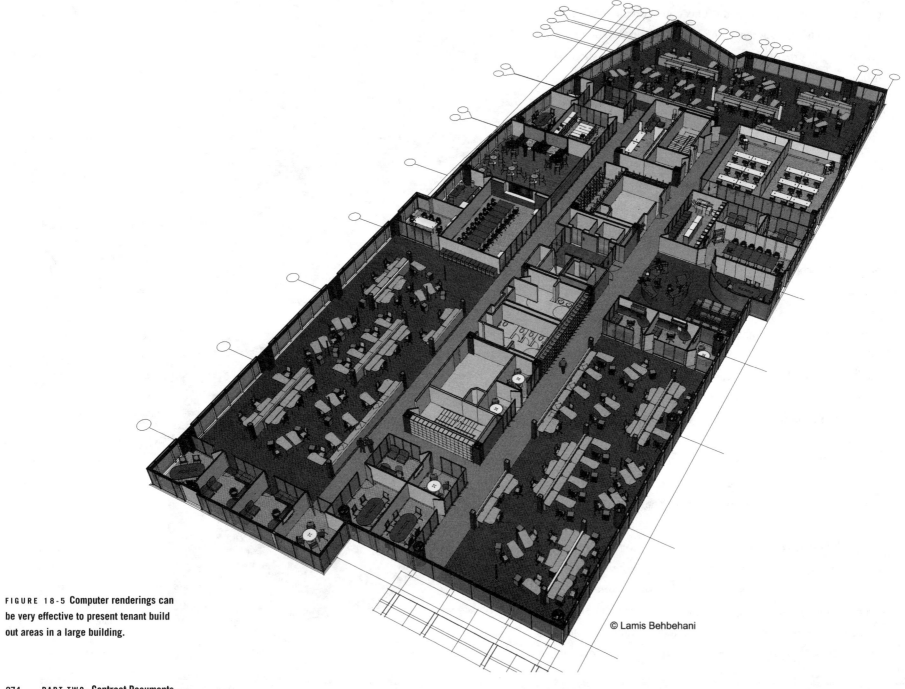

FIGURE 18-5 Computer renderings can be very effective to present tenant build out areas in a large building.

© Lamis Behbehani

18-4). However, large-scale machines are generally slower and more costly than the small ink-jet units. Now we are seeing more plot files e-mailed, rather than hand carried to the printer.

The other method of printing small drawings is by the process of a laser printer, which can accommodate the same sizes as the ink-jet system. Generally, laser printers can create more precise images and are often faster than the ink-jet printers.

Using Computers for Design, Communication, and Drafting

The use of computers has increased in design schools and the professional office. Computers are fast and very accurate, which has increased their use for complicated procedures. Originally, computers were used for drafting to produce construction drawings, and only occasionally for design process drawings. Today, with ever evolving software and the reduction in size and cost of computers, many designers and students use CAD systems throughout the design process. The computer is used to create preliminary design, photorealistic renderings, and construction drawings. Besides CAD, a wide variety of programs are for estimating, tracking time on projects, word-processing, creating data spreadsheets, exchanging e-mail, and many other uses. Some of the programs are effective for increasing productivity, where others—such as games and other accessories—offer a refreshing break from our everyday work schedule.

Many designers still find it quicker to create a rough drawing in sketch form by hand than with a CAD system. They prefer to use CAD for more photorealistic renderings and complex drawings, particularly ones that involve repetitive operations or similar shapes. CAD can also be more effective and faster than manual drafting for making changes to drawings. Editing files allow the designer to change only part of the file or drawing, or enlarge/reduce something very quickly. In addition its use for repetitive and other time-saving needs, the computer is also very effective as a design and presentation tool for creating and drawing three-dimensional objects and spaces (Figure 18-5). Larger memories and processor speeds have enabled designers to create very realistic and accurate images, which can also be explored in movement or what is termed *virtual reality*. For example, buildings and their interiors can be created on screen in real-time three-dimensional space, allowing the observer to "walk" through them. Some programs are interactive, allowing the transformation of objects and spaces in accordance with the viewer's directives.

CAD programs allow the designer to assign lines and objects their own unique layer. Each layer can then be assigned its own individual line weight, or thickness. In this layering system, line work can be easily controlled. The designer can "turn off" layers that are not needed in a particular drawing. These types of programs allow the base drawings to serve as the "reference" drawing for all others to build from. For example, in the AutoCAD® programs, the floor plan can serve as the base drawing for the electrical plan and the furniture-installation plan. When a change is made to the floor plan, it will automatically update the configuration of the electrical and furniture-installation plans, by using the cross-referencing command.

CAD drawings and programs also allow a designer to share files with others, such as clients, vendors, colleagues, and consultants. These files can be stored on disks or flash drives and given to other parties for viewing, printing, and even modifying. Today, however, we see more of this sharing done electronically by e-mail or over the Internet.

CAD programs are becoming increasingly interconnected, so that one can change a three-dimensional drawing and automatically cause a related change in the two-dimensional drawing stored in the program. This dynamic linking can also produce automatic changes in the 3-D drawing as the designer changes the 2-D drawing. This is a distinct advantage of programs that use building information modeling (BIM), as they link the 2-D drawings, 3-D drawings, as well as schedules and quantity spread sheets.

Although we speak of the interconnectivity of the programs, today's computer hardware is becoming more "unconnected" or wireless. Networking of computers and other devices has been accomplished primarily through the use of cables, wiring, and optical lines. Now, more and more devices are being "unplugged" by the use of wireless technology—using transmitting and receiving technology to connect multiple devices. This allows us to be less hindered by the hardwiring of our individual components, with the freedom to use a basic server that can wirelessly present through a portable video screen or input to a laptop—unfettered with wiring connections.

Again, it was not the intent of this chapter to present or review all the hundreds of software and hardware selections available today. New developments in computers and programs are made every six months or less, complicating the timing of discussion of items that may have changed drastically since the date of this writing. In some cases, new software is introduced and other software is discontinued. The computer will no doubt continue to improve our work habits and needs, affecting how we design and communicate to others. But, behind these wonderful machines is still the need for input and direction from a human designer.

Example Numbering for Simple Interior Project
Table of Contents

APPENDIX A

DIVISION 23   HEATING, VENTILATING, AND AIR-CONDITIONING (HVAC)

    23 31 00   HVAC Ducts and Casings

    23 37 00   Air Outlets and Inlets

DIVISIONS 24 TO 25 – NOT USED

DIVISION 26 – ELECTRICAL

    26 20 00   Low-Voltage Electrical Distribution

    26 51 00   Interior Lighting

DIVISIONS 27 TO 29 – NOT USED

SITE AND INFRASTRUCTURE SUBGROUP – Not Used

PROCESS EQUIPMENT SUBGROUP – Not Used

MasterFormat™ – 2004 Edition
Level 1 and 2 Numbers and Titles

PROCUREMENT AND CONTRACTING REQUIREMENTS GROUP

DIVISION 00 – PROCUREMENT AND CONTRACTING REQUIREMENTS

INTRODUCTORY INFORMATION PROCUREMENT REQUIREMENTS

00 10 00	**SOLICITATION**
00 11 00	Advertisements and Invitations
00 20 00	**INSTRUCTIONS FOR PROCUREMENT**
00 21 00	Instructions
00 22 00	Supplementary Instructions
00 23 00	Procurement Definitions
00 24 00	Procurement Scopes
00 25 00	Procurement Meetings
00 26 00	Procurement Substitution Procedures
00 30 00	**AVAILABLE INFORMATION**
00 31 00	Available Project Information
00 40 00	**PROCUREMENT FORMS AND SUPPLEMENTS**
00 41 00	Bid Forms
00 42 00	Proposal Forms
00 43 00	Procurement Form Supplements
00 45 00	Representations and Certifications

CONTRACTING REQUIREMENTS

00 50 00	**CONTRACTING FORMS AND SUPPLEMENTS**
00 51 00	Notice of Award
00 52 00	Agreement Forms
00 54 00	Agreement Form Supplements
00 55 00	Notice to Proceed
00 60 00	**PROJECT FORMS**
00 61 00	Bond Forms
00 62 00	Certificates and Other Forms
00 63 00	Clarification and Modification Forms
00 65 00	Closeout Forms
00 70 00	**CONDITIONS OF THE CONTRACT**
00 71 00	Contracting Definitions
00 72 00	General Conditions
00 73 00	Supplementary Conditions
00 90 00	**REVISIONS, CLARIFICATIONS, AND MODIFICATIONS**
00 91 00	Precontract Revisions
00 93 00	Record Clarifications and Proposals
00 94 00	Record Modifications

SPECIFICATIONS GROUP

DIVISION 01 GENERAL REQUIREMENTS

01 00 00	**GENERAL REQUIREMENTS**
01 10 00	**SUMMARY**
01 11 00	Summary of Work
01 12 00	Multiple Contract Summary
01 14 00	Work Restrictions
01 18 00	Project Utility Sources
01 20 00	**PRICE AND PAYMENT PROCEDURES**
01 21 00	Allowances
01 22 00	Unit Prices
01 23 00	Alternates
01 24 00	Value Analysis
01 25 00	Substitution Procedures
01 26 00	Contract Modification Procedures
01 29 00	Payment Procedures
01 30 00	**ADMINISTRATIVE REQUIREMENTS**
01 31 00	Project Management and Coordination
01 32 00	Construction Progress Documentation
01 33 00	Submittal Procedures
01 35 00	Special Procedures
01 40 00	**QUALITY REQUIREMENTS**
01 41 00	Regulatory Requirements
01 42 00	References
01 43 00	Quality Assurance
01 45 00	Quality Control
01 50 00	**TEMPORARY FACILITIES AND CONTROLS**
01 51 00	Temporary Utilities
01 52 00	Construction Facilities
01 53 00	Temporary Construction
01 54 00	Construction Aids
01 55 00	Vehicular Access and Parking
01 56 00	Temporary Barriers and Enclosures
01 57 00	Temporary Controls
01 58 00	Project Identification
01 60 00	**PRODUCT REQUIREMENTS**
01 61 00	Common Product Requirements
01 62 00	Product Options
01 64 00	Owner-Furnished Products
01 65 00	Product Delivery Requirements

08 56 00	Special Function Windows	09 28 00	Backing Boards and Underlayments	09 91 00	Painting
08 60 00	**ROOF WINDOWS AND SKYLIGHTS**	09 29 00	Gypsum Board	09 93 00	Staining and Transparent Finishing
08 61 00	Roof Windows	09 30 00	**TILING**	09 94 00	Decorative Finishing
08 62 00	Unit Skylights	09 31 00	Thin-Set Tiling	09 96 00	High-Performance Coatings
08 63 00	Metal-Framed Skylights	09 32 00	Mortar-Bed Tiling	09 97 00	Special Coatings
08 64 00	Plastic-Framed Skylights	09 33 00	Conductive Tiling		
08 67 00	Skylight Protection and Screens	09 34 00	Waterproofing-Membrane Tiling	DIVISION 10	SPECIALTIES
08 70 00	**HARDWARE**	09 35 00	Chemical-Resistant Tiling	10 00 00	**SPECIALTIES**
08 71 00	Door Hardware	09 40 00	Unassigned	10 01 00	Operation and Maintenance of Specialties
08 74 00	Access Control Hardware	09 50 00	**CEILINGS**	10 05 00	Common Work Results for Specialties
08 75 00	Window Hardware	09 51 00	Acoustical Ceilings	10 06 00	Schedules for Specialties
08 78 00	Special Function Hardware	09 53 00	Acoustical Ceiling Suspension Assemblies	10 08 00	Commissioning of Specialties
08 79 00	Hardware Accessories	09 54 00	Specialty Ceilings	10 10 00	**INFORMATION SPECIALTIES**
08 80 00	**GLAZING**	09 56 00	Textured Ceilings	10 11 00	Visual Display Surfaces
08 81 00	Glass Glazing	09 57 00	Special Function Ceilings	10 12 00	Display Cases
08 83 00	Mirrors	09 58 00	Integrated Ceiling Assemblies	10 13 00	Directories
08 84 00	Plastic Glazing	09 60 00	**FLOORING**	10 14 00	Signage
08 85 00	Glazing Accessories	09 61 00	Flooring Treatment	10 17 00	Telephone Specialties
08 87 00	Glazing Surface Films	09 62 00	Specialty Flooring	10 18 00	Informational Kiosks
08 88 00	Special Function Glazing	09 63 00	Masonry Flooring	10 20 00	**INTERIOR SPECIALTIES**
08 90 00	**LOUVERS AND VENTS**	09 64 00	Wood Flooring	10 21 00	Compartments and Cubicles
08 91 00	Louvers	09 65 00	Resilient Flooring	10 22 00	Partitions
08 92 00	Louvered Equipment Enclosures	09 66 00	Terrazzo Flooring	10 25 00	Service Walls
		09 67 00	Fluid-Applied Flooring	10 26 00	Wall and Door Protection
DIVISION 09	FINISHES	09 68 00	Carpeting	10 28 00	Toilet, Bath, and Laundry Accessories
09 00 00	**FINISHES**	09 69 00	Access Flooring	10 30 00	**FIREPLACES AND STOVES**
09 01 00	Maintenance of Finishes	09 70 00	**WALL FINISHES**	10 31 00	Manufactured Fireplaces
09 05 00	Common Work Results for Finishes	09 72 00	Wall Coverings	10 32 00	Fireplace Specialties
09 06 00	Schedules for Finishes	09 73 00	Wall Carpeting	10 35 00	Stoves
09 08 00	Commissioning of Finishes	09 74 00	Flexible Wood Sheets	10 40 00	**SAFETY SPECIALTIES**
09 10 00	Unassigned	09 75 00	Stone Facing	10 41 00	Emergency Access and Information Cabinets
09 20 00	**PLASTER AND GYPSUM BOARD**	09 76 00	Plastic Blocks	10 43 00	Emergency Aid Specialties
09 21 00	Plaster and Gypsum Board Assemblies	09 77 00	Special Wall Surfacing	10 44 00	Fire Protection Specialties
09 22 00	Supports for Plaster and Gypsum Board	09 80 00	**ACOUSTIC TREATMENT**	10 50 00	**STORAGE SPECIALTIES**
09 23 00	Gypsum Plastering	09 81 00	Acoustic Insulation	10 51 00	Lockers
09 24 00	Portland Cement Plastering	09 83 00	Acoustic Finishes	10 55 00	Postal Specialties
09 25 00	Other Plastering	09 84 00	Acoustic Room Components	10 56 00	Storage Assemblies
09 26 00	Veneer Plastering	09 90 00	**PAINTING AND COATING**	10 57 00	Wardrobe and Closet Specialties
09 27 00	Plaster Fabrications			10 60 00	Unassigned

10 70 00	EXTERIOR SPECIALTIES	11 30 00	RESIDENTIAL EQUIPMENT	11 90 00	OTHER EQUIPMENT
10 71 00	Exterior Protection	11 31 00	Residential Appliances	11 91 00	Religious Equipment
10 73 00	Protective Covers	11 33 00	Retractable Stairs	11 92 00	Agricultural Equipment
10 74 00	Manufactured Exterior Specialties	11 40 00	FOODSERVICE EQUIPMENT	11 93 00	Horticultural Equipment
10 75 00	Flagpoles	11 41 00	Food Storage Equipment	DIVISION 12	FURNISHINGS
10 80 00	OTHER SPECIALTIES	11 42 00	Food Preparation Equipment	12 00 00	FURNISHINGS
10 81 00	Pest Control Devices	11 43 00	Food Delivery Carts and Conveyors	12 01 00	Operation and Maintenance of Furnishings
10 82 00	Grilles and Screens	11 44 00	Food Cooking Equipment	12 05 00	Common Work Results for Furnishings
10 83 00	Flags and Banners	11 46 00	Food Dispensing Equipment	12 06 00	Schedules for Furnishings
10 86 00	Security Mirrors and Domes	11 47 00	Ice Machines	12 08 00	Commissioning of Furnishings
10 88 00	Scales	11 48 00	Cleaning and Disposal Equipment	12 10 00	ART
10 90 00	Unassigned	11 50 00	EDUCATIONAL AND SCIENTIFIC EQUIPMENT	12 11 00	Murals
DIVISION 11	EQUIPMENT	11 51 00	Library Equipment	12 12 00	Wall Decorations
11 00 00	EQUIPMENT	11 52 00	Audio-Visual Equipment	12 14 00	Sculptures
11 01 00	Operation and Maintenance of Equipment	11 53 00	Laboratory Equipment	12 17 00	Art Glass
11 05 00	Common Work Results for Equipment	11 55 00	Planetarium Equipment	12 19 00	Religious Art
11 06 00	Schedules for Equipment	11 56 00	Observatory Equipment	12 20 00	WINDOW TREATMENTS
11 08 00	Commissioning of Equipment	11 57 00	Vocational Shop Equipment	12 21 00	Window Blinds
11 10 00	VEHICLE AND PEDESTRIAN EQUIPMENT	11 59 00	Exhibit Equipment	12 22 00	Curtains and Drapes
11 11 00	Vehicle Service Equipment	11 60 00	ENTERTAINMENT EQUIPMENT	12 23 00	Interior Shutters
11 12 00	Parking Control Equipment	11 61 00	Theater and Stage Equipment	12 24 00	Window Shades
11 13 00	Loading Dock Equipment	11 62 00	Musical Equipment	12 25 00	Window Treatment Operating Hardware
11 14 00	Pedestrian Control Equipment	11 65 00	ATHLETIC AND RECREATIONAL EQUIPMENT	12 30 00	CASEWORK
11 15 00	SECURITY, DETENTION AND BANKING EQUIPMENT	11 66 00	Athletic Equipment	12 31 00	Manufactured Metal Casework
11 16 00	Vault Equipment	11 67 00	Recreational Equipment	12 32 00	Manufactured Wood Casework
11 17 00	Teller and Service Equipment	11 68 00	Play Field Equipment and Structures	12 34 00	Manufactured Plastic Casework
11 18 00	Security Equipment	11 70 00	HEALTHCARE EQUIPMENT	12 35 00	Specialty Casework
11 19 00	Detention Equipment	11 71 00	Medical Sterilizing Equipment	12 36 00	Countertops
11 20 00	COMMERCIAL EQUIPMENT	11 72 00	Examination and Treatment Equipment	12 40 00	FURNISHINGS AND ACCESSORIES
11 21 00	Mercantile and Service Equipment	11 73 00	Patient Care Equipment	12 41 00	Office Accessories
11 22 00	Refrigerated Display Equipment	11 74 00	Dental Equipment	12 42 00	Table Accessories
11 23 00	Commercial Laundry and Dry Cleaning Equipment	11 75 00	Optical Equipment	12 43 00	Portable Lamps
11 24 00	Maintenance Equipment	11 76 00	Operating Room Equipment	12 44 00	Bath Furnishings
11 25 00	Hospitality Equipment	11 77 00	Radiology Equipment	12 45 00	Bedroom Furnishings
11 26 00	Unit Kitchens	11 78 00	Mortuary Equipment	12 46 00	Furnishing Accessories
11 27 00	Photographic Processing Equipment	11 79 00	Therapy Equipment	12 48 00	Rugs and Mats
11 28 00	Office Equipment	11 80 00	COLLECTION AND DISPOSAL EQUIPMENT	12 50 00	FURNITURE
11 29 00	Postal, Packaging, and Shipping Equipment	11 82 00	Solid Waste Handling Equipment	12 51 00	Office Furniture

23 73 00	Indoor Central-Station Air-Handling Units
23 74 00	Packaged Outdoor HVAC Equipment
23 75 00	Custom-Packaged Outdoor HVAC Equipment
23 76 00	Evaporative Air-Cooling Equipment
23 80 00	DECENTRALIZED HVAC EQUIPMENT
23 81 00	Decentralized Unitary HVAC Equipment
23 82 00	Convection Heating and Cooling Units
23 83 00	Radiant Heating Units
23 84 00	Humidity Control Equipment
23 90 00	*Unassigned*

DIVISION 25 INTEGRATED AUTOMATION

25 00 00	INTEGRATED AUTOMATION
25 01 00	Operation and Maintenance of Integrated Automation
25 05 00	Common Work Results for Integrated Automation
25 06 00	Schedules for Integrated Automation
25 08 00	Commissioning of Integrated Automation
25 10 00	INTEGRATED AUTOMATION NETWORK EQUIPMENT
25 11 00	Integrated Automation Network Devices
25 12 00	Integrated Automation Network Gateways
25 13 00	Integrated Automation Control and Monitoring Network
25 14 00	Integrated Automation Local Control Units
25 15 00	Integrated Automation Software
25 20 00	*Unassigned*
25 30 00	INTEGRATED AUTOMATION INSTRUMENTATION AND TERMINAL DEVICES
25 31 00	Integrated Automation Instrumentation and Terminal Devices for Facility Equipment
25 32 00	Integrated Automation Instrumentation and Terminal Devices for Conveying Equipment
25 33 00	Integrated Automation Instrumentation and Terminal Devices for Fire-Suppression Systems
25 34 00	Integrated Automation Instrumentation and Terminal Devices for Plumbing
25 35 00	Integrated Automation Instrumentation and Terminal Devices for HVAC
25 36 00	Integrated Automation Instrumentation and Terminal Devices for Electrical Systems

25 37 00	Integrated Automation Instrumentation and Terminal Devices for Communications Systems
25 38 00	Integrated Automation Instrumentation and Terminal Devices for Electronic Safety and Security Systems
25 40 00	Unassigned
25 50 00	INTEGRATED AUTOMATION FACILITY CONTROLS
25 51 00	Integrated Automation Control of Facility Equipment
25 52 00	Integrated Automation Control of Conveying Equipment
25 53 00	Integrated Automation Control of Fire-Suppression Systems
25 54 00	Integrated Automation Control of Plumbing
25 55 00	Integrated Automation Control of HVAC
25 56 00	Integrated Automation Control of Electrical Systems
25 57 00	Integrated Automation Control of Communications Systems
25 58 00	Integrated Automation Control of Electronic Safety and Security Systems
25 60 00	*Unassigned*
25 70 00	*Unassigned*
25 80 00	*Unassigned*
25 90 00	INTEGRATED AUTOMATION CONTROL SEQUENCES
25 91 00	Integrated Automation Control Sequences for Facility Equipment
25 92 00	Integrated Automation Control Sequences for Conveying Equipment
25 93 00	Integrated Automation Control Sequences for Fire-Suppression Systems
25 94 00	Integrated Automation Control Sequences for Plumbing
25 95 00	Integrated Automation Control Sequences for HVAC
25 96 00	Integrated Automation Control Sequences for Electrical Systems
25 97 00	Integrated Automation Control Sequences for Communications Systems
25 98 00	Integrated Automation Control Sequences for Electronic Safety and Security Systems

DIVISION 26 ELECTRICAL

26 00 00	ELECTRICAL
26 01 00	Operation and Maintenance of Electrical Systems

26 05 00	Common Work Results for Electrical
26 08 00	Commissioning of Electrical Systems
26 09 00	Instrumentation and Control for Electrical Systems
26 10 00	MEDIUM -VOLTAGE ELECTRICAL DISTRIBUTION
26 11 00	Substations
26 12 00	Medium-Voltage Transformers
26 13 00	Medium-Voltage Switchgear
26 18 00	Medium-Voltage Circuit Protection Devices
26 20 00	LOW -VOLTAGE ELECTRICAL DISTRIBUTION
26 21 00	Low-Voltage Overhead Electrical Power Systems
26 22 00	Low-Voltage Transformers
26 23 00	Low-Voltage Switchgear
26 24 00	Switchboards and Panelboards
26 25 00	Enclosed Bus Assemblies
26 26 00	Power Distribution Units
26 27 00	Low-Voltage Distribution Equipment
26 28 00	Low-Voltage Circuit Protective Devices
26 29 00	Low-Voltage Controllers
26 30 00	FACILITY ELECTRICAL POWER GENERATING AND STORING EQUIPMENT
26 31 00	Photovoltaic Collectors
26 32 00	Packaged Generator Assemblies
26 35 00	Power Filters and Conditioners
26 36 00	Transfer Switches
26 40 00	ELECTRICAL AND CATHODIC PROTECTION
26 41 00	Facility Lightning Protection
26 42 00	Cathodic Protection
26 43 00	Transient Voltage Suppression
26 50 00	LIGHTING
26 51 00	Interior Lighting
26 52 00	Emergency Lighting
26 53 00	Exit Signs
26 54 00	Classified Location Lighting
26 56 00	Exterior Lighting
26 60 00	*Unassigned*
26 70 00	*Unassigned*
26 80 00	*Unassigned*
26 90 00	*Unassigned*

34 42 00	Railway Signaling and Control Equipment	35 43 00	Waterway Scour Protection	40 32 00	Bulk Materials Piping and Chutes
34 43 00	Airfield Signaling and Control Equipment	35 49 00	Waterway Structures	40 33 00	Bulk Materials Valves
34 50 00	**TRANSPORTATION FARE COLLECTION EQUIPMENT**	35 50 00	**MARINE CONSTRUCTION AND EQUIPMENT**	40 34 00	Pneumatic Conveying Lines
34 52 00	Vehicle Fare Collection	35 51 00	Floating Construction	40 40 00	**PROCESS PIPING AND EQUIPMENT PROTECTION**
34 54 00	Passenger Fare Collection	35 52 00	Offshore Platform Construction	40 41 00	Process Piping and Equipment Heat Tracing
34 60 00	*Unassigned*	35 53 00	Underwater Construction	40 42 00	Process Piping and Equipment Insulation
34 70 00	**TRANSPORTATION CONSTRUCTION AND EQUIPMENT**	35 59 00	Marine Specialties	40 46 00	Process Corrosion Protection
34 71 00	Roadway Construction	*35 60 00*	*Unassigned*	40 47 00	Refractories
34 72 00	Railway Construction	35 70 00	**DAM CONSTRUCTION AND EQUIPMENT**	*40 50 00*	*Unassigned*
34 73 00	Airfield Construction	35 71 00	Gravity Dams	*40 60 00*	*Unassigned*
34 75 00	Roadway Equipment	35 72 00	Arch Dams	*40 70 00*	*Unassigned*
34 76 00	Railway Equipment	35 73 00	Embankment Dams		
34 77 00	Transportation Equipment	35 74 00	Buttress Dams	40 80 00	**COMMISSIONING OF PROCESS SYSTEMS**
34 80 00	**BRIDGES**	35 79 00	Auxiliary Dam Structures	40 90 00	**INSTRUMENTATION AND CONTROL FOR PROCESS SYSTEMS**
34 81 00	Bridge Machinery	*35 80 00*	*Unassigned*		
34 82 00	Bridge Specialties	*35 90 00*	*Unassigned*	40 91 00	Primary Process Measurement Devices
34 90 00	*Unassigned*	DIVISION 40	PROCESS INTEGRATION	40 92 00	Primary Control Devices
DIVISION 35	WATERWAY AND MARINE CONSTRUCTION	40 00 00	**PROCESS INTEGRATION**	40 93 00	Analog Controllers/Recorders
		40 01 00	Operation and Maintenance of Process Integration	40 94 00	Digital Process Controllers
35 00 00	**WATERWAY AND MARINE CONSTRUCTION**	40 05 00	Common Work Results for Process Integration	40 95 00	Process Control Hardware
35 01 00	Operation and Maintenance of Waterway and Marine Construction	40 06 00	Schedules for Process Integration	40 96 00	Process Control Software
35 05 00	Common Work Results for Waterway and Marine Construction	40 10 00	**GAS AND VAPOR PROCESS PIPING**	40 97 00	Process Control Auxiliary Devices
		40 11 00	Steam Process Piping	DIVISION 41	MATERIAL PROCESSING AND HANDLING EQUIPMENT
35 06 00	Schedules for Waterway and Marine Construction	40 12 00	Compressed Air Process Piping	41 00 00	**MATERIAL PROCESSING AND HANDLING EQUIPMENT**
35 08 00	Commissioning of Waterway and Marine Construction	40 13 00	Inert Gases Process Piping	41 01 00	Operation and Maintenance of Material Processing and Handling Equipment
35 10 00	**WATERWAY AND MARINE SIGNALING AND CONTROL EQUIPMENT**	40 14 00	Fuel Gases Process Piping		
		40 15 00	Combustion System Gas Piping	41 06 00	Schedules for Material Processing and Handling Equipment
35 11 00	Signaling and Control Equipment for Waterways	40 16 00	Specialty and High-Purity Gases Piping		
35 12 00	Marine Signaling and Control Equipment	40 17 00	Welding and Cutting Gases Piping	41 08 00	Commissioning of Material Processing and Handling Equipment
35 13 00	Signaling and Control Equipment for Dams	40 18 00	Vacuum Systems Process Piping		
35 20 00	**WATERWAY AND MARINE CONSTRUCTION AND EQUIPMENT**	40 20 00	**LIQUIDS PROCESS PIPING**	41 10 00	**BULK MATERIAL PROCESSING EQUIPMENT**
		40 21 00	Liquid Fuel Process Piping	41 11 00	Bulk Material Sizing Equipment
35 30 00	**COASTAL CONSTRUCTION**	40 22 00	Petroleum Products Piping	41 12 00	Bulk Material Conveying Equipment
35 31 00	Shoreline Protection	40 23 00	Water Process Piping	41 13 00	Bulk Material Feeders
35 32 00	Artificial Reefs	40 24 00	Specialty Liquid Chemicals Piping	41 14 00	Batching Equipment
35 40 00	**WATERWAY CONSTRUCTION AND EQUIPMENT**	40 25 00	Liquid Acids and Bases Piping	41 20 00	**PIECE MATERIAL HANDLING EQUIPMENT**
35 41 00	Levees	40 26 00	Liquid Polymer Piping	41 21 00	Conveyors
35 42 00	Waterway Bank Protection	40 30 00	**SOLID AND MIXED MATERIALS PIPING AND CHUTES**	41 22 00	Cranes and Hoists
				41 23 00	Lifting Devices

41 24 00	Specialty Material Handling Equipment
41 30 00	**MANUFACTURING EQUIPMENT**
41 31 00	Manufacturing Lines and Equipment
41 32 00	Forming Equipment
41 33 00	Machining Equipment
41 34 00	Finishing Equipment
41 35 00	Dies and Molds
41 36 00	Assembly and Testing Equipment
41 40 00	**CONTAINER PROCESSING AND PACKAGING**
41 41 00	Container Filling and Sealing
41 42 00	Container Packing Equipment
41 43 00	Shipping Packaging
41 50 00	**MATERIAL STORAGE**
41 51 00	Automatic Material Storage
41 52 00	Bulk Material Storage
41 53 00	Storage Equipment and Systems
41 60 00	**MOBILE PLANT EQUIPMENT**
41 61 00	Mobile Earth Moving Equipment
41 62 00	Trucks
41 63 00	General Vehicles
41 64 00	Rail Vehicles
41 65 00	Mobile Support Equipment
41 66 00	Miscellaneous Mobile Equipment
41 67 00	Plant Maintenance Equipment
DIVISION 42	PROCESS HEATING, COOLING, AND DRYING EQUIPMENT
42 00 00	**PROCESS HEATING, COOLING, AND DRYING EQUIPMENT**
42 01 00	Operation and Maintenance of Process Heating, Cooling, and Drying Equipment
42 06 00	Schedules for Process Heating, Cooling, and Drying Equipment
42 08 00	Commissioning of Process Heating, Cooling, and Drying Equipment
42 10 00	**PROCESS HEATING EQUIPMENT**
42 11 00	Process Boilers
42 12 00	Process Heaters
42 13 00	Industrial Heat Exchangers and Recuperators

42 14 00	Industrial Furnaces
42 15 00	Industrial Ovens
42 20 00	**PROCESS COOLING EQUIPMENT**
42 21 00	Process Cooling Towers
42 22 00	Process Chillers and Coolers
42 23 00	Process Condensers and Evaporators
42 30 00	**PROCESS DRYING EQUIPMENT**
42 31 00	Gas Dryers and Dehumidifiers
42 32 00	Material Dryers
42 40 00	*Unassigned*
42 50 00	*Unassigned*
42 60 00	*Unassigned*
42 70 00	*Unassigned*
42 80 00	*Unassigned*
42 90 00	*Unassigned*
DIVISION 43	PROCESS GAS AND LIQUID HANDLING, PURIFICATION, AND STORAGE EQUIPMENT
43 00 00	**PROCESS GAS AND LIQUID HANDLING, PURIFICATION, AND STORAGE EQUIPMENT**
43 01 00	Operation and Maintenance of Process Gas and Liquid Handling, Purification, and Storage Equipment
43 06 00	Schedules for Process Gas and Liquid Handling, Purification, and Storage Equipment
43 08 00	Commissioning of Process Gas and Liquid Handling, Purification, and Storage Equipment
43 10 00	**GAS HANDLING EQUIPMENT**
43 11 00	Gas Fans, Blowers and Pumps
43 12 00	Gas Compressors
43 13 00	Gas Process Equipment
43 20 00	**LIQUID HANDLING EQUIPMENT**
43 21 00	Liquid Pumps
43 22 00	Liquid Process Equipment
43 30 00	**GAS AND LIQUID PURIFICATION EQUIPMENT**
43 31 00	Gas and Liquid Purification Filtration Equipment
43 32 00	Gas and Liquid Purification Process Equipment
43 40 00	**GAS AND LIQUID STORAGE**
43 41 00	Gas and Liquid Storage Equipment
DIVISION 44	POLLUTION CONTROL EQUIPMENT
44 00 00	**POLLUTION CONTROL EQUIPMENT**

44 01 00	Operation and Maintenance of Pollution Control Equipment
44 06 00	Schedules for Pollution Control Equipment
44 08 00	Commissioning of Pollution Control Equipment
44 10 00	**AIR POLLUTION CONTROL**
44 11 00	Air Pollution Control Equipment
44 20 00	**NOISE POLLUTION CONTROL**
44 21 00	Noise Pollution Control Equipment
44 40 00	**WATER TREATMENT EQUIPMENT**
44 41 00	Packaged Water Treatment
44 42 00	General Water Treatment Equipment
44 43 00	Water Filtration Equipment
44 44 00	Water Treatment Chemical Systems Equipment
44 45 00	Water Treatment Biological Systems Equipment
44 46 00	Sludge Treatment and Handling Equipment for Water Treatment Systems
44 50 00	**SOLID WASTE CONTROL**
44 51 00	Solid Waste Control Equipment
DIVISION 45	INDUSTRY-SPECIFIC MANUFACTURING EQUIPMENT
45 00 00	**INDUSTRY-SPECIFIC MANUFACTURING EQUIPMENT**
45 08 00	Commissioning of Industry-Specific Manufacturing Equipment
45 11 00	Oil and Gas Extraction Equipment
45 13 00	Mining Machinery and Equipment
45 15 00	Food Manufacturing Equipment
45 17 00	Beverage and Tobacco Manufacturing Equipment
45 19 00	Textiles and Apparel Manufacturing Equipment
45 21 00	Leather and Allied Product Manufacturing Equipment
45 23 00	Wood Product Manufacturing Equipment
45 25 00	Paper Manufacturing Equipment
45 27 00	Printing and Related Manufacturing Equipment
45 29 00	Petroleum and Coal Products Manufacturing Equipment
45 31 00	Chemical Manufacturing Equipment
45 33 00	Plastics and Rubber Manufacturing Equipment
45 35 00	Nonmetallic Mineral Product Manufacturing Equipment
45 37 00	Primary Metal Manufacturing Equipment

45 39 00 Fabricated Metal Product Manufacturing Equipment

45 41 00 Machinery Manufacturing Equipment

45 43 00 Computer and Electronic Product Manufacturing Equipment

45 45 00 Electrical Equipment, Appliance, and Component Manufacturing Equipment

45 47 00 Transportation Manufacturing Equipment

45 49 00 Furniture and Related Product Manufacturing Equipment

45 51 00 Other Manufacturing Equipment

45 60 00 *Unassigned*

45 70 00 *Unassigned*

45 80 00 *Unassigned*

45 90 00 *Unassigned*

DIVISION 48 ELECTRICAL POWER GENERATION

48 00 00 **ELECTRICAL POWER GENERATION**

48 01 00 Operation and Maintenance for Electrical Power Generation

48 05 00 Common Work Results for Electrical Power Generation

48 06 00 Schedules for Electrical Power Generation

48 08 00 Commissioning of Electrical Power Generation

48 09 00 Instrumentation and Control for Electrical Power Generation

48 10 00 **ELECTRICAL POWER GENERATION EQUIPMENT**

48 11 00 Fossil Fuel Plant Electrical Power Generation Equipment

48 12 00 Nuclear Fuel Plant Electrical Power Generation Equipment

48 13 00 Hydroelectric Plant Electrical Power Generation Equipment

48 14 00 Solar Energy Electrical Power Generation Equipment

48 15 00 Wind Energy Electrical Power Generation Equipment

48 16 00 Geothermal Energy Electrical Power Generation Equipment

48 17 00 Electrochemical Energy Electrical Power Generation Equipment

48 18 00 Fuel Cell Electrical Power Generation Equipment

48 19 00 Electrical Power Control Equipment

48 20 00 *Unassigned*

48 30 00 *Unassigned*

48 40 00 *Unassigned*

48 50 00 *Unassigned*

48 60 00 *Unassigned*

48 70 00 **ELECTRICAL POWER GENERATION TESTING**

48 80 00 *Unassigned*

48 90 00 *Unassigned*

Sample ADA Guidelines

The Americans with Disabilities Act (ADA) was enacted into law in 1990 to establish Accessibility Guidelines for commercial and public facilities. These guidelines are set forth in civil rights legislation and outline many specifics that must be addressed in new and remodeled buildings. The drawings that follow illustrate some common areas within these facilities that are outlined in the ADA Guidelines. More specific information and drawings of the ADA may be found on the United States Government website.

STAIR HANDRAILS

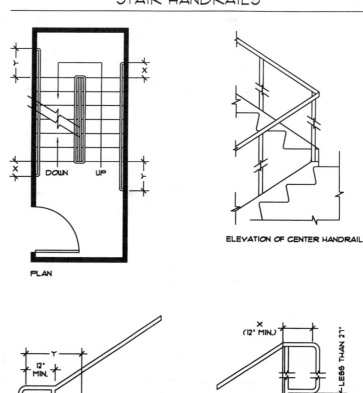

PLAN

ELEVATION OF CENTER HANDRAIL

EXTENSION AT BOTTOM OF RUN

EXTENSION AT TOP OF RUN

NOTE:
X IS THE 12" MIN. HANDRAIL EXTENSION REQUIRED AT EACH TOP RISER
Y IS THE MIN. HANDRAIL EXTENSION OF 12" + THE DEPTH OF ONE TREAD (TR) THAT IS
REQUIRED AT EACH BOTTOM RISER

FRONT APPROACHES - SWINGING DOORS

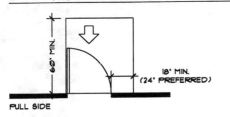

PULL SIDE

60" MIN.

18" MIN.
(24" PREFERRED)

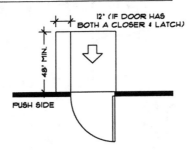

PUSH SIDE

48" MIN.

12" (IF DOOR HAS
BOTH A CLOSER & LATCH)

FRONT APPROACHES - SWINGING DOORS

PULL SIDE

60" MIN.

18" MIN.
(24" PREFERRED)

PUSH SIDE

48" MIN.

12" (IF DOOR HAS
BOTH A CLOSER & LATC

HINGE SIDE APPROACHES - SWINGING DOORS

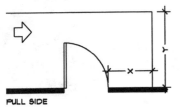

PULL SIDE

Y

X

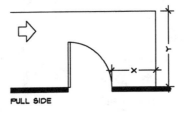

PUSH SIDE

54" MIN.

42" MIN.

NOTE:
X = 36" MIN. IF Y = 60"±
X = 42" MIN. IF Y = 54"

HINGE SIDE APPROACHES - SWINGING DOORS

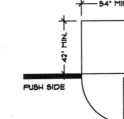

PULL SIDE

Y

X

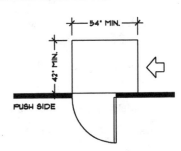

PUSH SIDE

54" MIN.

42" MIN.

NOTE:
X = 36" MIN. IF Y = 60"±
X = 42" MIN. IF Y = 54"

LATCH SIDE APPROACHES - SWINGING DOORS

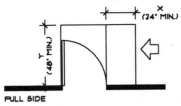

PULL SIDE

X
(24" MIN.)

Y
(48" MIN.)

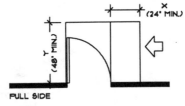

PUSH SIDE

X
(24" MIN.)

Y
(42" MIN.)

NOTE:
Y = 54" MIN. IF DOOR HAS CLOSER

NOTE:
Y = 48" MIN. IF
DOOR HAS
CLOSER

NOTE:
ALL DOORS IN ALCOVES SHALL COMPLY WITH THE CLEARANCES FOR FRONT APPROACHES

LATCH SIDE APPROACHES - SWINGING DOORS

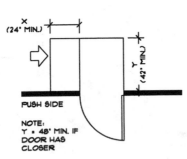

PULL SIDE

X
(24" MIN.)

Y
(48" MIN.)

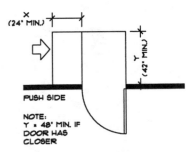

PUSH SIDE

X
(24" MIN.)

Y
(42" MIN.)

NOTE:
Y = 54" MIN. IF DOOR HAS CLOSER

NOTE:
Y = 48" MIN. IF
DOOR HAS
CLOSER

NOTE:
ALL DOORS IN ALCOVES SHALL COMPLY WITH THE CLEARANCES FOR FRONT APPROACHES

CLEAR FLOOR SPACE AT LAVATORIES

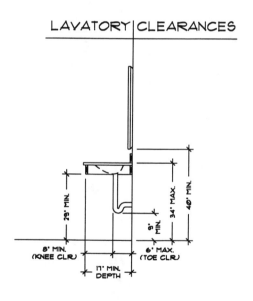

LAVATORY CLEARANCES

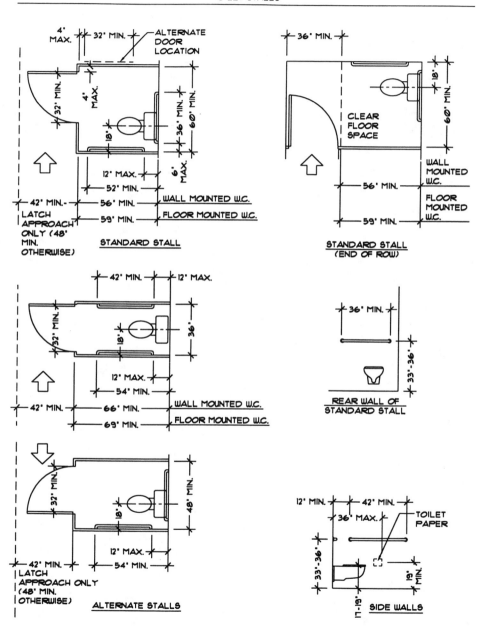

STANDARD STALL

STANDARD STALL
(END OF ROW)

WALL MOUNTED W.C.
FLOOR MOUNTED W.C.

REAR WALL OF
STANDARD STALL

WALL MOUNTED W.C.
FLOOR MOUNTED W.C.

ALTERNATE STALLS

SIDE WALLS

Abbreviations for Construction Drawings

AB	Anchor Bolt	CIR	Circle	DIN. RM.	Dining Room	FFE	Finished Floor Elevation
AC	Acoustical	CJ	Control Joint	DISP	Garbage Disposal	FHS	Fire Hose Station
A/C	Air Conditioning	CK	Check	DN	Down	FIN	Finish
ACT	Acoustical Tile	CLG	Ceiling	DP	Dam proof	FIX. GL	Fixed Glass
ADJ	Adjacent/Adjustable	CLK	Caulk	DR	Door	FLR	Floor
AFF	Above Finished Floor	CLOS	Closet	DTL	Detail	FLUR	Fluorescent
AL	Aluminum	CLR	Clear	DW	Dishwasher	FND	Foundation
ASPH	Asphalt	CLS	Close or Closure	DWG	Drawing	FOC	Face of Concrete
AUTO	Automatic	CM	Centimeter	DWR	Drawer	FOM	Face of Masonry
		CMU	Concrete Masonry Unit			FOS	Face of Studs
BR or BDRM	Bedroom	CNTR	Counter			FPL	Fireplace
BD	Board	C.O.	Cleanout	E	East	FR	Frame
BEL	Below	COL	Column	EA	Each	FTG	Footing
BET	Between	CONC	Concrete	EF	Each Face	FURR	Furred/Furring
BIT	Bituminous	CONST	Construction	EL	Elevation		
BLK	Block	CONT	Continuous	ELEC	Electrical	GA	Gauge
BLDG	Building	CONTR	Contractor	EWC	Electric Water Cooler	GB	Grab Bar
BLKG	Blocking	CPT	Carpet	ELEV	Elevator	GC	General Contractor
BM	Beam	CS	Counter Sink	EMERG	Emergency	GFI	Ground Fault Interrupter
BOT	Bottom	CSMT	Casement	ENCL	Enclose/Enclosure	GFIC	Ground Fault Interrupter
BRG	Bearing	CT	Ceramic Tile	EQ	Equal		Circuit
BRZ	Bronze	CTR	Center	EQP	Equipment	GI	Galvanized Iron
BRK	Brick			ESC	Escalator	GLS	Glass
BSMT	Basement	D	Drain	EX	Existing	GYP	Gypsum
BVL	Bevel	DBL	Double	EXH	Exhaust	GYP BD	Gypsum Board
		DEM	Demolish	EXT	Exterior		
CAB	Cabinet	DH	Double Hung			HB	Hose Bib
CEM	Cement	DIA	Diameter	FD	Floor Drain	HBD	Hardboard
CER	Ceramic	DIAG	Diagonal	FFCE	Finish Face	HC	Hollow Core
CI	Cast Iron	DIM	Dimension	FF	Finish Floor	HDR	Header

HDW	Hardware	MISC	Miscellaneous	RAD	Radius	SUSP	Suspended
HM	Hollow Metal	MLD	Molding	RAG	Return Air Grille	SYM	Symmetrical
HOR	Horizontal	MM	Millimeter	RAFT	Rafter	SYN	Synthetic
HT	Height	MOD	Modular	REF	Reference	SYS	System
HT'G	Heating	MTL	Material	REFR	Refrigerator		
HVAC	Heating, Ventilating, Air	MULL	Mullion	REM	Remove	T	Tread
	Conditioning			REQD	Required	TEL	Telephone
HWD	Hardwood	N	North	RET	Return	TEMP	Tempered
		NO or #	Number	REV	Revise/Revision	T&G	Tongue and Groove
ID	Inside Diameter	NIC	Not in Contract	RFG	Roofing	THK	Thick(ness)
INCL	Include	NOM	Nominal	RFL	Reflected	THR	Threshold
INSUL	Insulate (ion)	NTS	Not to Scale	RH	Right Hand	THRU	Through
INT	Interior			RL	Rail	TRTMT	Treatment
		OC	On Center	RM	Room	TV	Television
JST	Joist	OD	Outside Diameter	RO	Rough Opening	TYP	Typical
JT	Joint	OH	Overhead	ROW	Right of Way		
		OPG	Opening	RR	Restroom	UNF	Unfinished
KIT	Kitchen	OPH	Opposite Hand	RWD	Redwood	UTIL	Utility
KO	Knockout	OPP	Opposite				
				S	South	V	Volts
LADR	Ladder	PAR	Parallel	SC	Solid Core	VAT	Vinyl Asbestos Tile
LAM	Laminate	PED	Pedestrian	SCH	Schedule	VERT	Vertical
LAUND	Laundry	PERI	Perimeter	SCN	Screen	VTR	Vent Thru Roof
LAV	Lavatory	PFB	Prefabricate	SEC	Section	VTW	Vent Thru Wall
LBL	Label	PKT	Pocket	SERV	Service	VNR	Veneer
LH	Left Hand	PL	Plate	S4S	Surfaced Floor Sides		
LIV. RM	Living Room	PLAS	Plastic	SHR	Shower	W/	With
LOC	Locate/Location	PLAST	Plaster	SHT	Sheet	W	West
		PNL	Panel	SIM	Similar	WC	Water Closet
M	Meter	PNT	Paint	SL	Slide (ing)	WD	Wood
MAS	Masonry	PT	Point	SOFT	Soffit	W/D	Washer/Dryer
MAX	Maximum	PTN	Partition	SPEC	Specification	WG	Wire Glass
MECH	Mechanical	PVC	Polyvinyl Chloride	SPK	Speaker	WH	Water Heater
MED	Medium	PWD	Plywood	SQ	Square	WH	Wall Hung
METL	Metal			S&R	Shelf and Rod	WM	Wire Mesh
MFR	Manufacturer	QT	Quarry Tile	SS	Service Sink	WSCT	Wainscot
MILWK	Millwork			STD	Standard	WWF	Welded Wire Fabric
MIN	Minimum	R	Riser	STL	Steel		
MIR	Mirror	RA	Return Air	STR	Structure(al)		

Acoustical Tile: A fiberboard, fiberglass, or similar materials used to absorb sound rather than reflect it. Often used as a ceiling material.

Air exchanger: An HVAC unit designed to exhaust stale air and draw in fresh air. In cold climates, the units often capture latent heat in the air and redirect it to the heating system.

Acrylic paint: A water-based paint made with synthetic resins.

Alcove: Recessed niche or space connected to the side of a larger space or room.

Alloy: A substance produced by the combination of two or more metals, or a nonmetal fused with a metal.

Ampere: The unit used to measure the rate of flow of electrical current.

Anchor bolt: A threaded rod cast or shot into concrete (or masonry) and used for anchoring—e.g., securing a sill plate to the foundation.

Anodize: Using an electrolytic process and a combination of chemicals to place a protective oxide film on metal.

Architect: A professional who designs and draws up instruments such as construction drawings for buildings and other structures in the built environment.

Areaway: An open area below grade that allows light and ventilation into a basement door or window.

Ashlar: Stone that is cut in rectangular shapes and fitted together.

Ash pit: A recessed pit below a fireplace hearth that is used to collect ashes.

Atrium: An open space or court within a building.

Attic: A space between the ceiling and roof of a building.

Awning: Covering made of canvas, metal, or another material. The term is also used to describe a window that is hinged at the top and swings outward.

Baffle: A device used to block the flow of sound, light, or wind.

Balustrade: A row of posts that supports a rail, such as a handrail used on a stairway.

Banister: Another term for a handrail.

Baseboard: A finish and protective board (or other material) covering where a wall and floor meet.

Basement: Lowest story of a building, generally entirely (or partially) below-ground.

Base plate: A steel plate used at the bottom of a column to spread out vertical loads and anchor the column to the floor.

Batt: A blanket of insulating material (such as fiberglass) manufactured in specific widths to be installed between framing members.

Batten: A narrow strip of material (usually wood) that conceals the spacing between larger boards—such as in board and batten siding.

Batter: A wall that slopes away from perpendicular and is seen mostly in concrete or masonry construction.

Bay window: A window element projecting from a building that generally has three sides.

Beam: A horizontal structural member that supports loads.

Beam ceiling: A ceiling treatment that exposes ceiling beams to view.

Bearing wall: A wall that supports vertical loads.

Bib: A faucet with threads for the attachment of a water hose. Also called a hose bib.

Blocking: Wood framing pieces used to reinforce, secure, or provide backing for other members or materials.

Board and batten: A siding technique using narrow strips of wood (battens) placed in a pattern over wooden siding. The original intent of the battens was to hide the cracks between the vertical boards.

Bookmatch: A wood veneer pattern produced by alternating sheets (flitches) similar to the leaves of a book.

Brick veneer: A facing of brick installed in front of a frame, concrete, or concrete block wall.

Btu: An abbreviation for "British Thermal Unit" which is the standard measurement for heat loss and gain.

Building inspector: An official whose job is to inspect remodeling or new building construction for safety and compliance with various building codes.

Built-up beam: A roofing type composed of several smaller beams, all secured together.

Built-up roof: A roofing type composed of layers of felt and asphalt, commonly top-coated with gravel.

CAD: Computer-aided design

CADD: Computer-aided design & drafting. However, this term is not used as much as the former designation.

Cantilever: A projected structure that is supported only at one end.

Cant strip: A triangular strip of material used to support or eliminate sharp turns in roofing materials or flashings.

Carriage: The supporting linear frame that holds the treads and risers in a staircase.

Casement: A window that is hinged on the vertical side.

Casing: The frame around a window or door.

Caulking: A waterproof material used to seal small spaces between adjoining surfaces.

Cavity wall: A hollow wall made up of two layers of masonry walls constructed a few inches apart.

Cement: An adhesive masonry material.

Circuit breaker: A device that opens or closes an electrical circuit. It opens (breaks) a circuit automatically if an unusually high level of current passes through it.

Chamfer: An easing or angling of the edge of two adjoining planes, often at a 45 degree angle.

Channel: A standardized structural steel shape, which resembles a "u" form.

Chase: A space within a building for routing pipes, ducts, wiring, or other utilities.

Checking: Cracks or splits in a board. It is caused by drying or seasonal changes.

Chimney: A flue used to exhaust gases and smoke from a building. See also Flue.

Chord: The bottom, top, or diagonal member of a truss.

Cinder block: A concrete masonry unit made of cinders and cement.

Cleanout: A removable cover or insert in a sewer waste line for cleaning or inspection of the line.

Clerestory: High windows placed in an interior or exterior wall, used mostly for admitting light to a space.

Collar beam: A horizontal member used to connect opposing rafters in roof framing.

Column: A perpendicular load-carrying member.

Concrete: A mixture of cement, gravel, sand, and water that hardens to a strong solid state.

Concrete block: A precast hollow or solid masonry unit of concrete. See also Cinder block.

Concrete masonry unit (CMU): A concrete block made of hardened concrete, with or without hollow core cells.

Conduit: An outer channel (primarily of metal) used to contain electrical wiring for protection and safety.

Control joint: A groove troweled or cut in concrete slabs that permits the regulation of cracks.

Corbel: The projecting of masonry construction by placing courses cantilevered beyond the lower ones.

Cornerbead: A metal molding used in plaster or drywall construction to protect and finish corners.

Cornice: The projecting element of a roof or wall.

Course: The continuous row of masonry with the same uniform height.

Court: A partial or full open space within a building.

Cripple: The vertical structural member in a door or window that is less than full height.

Curtain wall: The exterior portion of a building that does not support loads.

Customer's own material (C.O.M.): The customer purchases upholstery from another party rather than the furniture manufacturer.

Damper: The adjustable plate in a chimney or air duct that regulates the draft or air flow.

Diffuser: A device that scatters (diffuses) air, light, or sound into a space.

Dimension line: A line that shows the distance (in measured increments) between two points. It consists of a line and arrowheads, dots, or slash marks to mark the exact point of reference.

Dormer: A housing projecting from a sloping roof that accommodates a window.

Double-hung: A window that has bottom and top sashes; either or both of which can be slid up and down.

Drip: A groove or projecting edge incorporated below a surface to carry water or cause it to drip away from a vertical surface below.

Drywall: Construction using pre-made gypsum board panels (versus lath and plaster, which is a wet system).

Duct: A rectangular or circular shaped material (metal, fiberboard, etc.) that is used to transfer air from one space to another.

Eave: The section of a roof that projects over a wall below.

Edge band: A thin veneer of material (such as wood) applied to the edge of a panel, such as plywood.

Efflorescence: A powdery deposit on the surface face of masonry. It is a result of water leaching to the surface and transporting chemical salts from within the structure.

Elevation: The drawing of the front, side, or rear of an object.

Escutcheon: A cover plate on door hardware; or cover for the gap around piping where it enters a surface.

Exterior insulation and finish system (EIFS): A coating system of reinforced stucco applied to the surface of an insulated plastic foam board.

Fascia: A vertical band (wood or other material) secured to the cornice or roof overhang.

Fenestration: The placement of windows on a wall surface.

Finished lumber: Wood that has been dressed (milled or sanded) to be used for constructing cabinetwork and other building trim.

Firebrick: A brick that is hard and withstands great heat. It is used to line fireplaces, furnaces, etc.

Fire door: A door that resists fire and prevents it from spreading between spaces. Fire doors are rated as 20-minute, 1-hour, 2-hour, etc.

Fire resistant: Capable of slowing the spread or providing a barrier to fire.

Firestopping: Fire-resistive material installed to close the opening through or around the edge of a floor, to prevent the spread of fire between levels.

Firewall: A wall assembly that prevents fire from spreading between adjacent spaces. Firewalls are rated as 1-hour, 2-hour, 3-hour, and 4-hour.

Fixed window: A sealed, non-opening window or glass section.

Fixture: An item of plumbing or electric equipment. The term is also used to denote other specialty items such as medical, laboratory, and display elements (as used in retailing and commercial facilities).

Flagstone: A flat stone used for flooring, steps, walls, and walks.

Flange: The horizontal top and bottom sections of a steel beam.

Flashing: The sheet metalwork used to make a construction assembly weathertight.

Flitch beam: A structural beam utilizing a steel plate sandwiched and bolted between two wood members.

Float: A process using a trowel (or tool called a float) to spread cement, stucco, plaster, gypsum joint compound, or other workable materials.

Floor joist: A horizontal structural member that supports and distributes floor loads.

Floor plan: A view from above in a building where an imaginary horizontal cut has been made about 4 feet above the floor plane.

Flue: A vertical shaft that exhausts smoke from a wood or gas fireplace; also, the piping used to exhaust gases from water heaters and furnaces.

Flush: Aligned, level, or even.

Footing: An enlarged base that supports a wall, pier, or column and distributes the weights of a structure onto the ground.

Framing: The wood or steel construction of a building's framework.

French door: A pair of glazed doors hinged at the door frame jambs, and swinging to meet in the center of the opening.

Frieze: A decorative board of cornice trim fastened to a structure.

Frost line: The depth at which frost penetrates the ground during the winter season.

Furred: The construction of a separate surface on a wall, ceiling, or other assembly.

Furring: Narrow strips of wood or metal secured to a wall or ceiling for the purpose of providing a new ground (surface) to attach other finish materials.

Galvanized: A process of treating a material (metal) with zinc and lead to prevent rusting.

Gauge: A measure designation of the diameter of a wire or thickness of a sheet of material, such as metal.

Glass block: A masonry unit made of glass, with a hollow center.

Glazing: Installing glass in windows or doors.

Glue-laminated beams: Structural beams composed of layers of wood glued together under pressure; abbreviated as glulam.

Grain: The direction of longitudinal axes of wood grain fibers found in wood members.

Ground fault interrupter circuit (GFIC): An electrical device in a circuit that quickly disconnects when current is leaked to ground—often used in moist spaces.

Grout: A pastelike mixture of cement, sand, and water used for laying and filling joints in masonry construction

Gusset plate: A metal plate used to connect various portions (chords) of a truss.

Gypsum: A material made of hydrated sulfate of calcium, used to make sheets of wallboard.

Hardboard: A sheet material made by compressing and gluing fine fibers of wood.

Head: The top of a door or window.

Hearth: A noncombustible horizontal surface immediately outside of a fireplace opening.

Heartwood: The center region of cells in a tree trunk.

Heat pump: A mechanical unit that can heat or cool buildings using refrigeration cycles of air or liquid mediums.

Hollow-core door: A door made with face veneers separated by an inner core of gridded spacers, with solid material around the four edges.

Hose bib: An exterior-mounted water faucet. It is frost-proofed in cold climates.

Insulation: Various materials used primarily for the reduction of heat gain or loss through floors, walls, and ceilings of buildings.

Jalousie: Horizontal windows composed of a number of long, hinged glass panels that are operated in unison.

Jamb: The vertical side of a door or window.

Joist: Structural members of wood, steel, or concrete used to support floors, ceilings, and roofs.

Kiln dried: Refers primarily to lumber that has been dried in a kiln to reduce its moisture content.

Knee brace: A short diagonal brace joining a beam and column.

Lag screw: A large structural wood screw turned with a wrench; has hexagonal or square head.

Laminated veneer lumber (LVL): Thin wood veneers glued together to make a larger structural member.

Landing: A platform at the beginning and end of stairs, or between runs.

Lath: A base material (often metal) that serves as a base for plaster or stucco.

Lattice: Open framework of wood or other material arranged in a grid-like pattern.

Lavatory: The washbasin in a bathroom. The term "sink" is often reserved for kitchens, laundry rooms, and other spaces.

Lintel: The horizontal structural member that spans openings and supports loads from above, such as at a doorway or above a window.

Live load: The nonstatic weights of people, snow, furniture, and equipment on a floor, roof, or structural member.

Lockset: The hardware assembly for a door, which includes a deadbolt and latch.

Louver: An assembly used to admit or exhaust air, such as a gable vent or other device.

Mantel: Decorative trim piece or member around a fireplace opening.

Masonry: Materials of brick, stone, concrete block, and burned clay (such as ceramic tile).

Masonry veneer: A layer of masonry units such as brick, stone, or tile facing a frame or masonry wall.

MDF: Medium-density fiberboard.

Metal lath: An expanded metal mesh used as a base for applying stucco or plaster.

Millwork: Wood building products used for finish work, such as cabinetry, moldings, and other trim.

Moisture barrier: Sheathing made of various materials that retards transfer of water vapor through walls, floors, and ceilings in buildings.

Mullion: The vertical divider(s) placed between doors or windows.

Muntin: Thin divider trim that separates panes of glass in a window assembly.

Newel: A post that serves as termination for guardrails and handrails.

Nominal: Refers to common size terminology for standard items, rather than their actual size, such as a 2 x 4 stud, which is actually 1.5 inches by 3.5 inches.

Nonbearing wall: A wall that has no load-bearing capacity to support other elements other than its own weight.

Nosing: The portion of the stair tread that projects beyond the riser below. Also used to describe projection of front edge of a countertop.

Ogee: An S-shaped curve mostly found in trim and roof gutters.

Oriented strand board (OSB): Construction panel composed of adhesives and shreds/flakes of wood fiber that is oriented in specific directions.

Parapet: The portion of a building's exterior wall that extends above the roofline.

Pier: A concrete or masonry footing used to support a load from above, such as a column.

Pilaster: A vertical column-like element in a wall that provides support or stiffening.

Pitch: The incline of a roof or other plane expressed as a ratio of the span to the height.

Plaster: Cementitious material made with Portland cement or gypsum. It is applied in paste form to a substrate of lath or masonry, and hardens to a finishable surface.

Plate: A horizontal bottom or top member in wall framing.

Plenum: The space used primarily for HVAC ducting. Usually found between ceiling of a space and floor above, or an elevated area constructed for HVAC purposes.

Plumb: Vertical.

Rafter: A structural member that supports the roof assembly and its finished roofing material.

Raze: To demolish an existing construction.

Register: A grille installed at the termination of a mechanical duct for supplying, returning, or exhausting air flow, usually in a directional manner.

Reinforced concrete: Concrete that has steel reinforcing added to increase its ability to handle various loading forces.

Riser: The vertical part of a stair step.

Rough opening: The initial framing size of an opening used to accept a door, window, or other assembly.

Rowlock: In masonry construction, a brick laid on its long edge, with the end exposed in the wall face.

Run: The horizontal distance of a stair.

R-value: A numerical measurement of a material's resistance to the flow of heat.

Sash: The frame that holds window glass in place.

Scribe: The process of fitting materials such as woodwork or counter backsplashes to irregular faces of a wall or floor surface.

Sealer: A coating that closes the porous surface of a material, such as concrete.

Shim: A tapered piece of wood or other material used between two parts for filling voids and to aid in leveling.

Sill: The lowest part or bottom of a window or door; also can refer to a rough wood member that rests on a foundation wall.

Soffit: The horizontal exposed part of a building overhang, such as a roof or balcony.

Soldier: A term used in masonry that describes a brick (or other masonry unit) laid on its end, with the narrow face to the outside or finished wall face.

Specifications: Written documents that accompany drawings and contain specific information that cannot be conveyed by the drawings alone. They address the materials and the workmanship needed to construct various parts of a building.

Spline: Thin material inserted in grooves cut in two joining pieces of material—used to hold or align the mating materials.

Split jamb: A preassembled door frame that is made in two halves, installed, and locked from opposite sides of an opening.

Sprinkler head: A wall or ceiling device that sprays water in a predetermined coverage pattern, primarily for extinguishing fire.

Stile: The vertical piece in a door panel.

Stringer: The sloped member of a stairway that supports the treads and risers.

Strip flooring: Finished wood flooring manufactured in narrow widths of tongue and groove boards.

Stucco: A mixture of Portland cement base and sand, which is applied to the exterior of a building. A similar coat applied to the interior of a building is called plaster.

Stud: A vertical wood or steel framing member that is primarily used to build walls.

Subfloor: The under-floor sheathing that provides the proper surface for the finished flooring.

Tempered glass: Heat-treated glass that resists breakage.

Terrazzo: Durable flooring made of small stone or other materials embedded in a strong cement-bonding agent and ground smooth.

Thermostat: An electrical or mechanical device that controls the HVAC system by maintaining a preset temperature or providing an override setting.

Threshold: The strip of material used under the bottom of doors to cover the joint between the finished floor and sill.

Thru: An architectural slang and abbreviation for the word "through."

Timber: Wood that is larger in cross-section size than 4 inches by 6 inches (102 mm by 152 mm).

Top plate: The horizontal framing member on top of a stud wall.

Transom: A small window located directly above a door.

Tread: The horizontal plane of a stairway that one steps on.

Truss: A structural assembly of wood or steel used to span great distances with the minimum amount of material.

Type X gypsum board: A specialized type of gypsum board used for greater fire resistance.

Vapor barrier: Material, generally a sheeting, that prevents water vapor migration into unwanted areas of a building.

Varnish: A tough transparent coating made of a combination of resinous substances with alcohol or oil. It is applied with a brush or sprayer.

Veneer: Thin sheets of wood or other material used in surface applications to other materials.

Vent: The vertical pipe in a plumbing system that exhausts sewer gas and provides pressure equalization.

Vestibule: The entry or open area dedicated to the entrance of a building.

Waferboard: Sheathing material or panel made by pressing and gluing flat flakes of wood.

Wainscot: The lower section of a wall finish, which is usually a different material than the upper section.

Water closet: The common name for a toilet that contains a bowl of water.

Water-resistant gypsum board: A panel of gypsum board that is manufactured to resist dampness. It is often used in bathrooms as a subsurface for ceramic tile.

Weep hole: A small aperture in masonry construction that allows the drainage of water to the exterior of the building.

Weld: The fusing together of two pieces of metal using intense heat from an electrode or rod to melt an additional metal.

Welded wire fabric (WWF): Concrete slab reinforcing, made of various diameters and strengths welded together.

Winder: The triangular tread found on a stairway.

Wood molding: Shapes of wood assemblies curved or angled in various convex or concave shapes—used for trim.

Wrought iron: Soft, malleable iron that can be forged into different shapes.

Zero-clearance fireplace: A metal prefabricated fireplace designed to be placed directly against wood framing, without causing combustion of the wood.

INDEX